Democracy

Democracy

History, Theory, Practice

Sanford Lakoff

WestviewPress

A Division of HarperCollinsPublishers

Copyright © 1996 by Westview Press, A Division of HarperCollins Publishers, Inc.

Published in 1996 in the United States of America by Westview Press, 5500 Central Avenue, Boulder, Colorado 80301-2877, and in the United Kingdom by Westview Press, 12 Hid's Copse Road, Cumnor Hill, Oxford OX2 9JJ

Library of Congress Cataloging-in-Publication Data
Lakoff, Sanford A.
    Democracy : history, theory, practice / by Sanford Lakoff.
        p.   cm.
    Includes bibliographical references and index.
    ISBN 0-8133-3227-3 (hc.) — ISBN 0-8133-3228-1 (pbk.)
    1. Democracy.   I. Title.
JC423.L295   1996
321.8—dc20   96-24373
                                                                                      CIP

The paper used in this publication meets the requirements of the American National Standard for Permanence of Paper for Printed Library Materials Z39.48-1984.

10   9   8   7   6   5   4   3   2   1

For Evelyn

Contents

Preface and Acknowledgements

Alexis de Tocqueville remarked that whereas in aristocratic times the attention of historians is drawn to the role of powerful individuals, in democratic times they are likely to concentrate too much on great events and general theories, until they mistakenly assume that democracy is an irresistible force. I have tried to keep Tocqueville's admonition in mind, all the more so because failures of democratization in recent times have sometimes had terrible consequences—consequences he feared and forecast.

To walk in Tocqueville's footsteps is also to see democracy as a multidimensional subject—political, moral, sociological, economic, anthropological, and psychological. When he blazed this pioneering trail, it took his imagination, originality, and boldness to penetrate and map an unmarked terrain. More than a century and a half later, democratic experience encompasses a wide range of countries and cultures, and a vast literature has grown up around it. The effort to understand this experience still demands imagination, but now originality and boldness must be tempered by humility and caution so that what is already known is taken into account. I am indebted to those whose writings are cited here and aware that because of its broad scope this book does not always do full justice to the nuances of more specialized studies. Chapter ten in particular includes a *tour d'horizon* of contemporary developments treated in much greater detail in more focussed accounts and still far from settled. Only by juxtaposing history, theory, and practice, however, can we grasp the subject in its wholeness and complexity.

In at least one important respect, the analysis to be offered here differs from Tocqueville's. He discerned the impulse behind democracy in the tendency toward "equality of conditions." By this deliberately ambiguous term he meant to suggest in the first instance a broad rejection of the ascriptive or status distinctions characteristic of the "old regime" in Europe. He was apprehensive that the democratic passion for equality might lead to the abolition of private property and then, by overwhelming the presumably weaker democratic attachment to liberty, to a tyranny of the majority. Although he was right to emphasize the generally egalitarian character of democracy, Tocqueville did not give enough weight to the influence of natural-rights liberalism in shaping the character of this egalitarianism. For me, as for other students of the subject, the unifying impulse behind modern democracy is not an undifferentiated passion for equality, but the quest for equal liberty, or, in other words, the aspiration to universal autonomy or self-government. The most compelling argument on behalf of democracy as an ideal is that it embodies a well-recognized truth about the human condition, best explained by Immanuel Kant but apparent to common sense (as Kant himself pointed out). This elemental truth is that human beings in full possession of their faculties are capable of moral autonomy.

But the aspiration toward autonomy finds expression in three ideal-typical variations, which will be described here as communal, plural, and individual. Communal autonomy, the oldest form, emphasizes the self-determination of a cohesive political unit, such as a city-state or a nation-state. It is evident in the exaltation of citizenship in Periclean Athens and in its modern echo, the call for a communitarian "civic republicanism." Plural autonomy emphasizes the need to accommodate and balance self-determining sub-groups, often by formal power-sharing arrangements. In the "mixed constitution" of the Roman republic, two such groups, the patrician and plebeian "orders," shared authority and struggled for supremacy. In the early modern republics, a similar separation and tension existed between the wealthy and the poor. In present-day democracies, demands for plural autonomy arise on the basis of various cleavages: language, culture, religion, ethnicity, region, and shared interest. Individual autonomy, the most modern form, emphasizes personal self-determination, defined since the eighteenth century in terms of universal natural or human rights. To theorize about democracy is therefore first of all to establish the dimensions by which social and political systems embodying these various forms of autonomy can be distinguished from autocratic alternatives. These alternatives will be designated here as oligarchic, (absolute) monarchic, authoritarian, and totalitarian.

As for any social process, theorizing requires both static and dynamic analysis. The static theory of democracy aims to define its dimensions in normative, institutional, and procedural terms. The *normative* dimension considers the justification of autonomy and the role of the civic culture in promoting acceptance of democratic norms. The *institutional* dimension is twofold, containing the forms of autonomy that find expression in civil society, understood as the private sphere of life, and those that apply to public government, or the sphere of the state. Interest groups, political parties, and communications media link the two spheres. The *procedural* dimension takes shape in electoral and judicial systems. Modern democracy is a compound in which these three dimensions interact and reinforce each other. The dynamic theory aims to describe the process by which democratization occurs, takes hold, and fails, and the consequences for international relations. It includes consideration of such dimensions as the role of economic development, changes in social structure, the spread of literacy and education, expanding means of communication, and the influence of ideology and political institutions.

The theoretical inquiry has practical implications—negative as well as positive. In societies in which economic and educational deprivation put the opportunity for meaningful individual autonomy beyond the reach of the great majority, democracy is unlikely to be achieved or sustained. The machinery of constitutions, elections, political parties, and the rest will be readily manipulated for the benefit of a powerful few. Similarly, where cleavages along group lines are deep-seated but the aspirations of sub-groups for autonomy are denied, democracy may also be hard to establish and maintain. But where demands for individual and plural autonomy become so intense as to override the need for comprehensive, cross-cutting allegiances, most commonly those of nation-states, democracy will tend to yield either to anarchy or to autocracy. And even when practice conforms to norms, the pursuit of autonomy can lead to conflicts—between rights and duties, between the individual and society, between sub-groups and collectivities, between unequal economic resources and formal political equality, between the mass appeal of popular culture and the democratic need for educated and elevated citizens, between national self-interest and interdependence—a problem as much for fraternal democracies as for other states.

The art of democratic politics consists in mediating these conflicts through structures of government—local, national, and international—and by the processes of education, accommodation, and peaceful dispute settlement. To be successful, democratic politics also requires a vigorous civic culture that habituates citizens to perform civic duties and to accept democratically determined outcomes. The greatest dangers to democracy arise from failures to achieve the various forms of autonomy and to maintain a balance among them that accords with the particular needs of differing societies.

This book amounts to a series of meditations and reflections on these themes. After the introduction (chapters one and two) the text reviews the historical development of democracy and the backlash against it (chapters three to six), the theoretical character of modern democracy (chapters seven through nine), the practical problems of establishing and maintaining democracy (chapters ten through twelve), and concludes with a review of the meaning of democracy and its prospects (chapter thirteen).

In the years during which this work has been done, many friends have given help and encouragement. I am especially mindful of my debt to Maurice Cranston, whose sudden death as this book was being completed has left me bereft of two inestimable benefits: the pleasure of his company and the value of his comments on my work. Colleagues in the Department of Political Science at the University of California, San Diego, have stimulated my thinking by their work and by the views they have expressed, formally and informally. Paul Drake, Alan Houston, and Arend Lijphart commented on drafts of parts of the manuscript. They also shared drafts of work in progress, as did Philip G. Roeder. Several friends elsewhere, Barry M. Casper of Carleton College, Athanasios Moulakis of the University of Colorado, and Jean Edward Smith of the University of Toronto, also read drafts of various chapters. Theodore J. Stahl and Karl-Erik Hansson thoughtfully called my attention to materials I might have overlooked. I am also grateful to Spencer Carr, Elizabeth Lawrence, and Cindy Rinehart of Westview Press for their encouragement, and to Jeff Calcara for his skill and patience in formatting this typescript.

Earlier versions of parts of some chapters have appeared in a volume of *Nomos*, in *The Review of Politics*, in the journal *Publius* and in papers prepared for meetings of the International Institute of Political Philosophy. I thank my students for their thoughtful term papers and probing questions, as I do Sara Piazza for her research assistance, the ever-helpful university librarians, and Joan Brunn and Kathy Klingenberg for their secretarial assistance.

My wife, to whom this book is dedicated, might have preferred another small teddy bear to add to her collection; I hope she finds this token of affection less fuzzy but almost as comforting.

Sanford Lakoff
La Jolla, California

1

The New Appeal of an Old Ideal

Chairman's tomb and Emperor's palace
*   face each other across the square,*
One great leader in his wisdom
*   made our countless futures bare,*
Each and every marble staircase
*   covers heaps of bones beneath.*
From the eaves of such fine buildings
*   fresh red blood drops everywhere.*
——anonymous poem posted on the Democracy Wall, Beijing, 1978[1]

At the turn of the fourth century B.C., after a democratic counter-revolution had dislodged the Athenian oligarchy known as "The Thirty," the philosopher Plato repented his earlier disdain for the democratic constitution. Although some of his own friends and family had been prominent members of the oligarchical conspiracy, Plato observed that by their oppressive behavior "they showed me in a short time that the preceding constitution had been a precious thing."[2] Centuries later, in Renaissance Florence, the statesman and historian Francesco Guicciardini offered a similar observation: "Great defects are inherent in popular government. Nevertheless, the wise and good citizens of our city prefer it as a lesser evil."[3] In recent times, too, democracy has won favor by default, after bad experience with alternatives, but the latest appeal of this venerable ideal also reflects a more positive appreciation of its advantages.[4] The most fundamental of these is surely that of all social and political systems democracy alone holds out the promise of personal and political freedom to the fullest practical extent and as a matter of constitutional right, not governmental caprice. Although the word "democracy" signifies in the most literal sense only "rule by the people," it has come to represent, from earliest times and even more in the modern period, the belief in autonomy, or self-determination, for

1

individuals and the collectivities to which they belong. Dictatorial systems may promise order and sometimes provide it, but the price they exact is the deprivation of freedom for most if not all of those they rule, except for privileges the rulers deign to allow and can retract at will. Those who live under such systems are subjects who are acted upon, but not also citizens, who may act for themselves and confer the powers of government upon accountable public servants. Even a "good despotism," as John Stuart Mill remarked, is debilitating: "The despotism of Augustus prepared the Romans for Tiberius. If the whole tone of their character had not first been prostrated by nearly two generations of that mild slavery, they would probably have had spirit left to rebel against the more odious one."[5]

Democracy offers the radically different promise that freedom need not be sacrificed for order because the constitution guaranteeing both is supported not by force alone but also by the express and regular consent of the governed. This promise of freedom accounts above all else for the new appeal of democracy, especially in the wake of modern experience with various specimens of autocracy, ranging from oligarchy and authoritarianism to the most extreme form, totalitarianism, in which the aim is to control virtually the whole of social life.

The latest appreciation of the dependence of freedom upon democracy appeared in the aftermath of the Second World War. The tragic consequences of that war, suffered on so unprecedented a scale, produced a revulsion against dictatorship, especially in societies which had experienced alternatives, and inspired a new appreciation, reminiscent of Plato's, of the benefits of democracy. One of the best known expressions of this new appreciation is the backhanded encomium of Winston Churchill. His comment is especially noteworthy because it came from a politician of such experience and renown and in circumstances that might have led him to feel angry and resentful toward democracy. A half century earlier he had been a liberal on domestic policy but an imperialist who shared commonly held racist views and was bent on denying democracy to the colonies.[6] Now he had been dealt a humiliating electoral defeat after rallying his countrymen in the "finest hour" of their history. Speaking in the House of Commons as leader of the opposition, Churchill accepted defeat with extraordinary grace and thoughtfulness in this often quoted observation: "Indeed, it has been said that democracy is the worst form of Government except all those other forms that have been tried from time to time; but there is the broad feeling in our country that the people should rule, continuously rule, and that public opinion, expressed by all constitutional means, should shape, guide, and control the actions of Ministers who are their servants and not their masters." Whether he had changed his mind about the suitability of democracy for the colonies is doubtful.[7] The fact that he identified his encomium for democracy with beliefs held "in our country" may well mean that he did not intend to encourage the universal adoption of democracy. Still, his words have been taken to apply generally.

At about the same time, the novelist E. M. Forster added another strong if somewhat qualified endorsement. Offering "Two Cheers for Democracy" because it provides the best setting for creativity and liberty, Forster observed that democracy

> is less hateful than other contemporary forms of government, and to that extent it deserves our support. It does start from the assumption that the individual is important, and that all types are needed to make a civilization. It does not divide its citizens into the bosses and the bossed—as an efficiency-regime tends to do. The people I admire most are those who are sensitive and want to create something or discover something, and do not see life in terms of power, and such people get more of a chance under a democracy than elsewhere. They found religions, great or small, or they produce literature and art, or they do disinterested scientific research, or they may be what is called "ordinary people," who are creative in their lives, bring up their children decently, for instance, or help their neighbours. All those people need to express themselves; they cannot do so unless society allows them liberty to do so, and the society which allows them most liberty is democracy.

Two cheers for democracy, then, "one because it admits variety and two because it permits criticism." Not three, because "only Love the Beloved Republic deserves that."[8]

Such approving comments were widely endorsed. In Latin America, belief in democracy "as a central symbol with almost universal resonance" emerged in the period during and after the Second World War, although it meant different things to different adherents.[9] In Asia, during negotiations brokered by the United States in 1945, Mao Zedong and Chiang Kai-shek agreed to endorse and publish a set of principles including the need for political democracy, which was to be achieved in the transitional manner envisaged earlier by Sun Yat-sen.[10] Everywhere in the world, in fact, democracy seemed to be in favor. In 1949, the United Nations Economic and Social Council circulated a questionnaire among scholars in many countries soliciting their views of democracy. The agency found that although they thought the term ambiguous, both as an ideal and as a practical system, they were unanimous in endorsing it: "There were no replies averse to democracy. Probably for the first time in history, 'democracy' is claimed as the proper ideal description of all systems of political and social organization advocated by influential proponents."[11]

These indications of acceptance did not last very long after the war, however. The shadow of totalitarian communism fell over eastern Europe and a large part of Asia. Hopes for democratization in the newly decolonized states of Africa and in many Latin American countries were dashed one after another by the appearance or reappearance of dictators or juntas. As a result, the new appreciation of democracy was tempered by skepticism. One fear was that it could be established or maintained only where liberal values were well established. A related concern was that where rates of poverty and illiteracy were too high and democracy seemed to threaten the interests of powerful social forces both domestic and international, it could not be established. Some theorists concluded that wherever the overriding concern was to achieve a rapid modernization, only repressive government would be suitable, and dictators were quick to take advantage of this supposition, sometimes masking their autocracy by names like the "guided democracy" of Sukarno in Indonesia. As a result, a general pessimism became commonplace among the best-informed specialists. By 1984, Freedom House could classify fifty-one countries as democratic, representing just over a third of the world's population, but Arend Lijphart pointed out that in only twenty-one of the countries could democracy be considered well established.[12] In the same year, Samuel P. Huntington, one of the most acute students of comparative political development, expressed skepticism about prospects for democracy outside Western Europe and North America. After noting that by the measures used by Freedom House, the percentage of the world's population living in what were defined as free states had barely risen over twenty years from 32 percent to 36 percent, Huntington concluded that "with a few exceptions, the limits of democratic development in the world may have been reached."[13]

Why did this widely held pessimistic judgment prove to be unwarranted? Perhaps the most important reason, because of its real and symbolic influence, is the stagnation, and then the unexpected dramatic collapse, of the communist dictatorships of eastern Europe. Until the sudden fall of these regimes, they seemed to be functioning alternatives to "Western-style democracy" providing a more attractive model for developing societies. The demonstrated failure of command economies both in the Soviet Union and in many developing countries has led to a disenchantment with the dictatorial path to modernization. In the case of Iran, the reaction has taken the form of a rejection of modernization in favor of a return to traditional religious values, including the admonition against taking or paying interest on loans. Elsewhere, however, pragmatic considerations produced a bandwagon effect: regimes no longer able to play off East against West recognized that it would be prudent to privatize their economies, heed the recommendations of the World Bank and the International Monetary Fund, and pay at least lip service to the ideals of human rights and democratic government. And ironically, in developing countries like South Korea where autocracy succeeded in promoting economic growth, that very economic success often engendered a demand for political freedom from those who have benefited most from economic growth and upon whom further growth depends—middle-class business people and professionals, and the students who aim to join their ranks.

Willingness to pay lip-service to democratic and free-market nostrums is, of course, no guarantee that change can be achieved. Democratic rhetoric may mask elite rule. In societies accustomed to state control and saddled with inefficient state-run enterprises, economic "shock therapy" unaccompanied by social cushioning may cause such short-term hardships as to evoke demands for a return to autocratic leadership and more paternalistic social policy. These difficulties are exacerbated by the likelihood that a less repressive government will find it hard to maintain law and order and prevent racketeering and the corrupting effects of buccaneer capitalism. The formidable problems of uncontrolled population increase, imbalanced economies, and lack of infrastructure and educational opportunities continue to block economic development in many poor countries. Which if any of the regimes recently drawn to democratic ideals will succeed in implementing them remains to be seen.

There are also other reasons for the new appeal of democracy, including advances in travel and communications technology, which have enabled people everywhere to compare their own ways of life with others and not just with their own previous circumstances. Thanks to travel, film, and television, as well as satellite-linked cellular telephones and fax transmission, the "demonstration effect" of the Western model combining political democracy with the market economy has had a worldwide impact on expectations. The "transparency" wrought by modern means of communication leads people in one country to compare their situation more readily to conditions elsewhere and not just to what it was in the past. By itself, however, communication does not necessarily universalize attitudes and behavior so much as it does expectations of standards of living. Democratic modes of behavior are apt to be adopted widely only after hard experience with alternatives and after they have been learned directly.

The perceived connection between the failure of command economies and the clamor for democracy has prompted some observers to contend that many who have come to favor democracy do so because they suppose it will bring economic benefits rather than because they value political freedom. In other words, they associate democracy with the benefits of Western-style capitalism and therefore look to it solely for the consumer benefits it supposedly brings. The crowds demonstrating at the end of the 1980s in Berlin, Prague, and Budapest, it has been said, were not "inebriate with some abstract passion for freedom, for social justice," as that ideal was defined by philosophers like John Stuart Mill, but rather with intoxicating visions of the consumer paradise they identified with the West. Their "new temples to liberty will be McDonald's and Kentucky Fried

Chicken" and other shrines to the "California-promise" marketed by Western films, television serials, and advertisements "to the common man on this tired earth."[14]

This interpretation seriously misses or misconstrues the point. Some of those who took part in these demonstrations, including leaders like the Czech writer Vaclav Havel, had been persecuted as political dissenters, and were therefore well aware of the importance of democracy to liberty of conscience. But even if the mass of demonstrators were moved by hope for material improvements, that hope is also rooted in a concern for liberty. Those who disparage these movements fail to appreciate that democracy aims to empower ordinary people as economic actors as well as voters and that, as Mill was among the first to point out, a civil society in which people enjoy the benefits of private ownership and the free market—however regulated and combined with public sector enterprises—is indispensable to liberty. The attitude of modern skeptics echoes that of critics of democracy since Plato who have complained that at bottom democracy is an expression of envy and materialism on the part of those unwilling to be ruled by their superiors and incapable of rising above their appetitive drives. The understanding of democracy by those who have embraced its tenets has always been very different. For them, its aim is to allow all citizens the same freedom to pursue their own ends and manage their own lives, separately and collectively, that only a few may enjoy under other systems. From this broad perspective, economic freedom is as much a part of democracy as any other freedom. Like other freedoms, it can sometimes lead people to become so absorbed in personal and private pursuits that they become indifferent or even hostile to the rights and welfare of others. In undemocratic systems, however, the denial of freedom is pervasive and indifference to rights is as endemic as government is unaccountable.

The disillusionment with Soviet-style socialism welled up not simply because of a failure of communist systems to produce the plenty that was promised; it was at the same time a reaction to the denial of liberty embedded in Marxian ideology as in other statist value systems. The privileges of the *nomenklatura* came at the cost both of the welfare and of the liberty of the masses whose self-appointed "vanguard" they claimed to be. As Frank E. Manuel has observed in an essay otherwise sympathetic to Marx's socialist ideals, "The regimes that spoke in his name derived their justification from the idea that the individual was of no moment in the period before the dawn of true human history, the coming of the age of unalienated labor; and if one Soviet state after another denied the meaningfulness of individual lives during the transition, Marx cannot be spared the world-historical verdict of complicity in their crimes."[15] Complaints about the failure of state socialist systems to "deliver the goods" consumers wanted were only one facet of a larger disillusionment with systems that denied individuals the rights and opportunities they came to understand were enjoyed in democratic societies. Thanks to advances in the means of communication, people in eastern and central Europe and in east Asia came to know not only "the ideology of consumerism, but the culture of democracy"[16] in which it is embedded.

It is just the centrality and radical character of the new recognition of the link between democracy and individual liberty that has led other observers to adopt the optimistic view that the result of the recent upsurge in belief in democracy will promote an historic transition away from autocracy toward more liberal systems—systems that combine representative government with market economies and social pluralism.[17] Along with the belief in such a transition, it is also tempting to hope that as it occurs, a global peace dividend will also be experienced as a fractured and conflict-ridden world order will be replaced by a dominant federation of democracies, more or less as prophesied at the end of the eighteenth century. Skeptics understandably demur, afraid that countervailing forces such as ethnicity, nationalism, and the continued existence of separate sovereign states will ensure that conflict continues, but even they are likely to admit that the spread of belief in democracy as an ideal represents a change, and an opportunity, of historic dimensions.

Why Autocracies Lose Favor

At bottom, then, the ideal of democracy is gaining in appeal in so many countries because of a growing awareness that the autocratic alternatives are all unappealing as a long-term political formula. Tyrants sometimes rise to power on the wings of popular adulation, but before long their ruthless appetite for power and self-aggrandizement at the expense of any other concern becomes all too apparent. The order they promise is likely to be appreciated in societies devastated by war and economic hardship or riven by various forms of civil strife. Whether appreciated or not, autocratic power is always dangerous to resist. But such forms of rule are bound to arouse resentment among elements of the populace, and in many cases among a great majority. Autocrats usually protect privileged groups and sometimes create new ones in order to prop up their power. They proscribe dissent, and exile and persecute dissenters. Their obsession with order often produces an economic and psychological stagnation that can be overcome only by fomenting fear of attack from without as a rationale for military adventurism. The bloated military establishments that usually accompany autocracies have the latent purpose of protecting the regime against internal threats, but sometimes they become a catalyst for change, either because they involve their societies in protracted and unpopular wars or because ambitious officers carry out coups d'état, sometimes bringing down governments they are unable to replace. Feared and hated secret police agencies help preserve such regimes (though they can also threaten to subvert them), but when dictators must appeal for public support, hatred of the secret police often turns against the regime itself.

The repressive controls autocratic regimes try to impose may be considered necessary to enforce the social discipline and mobilize the resources required for an economic "take off," especially where parochialism, traditionalism, and pre-industrial attitudes combine to resist rapid modernization campaigns. If democratization is attempted before a rapid rate of economic growth is achieved, it may generate pressures for immediate consumption preventing a high rate of investment. Autocratic regimes can enforce savings and channel investment into sectors of the economy with the greatest long-term benefit.[18] The prosperity achieved under "free-market authoritarianism"[19] in countries like Singapore, Taiwan, and South Korea is often cited in support of this contention, though special cultural factors such as Confucian regard for hierarchy may be more important than the structure of the regime in these cases. "Many of the most impressive economic growth records in the last 150 years," Francis Fukuyama has noted, "have been compiled not by democracies, but by authoritarian states with more or less capitalist economic systems. This was true of both Meiji Japan and the German Second Reich in the latter half of the nineteenth century, as well as any number of more recent modernizing authoritarian regimes such as Franco's Spain, post-1953 South Korea, Taiwan, Brazil, Singapore, or Thailand."[20] In many other instances, however, authoritarianism has produced only economic stagnation. Adam Przeworski and Fernando Limongi observe that "the world is replete with authoritarian regimes that are dismal failures from the economic point of view."[21] In India, Lloyd I. Rudolph and Susanne Hoeber Rudolph have pointed out, "both good and bad economic performance occurred under both authoritarian and democratic regimes."[22] Reviewing studies of the relationship between regime type and economic development, Przeworski and Limongi note that "eight found in favor of democracy, eight in favor of authoritarianism, and five discovered no difference." What seems to matter is not the type of regime but whether the state is committed to economic development and sufficiently free of political pressures working against it.[23] As Pranab Bardhan puts the same thought, the question is whether development-minded decision-makers are well insulated "against the ravages of short-run pork-barrel politics" and are able to "use the discipline of the market (guided possibly by world market signals) against the inevitable lobbies of group predation."[24]

Although the evidence is thus inconclusive with respect to the inception of economic growth, the high correlation between democracy and sustained economic growth[25] suggests that over the long run, the two are interdependent. Even when autocracy is economically successful, the repression it entails is likely to become a barrier to economic progress at an advanced stage. This repression stifles initiative, arouses labor unrest, and serves to protect state power and the privileges of ruling groups rather than the needs of the society as a whole and of most of its members. Whether achieved under autocratic or democratic auspices, economic growth requires higher levels of education, and education is likely to arouse more demands for the protection of fundamental human rights, if only because more and more people become conscious of the existence of alternative options and better able to articulate demands and organize to advance their interests.

Autocracies must resist such demands because they are incompatible with the leadership's retention of absolute power. In totalitarian settings, even to voice them is to challenge the insistence on conformity and subordination which is the premise of the regime. Whereas traditional autocracies often allow their subjects the opportunity to go about their daily business as they choose, provided only that they do not conspire against the regime or the status quo, modern totalitarian regimes have been far more intrusive, out of an inner compulsion to achieve total control of belief and behavior. Because of the same appetite for power, these regimes have usually been expansionistic and scornful of the claims to sovereignty and independence of neighboring peoples.

Democracies, whatever their flaws and whatever exact principles they may be said to follow, are, just as E. M. Forster noted, systems of government and society in which people are encouraged to exercise initiative, both in the private and the public sphere. People may not always take advantage of the opportunity, if pressures to conform to prevailing public opinion are too strong and the social cost of non-conformity is too high. But the opportunity is available and legally protected. In democracies, people of any social standing can make claims to legal protection of a variety of human rights and expect judicial redress in case their rights have been violated under color of law. Because of such constitutional protections, and because the representative system relied upon by modern democracies helps makes government permeable and responsive, no one need passively endure wrongful discrimination. Ironically, one of the dangers in a flourishing democracy is that demands for the protection of rights can go so far as to be self-defeating. The proliferation of rights and the effort to resolve all social tensions by defining them as conflicts of rights can lead to an obsession with litigation and to paradoxical outcomes like interference with freedom of speech and more solicitude for the rights of those prone to violence than for their actual or intended victims. But even such excesses are evidence that modern democracy and liberty are intertwined.

Finally, it is a striking fact that with only arguable exceptions, "democratic states never fight each other";[26] though they have sometimes behaved imperialistically toward non-democratic societies and rationalized their imperialism as a way of spreading democracy. Of the 353 wars fought since 1819, none has been fought between established democracies.[27]

These increasingly well-understood contrasts surely account for the rising appeal of democracy. But such explanations are very general and they do not reveal why there should be such sharp contrasts between democratic and undemocratic systems or whether there is some pattern in the process of political development which favors one or the other at particular times or in the long run. Nor do they take account of many criticisms of democracy, fair and unfair. More elaborate explanation, drawing on the historical record, is clearly needed if democracy is to be valued for its own sake and not merely as the lesser of evils—and if it is to be shown to be a practical ideal under most circumstances. First, however, the term itself must be defined.

2

Democracy as the Quest for Autonomy

Although some analysts would prefer to avoid having to use the word "democracy" altogether in discussing actual rather than ideal systems of popular government, it has historical associations and a continuing acceptance that make its use all but unavoidable. Provided it is defined in reasonably coherent terms, with due attention to variations and ambiguities, there is good reason to use it to denote both a social and political ideal and a set of institutions and practices. This chapter will examine criticisms of the term and attempts to replace it with other terminology. It will also discuss both the differences and continuities in ancient and modern usage, try to rebut the contention that democracy rests on a principle of exclusivity, stress the importance to modern democracy of the belief in human rights, and point out the disappearing differences in usage between "democracy" and "republic." Finally, it will offer a working definition of the term as the expression of the universal human quest for autonomy—and some reflections on the tensions among the forms autonomy takes in democracy.

Neologism, Criticisms, and Defenses

Because the word conjures up a standard of perfect self-government that has never been achieved and is inherently unattainable, Robert A. Dahl, the most influential contemporary analyst of political democracy, has gone so far as to coin a new word, "polyarchy," for empirical purposes; the word "democracy" would be restricted to normative use.[1]

When first introduced, polyarchy was defined as any political system in which leaders are controlled by non-leaders and which exhibits two essential characteristics: competition for office and a relatively inclusive electoral system. These characteristics have led other analysts of an empirical bent to describe it favorably as a "stipulative" definition, or one with clear empirical referents.[2]

Despite this distinct virtue, polyarchy has not been universally accepted as a substitute for democracy. Giovanni Sartori, another major modern theorist of democracy, has objected that such a distinction between the empirical and the normative does not take account of the dynamic interplay of these two dimensions of political reality: "What democracy *is* cannot be separated from what democracy *should be*. A democracy exists only insofar as its ideals and values bring it into being . . . Dahl's polyarchies are as they are because they embody ideals."[3]

As fruitful as Dahl's concept has been for the study of comparative government, Sartori's point is well taken. Although the job of empirical analysis may be more complicated if ideals as well as measurable practices and institutions must be taken into account, it is unrealistic to suppose that the normative dimension can be neatly separated from the empirical. To do so is to remove a dynamic or dialectical element from the political process which often plays a role in efforts to change realities. Systems characterized by nothing more than electoral competition and electoral inclusiveness, moreover, do not necessarily protect the civil liberties and rights of citizens—particularly since the definition makes no reference to laws and judicial systems. Unless there are institutional safeguards against abuse, even a vigorously competitive and very inclusive election may put into power a regime bent on destroying democracy. Democratic revolutions and civil rights movements, moreover, are sparked by norms no less than by interests. As Sartori suggests, it is the interplay between these dimensions that provides the fullest view of the political process. Dahl himself appears to have recognized the merit of the criticism in broadening the definition of polyarchy to include normative elements, bringing it closer to the conventional understanding of political democracy.[4]

Polyarchy, moreover, is a definition that deliberately separates political from socioeconomic considerations. But a political system that provides contestation and participation under conditions in which the mass of the people is mired in poverty and illiteracy is apt to be democratic in form but not in reality.[5] Effective contestation and participation will be as restricted as it would be under oligarchy, except for the need to manipulate and mobilize mass support. Dahl and many others treat these socioeconomic considerations as conditions either favorable or unfavorable to the establishment and maintenance of polyarchy. An alternative is to adopt a more multidimensional definition than polyarchy provides, one that includes socioeconomic considerations. Democracy, understood to require appropriate social, political and economic conditions, serves that purpose. Whichever term is used, however, there is no disagreement that successful democratization requires appropriate, even symbiotic, socioeconomic relationships. "Nothing is more obvious even to the casual observer," Robert Putnam has noted, "than the fact that effective democracy is closely associated with socioeconomic modernity, both across time and across space."[6]

Others have denied the validity of "democracy" as a term of analysis on a variety of grounds. Linguistic analysts maintain that it rests on metaphysical foundations so ambiguous as to be meaningless. (T. D. Weldon has observed of such statements as "All men are created free and equal" and "Men are always to be treated as ends and never as means": "Nothing follows from these high abstractions, or if you like anything does."[7]) Democracy is also held to be one of those philosophical concepts too "essentially contested" to be used without qualification or without specification among its various forms.[8]

But almost all important political terms involve ambiguous notions, are often contested, and need specification. The difficulty in defining democracy is no worse than in the case of many other concepts widely used in discussing politics and government. Thomas L. Thorson has suggested that the very relativity of values makes democracy the best basis for social organization because the "logic of democracy" (like the logic of science) denies that absolute truth can be known with certainty, and therefore allows for diversity, tolerance, and openness to change and recognition of error.[9] Others prefer to define democracy in terms of its procedural requisites so as to avoid the problem posed by the relativity of values. Joseph A. Schumpeter rejects the "classical theory of democracy," with its emphasis on direct popular government aimed at achieving the "common good" in favor of an approach stressing the "democratic method," an "institutional arrangement for arriving at political decisions in which individuals acquire the power to decide by means of a competitive struggle for the people's vote."[10] From a different perspective, Jürgen Habermas also grounds democracy as a commitment not to any abstract value principles but rather to rational discourse among equally empowered and enlightened citizens.[11] The "anti-foundationalist" Richard Rorty, who agrees with Habermas' objective, would substitute a freely arrived at consensus on pluralism for the principled foundation he thinks cannot be ascertained.[12] Brian Barry too contends that democracy is best understood in procedural terms, without "any constraints on the content of the outcomes produced, such as substantive equality, respect for human rights, concern for the general welfare, personal liberty or the role of law." The only exceptions are those required by democracy itself as a procedure, such as the freedom to form and express political preferences.[13] Barry Holden, not content with only a procedural formula, has shown that linguistic analysis can be used to identify universal needs and aspirations such as liberty and equality, and that these can serve as benchmarks in identifying and evaluating democratic systems.[14]

These efforts of reformulation show that however open to variation and differences of emphasis the concept of democracy undoubtedly is, it retains a core meaning in actual usage that becomes very clear when contrasts are drawn between democratic and non-democratic systems and when criteria are identified for distinguishing between them. As William E. Connolly has observed, in discussing such concepts, "'Democracy'— and other concepts like it—displays in our discourse over a normal range of cases a close connection between its criteria and its normative point. The relation is close enough to allow us to say that if that connection were somehow abrogated by a large number of people for a large number of cases over a long period of time, the concept itself would either fall into disuse or undergo fundamental change."[15] The fact that the term has neither fallen into disuse nor undergone fundamental change is, as Connolly suggests, a good *prima facie* reason for retaining it, provided its meaning and various dimensions are specified in particular uses and related to historical context. In order to obtain criteria for identifying and comparing democratic and non-democratic systems, it is necessary to distinguish among democratic ideals, democratic institutions, and democratic procedures. In order to assess the likelihood that a transition to democracy will succeed, it is also necessary to take account of the socioeconomic context.

Etymology and Usage: Differences and Continuities

In terms of historical usage, the term "democracy" certainly has different denotations and connotations now than it had when it was first introduced in ancient Greece. Then it was understood to denote direct popular government by assembled citizens; today it usually denotes mainly representative self-government. The connection between ancient and modern usage, moreover, is hardly unbroken, as Athanasios Moulakis has rightly noted:

> There is no real filiation linking modern with ancient democracy. There is no institutional continuity, no handing down of practices leading from the ancient city-states to today's regimes. Ancient democracy is known to the modern Western mind only through books. That is by no means nothing, but it is not the same kind of ancestry as that which links our democratic institutions with the charters and the Joyous Entries, the guilds and the corporations, the monasteries with their elected abbots, the parlements and the remonstrances and the bills of rights of our continuous European past. The modern European states and, at a further remove, their offshoots across the seas, grew out of medieval patterns of life and thought that were, in the course of events, reformed and revolutionized into what we now feel entitled, for some good and for some bad reasons, to call democracies. But "no taxation without representation" would have been unintelligible to the Greeks.[16]

More important than filiation, however, from the point of view of ascertaining the meaning of political terms, are family or morphological resemblances and connotations. By many concrete practical measures, the institutional, behavioral, and cultural similarities are sometimes striking among systems called democratic. What could be more familiar for modern democratic usage, for example, than the following set of rules adopted in Athens some 2,500 years ago? "Anyone addressing the *Boule* (steering-committee) or *Ecclesia* (assembly) must keep to the matter in hand, must not deal with two separate matters together, and must not speak twice on the same matter at any one meeting; he must not engage in slanders or scurrility, or interrupt others; must speak only from the platform and must not assault the presiding officer . . ."[17] Any parliament or committee operating under Robert's *Rules of Order* is following precepts similar to those adopted by Athenians centuries earlier. Such rules are essential for the success of "government by discussion," the principle Walter Bagehot thought the very essence of parliamentary government.[18] Parliaments, it is true, may be less than fully representative, and such rules are therefore necessary but not sufficient conditions for democracy. In spirit, however, government by discussion—in other words by free debate and negotiation among all parties—is very close to a definition of the aim of democratic government.

In numerous other respects, too, there are remarkable resemblances, despite the lack of continuity, many of which have to do with the use of voting to make or accept policies and choose officials. Political parties in the sense of persistent, relatively impersonal associations were unknown until the eighteenth century, when they began to appear in the form of parliamentary clubs and became essential in uniting voters, but factions, their predecessors, were common in the assemblies of ancient Athens and Rome. It was just because factions had so bedeviled popular government in antiquity that James Madison gave them so much attention in *Federalist* 10 and considered parties no different from factions. Voting is a technique used for advisory purposes or for pro forma endorsement in non-democratic settings, but in its most meaningful form, as the expression of free choice by self-governing citizens, it is a hallmark of democratic systems, required in jury trials, legislative assemblies, and in elections to public office. The word "candidate" comes from the Latin for "dressed in white," because Romans running for office called attention to themselves by whitening their togas with chalk when they paraded the city streets canvassing support in election campaigns during the last twenty-four days preceding the vote.[19] The introduction of the secret ballot in ancient Rome and its reintroduction in more recent times was a major step in protecting the independence of the voter. The Athenian use of pebbles (*psephoi*) dropped into urns to record votes has led modern analysts of voting to refer to themselves as "psephologists." From ancient times, elections have been accompanied by the use of patronage and bribery—persistent though less savory characteristics of democracy.

The use of the jury system is another constant. Trial by a jury of one's peers—when peers are understood to be a random selection of fellow citizens, under conditions that guarantee procedural fairness—is characteristic of many democratic societies. To guard against jury tampering, the Athenians invented a machine, made first of wood, then of stone—the *cleroterion*—by which jurors were assigned to cases by random selection, apparently according to the drop of black or white spherical balls down a funnel at the end of which they landed next to name tickets affixed to slots on the machine.[20] Athenian jurors had more authority than modern jurors. In the absence of judges, they interpreted the law as well as the facts of the case and applied penalties. Athenian juries were also far larger than modern ones and had legislative review and investigative functions broader than those assigned to modern juries (with the partial exception of American grand juries). Despite such differences, the reliance on randomly-selected citizen jurors is certainly another striking similarity among some though not all democratic systems.

Freedom of speech is a *sine qua non* of democracy. Although the appearance of means of mass communication coincides with the development of large-scale political systems and is very much a modern phenomenon, this freedom—*isegoria* to the Greeks—is indispensable to democracy. In classical Athens it meant that ordinary citizens had the right to stand up in the Assembly and state their opinions when the president of the Assembly, in accordance with custom, would ask, "Who wishes to address the Assembly?"[21] Modern media, as the very name implies, serve to mediate among the participants in public debate; in ancient democracies communication was more "immediate" in the sense of being direct and unfiltered. Drama too served as "a form of public speech," Peter Euben has noted, because it "opened public life to debate, discussion, and criticism while helping to qualify citizens to participate intelligently in them."[22] Citizens who served on juries and voted in the Assembly also acted in and formed the audiences for the tragedies and comedies performed at periodic religious festivals. The tragedies explored the fundamental questions of human existence and the morality of political behavior and rules, while also depicting both the nobility of character and the flaws of character of mythic gods and epic heroes. The comedies satirized both the susceptibility of the *demos* to flattery and pay for jury service and the pretentiousness and self-interestedness of elites. As many as a thousand boys and men took part as actors and in the chorus during a festival; theaters held up to 14,000 spectators.[23] Often couched in polemical and satirical form, Athenian free speech sometimes showed a disrespect for authority that would have been a punishable offense in other systems. It was more in evidence there than in Rome, one of the reasons the Athenian system is thought to have been more democratic.[24]

Then, as now, the requirement of communication and consent has helped prevent elites from dominating masses of citizens by the exercise of force alone. The key to the relative stability of ancient Athenian democracy, Josiah Ober has suggested, is "the mediating and integrative power of communication between citizens—especially between ordinary and elite citizens—in a language whose vocabulary consisted of symbols developed and deployed in public arenas: the people's courts, the Assembly, the theater, and the agora."[25] Even apart from the exercise of the suffrage and the use of the lot, this discourse of democracy enabled the mass of Athenian citizens to exert an influence that amounted to "ideological hegemony."[26] The same holds true in modern democratic societies when leaders must appeal to followers by invoking common symbols and values—symbols and values that serve as constraints, even though they are subject to manipulation and do not necessarily control policy. Although democratically elected and accountable leaders can sometimes manipulate public opinion by "managing the news" and appealing to emotion rather than reason, the opportunity for criticism and exposure of manipulation makes such behavior harder to sustain than it is in undemocratic systems where this opportunity is deliberately denied.

As to "no taxation without representation," although the ancient world did not know representation in the modern sense, the need to extract financial and military contributions from the lower orders, especially in the Roman case, compelled ancient oligarchs no less than modern autocrats to make concessions which gave the populace greater access to political power.

Similarities are also evident in a host of other particular practices and institutions. Contemporary Americans not as well versed in the history of democracy as the framers of their constitution were may suppose that the requirement that the Senate give its "advice and consent" to high-level executive appointments such as Supreme Court justices is a provision invented in the Philadelphia located in Pennsylvania. But the framers were careful students of classical history and may have been aware of the Athenian practice known as the *dokimasia* whereby appointees were given preliminary scrutiny by the *Boule*, the Assembly, and/or by the popular courts. Drawing on Aristotle's account of the practice, E. S. Staveley describes the *dokimasia* of the nine archons, the chief Athenian magistrates, in terms that—despite the differences in the matters of concern—will be recognizable to anyone familiar with a United States Senate confirmation hearing:

> The potential officer was required to establish that his family had been citizens for three generations, and to show that he had a family tomb and observed the traditional religious rites of Apollo and Zeus. He also had to submit to questioning on such matters as whether he had paid his taxes, whether he had done his prescribed period of military service, and whether he treated

his parents with respect. After witnesses had been produced to give evidence on these points, an open invitation was extended to any of those present to challenge the candidate's credentials or to lodge a complaint; in the event of a complainant coming forward, a form of legal trial was staged, involving the use of both prosecution and defence counsel, before a final verdict on the candidate's suitability was taken by vote.[27]

The same sense of familiarity applies to the lexicographic and etymological meaning of the term democracy. In use and origin, it means the rule or power (*kratos*) of the people (the *demos*), which in Greek usage connoted rule by the mass of citizens rather than by the rich and well-born. It drew upon and fulfills the Greek belief in *isonomia* or equal justice that seems to have been its immediate predecessor.[28]

The Problem of Exclusivity

Admittedly, the connotation of the term "democracy" suffers from ambiguity because of a record of practical usage in which supposedly democratic societies deviate from the formal ideal of equality. In excluding slaves and resident aliens from citizenship, and female citizens from political participation, Athenian democracy was marred by a very restrictive conception of fitness to rule. Even among formally equal male citizens, eligibility for public office was limited to those who met a high though steadily decreased property qualification. The Athenian philosophers rationalized exclusions from citizenship and political participation by making the barriers depend upon supposedly natural differences in rational capacity, even though these same philosophers had drawn a far more fundamental difference on this score between all human beings and other animals. Republican Rome adopted a much more inclusive notion of citizenship in order to suit its expansionist ambitions, but the proletarian masses were effectively denied power and slavery was practiced on a sometimes massive scale. Still, Rome's extension of citizenship to people of many different racial, ethnic, and religious affiliations is in this respect even more a foretaste of modern democracy than the ethnically-bounded Athenian notion of citizenship.

Later political systems similarly democratic in tendency were also restrictive in establishing criteria for citizenship, even after advances in philosophic and scientific thinking had discredited categorical distinctions among human beings. Europeans continued to trade in African slaves and to maltreat native populations in Africa, the Americas, and Asia as though they were incorrigible savages for decades after philosophers pronounced human rights natural and universal. Property and gender qualifications limited the right to vote even longer. In the United States, where property qualifications were dropped early in the nineteenth century, most

African-Americans were kept enslaved and denied the right to vote until after the Civil War. Even then, despite the amendments to the Constitution, discriminatory practices in the southern states, such as the poll tax and literacy test, effectively denied the franchise to freed slaves and their descendants for another century. Full universal adult suffrage was first adopted in the Norwegian constitution of 1905; other democratic countries only extended the suffrage to women after World War I[29]—Switzerland, only in 1971.

These serious limitations and inconsistencies in application should not be confused with, or allowed to detract from, the meaning of democracy as an ideal. Democracy meant to Athenians, as it meant to Abraham Lincoln, "government of the people, by the people, and for the people." How that ideal is translated into reality is, as Sartori rightly suggests, a constant and necessary problem in the construction and development of democratic systems. Pericles defined Athenian democracy as a form of government "run with a view to the interests of the majority, not of the few," and he took steps such as the introduction of pay for jury service to assure that all classes would participate in the democratic process; but as Martin Ostwald has noted, although the welfare of the masses was taken to be the object of policy, the majority of the people continued to suffer from certain political disabilities, notably exclusion from the highest offices.[30] Then as now, the democratic ideal was imperfectly realized.

Even more seriously than the use of economic qualifications for office, the restriction of citizenship, whether by ancient Athens or in the United States at its founding, inhibits a realization of the universal egalitarian ideal at the core of democratic belief. It does so by severing the link between recognition of the inherent human capacity for rationality and communication, which all human beings share to a far greater degree than other species, and an acceptance of the principle of self-government as the expression of that capacity.

Societies in which some categories of people in full possession of their mental faculties are classified as incapable or undeserving of citizenship will inevitably deny full educational opportunity and foreclose the most prestigious careers to those so classified, making the claim a self-fulfilling prophecy. As a practical matter, the stability and efficiency of democratic regimes depends critically on the ability of the general electorate to understand the issues confronting it and to make judgments about those issues and about the qualifications of candidates for office. Universal education is therefore as important for democracy as a more restricted, status-based system of education is for aristocratic societies. Such revolutionary republicans as Charles Maurice de Talleyrand and Antoine-Nicolas de Condorcet in France and Thomas Jefferson in America, understood this when they sought to make the cause of universal public education virtually the first order of post-revolutionary business. They were well aware that democratic society also needed to nurture a natural aristocracy, to provide leadership in politics as well as in the sciences, the arts, and commerce, but they recognized that republican government could succeed only if ordinary citizens could tell the real natural aristocrats from charlatans and demagogues, and if they had enough education not to be gulled, as previous generations had been, by those who claimed occult wisdom or metaphysical authority in order to exploit their ignorance.

To contend that democracy requires the utterly unrealistic assumption that everyone will acquire the same level of understanding of all subjects is to box against a shadow. Democracy *is* incompatible with the view that the great majority of people are born hopelessly irrational and are destined to remain ignorant and incompetent, regardless of the education they receive. It also requires denial of the view that only those capable of the highest levels of rationality can distinguish right from wrong or vote from considerations of self-interest and public interest. It rests on the belief that "common sense" and the wisdom gained from nothing more than the experience of living in conditions of freedom can serve as guides to judgment in many matters, and that enough formal education can equip people to come to grips with the most basic issues of public policy and appraise the advice of experts. Provided there is a serious social commitment to education, exclusion from the rights and responsibilities of citizenship on grounds of inferior intelligence is as unjustified in terms of democratic principle as would be the exclusion of those with superior intelligence. The fact that intellectual ability, or for that matter artistic talent, is likely to be unequally distributed needs to be acknowledged and taken into account by a democratic society, but only so that the natural capacities of the gifted can be nurtured for social benefit. With widespread education, a democratic citizenry can, as Condorcet put it, "confide the care of government to the ablest of their number but . . . not be compelled to yield them absolute power in a spirit of blind confidence."[31]

It does not follow, however, that because those who professed early and even more recent versions of democracy did not fully respect this commitment to equality, and practiced unjustifiable discrimination, "there is something evil at the very core of this great system of governance," as Orlando Patterson argues. Although he is very appreciative of the virtues and strengths of democracy, Patterson contends that democracy rests *in principle* on the exclusion of some "other:" "We, the citizens, the people, the free—those whom we 'hold dear,' those whom we marry, kith, kin, 'not in bondage, noble, glad, illustrious,' 'beloved'—we the politically free body of men, always, it would seem, tragically require the *them* who do not belong: the ignoble, the nonkith, the nonkin, the people we do not marry, the alien within—the serf, the Jew, the Slav, the slave, the Negro, the people who cannot vote—who demarcate what *we* are, the domestic enemy who defines whom *we* love."[32]

This criticism confuses the possible origins of a sense of freedom with the transformation the understanding of freedom began to undergo when political democracy institutionalized equal citizenship, limited as it was at first. The idea of freedom may conceivably have originated in the tribal practice of enslavement, as Patterson suggests, though the fact that manumission enabled Athenian slaves to acquire personal freedom even as they were denied civic rights vitiates the supposition that there is always a neat binary and dialectical connection between the perception of one's own freedom and the enslavement of others.[33] In kinship-based societies, where any outsider is designated as "the other," someone who succeeds in subduing and enslaving an outsider may well define his own condition as free by contrast. The establishment of democracy in ancient Greece represented an advance in the understanding of freedom because the concept of citizenship was not based on kinship, except in the attenuated sense of ethnic homogeneity. Although Athenian citizens were enrolled on tribal lists, the reform by which Cleisthenes created artificial tribes is an indication that the democratic *polis* had come to be something very different and more inclusive than the tribe. Women are excluded from Athenian (as from early modern) citizenship even though they are kith and kin. Those who do not meet a property qualification and are therefore denied full citizenship in incompletely democratic systems are also ethnic kin; to speak of them as "the alien within" only confuses the issue. "We may deplore the Athenians' exclusivist attitude," Ober has observed, "but moral censure should not obscure our appreciation of the fundamental importance of the new democratic political order. For the first time in the recorded history of a complex society, *all* native freeborn males, irrespective of their ability, family connections, or wealth, were political equals, with equal rights to debate and to determine state policy."[34] Similarly, American nativism arose in a nation which did not exclude from citizenship the same Roman Catholic immigrants against whom it was principally directed, but on the contrary adopted laws to promote immigration. Slavery, xenophobia, and other forms of discrimination in early and later democracies are better understood as atavistic survivals of an older understanding of freedom maintained in order to rationalize otherwise indefensible practices.

Democracy and Human Rights

A newer view of freedom arose in and through democracy because the effort to create popular government required that tribalism be replaced as a basis of organization by new social and political entities based less and less on kinship. The democratic city first and later the democratic nation-state became the focus of loyalty and belonging. These new entities can easily become parochial and therefore tribal in spirit, but the formal recognition of equal civic rights in democracy transforms the understanding of freedom. Eventually, if not immediately, freedom in democracies comes to be understood as a principle inconsistent with all forms of unjust discrimination, whether based on gender, religion, or race. When this principle of freedom, embodied in equal citizenship, is made prior to any civic entity—by reformulation in the ideal of universal natural rights—it becomes altogether incompatible with tribal enslavement and the older notion of freedom that slavery may have engendered or reinforced. As the understanding of freedom undergoes this evolution, racism and other denials of human rights are rejected as incompatible with democracy.

Although undemocratic sentiments and practices (as distinct from principled opposition to democracy on other grounds and self-interested opposition to democratization) persist, they do so not because of some evil inherent in democracy but because democratic consciousness has not fully succeeded in overcoming deep-set prejudices reinforced by ignorance, fear, and a variety of parochial forms of group identification. Insecurity and self-interest may continue to lead those who want the blessings of liberty for themselves to deny it to others, but a democratic consciousness promotes a belief in universal liberty that contradicts the will to dominate others. Thus, in the 1770s, even as the American colonists were beginning to rebel in the name of their natural right to liberty against the tyranny of imperial domination, their slaves were turning their own rhetoric against them. As one slave petition declared, "We have in common with all other men a naturel right to our freedoms without Being depriv'd of them by our fellow men as we are a freeborn Pepel and have never forfeited this Blessing by aney compact or agreement whatever."[35] As democratization succeeds in promoting greater self-confidence, in strengthening the bonds of citizenship, and in enlarging the bounds of civic identity—albeit at the risk of weakening the intensity of loyalty—the sense of insecurity is likely to diminish, removing any lingering rationale for denying the rights of others. Demands for equal liberty on the part of those denied it generate social tensions which can be alleviated only by conferring full rights of citizenship. Provided that democratic ideals are given institutional expression in pluralistic, competitive, and representative systems of government, the willingness to identify one's own interests with those of others, to compromise differences, and negotiate understandings and agreements can counteract lingering tendencies to see social intercourse as a zero-sum game in which the gain of one group must mean the loss of another.

A related and equally untenable charge against democracy, arising from the Terror in the French Revolution (and sometimes compared to the fanaticism of Girolamo Savonarola's apocalyptic Christian republicanism in Florence and of the repressive manifestations of Puritanism in England

and New England) is that democracy inevitably produces intolerance. The insistence on republican virtue is said to require that aristocrats, libertines, and even clergy be made to seem enemies of the people. But revolutionary periods, especially when they involve violence, produce polarization. Modern revolutions, which usually involve masses of people, inevitably make villains of those who can be depicted as enemies of the people. There is nothing specific to democracy—as Alexis de Tocqueville was among the first to point out[36]—that makes it inherently violent or fanatic, as the relatively bloodless examples of many other transitions to democracy show.

It is certainly paradoxical, as Patterson points out,[37] that John Locke, the first great exponent of natural rights liberalism, should have sanctioned enslavement as a just practice in case of war. It is also paradoxical that Locke should have denied full civic rights to women and servants and that he should have recommended compulsory labor for the landless poor, especially their children, so that they might acquire a work ethic. Locke was so influential, however, not because of his defense of these exclusionary and repressive practices, but rather because he championed religious toleration and denounced absolutism (and its supposed basis in patriarchalism and religion) as a form of enslavement. This attack was to have wider consequences than he himself could have imagined or may have intended.

Autonomy as the Core Value in the State and Civil Society

The source of the democratic belief in equal citizenship is the simple yet majestic moral principle of autonomy that the Athenians were the first to begin to appreciate—even though they restricted its application. That principle stems from the understanding that because all human beings share a capacity for reasoning, self-regulation, and communication which is different in degree, if not in kind, from that of all other animals, they ought to enjoy the opportunity for autonomy or self-government and will not be content to be denied that opportunity. The ancient Greeks did not have a fully developed understanding of autonomy, understanding the term to mean primarily the independence of a people rather than the self-determination of both individuals and collectivities, but they introduced a notion that would become, in fuller, more comprehensive form, the foundation of modern democracy. The history of that first democracy and of what happened in Greece more broadly, as the classicist W. G. Forrest has observed, is the record of "the gradual development . . . between 750 and 450 BC of the idea of individual human autonomy, of the idea that all members of a political society were free and equal, that everyone had the right to an equal say in determining the structure and activities of his society."[38] Although ancient Greeks thought of man, in Aristotle's terms, as by nature a *"polis animal"* rather than a solitary individual who might choose to live either within or apart from society, Athenians appreciated the distinction between public (*to koinon* or *demosion*) and private (*to idion*) and recognized the need for two kinds of freedom (*eleutheria*): "freedom to participate in political life and freedom from political oppression." This distinction was understood to mean that there were two sorts of social relationships: those of the *polis* and those of the private sphere, which included the family, the business, and other associations. What was missing, from the modern point of view, was a recognition of the rights of the individual as an individual.[39]

Later, as societies became larger and more complex and as representative government was instituted to take account of the change in size and complexity, perceptive analysts, beginning with Benjamin Constant in 1819, recognized the need to distinguish between the "ancient liberty" of the Greeks, with its emphasis on direct participation in government, and "modern liberty," the enjoyment of personal autonomy coupled with representative rather than direct self-government. But Constant appreciated the continuity of the underlying ideal of autonomy. "It is not to happiness alone, it is to self-development that our destiny calls us," he wrote, "and political liberty is the most powerful, the most effective means of self-development that heaven has given us."[40]

For just the reason Constant stressed, democracy is best understood to mean self-development in both social and political terms. The connection between democratic government and democratic society and character was well appreciated first by Plato and Aristotle and much later by such observers as the political sociologist Tocqueville, the poet Walt Whitman, and the philosopher John Dewey. Tocqueville saw democracy as the expression of a new ethos or set of mores (which he described nicely as "habits of mind and heart") affecting personal behavior, social relations in the family, the professions, and life in general as well as politics. The democratic ethos, he observed, "extends far beyond political mores and laws, exercising dominion over civil society as much as over the government; it creates opinions, gives birth to feelings, suggests customs, and modifies whatever it does not create."[41] Another way to put Tocqueville's thought, using the language of the modern study of comparative politics, is to say that "civil society" and "the state" or the public sector are interrelated.

This interrelationship, with its mutually reinforcing benefits as well as the tensions it engenders, is central to the modern meaning of democracy. In democracies, civil society consists of all relationships considered private, as distinct from those that unite all citizens in the sphere considered public. These relationships, which include those that arise in and from economic exchange, are considered to be exempt from public control, though not necessarily from regulation in the public interest and to protect basic human rights. The democratic state is the sphere of civic or public authority in which all citizens join together as equals in establishing constitutional rules and addressing common purposes, such as security and the general welfare. The autonomy of the individual is a basic value experienced in both spheres. Although the two spheres are analytically distinct, in practice the line between them is often difficult to draw sharply, especially because of the regulatory role of the state, but also because individuals and groups often seek authorization, support, and benefits from the state. Nevertheless, the existence of the separation as a matter of principle is a hallmark of democratic societies.

The Fragility of Democracy

The distinction between modern and ancient democracy is certainly an important one, but at least one common characteristic of both types is that democracy is a difficult system to establish. Athenian democracy led initially to the tyranny of Peisistratus. As Roman republicanism was on the verge of becoming more fully democratic, expansion and civil war brought Caesarism. The Bolsheviks hijacked the 1917 democratic revolution in Russia. Hitler came to power before democracy could be firmly established in the Weimar Republic. Democracy has often been compared to a slow-growing plant which must be carefully nurtured and sometimes even replanted before it is well enough rooted to survive—in Donald Kagan's phrase, "one of the rarest, most delicate and fragile flowers in the jungle of human experience."[42] In many cases, to extend the metaphor, the soil in which it is implanted proves hard and the climatic conditions resistant. Although democracy came to birth in the seventh century B.C., it died out after Athens was gravely weakened by the Peloponnesian War. It appeared again in different form in the Roman Republic, disappearing with the rise of imperial Rome, arose again in medieval times among the Swiss, and was revived on the Roman model in the aristocratic republic of Venice and the more fully mixed Florentine republic.[43] Several centuries later, it took root in northern Europe and the British colonies of North America in the seventeenth and eighteenth centuries. As these plantings survived and flowered, representative government assumed the name of democracy. Nevertheless, even after it seemed to be well established on two continents, the modern form of democracy was widely rejected in Europe and elsewhere in the nineteenth and twentieth centuries in favor of authoritarian and totalitarian alternatives. Only now does it seem to have broken out of these boundaries and to be proliferating almost everywhere in the world, but whether and where it will take hold outside North America and Western Europe remains uncertain.

Democracy and Republicanism

This history suggests both that over the long run there is something irrepressible about the appeal of democracy and that the flexibility of democratic institutions is their greatest strength, but also that in the short run a viable and stable democracy is hard to achieve and harder still to maintain. Because it was considered unstable and an invitation to mob rule, classical democracy acquired a pejorative connotation which led eighteenth century partisans of popular government to prefer to speak of republicanism as the alternative to monarchy, in the belief that forms of government modeled on the Roman were less open to criticism as inviting disorder and mob rule. The republicans of the seventeenth century, Stephen R. Graubard has pointed out, favored a "commonwealth" closely modeled on those of ancient Greece and Rome, "with an 'aristocracy of talent' governing in the name of the people."[44]

The "founding fathers" who created the American union were particularly leery of the word "democracy." To them it connoted the kind of direct self-rule considered practical only in small communities and derided by classical critics like Plato as the rule of the ignorant over the wise, or of appetite over reason. They preferred the word "republic," which also means rule by the people—literally, "the people's affair"—but did not then carry the same pejorative connotations as democracy. A republic was understood as an alternative to monarchy in which no one group, not even the majority of the people (the *demos*, in Greek usage), predominates, and in which those preeminent in civic virtue exercise a benevolent rule. In *Federalist* ten and fourteen, James Madison, who was anxious to avoid replacing the tyranny of absolute monarchy by a tyranny of the majority, boldly redefined republicanism so as to equate it with representative government. He argued in favor of a constitution rife with "checks and balances" that further weaken the possibility of majority rule by making the legislature bicameral, dividing powers among the three branches of government, and reserving certain powers to the states of the federal union.[45] He also rejected, as had David Hume several decades previously,[46] the conventional assumption that a large state could not be governed as a republic, arguing on the contrary that the existence of numerous factions would make it harder for any one to tyrannize over the rest. His definition of a republic, William R. Everdell has pointed out, was "in serious conflict with most historical examples of the phenomenon," which generally followed the Roman model.[47] In Rome, power was divided among several different assemblies, none of which was composed of representatives chosen in elections. The Italian and Swiss city states had republican constitutions designed to prevent both despotism and mass rule, but all power was concentrated in aristocratic senates. In Venice in 1797, out of a population of 137,000 residents and 2.2 million on its mainland, the right to participate in government was restricted to 1,090 noblemen.[48] In Geneva, which Jean-Jacques Rousseau celebrated as a model republic, only some 1,500 of 5,000 adult males were citizens and burgesses at the time of his birth in 1712. The rest of the inhabitants were divided into two categories—"natives" (Geneva-born sons of resident aliens) and "subjects" (mostly peasants living outside the city walls), and those in both categories were excluded from political as well as full civil rights. Effective political power was exercised by a small council on which every seat was monopolized by members of the social aristocracy.[49] Madison effectively redefined republicanism to make it a synonym for representative government based on the essentially democratic principle of individual rather than corporate representation, and by so doing erased much of the difference between traditional republicanism and the modern, representative form of democracy.

Republican sentiment arose in eighteenth-century France as a result of disenchantment with monarchy because there too the initial aim was to replace absolutism with a system of government that would divide power among the estates of the realm. The philosophers of the French Enlightenment shared Plato's revulsion for those common folk they referred to as the *canaille*, preferring an "enlightened despotism" similar to rule by philosopher-kings, with a technocratic twist. But the social criticism they unleashed in the name of rationalism helped make any form of despotism intolerable, whether it was the rule of some wise and well-advised monarch or the more subtle "legal despotism" advocated by the Physiocrats. Republicanism had long been recognized as the practical alternative to monarchy, even though, since the Roman Empire, the term "republican" had been used to describe polities ruled by monarchs. When the term was revived in the Renaissance and later, it was thought to refer to a type of government different from democracy and more suitable for larger societies because by dividing power among the different classes or estates it averted the danger of mob rule. Even such a champion of the social contract and popular sovereignty as Rousseau preferred Roman-style republicanism (complete with separate assemblies, tribunes, Censor, and a civil religion) to Athenian democracy. "If there were a nation of Gods," he observed, "it would govern itself democratically. A government so perfect is not suited to men."[50] Rousseau had more admiration for the Spartan spirit of community and asceticism than he did for the more contentious and hedonistic spirit of Athens. Condorcet too preferred republicanism to democracy. Struggling to square his belief in full citizen suffrage with a recognition that enlightenment was still not widespread, he concluded that the mass of citizens could be trusted to elect wise and impartial representatives, but that the deliberation of public policy should be left to these agents. Provided the laws of mathematical probability were applied to prevent assemblies from adopting decisions favored by minorities, the populace would have reason to suppose that the decisions arrived at by those they elected would be for the public good.[51]

This distinction between republics and democracies, then, was initially made by European and American reformers and revolutionaries who sought an alternative to monarchy that would not seem utopian or a danger to civilized standards and to property. The recovery of Roman history during the Renaissance had stimulated interest in the ancient republic as the alternative to monarchy and Caesarism. In England this interest had led to the creation of a school of opinion which adopted the English translation for republic of "commonweal" or "commonwealth." During the colonial period, American thinking was influenced by the writings of the Whig "commonwealthmen," and it is no accident that several of the states created in the New World were and still are called commonwealths.

Democracy became an especially pejorative word in England and America after it was invoked by the most radical leader of the French Revolution, Maximilien Robespierre. Although his principal aim was to defend representative democracy against the direct democracy the *sans-culottes* were clamoring for, he tainted the term by associating it with the use of terror against those stigmatized as enemies of the people. In a speech on the principles of political morality to the Convention in 1794, Robespierre used the word "democracy" eleven times in the space of 700 words. "Democracy," he said, "is a state in which the people, as sovereign, guided by laws of its own making, does for itself all that it can do well, and by its delegates what it cannot . . . Democracy is the only form of state which all the individuals composing it can truly call their country . . . The French are the first people in the world to establish a true democracy, by calling all men to enjoy equality and the fulness of civil rights; and that, in my opinion, is the real reason why all the tyrants allied against the Republic will be defeated."[52]

The ferocity of Robespierre's assault on the enemies of the revolution enabled critics to condemn democracy as the source of mob violence. By the end of the decade, however, the word had lost some of its association with the French Revolution, so that Americans could feel comfortable enough describing their system of government as a "democratic republic."[53] As the suffrage was extended, and the indirect election of the Senate and the president were abandoned, the two terms came to be used interchangeably. Although there may still be a whiff of ideological difference in the connotations of "Republican" and "Democrat" conveyed by the two major American political parties, members of both now regularly refer to the national political ideal as democracy, as do the French and Germans, even though they adopt the style of republic in their formal names. Other formally monarchical regimes are so in name only, having adopted the substance of republicanism and democracy while retaining the symbolic continuity of monarchy. In some contemporary usage, democracy is understood to refer to popular sovereignty, in the sense that constitutional or basic law and referenda reflect the direct will of the people, insofar as is practical, whereas the form of government is described as republican, in the sense that it is representative.[54] There is no real difference between this understanding of republicanism and what is otherwise commonly referred to as indirect democracy.

Toward a Working Definition—Normative, Institutional, and Procedural

As George Orwell noted in 1946, the word "democracy" had became a tool of propaganda: "In the case of a word like *democracy*, not only is there no agreed definition, but the attempt to make one is resisted from all sides. It is almost universally felt that when we call a country democratic we are praising it: consequently the defenders of every kind of régime claim that it is a democracy, and fear that they might have to stop using the word if it were tied down to any one meaning. Words of this kind are often used in a consciously dishonest way."[55]

To avoid cynical propagandistic usages, criteria are needed which can be used to distinguish societies in which all citizens may be said to have a real opportunity, even if imperfectly enjoyed, to govern themselves, directly and indirectly, from those in which they are being denied such an opportunity. Otherwise there is bound to be uncertainty as to whether the oligarchs of Soviet-style regimes were entitled to call their system of rule a "people's democracy" because they claimed to reflect the will of the masses, or whether C. B. Macpherson was justified in referring to such regimes in developing countries as "vanguard democracies."[56] Otherwise, too, there will be uncertainty as to whether the term democracy can properly be applied to political systems in which there is effectively no competition for office, where one political party is the sole legitimate party, or where one party becomes so dominant that those in opposition have little hope of wresting power away from them even in free elections. These are hard enough questions as a matter of abstract theory, but they become even harder when democracy is made a term of propaganda intended to obscure distinctions between democratic and undemocratic practices.

Fortunately, the propagandistic use of the language of democracy has been sharply rejected in recent times. Advocates of political democracy in central and eastern Europe, Latin America, Asia, and Africa have made it abundantly clear that their understanding of it does not differ from that of Western Europeans and North Americans. Thanks especially to them, it is becoming clear that to call any political system democratic, in the modern sense of the term, which does not allow its people the opportunity to exercise regular electoral choice and a means of informing and expressing themselves without fear of intimidation and reprisal, is to indulge in cynical manipulation. "What is true democracy?" asked Wei Jingsheng, the most prominent spokesman for the democracy movement in China, on a wall poster of December 5, 1978. His answer was the same as would now be given anywhere else: "It means the right of the people to choose their representatives [who will] work according to their will and in their interests. Only this can be called democracy. Furthermore, the people must also have the power to replace their representatives any time so that these representatives cannot go on deceiving others in the name of the people."[57]

This definition implies an underlying belief that democracy rests on the universal human right to equal liberty—a right that undemocratic regimes systematically deny. Whatever differences there may be between the Anglo-Saxon emphasis on "negative" liberty and the French and continental emphasis on "positive" liberty, Philippe Lauvaux has observed, the association between liberty and democracy makes the use of the term democracy for regimes that deny the people the liberty to choose their governments in free, regular, and competitive election not only cynical but fraudulent.[58] In Philippe Bénéton's precise words, the so-called "people's democracies" of eastern Europe were "fictitious democracies" because in them "an imaginary people holds power while the real people is subject to it."[59] This basic criterion of the right to vote in free elections would rule out dictatorships but not necessarily "uncommon democracies"[60] which have one-party dominant systems. These systems are not the most desirable form of political democracy because a dominant party is certain to be less accountable and likely to be open to the corruptions of power and the hegemony of one segment of the population group over others in a divided society. Alternation of office holders and/or power-sharing arrangements such as coalitions are more desirable but they are not absolutely necessary to suit the definition.

Norms. In its normative dimension, then, democracy embodies the belief that all human beings ought to enjoy the opportunity for self-government or autonomy. This norm may be grounded on various philosophic assumptions: a belief in an innate moral sense, in the capacity for moral choice inherent in human rationality, in rational self-interest, or in the pragmatic need to acknowledge the subjectivity of values. The aim of promoting autonomy implies a social responsibility for promoting conditions which enable citizens to acquire the education and information they need to make informed choices, both in civil society and in public government. It implies the development and inculcation of a civic culture in which the norm will be recognized and transmitted. It requires a system of law in which rights designed to promote autonomy will be protected. But autonomy can take different forms: individual, plural, and communal. Individual autonomy is the acknowledged right of all mature citizens to regulate their own conduct as they see fit, providing only that in so doing they do not deny others the same opportunity. Plural autonomy is the acknowledged right of social sub-groups, formed by cultural affinity and voluntary association, to regulate their own affairs and pursue their own ends, subject only to the same limit. It is sometimes given political expression in electoral arrangements for proportional representation, in executive power-sharing arrangements, in federalism, and in public support for parochial education. Communal autonomy is the acknowledged right of more inclusive political associations to collective self-determination, whether by majority rule or by consensus. These forms of autonomy are compatible, but they may also give rise to tensions.

Institutions. The institutional dimensions of modern democracy appear in two spheres: the private sphere of civil society and the public sphere of citizenship and representative government. Civil society embodies such forms of autonomy as the family, the private economic enterprise, churches, trade unions, professional associations and privately owned media of information and opinion. The public or state sector embodies representative legislatures, independent judicial systems, and accountable executives and civil servants. Political parties, pressure groups, and mass media serve as intermediaries between the two institutional sectors, focussing public opinion on issues of social concern and organizing the electoral process. The large size of modern democracies makes representative rather than direct self-government a virtual necessity and federalism desirable, but some provision may appropriately be made for direct or participatory democracy, as in party nominating or primary elections and referenda, both to ascertain the public will and to assure that electors experience self-government.

Institutional democracy is a more rigorous requirement in the political sphere than in civil society. Because membership in civil associations is voluntary, members may agree to unequal shares in influence and control. But it is misleading to suppose that in democratic societies, the prevailing norms can be restricted to political institutions.[61] As analysts from Plato and Aristotle to Tocqueville and many modern political sociologists have implied or explicitly asserted, democratic values are bound to find expression in many of the institutions and behavior patterns of civil society. It would be too much to expect (and dangerous to liberty and efficiency) all the institutions of civil society to be as democratic in form as those in the public sector. The requirements of liberty and efficiency should allow unaccountable, hierarchical, and otherwise undemocratic institutions to persist in civil society, especially where the adoption of standards of qualification for those admitted to membership is critical. Business corporations, hospitals, universities, churches, and scientific societies must be allowed to govern themselves hierarchically, and to admit members on criteria of selection that would be unacceptable in the political sphere. Nevertheless, it is also highly likely that adoption of the democratic political norm will produce pressures for democratization in civil society (such as the openness demanded to protect shareholders in corporations, the right of informed consent for patients receiving medical treatment, the self-government by faculty and to a lesser extent by students characteristic of universities in democratic societies, and the tendency for lay participation and toleration of dissent in even the most hierarchical churches). When these pressures undermine the integrity of the institutions and associations of civil society by stipulating the adoption of considerations which are not appropriate but may seem to satisfy some political objective (such as ethnic or gender quotas), the line between public and private may be breached and individual rights put in jeopardy. In this sense, there may well be tensions between political democracy and the civil associations of democratic society, though these practical strains are not inherent from a theoretical point of view.

Procedures. In procedural terms, democracy requires that government be in accordance with popularly adopted and amendable constitutional rules, that individual rights be protected by due process of law, that elections be fairly conducted and arranged so as to protect voters from intimidation, and that many other rules be adopted, which may vary from one system to another, to assure fair representation, the accountability of public officials, and the regulation of private activities in the public interest. Democratic electoral rules must embody the principle of equality for all citizens in the right to vote, and the general presumption must be in favor of majority rule, indeed of super-majorities for constitutional change, but the electoral rules may be arranged to allow for representation of minorities (as in proportional representation and power-sharing arrangements) and for federalism.

Democracy is thus a process of self-government in which individuals operate upon their environment directly and indirectly—directly as they make decisions for themselves, pursue careers, enter into relationships with others, and otherwise live their lives, indirectly through political representatives accountable to them. The system of government makes possible centralized decision-making and rule-setting in matters that affect all citizens, and decentralized decision-making and rule-setting in those best addressed on the local level. It is, in short, a social and political system characterized by a high degree of personal liberty and an equally high degree of political liberty, manifested in regular and free competitive elections, protected by a legal system based upon a constitution, and often articulated by means of federalism. Like other political systems, it cannot avoid the need for bureaucracy, but civil services must be subject to political accountability and arranged so as to serve the citizens, not dominate or frustrate them.

Democratic societies face a special dilemma in that the concern for popular participation in government must be balanced by a recognition of the need for political leadership of a kind that will make use of knowledge and abilities superior to those of most voters, induce them to confront hard choices, and propose and carry out policies designed to address public needs which may impose unpopular burdens and sacrifices. The point is underscored by Kagan in a study of the leadership provided by Pericles to Athenian democracy:

> The paradox inherent in democracy is that it must create and depend on citizens who are free, autonomous, and self-reliant. Yet its success—its survival even—requires extraordinary leadership. It grants equal rights of participation to citizens of unequal training, knowledge, and wisdom, and it gives final power to the majority, which is certainly inferior in these qualities to an elite. It gives free reign to a multiplicity of parties and factions, thereby encouraging division and vacillation rather than unity and steadfastness. In antiquity, this led critics to ridicule democracy as "acknowledged foolishness"; in the modern world, it has been assailed as inefficient, purposeless, soft, and incompetent. Too often in this century its citizens have lost faith in times of hardship and danger and allowed their democracies to become tyrannies of the right or left.[62]

The Ambiguities of Autonomy

Democracy, as Churchill implied and Forster made more explicit, ought not to be thought a panacea. It is, however, an opportunity for ordinary people to take a measure of control of their own destinies, to put the burdens where they belong, not in their stars or in some heroic demigod, not in the laws of history or the imperatives or race or religion, but in the common capacity they share as human beings to direct their own lives and cooperate in setting rules for the common good. That is why, throughout the long, often tragic and folly-ridden evolution of civilization, democracy has been and continues to be humanity's best hope. Its foundation, its open secret, is the commitment to the fullest possible autonomy for all. "The power and appeal of Democracy," John Dunn has rightly emphasized, "comes from the idea of autonomy—of choosing freely for oneself."[63]

Autonomy, however, is not an unambiguous ideal. In its earliest expression, in ancient Athens, *autonomia* was mainly understood to mean the independence of the community. In republican Rome and the more modern forms of mixed government modeled upon it, autonomy was understood in plural terms, as the right of groups to share in political power. Liberal democracies so exalt the autonomy of the individual as to make the rights of the individual limits on majority rule and the authority of government. Modern democracies tend to be composites of all three forms of autonomy. On the whole, the combination of the three forms of autonomy results in a strong and resilient social and political system, in which individuals and groups are free to regulate their own behavior insofar as it does not affect the rights of others, but in which all citizens cooperate in determining questions that affect them all.

The tensions among the three forms find expression, however, in sometimes difficult problems of practical application. The communal autonomy of the state may lead a majority to impose measures of taxation, regulation, and conscription which minorities may find coercive and even illegitimate. Communal autonomy may be thought by some to require common systems of public education, while respect for plural autonomy may be thought by others to warrant public support for separate forms of schooling, based upon religious affiliation. The choice of proportional representation or "winner take all" systems of election inevitably raises the question of whether individuals or groups are to be represented. Efforts to promote pluralistic "diversity" in the work place and schools may impose standards discriminatory to individuals. In extreme instances, individuals and groups may challenge the legitimacy of the autonomous community, leading to its breakup and reconstitution in the form of new states and nationalities. In these and a host of other ways, democracy remains problematic, even when well established. The art of democratic politics consists in a continual mediation among the forms of autonomy in order to preserve balance and maintain social harmony. Success is not guaranteed, and breakdown may lead to the adoption of authoritarian and totalitarian alternatives, as historical experience makes all too clear.

History

3

Communal Autonomy:
Athenian Democracy

The first efforts to replace monarchy and aristocracy by popular self-government were made among the ancient Greeks, who invented both the word "democracy" and the constitution it signified. The Athenians, who brought democracy to its highest early development, understood it to mean the self-government or autonomy of the community or *polis*. Although they also came to appreciate the need to respect the autonomy of the individual, they restricted this form of autonomy to male citizens, and generally believed that the autonomy of the *polis* took precedence over that of the individual. The subdivisions of the *polis*—the family, the village and the tribe—were understood to be integral parts of the whole, rather than independent components, and there was no separation of religion and society. The emphasis was therefore very much on communal autonomy. Athenians put so much emphasis on communal autonomy, i.e., the autonomy of the *polis*, that they failed to develop an understanding of democracy that would have had broader appeal and would have balanced communal autonomy with the autonomy of individuals and sub-groups.

By the time of Pericles, the citizens of Attica (the territory controlled by the Athenian *polis*) actually enjoyed a considerable degree of freedom in their personal lives as well as an altogether remarkable degree of self-government. This system may well have enabled them to make war more effectively than they had been able to under tyrannical rule (as Herodotus claims[1]). Ultimately, however, they paid a high price for restricting the benefits and responsibilities of democracy to those of Athenian stock and denying it to others under their influence and control. By not abolishing slavery or consistently extending citizenship to long-resident aliens, not to mention women born to citizens, they limited the contribution much of the populace could make to the welfare of the *polis* and compromised the egalitarian moral premise of democracy. It may be that the very nature of the

Athenian *polis*, as a homogeneous unit, made greater inclusiveness impossible, but the cohesiveness that so often sustained the city in times of adversity may well have been its ultimate undoing. The failure to abjure imperialism and grant other Greek communities the autonomy the Athenians claimed for themselves, by creating a federal commonwealth of democratic city-states instead of a hegemonic league, may have cost them the allegiance of others who could have helped them to resist Sparta and then Macedonia more effectively. Democracy in Athens depended to some degree, moreover, both on slave labor and on imperial revenues. The fact that pay for jury service and attendance at meetings of the assembly and council, as well as for attendance at festivals, enabled poorer citizens to take part in public life, gives some credence to the argument that Athenian democracy was partly subsidized by slave labor and tribute from the subject peoples of other member states of the Athenian League.

From the point of view of the history of democracy, the limitations of Athenian democracy are therefore as cautionary as its achievements are inspiring. However "unhistorical" it may seem to judge Athenian practices by later standards, especially since Athenians would hardly have been Athenians had they not been fiercely attached to their *polis* and dedicated to its preservation, the long-term fate of democracy requires that the limitations of the Athenian precedent be recognized. As it is proper to recall the celebration of Athenian freedom Thucydides ascribed to Pericles, so it would be imbalanced to forget that Pericles also thought that future generations would consider Athens to have been a great civilization because "we of all the Greeks ruled over more Greeks than anyone,"[2] and that Athenians sometimes defined freedom as "rule over others," a phrase Thucydides puts in the mouth of another speaker.[3]

The Early Period: Tribalism and Monarchy

The earliest period of Greek history of which there is any record appears to have been a long era in which tribal societies were transformed into monarchical states, in the anthropological sense of the term state, but states that did not succeed in creating a truly unitary system of rule. The result was that Greece experienced a fragmentation into regional agglomerations of villages which experimented with different forms of rule, either monarchic or oligarchic. The Homeric epics likely reflect practices and beliefs prevalent from at least the thirteenth to the eighth century B.C., by which time the influence of the social system the epics depict began to wane. In the *Odyssey*, the tribal chief is known as *basileus*, the same title used to denote the subordinate chiefs. There is normally one highest chief or king, whose office ordinarily descends by inheritance to one of his children. The example of Telemachus, who must fight to gain a chieftainship that is presumably his by birthright seems to show

that although birth may confer a presumptive claim, it does not necessarily settle the question.[4]

The chief is advised by a council of elders, nobles, and eminent warriors
which has no independent authority; no votes are taken in it except at the
order of the chief. Because it is a venue in which rhetorical skill matters, it
is an important step in a long process which leads to a wider sharing of
authority and eventually to popular and representative government. In an
oral culture in which participation is limited to those who take part in deliberations, such an ability is especially critical to political success, but it
remains important even as forms of expression and communication change,
as the Sophist teachers of rhetoric recognized. In this respect there is continuity between the monarchical council and the later democratic councils,
assemblies, and juries.

During the monarchical period, the place of the other warriors in the
social hierarchy was very likely a function of their role in warfare and their
possession of wealth, especially landed property. Wherever Greek chiefs
and nobles fought like Homer's heroes from horse-drawn war-chariots,
they were undoubtedly superior in status and power to kinsmen who lacked
the resources to enhance their physical strength. As metallurgy made iron
weapons cheaper and more widely available, those who could use such
weapons in warfare acquired higher status and with it a new claim on
political power. Athenian democracy, especially under the reforms of
Cleisthenes, was made possible by the support he could count on from the
infantrymen (hoplites) who had become a critical component of Athenian
military power.

But military and economic considerations are always closely linked in
tribal societies to the structure of kinship relations, and these are all but
invariably patriarchal. This patriarchal social structure is at first reflected
in kingship and then in rule in the oligarchies composed of the patriarchs
of the leading families. In the family unit, paternal authority appears to
have been absolute over all family members. Fathers had the authority to
betroth and divorce any of their children at will, and to punish disobedience by inflicting even the penalty of death. The father's estate apparently
passed on his authority to a male heir, except that in the absence of such an
heir, authority passed to an agnate—the nearest high-ranking male. These
families were grouped into larger bodies held together by a supposed common kinship. The *genos* or clan is thus an extension of the family which
may include household dependents who are not blood relatives. In Attica,
the social hierarchy was long based on relationships of dominance and
subordination among different *gene* determined by claims to noble ances-
try and possession of landed wealth.[5]

In pre-democratic Athens, political development produced a threefold
division among chief or king, subordinate chiefs of eminent families, and

the *demos*, the "many" of free males. This triad came to be understood in Greek political theory as the basis of three types of government: monarchy, aristocracy, and democracy. Much speculation was devoted to the pattern of succession among these forms. As kings became oppressive, it was thought, their hold on power would be challenged by the noble families. In the *Republic* Plato speculated that if the ideal form of government, rule by philosopher-kings, were to be lost, the aristocracy that would likely replace it would become a militaristic "timocracy," which would in turn be succeeded by oligarchy, or the rule of the wealthy. Democracy would arise next as the commoners, or *demos*, rebelled against the wealthy, leading to tyranny as they proved incapable of maintaining order and turned to a demagogue.[6] Degeneration from monarchy to aristocracy, aristocracy to oligarchy, oligarchy to democracy, and democracy to mob rule and tyranny, was considered "natural" by the Greek chronicler of Rome, Polybius, who also thought the process was cyclical.[7]

On the whole, the evidence of what actually happened points to the replacement of monarchy by forms of oligarchy mixing noble birth and wealth. Even in the passage from the *Iliad* to the *Odyssey*, it is noteworthy that the title *basileus* is first ascribed solely to the king and then in the later work to all chiefs, perhaps indicating that monarchy is no longer so venerated. In Athens, however, the pattern does seem to be similar to the one the theorists described. By 630 B.C., before Solon began the transition to democracy, rule seems to have passed from kings to the Council of the *Areopagus*, an assembly recruited from magistrates, the *archai* or archons, noblemen who were elected annually and afterward held their seats in the council for life. The *Areopagus* was thus the instrument of the *eupatridai* or noble families with land-based wealth.[8] Democracy came about in Athens as a result of a series of reforms in which the authority of these families was challenged and diminished and the Council of the *Areopagus* displaced as the locus of authority—so much so that in 462 B.C. its authority was reduced to the single function of serving as the court for homicide cases in which the victim was an Athenian citizen.[9]

The Importance of the Polis

Because it arose in the *polis*, Greek democracy acquired important elements of its character from the nature of this social setting. To call the *polis* a city-state is to impose an anachronism: the term "state" arose much later, in the sixteenth century, to connote a formal and enduring entity distinct from both the government and the existential community of citizens. Classical usage, Philip Brook Manville points out, gives a better idea of the reality by referring to the Athenian *polis* as "the Athenians" (*hoi Athenaioi*) rather than to Athens, the name of a place rather than a people.[10] Various factors probably influenced the concentration on this social and political unit, including a lingering tribalism, a polytheism which made particular deities the patrons of particular *poleis*, and the practical difficulties of maintaining control over wider areas, but three other considerations—economic, topographic, and military—may also have been influential. Given the economic reliance on small-scale agriculture and large-scale trade, the *polis* seemed to be the most manageable size for economic interaction, or for autarkic "self-sufficiency," the Aristotelian ideal.[11] A central authority was necessary because of the size, urbanization, differentiation, and complexity of social conditions, and to allow for military mobilization at a time when wars were frequent, but Greek economic conditions did not lend themselves to massive efforts of state-building by the control of agriculture, irrigation, and construction, as was the case in Egypt, where the management of Nile floods was critical to the entire population.[12] The often mountainous topography and the scattering of the population over islands, many of them small, as well as the mainland, made political integration difficult and predisposed the Greeks to focus their energies and ambitions on small localities that were readily coherent and could be made relatively defensible. Many of these communities were formed by waves of immigration, one from the collapsed Mycenaean civilization, others from other areas to the north, and others as colonies. There were some 750 *poleis* in Greece and at least 300 more founded by Greek colonists outside Greece proper.[13] Most of the settlements were "small nuclei with much land around them for them to occupy"[14] and with an average territory of less than 100 square kilometers and a citizen population of fewer than 1,000 adult males.[15] Sparta was exceptional in that it was a *polis* which came to control vast tracts of conquered territory and equally vast numbers of subjects, the helots, who were enslaved by their Spartan masters, and the *perioikoi*, subjects but not serfs. Athens was in territory the second largest after Lakedaimon, which was not a *polis* but a loose agglomeration of villages, and with its port of Piraeus it became a kind of *mega-polis* for Attica, a region of about 2,500 square kilometers. In effect, Athens was the capital of a region including many villages which were gradually united into a single political entity. Its (adult male) citizen population at the time of Pericles in the fifth century was about 60,000, and about 30,000 a hundred years later, during the time of Demosthenes,[16] when requirements for citizenship had been tightened.

Although the *polis* may originally have been constructed as a walled town offering greater protection than the open countryside, the large *polis* has a character that cannot fully be accounted for on military or for that matter economic grounds alone. Compared to the village, the division of labor possible in the *polis* allows for greater diversity, which in turn promotes much higher standards of art, learning, and craftsmanship and elaborately organized ceremonies, religious observances, and cultural activities. Because of its combination of advantages, the *polis* came to be understood by philosophers, notably Aristotle, as the highest form of social interaction—a unified community (*koinonia*) composed of households regulated by citizens which was somehow greater than the sum of its parts. Too large a community would not serve the same purpose because it would not be possible for all the citizens to assemble and act in concert. The *polis* may also confer autonomy (*autonomia*), a term originally understood to refer to the relative independence of one community from another but which comes to apply also to the political self-determination the citizens of a democratic community enjoy.[17] Like the other early city-states of Mesopotamia and Sumer, the Greek *poleis* were communities with urban centers, each with a keen sense of separateness from other communities and all with governments which legislated, collected taxes, declared war, and maintained boundaries excluding others from their territories.[18]

As Athenians achieved a greater sense of security and a civic as well as a village way of life, monarchy must have come to seem anachronistic and incompatible with the spirit of freedom they had begun to experience. But the Athenians also well understood that freedom required law, and that without a king to declare and enforce the law, some alternative would be needed that would protect them against arbitrary rule. The *polis* therefore became the setting for the creation of a constitutional order in which justice could be dispensed in accordance with established laws, divinely ordained, customary, and statutory. Humphrey Kitto captures this association between the *polis* and justice especially well in observing that in the plays of Aeschylus "the mature polis becomes the means by which the Law is satisfied without producing chaos, since public justice supersedes private vengeance; and the claims of authority are reconciled with the instincts of humanity."[19]

This maturity did not come easily, but it did come. Athens acquired its first written code of laws in 621 B.C., with the result that the *eupatridai* could not claim a monopoly of the knowledge of the law. But the codification was left to one Draco, whose severe punishments became eponymous for extremely harsh rules, and which were soon superseded.[20] At the end of the war between Athens and Sparta, toward the end of the fifth century, the conflict between the two warring factions within Athens, the *demos* and the "few," was settled, Martin Ostwald points out, by the drafting of "written laws and agreements, voluntarily accepted by a majority of both parties, that inhibited what rancor was still at large among the victims of the oligarchy and prevented it from disrupting the precarious unity of the state." After a long period in which popular sovereignty seemed in conflict or at least in tension with customary law, the two were now reconciled: "A new social and political order was created that retained the characteristic institutions of the Athenian democracy while subordinating the principle of popular sovereignty to the principle of the sovereignty of law."[21]

Popular sovereignty had been introduced gradually but vigorously. As a result of a series of reforms, Athenian government was made the function of the assembled citizens, and magistrates were given temporary responsibilities and held closely accountable by the citizenry. The move toward more popular rule was fairly widespread in Greece, although only Athens institutionalized it as a stable and long-term process. Except in Sparta, kingship was abolished in most of the Greek city states and replaced by oligarchy. By the time of Thucydides, there were few if any kings left in the Hellenic *poleis*.[22]

In Athens, the shift was gradual, and never completely overcame the initial tendency for oligarchy to replace monarchy. First, the monarchical office was shorn of a part of its power by the appointment of a *polemarch* or commander-in-chief distinct from the king. Then a third magistrate was appointed, who ultimately became chief executive for internal government, and the kingly office ceased to be hereditary. By the seventh century, about which there is better information, we learn that Athens, which is almost completely dependent on agriculture at this stage, is ruled by the *eupatridai* through the Council of the *Areopagus*, which made the key decisions on foreign and domestic policy. The executive power was vested in three archons—one for civil administration, one, the *polemarch*, for war, one for civil religion. There may have been an *ecclesia* or popular assembly, but if so it was still weak. Other cities had similarly aristocratic systems of rule. In some cases, the main powers of government were retained within a royal family. At Corinth, for example, a single house ruled for ninety years until the first half of the seventh century B.C.[23] though the Kypselid dynasts who replaced an oligarchy were considered tyrants rather than kings;[24] their rule, like that of Peisistratus in Athens, may therefore be considered a species of populist autocracy rather than traditional monarchy.

In the period that succeeded the early emphasis on tyranny, a struggle ensued among the Athenians between democracy and oligarchy, with the result that there was a general shift toward democracy, until in the latter half of the fourth century B.C. the Macedonian predominance introduces a completely changed environment. Had the domestic situation not been so strongly affected by external influences, including the power of Sparta, the rest of Greece might have moved more and more in the direction of democracy. From 480 B.C. to 336 B.C., there is a pronounced movement from oligarchy toward fully developed democracy. Aristotle made democratization in its "extreme form" a function of size of population,[25] but oligarchy was an eminently practical alternative, and there is some reason to suppose that even the democratic regimes of Athens were often effectively oligarchical.

Perhaps because he pursued his empirical bent by setting his students to collecting constitutional histories, Aristotle (in the *Politics*) is the best source for knowledge of what oligarchies were like. He notes that the mildest form, sometimes called timocracy, was one in which there were public assemblies and juries, as in a democracy, but in which participation was limited by a property qualification so that rule was confined to a minority of the citizens, though not a small minority. Sometimes the property qualification was not the only method of restricting access to power. The constitution might require that important decisions be made by a small elected body; sometimes vacancies were filled by cooptation. Magistrates were subject to a property qualification, and they might be elected rather than appointed by lot. In the most extreme form, magistracies were made hereditary. Oligarchy secured itself also by fining the wealthy for nonattendance and having a small council (in contrast to the 500-member *Boule* in democratic Athens) for initiating measures to be passed by the deliberative body.

The Reforms of Solon and Cleisthenes

The fullest development of democracy occurred in Athens during the fifth century, with the end result apparent in the fourth century. It is recounted in Aristotle's *Constitution of Athens*, recovered only in the nineteenth century and sometimes attributed to a pupil rather than to Aristotle himself.[26] The beginning was made by the *eupatrid* archon Solon in the early decades of the sixth century B.C., who became famous for stepping in as a mediator between the rich and the poor when economic changes had caused great hardship and tension. Solon is thought to have taken office as archon in 594 (although David Stockton suggests that he made his great reforms in the decade of the 570s[27]). He resolved the difficulties by arranging debt relief for the poor but without redistributing land, so that the nobles retained the basis of their wealth and status. He abolished enslavement for debt and decreed that henceforth no Athenian could mortgage his personal liberty. He also decreed that no individual could own more than a certain amount of land and that there should be limits on such things as funeral expenses and dowries. He forbade the export of grain so that the poor would not be deprived of the staff of life, making the export of olive oil the chief commodity by which Athenians traded. Because Athens was short of skilled labor, he encouraged the immigration of foreigners—*metoikoi* or metics—with skills, and encouraged fathers to teach their children a trade. In politics he extended the franchise to the poor but did not abolish the Council of the *Areopagus*, the stronghold of the nobles. Instead he balanced it by strengthening the *Ecclesia* and possibly also by setting up the *Boule* or Council of 400, which reportedly set the agenda for the *Ecclesia*, as the Council of 500 is known to have done later. Solon is also thought to have reformed the administration of justice by codifying the laws, setting up a people's court called the *Heliaia*, giving every party to a lawsuit the right to appeal to this court, and giving every citizen the right to initiate a prosecution either on behalf of an injured person or in the public interest.[28]

During Solon's reign, a system of classes, based on income, measured in produce rather than in monetary terms, was established. At the top were the *pentakosiomedimnoi*—so-called because they received income of at least 500 measures (the *medimnos* was a dry measure of about one and a half bushels of grain[29]) of produce. The *hippeis* or horsemen were formed of those who earned between 300 and 500 measures (whether or not they actually owned horses); the *zeugitai* (from *zeugos* for "pair" of oxen) or hoplites, of those who had between 200 and 300 measures (whether or not they owned oxen); the *thetes* or menial laborers, the lowest class, of those with incomes below 200 measures. This lowest group was ineligible to hold any public offices. Only those in the highest grouping were eligible for the top offices, including those of the nine archons. The fact that wealth was estimated in terms of dry measures probably indicates that the reforms were introduced at a time when Attic farmers mainly cultivated wheat rather than vines or olives.[30]

Solon is thought to have composed a verse in which he summed up his own achievements as a mediator between rich and poor:

> To the mass of the people I gave the power they needed,
> Neither degrading them, nor giving them too much rein:
> For those who already possessed great power and wealth
> I saw to it that their interests were not harmed.
> I stood guard with a broad shield before both parties and prevented either
> from triumphing unjustly.[31]

Plutarch also reports that Solon repealed the laws of Draco which applied the death penalty to all sorts of lesser crimes. According to Plutarch, Solon put so much emphasis on participation in politics as to decree that in the event of revolution, citizens must take one side or the other; anyone who remained neutral was to be disfranchised when the turmoil was over.[32]

Cleisthenes, the second great Athenian reformer, is given most of the credit for establishing the democratic constitution. He assumed power in 507 or 508 after taking a leading part in a campaign by returned aristocrats to expel the son of the tyrant Peisistratus, who had come to power despite Solon's reforms. Cleisthenes' rival, Isagoras, came to power first with the help of Sparta, and proceeded to strengthen his position by winning support from the aristocratic political associations or clubs known as *hetaireiai*. Cleisthenes succeeded in ousting him after recruiting support from the *demos* by promising reforms.[33] He then proceeded to introduce a constitution which was the first to be referred to by the Athenians as "democratic" and which resembled constitutions adopted at the same time in other *poleis*.[34]

The innovations introduced by Cleisthenes included several of a fundamental character and others that amounted to significant modifications of the Solonian reforms. One interesting feature that did not last but was repeated during the French Revolution many centuries later was reform of the calendar; in both instances the change of the calendar may well have reflected a sense that the political reforms were fundamental in character. Cleisthenes' reform relied on the solar rather than the lunar year.[35] Another, and perhaps the most important of Cleisthenes' reforms, also found an echo in the French Revolution, with its new division of France into electoral departments. It was aimed at counteracting the divisive effects of both kinship and regional loyalty. Alongside but in effect in place of the four old *phylai* or *phratres* (in which the *eupatridai* played a dominant role), he set up ten artificial tribes composed of thirty *trittyes* or electoral districts and 139 *demes* or wards. Each new tribe was an amalgam of several clusters of *demes* deliberately drawn from the city, the coastal, and the inland regions of Attica. The aim was to promote cooperation and a greater sense of civic loyalty rather than of merely kinship or local loyalty. Like Solon, Cleisthenes did not eliminate the Council of the *Areopagus*, perhaps because such a move would have driven the noble families to oppose his reforms.

In addition, Cleisthenes either created or renovated the *Boule* or Council of 500. Its members now came to consist of fifty citizens selected annually by lot from each tribe. From these 500, fifty were selected to serve for one-tenth of the year on *prytaneis*, or standing committees. Each standing committee was therefore both a more effective body than the larger *Boule* and broadly representative of the citizenry, as a result of its random composition. Cleisthenes set the rules that prevented anyone from holding high office more than twice and made office holders accountable for their performance.

Cleisthenes also established the novel system of ostracism ostensibly in order to prevent tyranny but perhaps also to enable him to remove rivals like Isagoras. Each year, the assembly voted on whether to hold an ostracism. If the motion passed, a time was set and citizens wrote the name of a candidate on *ostraka* or potsherds. The one who received the highest number was expelled from the city for ten years, though without forfeit of his property. The goal may have been to "let the people as a whole decide which of two major policies was to be adopted by temporarily banishing from the political scene the most prominent spokesman of one of them."[36] The fact that the exile's property was not confiscated indicates that he was not considered to have been convicted of a crime, and that the rationale for the practice was to prevent overly ambitious figures from developing a following large enough to threaten the fundamental structure of democracy. In practice, it more likely functioned as an instrument of factional conflict.

Later, Ephialtes and Pericles led the attack on the residue of oligarchy, and the progress of democracy was marked by the opening up of civil offices to all citizens and the introduction of payment for jury service. Jurors were assigned by lot, and in 487 it was decreed that the archons and the *polemarch* should no longer be chosen by direct vote but from among the people's nominees by casting lots. The use of the lot or sortition may have originated in Greek religion, where it was a way of leaving the outcome to the gods. In the fifth century, however, it was used to maintain the equality of all citizens and their equal right to rule.[37] It must not be supposed, however, that Athenian democracy made such a fetish of equality that it had no protection against incompetence or malfeasance in office. To guard against these dangers, the constitution put some emphasis on the scrutiny of magistrates prior to their assuming office and much more on holding them accountable afterward for their stewardship. The *dokimasia* or prior scrutiny assured their suitability for office by making sure that the official was a citizen, had discharged his private and religious duties, and had met his financial and military obligations; the *euthyna* or review was used to examine conduct in office by, among other things, going over financial ledgers within thirty days after officials had left office; and the *eisangelia* or prosecution before the Council, Assembly, or a jury court, was used to consider allegations of crimes against the state—such as impiety, embezzlement, treason, and conspiracy.[38]

Athenian democracy did not entail disrespect for traditional moral values. On the contrary, private vices could become a disqualification for public office. Prostitution might disqualify a man from all the prerogatives of public life. Anyone who sought to propose a decree was forbidden to speak to the Assembly if he had maltreated his parents or squandered an inheritance.[39]

The main offices for which the lot was not used were those of the ten chief military commanders, or *strategoi*. They were directly elected by the Assembly and were eligible for reelection. As a result, the position of general was very much a political position, and a powerful one at that. The leading member of the ten became a kind of prime minister for foreign policy. It was in this capacity that leaders like Themistocles and Pericles held office, Pericles for over two decades. Except for these offices and a few others, the rule the Athenians followed was that no one should hold office more than once in his lifetime. The aim was apparently to preserve "the overriding supremacy of the popular assembly" and prevent "the emergence of an identifiable governing class, whether represented in the Council or the magistracies, which would be strong enough to wrest control from the Assembly and maintain a general supervision of policy."[40] But the generals were held accountable for their conduct in office and sometimes severely punished—even vindictively—for failures of command. And just as they were popularly elected, they were the only public officials subject to scrutiny not from the Council, at least in the first instance, but from the *demos* itself in the Assembly.[41] Demosthenes bitterly criticized the use of the *eisangelia* to prosecute generals: "Things are nowadays so scandalous that every single general is judged in your court two and three times on charges of life and death, while not one of them has the guts to fight a single battle against the enemy for life and death. They prefer the death of kidnappers and cutpurses to a proper one: only criminals die by death sentences; generals ought to die in battle."[42]

The democratic constitution was sorely tested by military adversity, and critics blamed it for causing military defeats. Military disasters in 415-413 B.C. strengthened the hand of the oligarchical opposition, organized in upper-class *hetaireiai*, and led to a conspiracy which succeeded in overthrowing the democratic constitution by the use of terror and appeals to war-weariness. At an irregular meeting, the Assembly voted to abolish the democratic constitution and put the government in the hands of a Council of 400 chosen by the oligarchs. Their rule lasted only four months because the exiled Alcibiades, one of the leaders of the conspiracy, was unable to deliver on his promise of an alliance with Persia and because the sailors in the Athenian fleet refused to recognize the new regime. Democracy was reestablished after a badly needed naval victory in 410 B.C., but later military defeats led to capitulation to Sparta in 404 B.C. and an oligarchical restoration under the Commission of Thirty—whose malevolent rule, which included the execution of 1,500 citizens, earned them the name of the "Thirty Tyrants." Loyal democrats fled and organized an opposition led by Thrasybulus which defeated the Thirty, who regrouped as a Commission of Ten. Finally, after the Spartans intervened, a compromise was worked out whereby democracy was restored in 403 B.C. and the oligarchs were allowed to create their own little *polis* at Eleusis in western Attica. Two years later, Eleusis was recaptured and the oligarchical leaders executed, without Spartan intervention. The full restoration of democracy was symbolized by the deification of the constitution as the goddess *Demokratia*, to whose statue offerings were made.[43]

The Social Structure of Democratic Athens

The social structure of democratic Athens was hierarchical. Stockton pieces together the evidence, which he admits is thin, to arrive at "best guesses." By his reckoning, there were in 431 B.C. about 40,000 citizens, males over eighteen, of whom some 22,000 were *zeugitai* and 18,000 *thetes*. Metics numbered perhaps 10,000, or somewhat more. Estimates for the slave population are not well founded, but Stockton suggests that the figure for Periclean Athens can scarcely have been fewer than 100,000. The numbers vary considerably over time, waxing and waning with Athenian prosperity, as well as with losses due to war and disease.[44] A. H. M. Jones estimates that perhaps 60 percent of citizens in fourth-century Athens lived on small holdings of five acres or were skilled craftsmen, shopkeepers, or casual laborers.[45] No clamor for land reform or cancellation of debts is recorded, apparently because property was widely distributed among citizens. Whereas in most Greek *poleis* there was continuous class war, Athens had only two counter-revolutions, one supported by Sparta, both of which were short-lived.[46]

Citizenship was based on kinship determined by descent through the male line at first and then, in accordance with a law introduced by Pericles in 451/450 only to those born to parents who were both citizens. It could not be gained by mere residence, no matter how long, though aliens were sometimes naturalized by decree. Citizenship was conferred on eligible males once they reached the age of eighteen and were registered in the *deme* to which their fathers belonged. Registration was a formal process in which qualifications were examined by other members of the *demes* and subject to challenge in court and possible further scrutiny.[47] Once inscribed on a *deme* list, a citizen became eligible to exercise a variety of prerogatives:

> to participate in Athenian cults, festivals, and worship; to attend, speak, and vote in the popular assembly (*ekklesia*); to serve (after the age of thirty) as a juror in the law courts (*dikasteria*); to vote and (depending on age and eligibility) stand for elected and allotted offices (*archai*); to seek redress and receive protection under the laws; to have the capacity to own land in Attika; to receive public disbursements, whether for services provided, as special distributions, or as maintenance for hardships. The loyal Athenian might also be rewarded with public burial at state expense if he sacrificed his life on behalf of the polis.[48]

A citizen was obliged to obey the law and might forfeit civic rights and privileges for not doing so. Wealthy citizens were required to support various "liturgies" or literally "work on behalf of the community" such as maintaining warships or sponsoring dramatic festivals. Citizens were also required to perform military service and pay taxes, mostly indirect, obligations also imposed on metics. By the latter part of the fourth century, males between eighteen and twenty years of age were required to undergo two years of military training and afterward to supply the equipment required for their military duty, in accordance with their social rank.[49]

The total population was swelled by resident aliens or metics as well as slaves. The slaves were mainly imported as a result of the many wars fought by Athens and other Greek cities. The law distinguished among citizens, foreigners (*xenoi*), resident aliens (*metoikoi*), and slaves (*douloi*). Foreigners did not enjoy the rights or protections accorded to citizens. They gained status as metics by being sponsored by citizens; once granted this status they were required to pay a yearly tax, the *metoikion*, and were granted certain legal advantages, but not the right to marry an Athenian woman.[50]

A census taken at the end of the fourth century showed 10,000 metics compared to 21,000 (adult male) citizens. Some of the metics settled in Athens voluntarily; others were former slaves who acquired this status when freed. Their large number makes it evident they found conditions attractive. Although they could not own land, they contributed greatly to Athenian prosperity by their activities in commerce and banking and were liable for military service. Many also proved their loyalty in times of crisis by making generous gifts.[51]

As to slavery, it would be wrong to suppose that everyone in Athens, or even a majority, drew a living from slave labor. All well-to-do families had several slaves. In plays, slaves appear in poor households, but Jones suggests that this is artistic license: slaves were good stock characters. The hoplites very likely all had a slave to take care of their armor or they may have had to hire someone to perform that function. Probably a quarter of the population had slaves, but few were employed in agriculture. Most were domestic servants. Most farms were probably run by families too poor to own slaves. Slave artisans sometimes worked side by side with other artisans, either working for a master or paying him a commission. There were some "state slaves"—notably the 1,200 Scythian archers who policed the Assembly and the law courts and enforced decrees issued by the magistrates. In some cases slave gangs might be leased from a contractor. Slaves were also employed in industry, especially mining on a large scale. One slave contractor owned 1,000 slaves and leased them to a mine owner in the fifth century; conditions were apparently very bad in these mines. There is no good evidence for the total number of slaves in Attica but one source around 383 B.C. estimates there were 150,000 in the entire area. On the whole, then, slavery was an auxiliary economic institution in Athens rather than the economic basis of the society. The great majority of Athenians earned their living by their own hands. Most citizens seem to have taken slavery for granted as a condition that was "according to nature," though some Sophist theorists rejected this assumption.[52] Sometimes, in crises, male slaves of military age were freed to man the ships. Once, the Assembly almost voted to free slaves who had fought for the city.

Even without emancipation, however, there was reported to be good feeling between slaves and citizens, though slaves were regarded as items of property and were therefore without legal rights. It was against the law to kill a slave, although it was legal to extract evidence from a slave by torture in judicial proceedings (because otherwise he might not testify truthfully against his master). The provision seems to have been used more as a deterrent to lying by slaves (and to threats by their masters to punish them for doing so) than as routine practice. The "Old Oligarch" who was critical of democracy noted indignantly that it was illegal to strike slaves. In the *Republic* Plato too makes fun of democratic egalitarianism with respect to slaves.[53]

The Procedures of Athenian Democracy

In the mature Athenian democracy of the late fifth and early fourth centuries, authority rested in an Assembly open to all citizens of a certain age which was a governing body, not merely one that selected and controlled those who governed. The Assembly met regularly forty times a year, in addition to extraordinary emergency meetings, and conducted all the major business of the *polis*, including foreign policy and the initiation of legislation, convening in a sloping outdoor meeting place, the *Pnyx*, which could hold 6,000 people until it was enlarged to double its capacity—though it is unlikely such a large number could attend most meetings since most citizens lived far from the place of assembly. Any citizen not disenfranchised, whatever his vocation or wealth, might speak his mind in the Assembly. In the most moderate form of democracy, the function of the Assembly was limited to choosing magistrates, examining accounts, and leaving other matters to the elected magistrates and council. In its more radical form, the function was broadened to include debate and discussion of major issues. Finley describes it vividly:

> Athenian democracy was direct, not representative, in a double sense; attendance in the sovereign Assembly was open to every citizen, and there was no bureaucracy or civil service, save for a few clerks, slaves owned by the state itself, who kept such records as were unavoidable, copies of treaties and laws, lists of defaulting taxpayers, and the like. Government was thus "by the people" in the most literal sense. The Assembly, which had the final decision on war and peace, treaties, finance, legislation, public works, in short, on the whole gamut of governmental activity, was an outdoor mass meeting of as many as a thousand citizens, over the age of eighteen, as chose to attend on any given day. It met frequently throughout the year, forty times at a minimum, and it normally reached a decision on the business before it in a single day's debate in which, in principle, everyone present had the right to participate by taking the floor. *Isegoria*, the universal right to speak in the Assembly, was sometimes employed by Greek writers as a synonym for "democracy." And the decision was by a simple majority vote of those present.[54]

The *Boule* or Council prepared business for the Assembly, and Jones considers it the "administrative linch-pin of the constitution."[55] The offices of the magistrate and the *Boule* were distributed on the basis of the principle that "one man is as good as another." Attendance was compensated in the Council and ultimately in the Assembly as well. Participants in the Assembly were paid subsistence and Councillors received higher compensation.

Even though the exclusion of slaves and aliens from the citizenship kept the Assembly from being truly popular and majoritarian, it included many whose poverty prevented them from having the degree of leisure Aristotle thought essential for learning what was necessary to citizenship.

One important difference between the Athenian Assembly and modern legislatures should be particularly noted. Although the Assembly initiated legislation, it did not actually make laws or override laws by its decrees. That function was assigned to a large committee of perhaps 500 or 1,000 law-makers selected from the annual jurors. Thus the *Ecclesia* and the committees of *nomothetai* ("law makers") worked together to fashion laws or re-examine old ones. At the first assembly of each year, the established code was adopted by vote after a debate in which each citizen could propose changes, chapter by chapter. If any old law was vetoed, *nomothetai* were appointed to revise it. The proposer of a change meanwhile had to exhibit the old law and the new proposed one side by side "by the statues of the *Eponymoi*." Copies were given to an official who read them in public at several meetings of the assembly. By the fourth assembly, the people assigned the law makers, stipulating the time allowed them, the pay they were to receive, and also named five people to defend the existing law. Then, acting with a small group of the Council on each change, the *nomothetes* decided finally whether the new law should be enacted.

The proposer of a decree later judged contrary to previously existing law was subject to criminal proceedings. Under the practice called a *graphe paranomon*, anyone who introduced a proposal that was adopted by the Assembly but afterward judged contrary to the prevailing law could be tried and subjected to a heavy fine. This strange procedure—whereby the Assembly, which presumably had unlimited authority to adopt laws, allowed a popular jury chosen by lot to review laws it had adopted—served two important functions. First, by making those who promoted changes liable for violations of the constitution, the practice inhibited them from making frivolous or dangerous proposals that may have appealed to some passing passion but would not be likely to withstand calmer scrutiny. Second, the practice permitted the populace to reconsider laws accepted in the Assembly in the light of further reflection or of experience, by juries which were easier to convene than the Assembly.[56] One clearly persistent public speaker, Aristophon, claimed that he had been indicted, by *graphai paranomon* alone, seventy-five times.[57]

The obvious danger of this practice is that it enabled the populace to punish advisers rather than accept responsibility for its own bad decisions. Athanasios Moulakis points out that the historian Thucydides quoted one of the advisers as observing in criticism of the Athenian *demos*, "We are responsible advisers, while you are irresponsible listeners. Indeed, if not only those who gave advice but also those who followed it had to suffer alike, you would show greater prudence in your decisions; but as it is, whenever you meet with a reverse you give way to your first impulse and punish your adviser for his single error of judgement instead of yourselves, the multitude who shared in the error."[58] Moulakis also notes that the great frequency with which the *graphe paranomon* was resorted to suggests two considerations: "First, that the laws of Athens passed by the assembly were so contradictory, that nobody could keep track of them in an orderly fashion. It was therefore difficult to be sure that new laws were in accordance with existing laws. This incoherence was enhanced by the lack of differentiation between constitutional, procedural and substantive laws or decrees. Secondly, given this uncertainty, the *graphe paranomon* became a very convenient means to obstruct political action and to embarrass political opponents."[59]

The members of the Council of 500 were chosen by lot from among citizens over the age of thirty in the *demes* (wards or parishes) in proportion to their size. The Council's principal functions were to supervise and coordinate the activities of the magistrates—700 in number according to the pseudo-Xenophon[60]—and prepare an agenda for the Assembly. No question could be raised in the Assembly unless it had first been published in written form by the council and advertised, so as to preclude snap votes. On non-controversial questions, the Council drafted a motion, which had the effect of clearing away formal business. On controversial questions, the Council expressed no opinion. The presidency rotated by lot for a tenth of each year. To preclude undue influence, the presiding officer or foreman of the council was chosen anew daily from the members of the tribe in charge at the time. No one could serve as foreman of the council more than once.[61]

Most magistrates—who numbered about 350 in the later fourth century[62]—were chosen annually by lot from all qualified candidates who put themselves forward. The major exception to this rule, introduced in the fifth century, was for military officers, including the ten *strategoi* or generals, who were elected annually by the Assembly. The Assembly debated military policy and issued instructions to the generals, who were expected to adhere to them closely. In the fourth century, a few of the high financial officers were also elected.[63]

The law courts drew upon an annual panel of 6,000 jurors chosen by lot and assigned to cases by lot: an ingenious machine, the *cleroterion*, was used to draw the required number of jurors' metal name plates from those inserted. Juries did not sit only on civil and criminal cases but had a political function as well. They heard complaints against magistrates or those accused of deceiving the people in speeches to the Assembly. They could also quash any motion voted in the Assembly as unconstitutional (contrary to the laws) and punish its author.

There was an age qualification of thirty for jury service and election to the Council or to public office, though any duly registered male citizen over twenty could attend the Assembly.[64] A citizen might be disqualified from service by failure to pay debts owed the treasury. Every year, 6,000 jurors were impanelled by lot. They received a subsistence allowance while serving on juries. From the beginning of the fourth century, the size of juries was either 201 or 501, depending on the type of case, and courts were in session for some 300 days, all except for assembly and festival days.[65]

Although these institutions make Athens a model of direct democracy, outstanding citizens sometimes had more authority than others. Eminence was not simply a function of land ownership or the use of patronage, however. Because the nobles were rivals and none could assure himself a large enough following, the choice of leadership was made by the Assembly in consideration of rhetorical skills and proven administrative ability, especially as demonstrated in battle.[66] Pericles was elected and re-elected for twenty-five years until in 455 B.C., he was deposed and heavily fined. The ten *strategoi* might be re-elected without restriction and became far more important than the archons who served only for one year.

Athens has been faulted because the pay for jury service was drawn from the tribute paid by Athens' allies in the Delian League. Democracy is therefore said to have been parasitic on the empire. The citizens who served in these governmental capacities had leisure to do so because they were supported by the labor of slaves, and Athenian imperialism raised many citizens from poverty by providing them with land in the colonies. But Jones points out that democracy did not cease to function in the fourth century when Athens had lost the empire and that the Second Athenian League (377 to 357) was never a paying proposition.[67] Nevertheless, there is a sense in which Periclean democracy can be said to have supported itself by a policy of "social imperialism." Finley argues that Athens was free from civil strife, except for two episodes during the Peloponnesian War, for nearly two centuries because many of its citizens benefited from the supplementary income they received from the "extensive distribution of public funds, in the navy and in pay for jury duty, public office and membership of the Council, as well as the relatively large land settlement programme in subject territory."[68] The jury system is also open to criticism on other grounds. Juries may well have been too susceptible to emotional appeals, and the jurymen may have been swayed on occasion by fear that if they did not find a defendant guilty, and punish him by assessing a fine, there would not be enough money available to pay them for their service.

Athenian citizens properly took pride, however, in their civic loyalty. Their army was only average, not as disciplined as Sparta's, but since the Athenians were a naval power it is more to the point to note that their seamanship was excellent. Some 12,000 citizens of the class of *thetes* served as crews on Athenian triremes, which under Pericles numbered sixty on active service and 300 in dockyards.[69] A good deal of money was spent on public works, such as the Parthenon, and this expenditure gave employment to many poorer citizens. Athenian religious festivals were well and devotedly maintained, and its dramatic performances were unrivalled, all with public subsidy.

In view of the remarkable success of Athenian democracy, the most glaring deficiency in the record of the period is the absence of an explicit democratic theory. As Jones notes, "It is curious that in the abundant literature produced in the greatest democracy of Greece there survives no statement of democratic political theory." All the writers whose works survive were in various degrees sympathetic to oligarchy or, in the singular case of Plato, to rule by philosopher kings. Socrates, the wisest teacher of Athens, was hostile to democracy, according to both Plato and Xenophon, and his condemnation by a democratic jury became for Plato a symbol of the incompatibility of philosophy and democracy. Isocrates wrote panegyrics of Athens while young but grew embittered. Aristotle tried to balance positive and negative judgments, concluding that a mixed constitution was the best and most stable form. Among historians, only Herodotus is a democrat. Thucydides was hostile, preferring a regime that disfranchised two-thirds of its citizens. Xenophon admired Sparta. The orators of the fourth century, who were expected to flatter their public patron, were democrats, but only the speeches of Pericles and Lysias survive.[70] The largely hostile literary legacy does not reflect the views of most Athenians, who were deeply attached to their constitution. Counter-revolutions were the work of small cliques of the wealthy and the heads of noble families.

One of the most important critiques of Athenian democracy is contained in a piece of writing called "The Constitution of the Athenians" and preserved in antiquity among the writings of Xenophon. It is now accepted that he could not have written it, so the author is often described as the "Old Oligarch," an epithet which is misleading, as Stockton notes,[71] because much of the work is a defense of Athenian democracy. It is thought to have been written about 415-412 somewhere other than in Athens, but the author's close familiarity with Athenian institutions makes it likely he was himself an Athenian critical of democracy. He appears to have written the work to explain Athens to non-Athenians, particularly to explain why it was successful in maintaining itself. For all the criticism it contains, however, the work shows a grudging admiration for Athenian democracy, reflecting the Sophist view that what succeeds must be right.

The two most usual criticisms of democracy were first, that it produced a feckless liberty and second, that it dispensed equality to equals and unequals alike. Although the first charge was somewhat justified, Athenian citizens revelled in the liberty they enjoyed under the democratic constitution. While the prosecution of Socrates demonstrated the limits of Athenian toleration, it was a comparatively rare exception to the even-handed administration of justice in Athens, an exception which occurred largely because Socrates' favorite pupil Alcibiades had done more to ruin Athens in a recent war than anyone else. Socrates' pupil Critias had also been the ruthless ringleader of the Thirty, who had massacred thousands of Athenians a few years earlier. The condemnation nevertheless stands as a permanent rebuke to Athenian democracy, because it was based upon guilt by association and amounted to making a scapegoat of the city's most illustrious teacher and punishing him for military failures commit-ted by those like Alcibiades and Critias who may have studied with him but were in no way acting upon his instruction. Alcibiades in particular was an extremely popular leader whose conduct was based on decisions taken by the Assembly.

As to the issue of equality, Plato's charge is echoed by Isocrates and Aristotle, who distinguish between the equality that distributes the same to everyone and the equality that distributes different benefits in accor-dance with some standard. Demosthenes praised the equality of Athens because it gave each citizen a feeling that he had a share in equality and justice. Equality before the law was one of the fundamental characteristics which distinguished Athenian democracy from oligarchy. Under the Thirty, the right to a legal trial was available only to the 3,000 full citizens.

The principle of equality also applied fully in matters of government. Everyone had the right to speak and vote and assemble, as well as to serve in both the Assembly and Council. Plato argued that because government was an art demanding the highest skill, rule should be reserved for those most capable of exercising it, the properly educated select few, and not all citizens indiscriminately. Aristotle disagreed; he liked the idea of relying on collective wisdom and virtue even though he too thought that admin-istration was best left to the wisest. Politics, he argued, is one of those arts where the consumers are better judges than the producers.[72] In large mea-sure, the debate turns on the question of whether people can be trusted to know their own interests and make a proper judgment on a debated is-sue. Socrates argues that if it is inappropriate to appoint flautists or ship's captains or carpenters by lot, it is no less wrong to use the lot to select rulers. Unfortunately no reasoned defense of the lot (or sortition) has sur-vived. The most likely explanation of its popularity among democrats is, that contrary to Socrates (as reported by Plato), it was not used to select "rulers" but only officials charged with routine duties, for which little more than a sense of decency and fair play was required. As has been pointed out, office holders served for only one year, after passing a preliminary examination; their accounts were audited afterward and their steward-ship was subject to review in case allegations of misconduct were made.

Athenians did not ignore merit. It was said in a mock panegyric that Athenian democracy was in reality "an aristocracy with the approval of the majority. In most things the majority is in control of the city, and bestows office and power on those whom it thinks to be the best . . . There is one criterion: the man who is thought to be wise and good holds power and rule."[73] But the Athenian belief in equality among citizens also very likely reflected the view that since all were expected to sacrifice themselves, if necessary, for the sake of the city, all should share equally in its deliberations.

Another criticism sometimes put then and since is that because in a democracy the people is sovereign instead of the law, policy decisions can be arbitrary and changeable. There is some truth in the charge that democracy risks legal chaos: like the tyrant, the majority may habitually override existing laws. This very danger helps explain why the Athenian Assembly went to such extreme limits as making liable for punishment those who sponsored new laws in violation of old laws. The two greatest weaknesses of the classical democratic constitution from a modern perspective are that it did not make a distinction between basic law and statutory law and that the laws did not acknowledge human rights with a paramount claim to protection even from interference by the majority. Even so, the idea that Athenian democracy was as capricious with regard to law as tyranny is hardly supportable. Athenians, like other Greeks, believed that law was the embodiment of reason laid down by a wise legislator like Solon and Cleisthenes but might need to be clarified or supplemented from time to time. And over time, as Ostwald points out, popular sovereignty yielded to a conception of law or *nomos* as an overriding foundation for decision-making.[74]

Critics frequently complained that democracy in effect meant that the poor majority ruled over the rich minority in its own interest. While it is true that sometimes the rich were heavily taxed, especially in time of war, and that wealthy individuals were required to maintain triremes, the tax system was by no means expropriation. The war tax involved 5 or 6 percent of income and was widely imposed. Critics complain that the courts condemned the rich on trumped up charges and confiscated their property, but it is hard to say how common such practices were, and in any case, the rich had their own ways of evading the laws.[75]

Yet another criticism put by philosophers concerns the role of the *polis* in rearing citizens. The philosophers, especially Plato, tend to argue that human beings are naturally driven by the desire to gratify their appetites at the expense of others, and therefore that the function of education must first of all be to inculcate a sense of social responsibility. Plato in particular thought that authority should be given only to the wisest and most excellent, who would impose a just way of life on the rest by a rigid system of differential education and control over reproduction.

Athenian democrats had a more optimistic view of human nature. They too believed that education was critical to character as well as physical development, but they also believed that every citizen should be allowed to live his own life within the broad limits laid down by the law and that all should take part in government. They were not naive, however, about the temptations of power. They "were distrustful of human nature on its ability to resist the temptations of irresponsible power; hence their insistence on brief terms of office, regular review of the conduct of magistrates in office, and above all a searching scrutiny of the record of magistrates on completing their term." By contrast, "the philosophers are strangely blind to this danger, and are content to rely on the virtue of their usually hereditary or co-optative oligarchies of wise men."[76] Lysias, like Pericles, expressed the pride Athenians felt because their constitution protected liberty. Our ancestors, he said, "were the first and only men of that time who cast out arbitrary power and established democracy, holding that the freedom of all was the greatest concord, and sharing with one another their hopes and perils they governed themselves with free hearts, honouring the good and chastising the bad by law. They held it bestial to constrain one another by force, and the part of men to define justice by law, and to persuade by reason, and serve both by action, having law as their king and reason as their teacher."[77]

Thucydides faults democracy for Athenian military failures. He contends that the Athenians fought well so long as Pericles was in charge but suffered when he was rejected by the populace. Jones agrees that the Athenians often showed poor judgment but questions whether the system should be held responsible, inasmuch as the same poor judgment was exercised by oligarchies and kings. The Athenians held out against Sparta for thirty years and only lost because the Spartans traded the freedom of the Greeks to the rulers of Persia in return for subsidies. Thucydides also blames Athens for a cynical and brutal imperialism which ultimately proved costly in alienating allies she would have to call upon in times of danger. In particular, he criticizes the treatment accorded Naxos, the first ally which tried to secede, and the slaughter of the Melians in Sicily when they tried to resist Athenian demands. For the most part, the Athenians respected the autonomy of the satellites, but not when they dared to exercise it to secede from the alliance.[78]

Thucydides' critique of Athenian imperialism raises the question of whether democracy was responsible for the Athenians' failure to stop Philip of Macedon. The causes are more likely to have been the damage done by the Peloponnesian War and the added weakness due to the failure of the Greek *poleis*, including Athens, to achieve greater unity. Had the scattered communities of the lower peninsula achieved a better-integrated form of federation, they might have given a better account of themselves in the face of the Macedonian challenge. Otherwise, the evil Plato finds in democracy, notably *stasis* or internal war between the few and the many, the rich and the poor, is largely absent from democratic Athens. Donald Kagan has described Plato's assault on the character of Periclean Athens as a "travesty" because the people did not permit leaders to usurp power or hesitate to remove from office even the most powerful of them, and because they showed through the horrors of three decades of war, defeat, occupation, and a coup d'état, a civic commitment that enabled them to maintain their democratic form of government.[79]

Democratic Consciousness: The Origins of Autonomy

Reflecting on the institutions of democratic Athens almost compels the conclusion that this society must have engendered a belief system which served to rationalize and justify it. Educated Greeks of this period were so enamored of rationality that they wanted to account for virtually everything in philosophical terms. The very fact that Plato and Aristotle devote so much attention to the critique of democracy suggests that there must have been a democratic political consciousness, if not a fully developed democratic political theory. The speeches of Pericles and Lysias make it very clear that there was a democratic ethos—one that regarded the liberty of the citizen and his participation in the affairs of government as characteristics eminently compatible with the concern for good order and happiness which we know from Plato and Aristotle were of paramount concern but which Plato especially made to seem identical with aristocratic rule. Unfortunately, we can only guess at what this consciousness held from what is said about it by its critics—who, of course, are likely to have emphasized flaws rather than to have a drawn a balanced picture.

One way to approach the effort of understanding the views of the democrats is to suppose that they held ideals more or less the opposite of those their critics espoused. This is a helpful technique in some respects but not in all. One problem with it is that both Aristotle and Plato shared certain of the ideals of democracy. Another is that democrats may have had concerns which their critics simply ignored. A third is that it would be absurd to require that a democratic philosophy be the antithesis of everything Plato endorses in the *Republic*, including rationalism, the government of the wise, and equality for women. These caveats acknowledged, however, this procedure would lead along a clearly discernible path. A democrat, measured as the antithesis of Plato, would be skeptical of the principle that there is another world in which the true forms reside. He might suppose that there is no single truth about anything, but only the imperfect versions that human beings are capable of achieving by observation and reasoning. As Plato is an absolutist, he would be a relativist, except with respect to certain fundamental moral axioms. In Karl Popper's terms, as Plato advocates the closed society, the democrat would advocate the open society, premised on the notion that there is no one settled notion of truth and that all inquiries should be encouraged.[80] The democrat would therefore not prescribe rule by philosopher-kings. He might share with Plato the belief that the soul of the individual is only rightly ordered and happy when reason presides over the passions, but he would not suppose that the exquisitely developed reason of the philosopher would be necessary to regulate the affairs of the *polis*. Since all men are by definition capable of rationality, those who give evidence of being able to make practical use of their faculties ought to govern themselves, individually and collectively. Far from supposing that the mass of men are driven by their appetites and need to have those with reason sit on them, in Plato's image, as a rider on a horse, a democrat would contend that reason helps all people to fulfill their desires, whether these are the desire of the philosopher for comprehensive knowledge or of the ordinary man for practical wisdom and other kinds of happiness.

This approach may not be far off the mark. Perhaps the closest to a democratic philosopher, if Plato is the prototypical anti-democrat, is Protagoras, the Sophist whom Plato often attacks. We do not have Protagoras' own writings, only fragments and scraps in the writings of others which attribute various arguments to him. The most famous of his sayings, "Man is the measure of all things," has been variously interpreted. Plato saw it as a fallacious view that there is no reality beyond our perceptions. It may also mean that there is indeed a world outside man, but one that can only be understood by human reason, which would bring it closer to Plato's view except insofar as Plato's other world has an existence independent of human discovery. Protagoras' saying also suggests a kind of humanism with respect to standards of conduct. Plato's view is that the standard for human conduct is outside us; Protagoras seems to believe it must come from within. Democracy is critical to Protagoras because he sees human fulfillment as the effort to achieve autonomy. Plato, by limiting rule to the wise and restricting others to non-governmental functions, would deny the opportunity for autonomy to most people because they are supposedly incapable of achieving wisdom. According to Plato, Socrates complained that although Athenians deferred to the views of technical experts, such as architects, they felt free to express their own unqualified opinions about the laws that ought to govern society. Plato cites Protagoras as replying that Zeus gave various talents to people but a sense of decency and fair play to all, since otherwise society would be impossible:

> So, Socrates . . . that is why the Athenians and the others, when the debate is about architecture or any other technical question, think that few should take part in the discussion, and if anyone outside the few joins in, do not tolerate, as you say—rightly in my opinion. But when they come to discuss political questions, which must be determined by justice and moderation, they properly listen to everyone, thinking that everyone shares in these qualities—or cities wouldn't exist.[81]

For similar reasons, Plato also objected to the use of the lot in appointing magistrates. Because no reasoned defense of the use of the lot remains,[82] we can only speculate that democrats thought it justifiable because the role of the magistrates was to administer the laws, and for this purpose a sense of justice was all that was required, especially inasmuch as judicial procedures held office holders accountable.

Cynthia Farrar has examined Protagoras closely to this end—along with two others also considered sources for understanding Greek democratic consciousness: Thucydides, and the scientist, Democritus. Farrar begins from the premise that in all societies people's understanding of themselves as agents is shaped by their interactions with the world around them. For the Athenians, a major question arising out of this interaction was how to reconcile individual autonomy with political order. An evolution of thought took place in which many Greeks came to understand democracy as the proper form for this reconciliation. The Homeric view of life and the world is very different from the later view. Man is in considerable part understood as an instrument of the gods rather than as an autonomous agent. Still, man is expected to act in ways that do not violate tradition and jeopardize social order. Often the tragic hero is torn between necessity and personal responsibility. A major change comes when order is understood not as externally imposed but as something ratified and replicated by human agency. Thus the laws human beings make and impose upon themselves partake of the same character as the laws that govern the universe. They establish order and there is a mysterious link between them, but the laws of the *polis* are made by its citizens, not imposed by the gods or the fates or any mysterious forces. Farrar stresses that the change takes place first in the development of the oligarchic constitution:

> The transition from an externally-imposed order in which man figures as an all-but-unwitting agent to conscious participation in or ratification of an order still external and mysterious, and eventually to a self-determination which declares its virtual independence of *tuche* or external control, is ultimately a political transition. It is the political community, the *polis*, freed from the arbitrary, autocratic rule of nobles or tyrants and ordered by customary law (*nomos*) that expresses at once man's autonomy and his participation in a divine pattern. Divinely-sanctioned *nomos* is construed by the aristocrats and approved by the people. Political order is the image of intelligible (not

obscure or arbitrary) divine order, mediated by the traditional rulers, the nobles, whose authority was both religious and political . . . the significant contrast is not between democracy and oligarchy or tyranny, but between freedom on the one hand, and irresponsible, despotic (and narrowly self-interested) rule on the other.[83]

At first, she points out, both Spartans and Athenians saw the community as a form of order created by subservience to law, in contrast to the despotism represented by tyrants and the Persian king. The Athenians, however, went on to explore and revise this understanding of freedom and autonomy. When Solon mediated the conflict between rich and poor in the sixth century he not only eased the friction between them but transformed their relationship by making rich and poor equal citizens. These reforms were not enough, but when Cleisthenes strengthened them by making all inhabitants of Attica at the same time citizens of Athens, he laid the basis for the development of a stable democracy. Instead of defining themselves as nobles and commoners, or free men and slaves, Athenians defined themselves primarily as citizens or non-citizens. This identity was fully realized only in the fifth century, "when the institutional dominance of the elite came to an end, and political status was firmly distinguished from personal, social or economic attributes, and freedom and order were construed politically, as the product of the interaction of political equals."[84]

This strong sense of communal autonomy was expressed in the expanded role of the courts, which came to sit in judgment on the character and performance of public servants. Because jury service was compensated, large numbers of citizens could take part. Gradually the property qualification for holding office was also lowered and it is possible that magistrates too were compensated. Great emphasis was placed on freedom of speech in the Assembly. Political power came to reside in the ability to persuade the Assembly.[85]

This momentous development, she suggests, is reflected in the Greek theater, especially in the plays of Aeschylus, as in the *Oresteia* where the conflicting claims of the gods or tradition confront the claims of the community. Clearly, the aim of Aeschylus is to commemorate the transition from a juridical order based on blood feuding to one in which justice is embodied in impartial law reflecting the divine character of the *polis*. These plays may well depict the inner struggle of democratic societies to reconcile the conflicting claims of man as an individual with his role as a citizen and of man as part of the universe and as part of his community.[86] It was under the influence of this sort of concern that Protagoras formulated his views, having in mind both the speculative and the practical aspects of the question. The answer he came to is that the order of the universe is not transcendent as Plato argued but immanent in the world, and that knowledge is our understanding of the order implicit in the interaction of the elements that make up the universe, always with an eye toward understanding the basis of constancy and stability. By arranging our own lives in the form of democracy, we apply this knowledge to our own interrelationships with each other to achieve political order.[87] Unlike Plato, therefore, Protagoras emphasizes the importance of opinions and appearances, because in them we can discern this reality. Our understanding must begin in what we can know. Also unlike Plato, he accepts and advocates the Sophist approach to politics, which consists in helping people to articulate their own self-interests on the basis of what they themselves can know, suggesting questions to them, drawing on their own wider experience, but not denying the validity of their separate interests and perceptions. Democratic politics teaches them to accommodate their views to those of others, not to seek absolute knowledge but practical compromise—not, as Plato charged, in order to make the bad appear the good, but rather to arrive at political good—a relative, not an absolute good, one that would not have to be imposed but would be arrived at by the parties themselves. Participation in the *polis* helps socialize people because they notice their neighbors and respect their needs and views. Protagoras is therefore "so far as we know, the first democratic political theorist in the history of the world" and the philosophical counterpart of the dramatist Aeschylus, both of whom sought to show that "political action is both collective self-expression and collective self-restraint."[88] Unlike Plato, Protagoras and Aeschylus thought that ordinary people had the competence to make such judgments. Socrates had often used the image of the flute player to point out that in a just society only those who could play well would have the flutes. The Sophist answer was that if survival depended upon playing the flute, each citizen would teach the other how to play and by comparison with those altogether unskilled the citizens would be quite accomplished.[89] In such reflections as these, the democratic consciousness took shape, supplementing the institutions that very likely arose more from "untaught feelings" and pragmatic need than from rational deliberation.

Whether this interesting speculation about Protagoras is historically right or not, it rests upon a compelling premise, which is that the rise of democracy must have inspired a democratic ethos, and that this ethos very likely entailed a theory of man and society resting on a belief that ordinary people are capable, by virtue of their capacity for reasoning, of regulating their own lives. Indeed, as Pericles observed, the most distinctive feature of Athenian democracy was that it made public affairs of even more concern to citizens than their private business. Insofar as he rejected the democratic premise (which, arguably, he accepted to a considerable extent in the later dialogues), Plato was compelled to assert that rational capacity, which all Greeks believed to be the defining characteristic of human beings, was so lacking in most people that they would be better off being ruled by philosophers like himself. The same argument was used by ordinary Greek males to rationalize the exclusion of women from politics and the enslavement of "barbarians." The extraordinary achievements of Athenian civilization in its democratic period, both with respect to self-government and to the encouragement of philosophic criticism and introspective drama, are themselves the best refutation of Plato's argument, for these achievements were hardly impositions of the few wise upon the many ignorant; they were all made possible by the experience of democratic citizenship and the free dialogue democracy encouraged. As W. G. Forrest has remarked, the greatest achievement of the Athenians was to have created, "virtually *ab initio*, the idea of a state composed of citizens who by virtue of their citizenship alone had certain unquestionable rights and to do this without allowing either existing prejudices or existing institutions to interfere in any way with the exercise of those rights, without creating or permitting new prejudices and new institutions which might curb or distort their development. In a word, to invent the notion of an autonomous human being and to apply it rigorously throughout the society."[90]

The main problem of Athenian democracy was not that it led only to demagoguery and to hedonism (for which in any case the intellectual critics had the same weakness as others). The problem was rather that the preoccupation with communal autonomy prevented Athenians from recognizing the need to transcend their own parochialism. Instead of promoting democracy as an ideal suitable for all and cooperating with other *poleis* to create a federal system that might have better protected them all, they enslaved those they considered natural inferiors and practiced naked imperialism toward other Greek *poleis*. Having discovered the principle of autonomy, we might say, they became so enamored of it that they kept it too much for themselves. Only with the collapse of the *polis* and the rise of Stoicism, with its dreams of universal brotherhood and the ideal *cosmopolis*, did the principle of autonomy introduced earlier begin to find unbounded expression—as yet, however, only as an ethical ideal with no political implications.

4

Plural Autonomy: Roman and Later Republicanism

Athenian democracy—as the direct self-government of an entire community—did not set an example that later societies would seek to emulate; Roman republicanism—a form of balanced or mixed government in which public opinion had only a restricted role and in which power was divided among different assemblies, with an aristocratic senate the most important—did provide such a model. Although the republic was succeeded by an imperial monarchy, it provided a source book for republican government that was to be carefully examined centuries later, when monarchy came under attack and opponents sought a practical alternative.

Roman republicanism resembled Athenian democracy in locating ultimate authority in the citizenry, but differed in dividing legislative and elective authority among several assemblies. Because of the Roman example, a republic came to be understood as a system of mixed or divided government combining monarchy, aristocracy, and popular government in what was often thought to be the most stable political arrangement. The Roman constitution was also "mixed" in the sense that it distributed power among various constituencies, based upon kinship, status, place of residence, and wealth. In the popular assemblies, voting was by group rather than by individual suffrage. The balance or equilibrium among these constituencies was thought to provide a form of power sharing among the major groups composing society, but one that respected the need for social hierarchy. In recognizing the political legitimacy of these groupings or factions, Roman republicanism differed from Athenian democracy, which united all citizens in a single assembly and gave much less recognition to differences of wealth. It may therefore be thought of as introducing a form of "plural autonomy" modifying the communal autonomy claimed as much by the Roman *civitas* as by the Greek *polis*. As a result, when a Roman citizen went into battle to defend his city or to extend its power, he fought both as a proud Roman citizen, exhibiting patriotic "civic virtue," and as a member of a class-divided army carrying a banner inscribed *SPQR*, for "the Senate and People of Rome." At home, the same citizen would be identified with different parties whose struggle for control was sometimes so divisive as to lead to internecine warfare.

Along with its greater size and pluralistic character, other factors also made the Roman experiment more influential than the Athenian in later centuries. Rome lasted much longer and was regarded as the proud symbol and foundation of Western civilization for centuries after its collapse. The republic, because it created the conditions for Rome's successful expansion, could not be dismissed as a failed experiment contrary to human nature or a system of government fit only for a very small and homogeneous community. Memories of the grandeur that was Rome blended the spirit of republican citizenship with the might of empire and associated both with military and organizational prowess. When opponents of feudalism and absolutism sought an alternative that would create an operational and not merely theoretical form of popular sovereignty, they were able to point to the history of Rome and they found in Roman law and political practices a veritable handbook of procedure. The fact that the Roman Republic had been more oligarchic than Athenian democracy made it more congenial to aristocratic and upper middle class reformers who feared that unbridled popular sovereignty would lead to mob rule, but the fact that over time the powers of the plebeian assembly had been greatly strengthened also made it appealing to champions of a broadened franchise. The Roman model, with its elaborate constitutional engineering and its stress on law and the authority of magistrates, seemed less susceptible to demagoguery and incompetence than the Athenian, which had been roundly criticized by the city's own philosophers on that score. Rome had suffered even more than Athens from corruption, as Sallust and other historians had pointed out, but this could be guarded against by drawing lessons from Roman failures (especially by avoiding the conditions of poverty and dependence that helped produced Caesarism) and emulating its efforts to inculcate patriotic loyalty and an ethic of civic virtue. Outright democrats found Roman republicanism a source of inspiration because it yielded a more expansive concept of citizenship than the Athenian *polis* and because the struggle of the orders resulted in a gradual widening of popular participation, coming close, in the revolt led by the brothers Gracchi, to establishing a much more democratic constitution.

When later republicans sought to imitate the Roman example, they sought to emulate both its emphasis on civic virtue and its recognition of the pragmatic benefits of checks and balances, functional and social, in preventing any one group from monopolizing power. Under the influence of natural rights-social contract theory, however, the association of republicanism with social hierarchy was at first muted and then all but abandoned. What was retained was the commitment to functionally mixed government and a pluralism of sociopolitical groups—interests, factions, and parties—as well as the understanding that republican government requires civic virtue. When republicanism also became a synonym for popular representative government, often unicameral and based on universal suffrage, the difference between republicanism and democracy became more a matter of historical connotation than political reality.

Before the revival of republicanism, however, the entire Roman experience was put under a cloud because of the Christian denunciation of paganism teachings and the use made of religious teachings by the prime beneficiaries of feudalism. All that was Greek and Roman, and not merely their pantheism, was condemned as idolatrous, including attachment to the "earthly city," whether *polis* or *civitas*. A "great chain of being" was said to extend downward from the heavens and to assign everyone a place in the social hierarchy. As the unity of Christendom required subordination to a single church headed by a single bishop, so the unity of society was held to require subordination to a single temporal order under a Christian king.

Even within the idealized *"corpus Christianum,"* however, dissension had to be dealt with. When it was not ruthlessly suppressed in campaigns against heresy but allowed to express itself in church councils, the medieval church provided an experience of self-government that helped prepare the way for the reappearance of secular republicanism. The "conciliar movement" led by figures like Marsilius of Padua, Nicholas of Cusa, and John of Paris, championed representative government both for the church and for secular society. Some heretical movements repudiated episcopacy and called instead for covenentalism, a tendency which finally found political expression among groups like the Levellers among the English Puritans. When the Protestant revolt created a schism of faith that could not be resolved by the wars of religion, the way was finally open for the toleration and separation of church and state that became a bulwark of modern democracy. Substantively, Protestantism also provided powerful support for secular individualism, both in economic and political behavior, even though its leaders usually preached political quietism and support for Protestant princes.

The Rise of the Roman Republic

Rome differed from Athens in encompassing a larger territory with a more varied populace. "The difference between the Greek *polis* and the Latin *civitas*," A. N. Sherwin-White has pointed out, "corresponds to the difference between the mountains of Greece and the hills of Latium." Latium is a plain not broken by impassable mountains but encircled by hills. Whereas the Athenians had no choice but to remain within Attica and to found colonies and make alliances by seaborne expeditions, Rome could more readily expand to incorporate neighboring peoples.[1]

Like the Greek democracies and soon after them, the Roman Republic also arose after a long pre-history in which the immediately prior form had been monarchy. Originally a collection of villages on the banks of the Tiber, Rome is thought to have become a monarchical state as a result of Etruscan conquest in the middle of the seventh century B.C., not as legend would have it, because its eponymous founder, Romulus, had been a demi-god who passed without dying to the dwelling-place of the immortals.[2] The conquerors seem to have fused the mostly small villages into a single political unit, with an elective kingship that became hereditary.[3] The republic is thought to have arisen in 509 B.C. in a revolt led by patricians (from *pater* or father, connoting clan elders), a noble class of long standing, with the support of the royal military forces, against the tyrannical rule of the last Etruscan king, Tarquin the Proud. It reached the zenith of its power in the several centuries following the decline of the Athenian *polis*, during which the form of government that prevailed elsewhere in the Mediterranean world was dynastic. Unlike Athens, however, Rome went through a second transformation when the republican constitution was replaced, after it had lasted over 400 years, by an imperial monarchy, which eventually succumbed when the Gauls succeeded in invading and sacking Rome in 390.

Although Roman republicanism was at first more explicitly oligarchical than Athenian democracy, its development into a more popular form of government shows that oligarchy is hard to maintain once the principle of popular sovereignty is adopted. After much hard experience, the Romans came to understand as clearly as the Athenians that the great divide in forms of government is between autocratic and popular. The very term *res publica* implied that popular government is the only form in which all citizens could enjoy liberty. Even aristocrats saw monarchy as a form of domination analogous to the relationship between master and slaves.[4] Cicero expressed the Roman appreciation of the link between popular government and liberty, even as he also expressed the Roman view that popular government must be tempered by respect for superior merit:

> In a monarchy all except the king are too much excluded from the protection of the law and from participation in deliberative functions, though these rights belong to the whole people. In a government dominated by an aristocracy the mass of the people have hardly any share in freedom, since they have no part in common deliberative and executive powers. And when the state is governed by the people, even though they be just and self-disciplined, yet their very equality is inequitable in that it does not recognize degrees of merit. Therefore, even if Cyrus the Persian was a perfectly just and wise king, nevertheless the condition of the commons—that is, the commonwealth . . . does

not seem to have been one which we should particularly covet, since it was subject to the caprice of a single man. Similarly, even if our clients, the Massalians, are governed with the greatest justice by their oligarchy of nobles, still in a people so situated there exists something like slavery. And even if the Athenians at certain periods after the fall of the Areopagus conducted all public business through enactments and decrees of the people, still their state did not preserve its glory, since it failed to regard differences of worth.[5]

The Roman effort to achieve Ciceronian balance involved a constant struggle which ultimately failed when reliance on patronage made voting in the popular assemblies too dependent on bribery and when control over the armies passed from the Senate to military commanders. Internal conflicts among the orders led to a broadening of political participation which in some respects resulted in a stronger sense of unity, but the later shift toward populism exacerbated problems caused by corruption and helped open the way to demagoguery and the rule of generals who made themselves emperors. The republican constitution fell victim, the historian Sallust observed, mainly to a combination of avarice and ambition.[6]

Roman republicanism differed from Athenian democracy in several important respects. Like Athenian citizens, Roman citizens were divided into classes denominated by status and income with different military roles, but these distinctions were far more influential in the structure of Roman government than they were in the Athenian. The predominance of the Roman upper class, at first completely patrician and eventually also composed of wealthy plebeians, was reinforced by the institution of *clientela* (clientship), a form of personal dependence unknown in the Greek world. Clients performed a variety of services for their patrons in exchange for protection, and they also provided important political backing, by delivering their own votes and those of their friends.[7] At first the Roman republic had separate assemblies for patricians and plebeians (from *plebs* or common people, equivalent to the Greek *demos*) and property qualifications for all high offices. By not providing salaries for elected officials, Rome effectively barred its highest offices to all but the wealthy. Even the Roman notion of *aequitas*, or equality before the law, differed in connotation from the Athenian ideal of *isonomia*, its literal counterpart. Initially, Chaim Wirszubski points out, the plebeians did not enjoy the same civic rights as patricians and had no political rights. They therefore "attached great importance to equality before the law and to the fundamental rights of citizenship. But the right to govern was not considered a universal civic right. The Athenians sought to establish equality in respect of the right to govern, whereas the Romans sought to safeguard their rights against the power of government."[8] Although this understanding changed over time, as the plebeians gained full civic rights and a greater degree of authority and access to high office, Rome remained a largely oligarchical republic. A unique form of group voting, which had been introduced early on, continued to serve as a useful instrument for the elite to frustrate majority rule. A differential notion of civic rights allowing for variations in degrees of citizenship encouraged the affiliation of foreigners but was also used to vitiate the popular character of Roman republicanism. The Roman form of government became the model of the mixed constitution, celebrated by Polybius, who cited it as the reason for Rome's success, blending monarchy (the Consuls), aristocracy or oligarchy (the Senate), and popular government (the Tribunes and the plebeian council).

From Monarchy to Republic

Tacitus began his *Annals* with the categorical statement that the city of Rome was from its beginning in the hands of kings. This claim is considered highly doubtful by modern historians, even though they acknowledge that local kingships did exist in Italy before the Etruscans imposed monarchy and with it the status of a city-state or *civitas* on Rome.[9] All that it is known with reasonable certainty is that a period of monarchy arose during the Etruscan conquest and that the republic emerged afterward.

The Etruscan kings were said to have *imperium*—a term that came to sum up for Roman jurisprudence everything that would be connoted by the word sovereignty when it came into use in the sixteenth century. They used the symbol of the *fasces*, an axe bound with rods, which was of Etruscan origin. The king was not only a political authority, but at the same time the religious authority, military commander-in-chief, and chief justice. He held power by virtue of religious sanction and by force of arms, but not by popular concession. The *patres* or elders formed a Senate which the king might choose to consult and to which royal authority initially reverted on the death of the king. The Senate would appoint an *interrex* who would hold office for a short period before a new king could be nominated. Popular councils called *curiae* are reported to have had the role of giving approval to the nomination.[10] The king was assisted by several officials appointed by him.

Within early Roman society, the authority of the king was paralleled by the authority of the *pater familias*. These *patres* and their legitimate sons formed the patrician order and lived as landowners on the Seven Hills of Rome or in the countryside. The patricians had a standing in society that brought with it a sense of social superiority and a still uncertain sense of authority. They alone had *civitas optimo iure*, the full rights of citizenship, including personal freedom, *ius commercii*, the right to hold and exchange property, *ius conubii*, the right to intermarry with other members of the *gentes* or clans, *ius gentilitatis*, the right to share in the worship of the clan, and the political rights: *ius sufragii*, the right to vote, and *ius honorum*, the right to hold office. Foreigners who settled in Rome, either to better their conditions or because they had lived in conquered territory or had been freed from slavery, became the *clientes* of a patrician *patronus*, exchanging services and payments for the privileges this status accorded them.[11] Already during the monarchical period, a new order, the plebeian, had come into being, which at first did not have the same legal status as the patrician, but was considered a motley collection of outsiders, perhaps formed of conquered populations.

The penultimate Etruscan king, Servius Tullius, is reported by Livy to have established a census and used it to form five classes subdivided into "centuries" or hundreds, all based on wealth, and all with different military roles, rather like the four classes established under Solon and Cleisthenes in Athens, except that in Rome those whose fortunes did not meet the minimum were assigned to a single separate century exempted from military service. The cavalry centuries were raised from the First Class, and the burden of supporting the cavalry was said by Livy to have been borne by the rich.[12]

The process by which civic rights as well as duties were given the *plebs* may well have begun because the kings needed their financial assistance and wanted to use them to offset patrician pressure. The plebeians were apparently keen to make this bargain because it gave them a measure of protection for their persons and goods. They received *ius commercium* in full at an early period and won qualified citizenship when civic rights were granted on the basis of wealth and residence rather than exclusively by birth. The reforms were not the work of the Etruscan kings entirely, however, and came to full fruition only after they were expelled, during the sixth and fifth centuries B.C.[13] It was then that the plebeians were organized along with the patricians into four urban "tribes" and admitted to partial citizenship.

The expulsion of the Etruscan kings led at first to the replacement of monarchy by two chief executives, the *praetores*, who were chosen annually by the whole body of citizens—organized in various councils—and later given the title of consul. Other officials were also elected, including the *Censor*, whose function was to assess property, prepare registers of citizens according to tribe, class, and military organization, and who later acquired the function of moral guardianship. A certain number of plebeians were admitted to membership in the Senate, but these *conscripti* were given only a restricted role. Although kingship was retained, the function of that office became purely religious and ceremonial, until the early part of the fifth century when the king's religious role was removed and assigned to the *Pontifex Maximus*. To decrease the likelihood that the consulship would become a basis for a revival of kingship and tyranny, two consuls were elected to hold the office jointly, each having equal power (*par potestas*) and the right of mutual control (*intercessio*). The dual consulship was sometimes criticized for producing contradictory directives, especially harmful in war, but it reflected a belief in dividing power as a way of preventing arbitrary rule—a belief which has always been characteristic of republican polities. The consuls and all other magistrates, well over fifty by the time of Cicero, were elected annually by several assemblies, after the early period when they were elected by the military assembly, the *Comitia centuriata*.[14] The patricians recognized that a weak and disunited executive could be dangerous in an emergency, so to forestall that eventuality they early introduced the provision for the appointment of a constitutional dictator who would rule by decree as *Magister Populi* (afterwards *Dictator*) for a period of no more than six months.[15] The most famous such *Dictator* was Lucius Quinctius Cincinnatus, who was called by the Senate from his small farm to rescue the city, and after doing so gave up the office and returned to the farm—an example which led George Washington to form the Society of the Cincinnati when he refused to stand for reelection and instead returned to Mount Vernon.

At first the populace was organized in military form as the *Comitia centuriata*, which usually convened outside the city at the Campius Martius.[16] Although in origin a military organization, it gradually acquired political functions. The centuriate assembly gained importance because it was here that the consuls were elected and endowed with total control and that supreme decisions were taken over war and peace as well on laws. It also had the judicial function of hearing appeals of those condemned to death and pronouncing on their cases as the court of last resort.

The political version of the *Comitia centuriata* consisted of centuries, so called because they originally consisted of 100 soldiers. Even after they retired from active military service, members of the various centuries retained their membership in them for political purposes. The 193 centuries included eighteen of cavalry or *equites*, 170 of infantry, and five of militarily qualified non-combatants. The infantry centuries were subdivided into five classes based upon ownership of landed property, and one underclass of non-landowning *proletarii* (so called because their only possession was their offspring or *proles*). In each class, the centuries were further divided by age into senior and junior. Eighty of the infantry centuries were senior and junior centuries of the first class. Each century cast a single voice vote previously decided by the majority, and the votes were cast sequentially by class. Because the *equites* were asked to vote first, their centuries were called "prerogative," the origin of the term that would in later European history be used to denote the exclusive right of the sovereign. If the *equites* and the eighty first class infantry centuries were in agreement, they therefore controlled ninety-seven votes, one more than the necessary majority.[17] Over time, moreover, the political centuries ceased to be of uniform size, further advantaging the patricians and wealthy plebeians. Cicero reported that in his day there were more members of the one century enrolling proletarians than in all the first class centuries combined.[18] Initially, the centuriate assembly was almost as much an instrument of patrician control as the Senate. As pressures were felt to make Roman government more popular, the rules of the centuriate assembly were changed, but it remained in control of the upper classes.[19]

The republican constitution was completed by the addition to the Senate of a formally tri-cameral system of popular assemblies. Alongside the *Comitia centuriata* were recognized the *Comitia curiata*, composed of the thirty *curiae* or ten sub-divisions of each of the three original clans or tribes (the Tities, Ramnes, and Luceres), and the *Comitia tributa*, or tribal assembly. The *Comitia curiata* had been established under monarchy as an assembly of subjects convened to hear announcements and endorse initiatives. Under the republican constitution, it had the largely formal authority of confirming the authority of the magistrates to take auspices in their official capacity, and it soon seems to have lost much even of its limited significance.[20] The *Comitia tributa* included all male citizens, as listed in the census as belonging to thirty-five territorially defined *tributa* or "tribes" in the sense of administrative units and, after 471 B.C., voting districts based on domicile. Four of the tribes were urban, the rest rural. New citizens were assigned to tribes by the Censors. These new tribes were created to replace the old system of kinship tribes or clans represented in the *Comitia curiata*. The *tributa* were themselves also sub-governmental units with the task of collecting the citizen tax or *tributum*. The *Comitia tributa* gradually acquired the power to elect all the lower magistrates as well as certain judicial functions and an increasingly important role in legislation.[21]

This tribal assembly consisted of two bodies: the *Concilium plebis*, or plebeian assembly, probably the first of the two to be created, and the less formally recognized *Comitia populi tributa*, or tribal assembly of the whole people, as it was commonly called. Patricians were excluded from the former but they were influential in the latter, and even a *plebis scita* or resolution of the *plebs* at first required patrician sanction (*auctoritas patrum*) to acquire the force of law. By the third century B.C., however, the plebeian assembly had acquired the authority to legislate without restriction on behalf of the whole people.[22]

The patricians contained the power of the military assembly by imposing elaborate constitutional checks. Although the consuls were elected by the *Comitia centuriata*, their power had to be conferred in two stages. The *potestas* or right to deal with the people and Senate was conferred by the *Comitia centuriata*, but the *imperium*—the totality of civil, military and judicial power—could be conferred only by the *Comitia curiata*, which they controlled until the plebeians succeeded in achieving a greater share of authority and power. In effect, the *Comitia curiata* ratified the election of the consuls, who could only be chosen from the ranks of patricians and who had formal and informal power in the choice of successors. The outgoing consuls had to transmit the *auspices*—the religious legitimation of secular rule—to their successors by means of a definite statement on their part. In addition, because they served as presidents of the centuriate assembly, who had to name (*nominare*) candidates for the succession, they might refuse to announce names they disapproved of or to proclaim such a candidate if he were to be elected nevertheless. The *Comitia centuriata*, moreover, could only discuss bills the presiding Consul chose to put forward; it had no initiating power of its own. In these ways, the patricians sought more or less successfully to limit the authority of the *Comitia centuriata* in order to foreclose the possibility that the plebeians might make use of it to gain a stronger voice.

This patrician or oligarchical system might have persisted but for the fact that in the fifth century and the first half of the fourth century B.C., Rome was hard pressed by Etruscan and other enemies and by inhabitants of Latium who rebelled against its hegemony. The patriciate, which had been more open to new recruits earlier on, had become a closed caste which began to be depleted in numbers. As the patrician clans or *gentes* were depleted, their clients were released to swell the ranks of the plebeians. The patricians therefore had no choice but to turn for help to the *plebs*, who in turn insisted on greater power in recognition of their increased military and financial burdens. In 494, when Rome was engaged in a fierce struggle with the Aequi and the Volsci, the plebeian soldiers refused to march against the enemy until the patricians agreed to allow them to elect annually officials called tribunes (*tribuni plebis*).

As a result of concessions made to the *plebs*, differences between patricians and plebeians in respect of military service and tax obligations all but disappeared by the end of the fifth century B.C. All members of the *civitas* were required to serve in various capacities in the military and to pay taxes according to their means. As Rome expanded its control over the surrounding territories and then over most of Italy, those absorbed were granted a limited form of citizenship, becoming citizens without the vote (*cives sine suffragio*), which meant that they were required to serve in the Roman legions and pay taxes to Rome, and enjoyed certain civic rights in return, but could not vote in any of the assemblies.[23] The plebeians, once they had gained more civic rights, demanded that their voting right be given more influence over policy and that the disabilities limiting their participation in the Senate and magistracies be lifted. In particular, they insisted on a series of reforms: authority to legislate debt relief and agrarian reform; the establishment of a written legal code, common to all, a demand which led to the publication of the Twelve Tables, the first codification of Roman law; authorization of inter-order marriages; the right to serve as consuls and in other magistracies that might be created, and as members of the Senate; recognition of the legal validity of all plebiscites; the right to cast a secret written ballot; and the right of admission to the priesthood on the same terms as patricians.

Debt relief was of particular concern to the mass of small landholders who formed the bulk of the rural plebeians. They were compelled to borrow frequently at often usurious rates of interest; insolvency could result in enslavement or execution. The urban proletarians also demanded land and distributions of food to feed their children. Goaded by pressures from both quarters, the plebeian leadership aimed to achieve total equality of rights between patricians and plebeians in recognition of their equal share in the burdens of maintaining Roman security and power. Their ability to withhold critically needed support by calling a strike of taxpayers and soldiers put them in a strong position in which to make these demands.

The Struggle of the Orders

The result was the epic conflict known to classical scholars as "the struggle of the orders," a conflict which took both social and topographical form: because the patricians lived in the older parts of the city such as the Seven Hills, and the *plebs* in the newer quarters, the conflict of orders therefore also became a conflict of districts or neighborhoods. The patricians were clearly a social class, whereas the plebeians were a "pure multitude," in Michel Serres' imaginative contrast. The patricians had long "been perfectly organized; attached to agricultural property, domestic altars, the tombs of their ancestors, familial hierarchy, junior branches, clientele, servants, and slaves. There is an order. The plebs has no social order, no delimited agrarian terrain, no religion, no law, no magistrates. It is not a people, not a body, not a group; it is a true collective. It is the pure multitude. Crowd, aggregation, population, cloud, confusion, herd of cattle."[24] The struggle of the orders was therefore not a class war, Serres suggests, fought between two organized and disciplined groups, each with its own armed forces; it was rather a conflict between "a class and a nonclass." In the process "the classical patrician order resists, undoes itself, redoes itself, falls into disorder. The plebeian disorder fluctuates, organizes itself, orders itself, undoes itself, redoes itself, moves toward order, and falls back into disorder."[25] In more prosaic terms, the conflict forced the central governing apparatus controlled by the patricians to accept a series of compromises. These held the society together, but the unity of the *civitas* was often nearly lost in the struggle between the *optimates*—as the ruling oligarchs called themselves to emphasize their supposedly superior moral claims—and their less cohesive opponents, who had in common that they sought the support of the *populus* and were therefore called the *populares*.[26]

In pursuing their ends, the *plebs* sought and gradually won both more power for the *Concilium plebis* and greater opportunity to take part in the other bodies and offices on a more equal footing with the patricians. The *Concilium plebis* had gained formal recognition in a convention which was in effect a treaty of civic peace. Its leadership held office in the form of the tribuneship, a term derived from the word for tribal leader. Two such offices were created, a number later increased to ten. The plebeian assembly elected the tribunes, made decisions by plebiscites (which at first could apply only to plebeians), and exercised judgment in certain court cases. The tribunes had authority to represent the *plebs* both individually and as a group, and they used their "right of intercession" to "veto" (literally "I forbid") decisions of magistrates, including a consul, but only within the city.[27] The free exercise of this right was guaranteed by the legal inviolability of the tribune; challengers to the authority or personal safety of a tribune risked being outlawed or put to death.

The struggle of the plebeians for a greater share of power succeeded by several stages. The only specific civic right they enjoyed at first was that of *commercium*. Next they gained the civic rights of marriage, testament, and adoption. In the past these rights had been denied to them on the ground that they entailed religious acts from which plebeians, as strangers, were barred. New secular forms were devised to enable the plebeians to enjoy these rights. Another major advance took the form of the codification and publication of Roman law. In the middle of the fifth century, a tribune proposed that the laws be published in a code, and the Senate, after resisting, finally agreed to appoint a commission to study the codes of the Greek cities of southern Italy. Upon their return, a ten-member commission (*Decemviri*) was appointed in 451 to draft a new code, resulting after great struggle in the Laws of the Twelve Tables, celebrated by Livy as the foundation of all Roman public and private rights.[28] Prior to this action, Roman law had been based upon custom as interpreted by the patricians because of their virtual monopoly of the institutions of government. Publication of the laws did not make public the procedures by which the law was implemented and justice delivered, which continued to provide an opportunity for patrician manipulation, until, at the end of the fourth century, these too were set down and published. Shortly after the drafting of the Twelve Tables, in 445, it is thought, another tribune introduced a bill abolishing the prohibition of intermarriage between the classes, and it too was carried over the vehement opposition of the patricians.

The achievement of these civic rights emboldened the *plebs* to press for political rights as well. Its leaders demanded admission to the *Comitia curiata*, more influence in the *Comitia centuriata*, and more power for the *Concilium plebis*. They succeeded in gaining entrance into the *Comitia curiata*—when is not clear—and in gaining a larger role in the *Comitia centuriata* commensurate with their growing military responsibilities. In this council, however, wealth had been made such a key organizing principle that greater plebeian participation in effect meant that wealthy plebeians shared power with wealthy patricians. The new power of the *Concilium plebis* was recognized in a series of laws giving plebiscites the force of law provided they were subsequently ratified by the Senate. This law was later changed to provide that the Senate must first authorize laws, which would then be put to the vote of the people. It was changed again, finally, in the *Lex Hortensia* of 287 B.C., to eliminate the need for any Senatorial sanction. This was still a far cry from full democratization. No one but a magistrate could bring a bill before one of the popular assemblies for action, and the Senate usually found ways to maintain control over the magistrates.[29] In 445 B.C. a tribune demanded that the consulship be shared by plebeians and patricians. Instead, some of the powers of the consuls (notably the census and public works) were transferred to new magistrates and the consulship was replaced by the military tribuneship with consular power. These tribunes, who varied in number from three to six, might be chosen from either order. In 376 B.C., in one of the *Licinian* laws, however, a military exigency was met by reviving the consulship with the stipulation that one of the two annual posts should be reserved for plebeians. Once this barrier was overcome, the plebeians gained admission to all other magistracies. Eventually all offices, including the dictatorship and the priesthood, were open to them.

The end result of these changes was that the plebeians were admitted to membership of the Senate in 400 B.C. The plebeian minority in the Senate increased in size steadily until it became a majority by the end of the third century B.C. The ranks of the plebeians swelled with the annexations that resulted from the conquest of Latium and the unification of peninsular Italy and as Rome itself became more important as a center of trade. Rome's expansion increased the wealth and influence of some plebeian families. Military conquests also enhanced the power of the plebeians, who were the backbone of the army. With the passage of the *Lex Hortensia*, by which plebiscites no longer needed Senate approval, the plebeian assembly became more and more powerful.

With the resolution of the conflict of orders, all Romans except those foreigners who had been granted conditional citizenship became formally equal citizens with the same civic rights and obligations, though with military and political roles and power corresponding to their wealth. The city's political institutions were divided, so as to accommodate both patricians and plebeians, but combined, in order to prevent civil war. Each assembly was founded on a different principle: the *curiata* on the right of birth (based on membership in one of thirty clan sub-groups), the *centuriata* on military role as determined by wealth, the *tributa* on domicile. This complex system was made to work because a new elite emerged, a *nobilitas* composed of patricians and plebeians, which gave it unity, although each assembly had a faction unwilling to compromise with its old enemies. William R. Everdell sums up the system of shared power about as clearly as possible, given its complexity:

> The legislative power, based like ours on the theoretical sovereignty of the people, was vested in no less than four assemblies, each elected on a different pattern of constituencies. The old Comitia Curiata, divided by families, still met to elect the rex sacrorum or confer imperium (executive power) on a magistrate. The prerepublican Comitia Centuriata, divided by wealth, elected consuls, praetors, and quaestors, and retained the power to make law. Made supreme in 287 B.C., the Comitia Tributa, divided according to residence, made law, declared war and peace, and elected the tribunes and aediles. Finally, there was the Senate, composed entirely of former elected magistrates, which issued advices (*senatus consulti*) to both the consuls and the assemblies on foreign and military policy. To ensure that all these assemblies would maintain their representative character and that the members of the Senate would remain worthy despite life tenure, the Romans in 443 B.C. created the censorship, two magistrates with the uniquely long term of five years (later shortened to eighteen months). Their duty was to maintain and revise the census, or list of citizens, and to impeach members of the Senate.[30]

Social tensions persisted, and were met by a variety of policies. Usury continued and the burdens faced by poorer plebeians continued to rankle, leading to debtor rebellions. The moderate coalition tried to address the problem by easing conditions for the rural plebeians. In 326 B.C. a law was adopted abolishing the seizure of the person (*nexus*) for debt. Colonies were founded, mainly for the benefit of the rural plebeians. Booty from Roman conquests was also used to allay discontent.

Nevertheless, at the end of the fourth century B.C., a clever patrician die-hard, who might also be considered the first Tory democrat, Appius Claudius, succeeded in uniting the unreconciled patrician faction with populist elements among the plebeians. He did so by using the power he had acquired as a leading patrician to infiltrate plebeian allies into the institutions that had become the bastions of power for the coalition. The coalition succeeded in repelling his subversive efforts but the reforms adopted under plebeian pressure launched Rome in the direction of rural democracy. Despite these changes, the practical difficulties of achieving effective self-government by 250,000 to 300,000 citizens, many living great distances from Rome, whose assemblies were expected to make decisions affecting foreign regions of which they had no direct knowledge, enabled the Senate to continue as the effective seat of government.

The Ideology of Roman Republicanism According to Cicero

As the republic matured, it acquired an ideology. According to Cicero, the foremost spokesman for this ideology, the republic is the best form of government because it is held together by the twin strands of a common sense of right and self-interest. The commonwealth [*res publica*] is "the people's affair; and the people is not every group of men, associated in any manner, but is the coming together of a considerable number of men who are united by a common agreement about law and rights [*consensus juris*] and by the desire to participate in mutual advantages."[31] *Libertas* or freedom consists not in the power to do as one pleases but to live according to the law which applies equally to all, and the law is respected because it is understood to be extremely advantageous to all.[32]

Republican government, Cicero argued, is preferable to monarchy and aristocracy because in monarchy everyone but the king is excluded from the protection of the law and from participation in deliberation, whereas in aristocracies the mass of the people is excluded. Rule by the people, however, is also deficient, in that it does not recognize degree of merit.[33] Cicero was typically Roman and republican in believing that although equality before the law means that in principle democracy is the only government that deserves to be considered republican,[34] the success of popular government depends not on mass participation or majority rule, but on the willingness of the ablest citizens to take part in the political life of the *civitas* rather than withdraw to their private affairs. In an obvious allusion to the drastic remedy proposed by Plato for the ills of Athenian democracy, that of compelling the wise to take part in government, Cicero appealed to a sense of duty as well as self-interest:

> It is asserted . . . that political life attracts in general only utterly worthless men, to be compared with whom it is disgusting, and to contend with whom, especially when the mob is aroused, is deplorable and dangerous. Therefore, it is said, a wise man does not grasp the reins of government, since he cannot restrain the mad lunges of the untamed rabble, nor does a free man strive against vile and savage opponents, or submit to the lash of insult, or suffer injuries that a wise man should not bear. As if a good and brave and high-minded man could find a more honorable reason for entering public life than the desire to avoid the rule of scoundrels or to prevent them from rendering the commonwealth, while he himself, though eager to aid, looks impotently on![35]

Hierarchy, Pluralism, and the Republican Constitution

Although in principle the republican constitution was understood as government by the people, as in democratic Athens, there were important institutional differences as well as differences in understanding, especially of the degree to which inequalities of merit and wealth should be reflected in political authority. The Roman system did not provide direct self-government to the same extent as the Athenian system, but neither was it representative in the modern sense of elections based upon universal suffrage. All magistrates or public officials were elected for one-year terms in the various public assemblies. All legislation initiated by the magistrates had to be confirmed in the assemblies. Each of the assemblies, however, had a different character, though this character became more uniform in the course of time as the plebeians gained access to all of them. After the Ovinian Laws (339-312 B.C.), membership in the Senate was open only to those who had served as magistrates, offices for which only patricians were eligible. Only after much struggle did plebeians become eligible to enter the Senate. As the *Comitia centuriata* became more powerful, plebeians rose in power, but wealth continued to determine access to power and influence. The Senate and the other assemblies became in effect arenas in which the patricians and the plebeians struggled for control. In the process, wealth was gradually joined to social status and oligarchy succeeded aristocracy.

It is in the voting arrangements that Rome's emphasis on plural autonomy contrasts most plainly with the Athenian emphasis on communal autonomy. Rome's use of group voting set a precedent for the later use of districting in parliamentary elections and for the electoral college in American presidential elections.[36] The Athenians practiced voting by group in only one respect, when delegates to the Council of 500 were chosen by each of the artificial tribes created by Cleisthenes. The use of the system in Rome functioned both to make it more broadly reflective of the regional distribution of population, as the Athenian system did, and to confirm class divisions and open the electoral system to manipulation. As the Roman populace expanded to include people with full rights of citizenship who lived too far from the city to take part in the popular assemblies, the system of group voting created incentives for corruption and enabled oligarchy to survive a broadened franchise by means of patronage or clientship. Owing to group voting, a candidate for office in the various assemblies could succeed with the support of as few as a quarter of the voters. The votes of smaller elite groupings consistently outweighed the votes of the larger groups comprising poorer citizens. In the tribal assemblies, the powerful and influential could control the votes of blocs of followers, even though, unlike the procedure for recording and announcing votes in the military assembly, the order of voting was determined by lot. Anyone assured of the support of a bare majority of voters in half plus one of the regional districts could win election even without capturing a single vote in the remaining districts. The inflexibility introduced by the assignment of voters to district tribes made the system particularly disproportionate when the rural areas were depopulated in the second century B.C. and those who came to Rome were not reassigned to the urban districts or tribes. These new urbanites outnumbered those from the rural areas willing and able to make the journey to Rome to participate in the deliberations of the *Comitia tributa*. As Staveley explains,

> Those who migrated to Rome at this time appear to have retained their membership of the particular rural tribe in which they had been registered while they were still farming the land. Consequently, as their numbers grew, they found themselves in a position to outvote any fellow-tribesmen who happened to be present from their home areas, with the result that the *comitia* gradually came to be dominated by urban interests. This trend could very readily have been checked if the censors had taken the simple step of reassigning the immigrant urban population to one of the four city tribes; but there is no suggestion that they ever attempted to do so, or that the idea was ever seriously mooted.[37]

The censors' failure to reassign these voters very likely reflected the interest of those who secured their election.

Electorally and institutionally, Rome was a more divided society than Athens. More starkly than in Athens, *nobilitas* and *populus* and rich and poor stood apart from each other and opposed. The military assembly might have held a balance of power but it too was dominated by the patricians at first and then by the new patrician-plebeian elite. The existence of several assemblies with different qualifications for membership instead of one uniting all citizens on the same basis was in itself a formidable barrier to majority rule. But the patricians could not rule without any check because the plebeian assembly had the constitutional right to call magistrates to account after their term of office. By contrast, there is no case recorded of any but a unicameral legislature in Greece.[38]

Another peculiarly Roman institution which enabled the majority to check the power of the oligarchy was the tribunate. The power of the tribunes was not positive, as was that of the consuls, but only negative. Like modern-day ombudsmen, they could protect plebeians who were being badly treated by exercising a right of help or *auxilium*. They could forbid or veto any administrative act.

The Roman republican system functioned to preserve the *dignitas* of the nobility and at the same time the *libertas* of the common people.[39] Even this harmony, such as it was, did not come about by accident. It was the result of the power struggle in the republic between the old families and the new citizens or plebeians. The plebeians had in effect organized themselves into a kind of state within a state, with assemblies of their own under officials elected by themselves. (There is a similarity here with the struggle during the French revolution between the aristocracy and the new men of the third estate.) The plebeians fought hard enough to force the patricians to recognize the right of their officers to check the action of the senate or ordinary magistrates judged to be oppressive. They also forced them to accept the resolutions of the assembly as having the force of law.

Although the plebeians won considerable victories in the early phase of the history of the republic, a period lasting more than 150 years after the fall of the monarchy, the patricians retained the exclusive right to be elected as chief magistrates or consuls until 367 B.C. when the Licinio-Sextian law established that one of the two consuls must always be a plebeian.

Why was their victory not carried forward to establish a more complete form of democracy? Why in fact did the administration of Roman government remain substantially aristocratic while Rome was conquering much of the known world? During this period the plebeian assembly became a legislative body that normally worked in harmony with the Senate and under its influence, and the tribunate was changed from an office of opposition to a rung on the political ladder that led to the consulship and the Senate. This harmonization may have been due to the pressure of external conflict which led to a sense of the need for discipline and obedience on the part of the people. Another conceivable reason is that because votes in the plebeian assembly were decided not by the majority of individuals but by tribal units, the landowning rural element predominated. The more mixed-status, relatively poorer urban element of the population, in other words, was subordinated until the decay of the republic set in. As Rome's population swelled with annexation and conquests, landless citizens were given the right to vote, but they could exercise that right mainly in the four urban tribes which were readily outvoted. These urban tribes came to be the least prestigious, indeed the tribes in which the most despised members of the population were concentrated. Thus, as Sidgwick points out, when, after a prolonged struggle the plebeians had established a system of control over their governing class "so effective that, judged by Greek analogies, it seems likely to lead to complete democracy, they stopped at this point for the two centuries that decided the fate of Western civilisation; leaving the administration of affairs in the hands of what in Aristotle's sense as well as ours may be called an 'aristocratic' body."[40]

The struggles between the two social groups were not altogether one-dimensional. They involved a clash of economic interests, especially those dividing the poor farmers from those who had more land and sought to control even more. They also led to a struggle on the part of "new" families to gain access to high offices monopolized by the old. The victory of the plebeians in 367 B.C. led to the coalescence or cooptation of the leading plebeians with the old nobility. A new nobility was formed in which rank was given not by patrician extraction but by having ancestors who had held the highest offices. That left the old nobility with the lion's share of the offices but opened access to power for some previously excluded.

Rebellion and Imperial Monarchy

It is an intriguing question why this compromise worked for so long to quell the conflict between the plebeians and patricians until, in the latter half of the second century B.C., revolution broke out led by the Gracchi. Again, the answer may lie in the history of Rome's wars of expansion. As Italy was being subdued, the conquered were forced to cede a portion of their land. This land—considered *ager publicus* or public land—belonged in the first instance to the community, and large portions of it were distributed among Roman citizens who held it in complete ownership. This was done largely by founding colonies. Unlike Greek colonists, the settlers did not create new *poleis* but extended Rome's control over outlying territories. In other cases, those in conquered territories who held office could thereby acquire Roman citizenship. This system provided a network of garrisons and extended the Latin language in such a way that it protected Rome from assault and enabled the two assemblies to govern an extended imperial republic. Although there were tensions between the colonists and the natives, eventually Roman citizenship was broadly extended. By the middle of the second century B.C., therefore, the Rome located on the banks of the Tiber contained 328,000 citizens capable of bearing arms. When expansion stopped for a time, trouble developed. The demand of the poorer citizens for land could not be satisfied. A century of conflict, dissolution, and agony followed through which the republic was transformed into a monarchy. Land reform led to the enlargement of the number of citizens. The Senate pragmatically recognized that it had to accept these reforms, and sought in vain to cling to power. The wealthy and powerful surrendered all self-restraint and became a "gang of venal and avaricious tyrants. To keep their power, the plunderers of the provinces threw large handfuls of the plunder to the people at home. They distributed grain first at low price, then at merely nominal prices, they practiced wholesale bribery at elections, turning yeoman farmers into a metropolitan mob."[41] Sallust saw the underlying conflict as a struggle between the few and the many in which the balance of *dignitas* and *libertas* was destroyed: "For the nobility began to push to excess its claim to *dignitas*, the people its claim to *libertas*; everyone sought to draw or snatch everything to himself. And so everything fell to one side or the other, and the *res publica*, which was the bone of contention, was torn to pieces."[42] Rome moved from monarchy to republic, and then, after nearly 500 years, back to monarchy. In the period of republican expansion, the central power was held by the Senate. It had the power to assign provinces among magistrates and allocate troops, money and staff; consisting of ex-officials given life membership, it was in a better position than the consuls, who were appointed annually, to exercise continuous power. When the role of the consul was effectively replaced by that of the *princeps*, who was at the outset only the nobleman considered first among equals, and the principate became institutionalized under Augustus, republicanism became a veneer for monarchy.[43]

The transition from republic to imperial monarchy was in the first instance a function of the growing inadequacy of the republican form for the management of a far flung empire, but it was also due to internal difficulties which overwhelmed the republic's balance of power. The causes of change are many, having to do with the absorption of a larger population into citizenship; with the anomaly of a government based in Rome trying to rule over a large country and then a large empire; and with the change in the character and loyalty of the army. When the Roman legions were still composed of citizens in arms, their loyalty went to Rome; as they absorbed non-citizens, their allegiance shifted more to the commanders of the army units. The predominance of the city's government could not be maintained against those who were the masters of the Roman legions. At first the power of the proconsuls was increased. Finally the emperor succeeded in becoming chief of the Roman legions. Gradually the scaffolding of republican institutions fell away and the unlimited monarch stood revealed in the form of the Caesars. When, during the third century A.D., full Roman citizenship was bestowed on all subjects of Rome, the last relics of the distinction between Italy and the provinces fell away and the city-state disappeared into the empire.

The revolt of the Gracchi brought Rome to the brink of a fully democratic system, though it is impossible to know whether their success might actually have brought about greater democratization or merely their own personal control. They were tribunes who appealed to the principle of the sovereignty of the people in their demand for military and economic reforms. The result was civil war. The first brother was assassinated, the second who took up his banner fell in the civil war that followed. One of the causes they fought for, the enfranchisement of Italians under Roman rule, was eventually successful because the government needed the support of the provincials in war. But as the state was enlarged, and as the generals achieved a position in which to use their legions against the Senate and people, the way was open for the establishment of the rule of the Caesars. The Roman ideal of *libertas*, having once been understood to mean that Romans were their own masters, now underwent a complete change. "Now," Wirszubski starkly observes, "they were subjects whose welfare depended on the care of an absolute autocrat who ruled them by direct command. In the last resort their freedom depended on whether their ruler was kind and enlightened. All that remained of the res publica was government for the people."[44] In the hands of Nero and Caligula, unrestrained power turned into oppression on a grand scale, but even that terrible experience did not lead the Roman people to reestablish the republic. However much some may have wished to do so, the power of the military in the form of the Praetorian Guard was too great to overcome and the military insisted on maintaining the rule of a prince.

From the Respublica Christiana *to the* Ständestaat *and the Revival of Secular Republicanism*

With the collapse of the Roman Empire, the legacies of democratic Athens and republican Rome were buried, along with much else of classical civilization, beneath the tent poles of the barbarian invaders whose successes led Europe into feudalism. Before long, spokesmen for a triumphant Christianity disparaged the classical ideals of government as part of an erroneous and even sinful paganism and later went on to rationalize feudal hierarchy as the earthly reflection of heavenly order. The only republic of concern to medieval Christians was the *respublica christiana,* a term often used interchangeably with *ecclesia,* and signifying the social as well as spiritual unity of all Christians in the church. There was no place in this Christian ideal for independent secular entities of government, or for any form of self-determination, as William Bouwsma has well explained:

> The *respublica christiana* was necessarily organized as a hierarchical system in which lower ends were subordinated to higher, and inferior powers to superior; authority in the entire structure descended from above. Its systematic character meant that the clergy were superior to the laity and gave an ultimate supremacy, in temporal as well as spiritual matters (since the former ranked lower in the hierarchy of values) to the pope. And as subordinate members of a universal system men could be seen to have no right to govern themselves, and states no right to determine their separate courses of action. Self-determination, in this view, could only appear, in the deepest sense, a violation of the very structure of reality, and political duty appeared to consist only of patient submission and obedience. Man, in this system, was always and necessarily a subject; he could not be a citizen.[45]

This disparagement of popular government comported well with political reality over many centuries. In many places, European social structure lost the models of the *polis* and the *civitas* and followed the more traditional village pattern which was reshaped into the manorial economy. A system of infeudation established hierarchical, quasi-contractual, yet highly personal and familial linkages among the members of the landed nobility who occupied the privileged positions. Only from the fifteenth century onward did changes in economic, social, and political conditions promote a revival of democratic thinking, first in the Italian city-states and then in the new nation-states ruled by centralizing monarchs. During this long period, Christian teachings were usually interpreted in such a way as to defend and rationalize the feudal social order and monarchical rule. With the Reformation, however, they became an intellectual arsenal for democratic change.

Feudalism became entrenched because no single political force emerged to replace the Roman empire. The rise of the Carolingian dynasty in the eighth century revived the political framework of the empire but the would-be successors of the Roman emperors were unable to duplicate their degree of vertical control. The structural weakness of the Holy Roman Empire justified the hoary witticism that it was neither holy nor Roman nor an empire. The hallmark of feudalism became decentralization. The "network of interpersonal relations" created during the Middle Ages, Gianfranco Poggi observes, tended to shift the seat of effective power "downward toward the lower links in the chain of lord-vassal relations . . . making unified rule over large areas increasingly difficult."[46]

By the thirteenth century, however, a revival of trade and the development of craft guilds brought a major change in the feudal system as trading towns engendered a new local collective consciousness and offered an alternative both to the manorial economy and the system of personal fealty. The townspeople demanded autonomy for their corporations and introduced systems of self-government similar to those of earlier cities. As some of the new towns flourished, they emerged as city-states, notably in Italy, but also in Germany, where the slack control of the Holy Roman Empire allowed them to develop. These towns became enclaves partly or wholly immune from customary feudal practice and feudal law, but they could not become fully independent because they relied on food and raw materials supplied by the surrounding countryside and on the protection of territorial princes. In the late Middle Ages, therefore, a new system of rule was developed in most of western Europe which in effect removed the anomaly created by the rise of the towns by transforming the older system in which the territorial prince ruled through the sub-nobility. This new system has been called the "*Ständestaat*" because it entailed a sharing of power between rulers and organized bodies controlled by the estates or *Stände* (such as the French *parlements*). Under this regime, powerful individuals and groups would gather, either personally or through delegates, in periodic assemblies in which they would deal with the ruler or his agents, voice their protests, restate their rights, give advice, establish terms of collaboration with rulers, and exercise their share of the burdens of government.[47] Out of the clash of the estates and the absolute monarchy emerged constitutional monarchy and parliamentary government. As the parliamentary forces gained strength and demanded more power, they often adopted republicanism as an ideological goal.

Underlying this secular transformation was a prior development which was religious in character and centered on the question of the compatibility of Christianity and democracy. The change in the Christian attitude toward democracy in the wake of the Protestant Reformation was critical in making secular change possible. The Reformation created a climate in which democratic change seemed both appropriate and legitimate in moral terms. In response, Roman Catholic authorities at first resisted democracy, particularly when it was accompanied by a radical anti-clericalism, but their successors eventually came to terms with it. They even discovered values in democracy compatible with Christian belief—values which could be said to grow out of Christian universalism and natural law as defined by the greatest medieval Catholic thinker, Saint Thomas Aquinas. In retrospect, both modern republicanism and natural rights-social contract theory do indeed reflect the influence of Judaeo-Christian values, but this influence is complex and ambiguous, not only because Christian social teachings are subject to varying sectarian interpretation but also because the teachings have varied with the relationship of Christian churches to secular authorities.

At first, while their religion was still shaped by the attitude of opposition to prevailing polytheistic doctrines and Hellenistic values, Christian authorities were hostile to the civic doctrines of antiquity, as they were to all manifestations of "paganism." Christianity began as an apolitical faith. In accordance with the express pronouncement attributed to Jesus, "My kingdom is not of this world" (*John* 18:36), it redirected aspirations from the *polis* and the *civitas* to the eternal spiritual realm beyond the earthly city and beyond even the created cosmos. "The well known antagonism between early Christianity and the *res publica*," Hannah Arendt has pointed out, was well summed up in the formula of Tertullian, the church father, "*nec ulla magis res aliena quam publica* ("no matter is more alien to us than what matters publicly").[48] "Political activity," she observes, "which up to then had derived its greatest inspiration from the aspiration toward worldly immortality, now sank to the low level of an activity subject to necessity, destined to remedy the consequences of human sinfulness on one hand and to cater to the legitimate wants and interests of earthly life on the other." The life of the individual "now came to occupy the position once held by the 'life' of the body politic."[49]

Saint Augustine made the opposition between Christianity and Roman beliefs starkly clear by contrasting the city of man with the city of God— the one resting on self-love, the other on the love of God; the one celebrating earthly virtue and aiming for fame and power, the other piety and hope of eternal life after death. The city of man had been founded by Cain, the fratricide: "It is recorded of Cain that he built a city, but Abel, being a sojourner, built none. For the city of saints is above, although here below it begets citizens, in whom it sojourns till the time of its reign arrives, when it shall gather together all in the day of the resurrection . . ."[50] Between the two symbolic cities, he thought, there could be no Ciceronian compromise.

The Christian lived "like a captive and a stranger" in the earthly city and would remain so until the second coming.[51] Augustine was not simply attacking the Roman empire as a departure from republican civic virtue or deploring the corruption of Roman morals and manners. He was rejecting the very rationale for Roman citizenship as it had been stated by Cicero, following Plato, in maintaining that justice is the basis of the republic and that justice meant giving everyone his due. Augustine insisted that true justice meant not only giving all men their due but above all giving God His due, and therefore that pagan Rome was not a republic, as Cicero had claimed, because it was not founded upon justice.[52] Roman corruption was the inevitable consequence of a love of the earthly city. The Augustinian message held that humanity was faced with a radical choice between two loyalties, and that for Christians there could be no compromise between them. Submission to temporal authority was a religious obligation, but only because political authority was instituted as a remedy for sin, not because government was a natural necessity[53] or an opportunity to fulfill some divine gift for autonomy.

Despite this rejection of civic commitment, Christians were at first counselled not to disobey or rebel against the authorities of the pagan state so long as it did not prevent them from practicing their faith (in accordance with the injunction in *Romans* to "render unto Caesar what is Caesar's and unto God what is God's"). Following Augustine, government was said to be a consequence of human sinfulness and therefore necessary to restrain and punish the capacity for evil until sinfulness should be annulled in the second coming. Early Christianity can therefore be said to have been not only an apolitical creed but also one that counseled indifference to the civic function. In sharp contrast to the Greek and Roman perspective, the human relationship to the universe was redefined so that it did not include a relationship to the earthly city, except as a necessary and transitory evil. As a result, there was little in early Christian teachings that amounted to a political theory, and no concern at all that political authority be based in any way upon the consent of the governed.[54]

At the same time, however, there were other respects in which Christian teachings were to have profoundly different, even opposite, effects on subsequent political thought. One of these was the willingness of church authorities to give a positive sanction to political authority once Christianity had been adopted as the religion of the Roman empire. The tolerance toward political authority in the Gospels was exploited by the church authorities in the Gelasian doctrine of the "two swords" and further elaborated in the analogies that were drawn between the hierarchy of God and the angelic host and the hierarchy of feudal society. The feudal term "lord" accommodated both religious and social hierarchy. Later in the middle ages, when Aquinas revived Aristotle's philosophy and remodeled his political theory to suit Christian principles, this uneasy compromise between spiritual and temporal was transformed into a unification. The temporal order was said to have legitimate positive functions, and the highest of these was to make possible a Christian way of life.[55] Aquinas's willingness to accept a positive role for government and the civic order was a sign that theologians and church officials had become reconciled to a long wait for the second coming, and had in effect decided to Christianize the secular world, even though they continued to recognize a gulf between the temporal and the spiritual, or, more fundamentally, between the carnal or worldly and the spiritual spheres. When Dante called for a Christian king, he put the seal on this unification. Christianity thus became identified not only with the hierarchical world view of feudalism, which had long been the case, but also with secular absolutism, making the church and its doctrines inevitable objects of attack when the French revolutionaries set out to overthrow both the remnants of the feudal social order and absolute monarchy.

The Millenarians: Egalitarians or Proto-Totalitarians?

There was, and is, however, another dimension to the Christian tradition—the apocalyptic or eschatological—which makes its political associations more complex. When the drama of salvation was represented in earthly or secular terms, it often issued in a Christian doctrine that was much more political in its character and implications. Everything in the "carnal" world became a sphere for transformation or redemption in a succession of movements condemned as heretical by the church. The millenarian movements which first appeared in the second century, often stimulated by Gnostic accounts of the liberation of man from his alienation in the world, called for the overthrow of earthly principalities as foreseen in the apocryphal Book of Daniel. Sometimes, they inspired the creation of communities of the perfect, who separated themselves from society either to await redemption or to recover the lost innocence of Adam or create some new Jerusalem. In the Spiritual Franciscans of the twelfth century, this belief issued in an historicization of the Trinity by Joachim of Fiore—who divided the history of the world into successive periods identified with the persons of the Trinity, the ages of the father, the son, and the holy spirit. Joachimite prophecy influenced the left wing of the Reformation a century later and prefigured the historicist vision of Hegel, who thought of the historical process as a realization of freedom and, like Joachim, distinguished a three-stage evolution of religious consciousness: from the religion of the commanding father, Judaism, to the religion of the son and faith, Christianity, and finally to the religion of spirit and "mutual recognition," a kind of post-Christian fulfillment.[56] In the Puritan revolution, the left wing of the Reformation exhibits a decidedly apocalyptic side; Gerrard Winstanley leads the "Diggers" who take over a piece of common land and till it in common, claiming to be building the New Jerusalem, and may well be considered fore-runners of the modern socialist movement. But even the less politically and socially radical elements of the Puritan coalition believed in the ideal of the "holy commonwealth," blending sacred and spiritual in a belief in Christian redemption in the here and now. The same apocalyptic attitude toward social life is apparent in American Puritanism, where the covenant with God extends to the covenant among men, as in the precedent of ancient Israel, and the belief in the promised land is transferred onto the United States, and Boston or Providence is seen as the new Jerusalem.

In some respects, the medieval millenarian movements also prefigure a paradoxical dialectic linking democratization to the rise of totalitarianism.[57] Jacob Talmon has argued that this Christian apocalyptic tradition shaped a "political messianism," a belief in total transformation that emerged in the French Revolution and in subsequent movements of "totalitarian democracy," which were similarly aimed at achieving a return of primitive innocence and wiping out corruption—the social contract becoming a way back to the innocence and virtue of the state of nature despite the fall. The very ferocity of the pursuit of wickedness in the name of virtue is thought to justify the use of terror, whether by Savonarola and his bonfire of the vanities, by Calvin in his zealous campaign against luxury and heresy, or by "the incorruptible" Robespierre.[58]

Christianity and Equality[59]

The Christian teaching with the greatest implications for democracy is the belief that because humanity is created in the image of God, all human beings are of equal worth in the sight of God. Along with the Greek Stoic belief in equality as a reflection of the universal capacity for reason, this belief shaped an emerging democratic consciousness, as Alexis de Tocqueville noted when he observed in the introduction to his study of democracy in America that "Christianity, which has declared all men equal in the sight of God, cannot hesitate to acknowledge all citizens equal before the law."[60]

Neither Christian nor Stoic egalitarianism had an immediate political impact because both versions were at first understood to apply to the social order only in a remote past (the Golden Age for the Stoics, the era before the Fall for Christians) or to a future state in which original innocence might be restored. The accepted interpretation of the Christian teaching was that equality was a "spiritual" condition that was essentially different from and irrelevant to earthly hierarchy. But the very presence of a belief in equality, even if only the equality of souls, coupled as it was with the example of the brotherly fellowship of the apostles (even to the extent of a communism of possessions reflecting indifference to material things) promoted a very different view of equality as a social condition.

This alternative tendency burst into the open when the classical dualism was broken by the Reformation and the belief in an equality of believers replaced the sharp distinctions between clergy and laity. As worldly activities were sanctioned as spiritual vocations, the distinction between carnal and spiritual activities was also rejected. The result of these momentous changes was that in the form of Protestantism, Christian belief became much more receptive to democracy. This was not so much due to the intent of the Reformers as to the consequences of their religious revolt. "Modern Democracy," as the historian G. P. Gooch well observed, "is the child of the Reformation, not of the Reformers."[61] Martin Luther and John Calvin, to consider only the leading examples, did not call for the overthrow of monarchy, but they did promote a reform of the church that called ecclesiastical hierarchy into question, raising the question of whether secular hierarchy was any more legitimate. Luther's reliance on German princes for protection, however, had the effect of weakening the role of the church as a counterweight to secular rulers and therefore of promoting political authoritarianism. Calvin's Genevan republic, by combining elements of republicanism, aristocracy, and theocracy, drew his followers away from royalism and toward republicanism. Calvin's disciples, especially among the Huguenots and Scottish Presbyterians, explicitly allowed for a right of resistance to monarchs who did not allow them to worship according to their faith. The individualism of Protestant worship, coupled with the belief in the "priesthood of all believers," was also a powerful stimulus to the beliefs that were to express themselves politically in the demand for the protection of individual rights and the transfer of power to popular assemblies. The German Calvinist Johannes Althusius was perhaps the earliest political theorist in the seventeenth century to propound a popular framework of government. Although he was firmly opposed to rule by the mass of the people, Althusius laid the groundwork for the more expressly democratic theory to come by asserting that subjects had no obligation to obey any exercise of power other than that expressly granted to the ruler.[62]

Under pressure from Protestantism, the Catholic view also changed, as earlier conciliarist views (such as were expressed by Marsilius of Padua and Nicholas of Cusa) were revived with respect to church government, and natural law was reinterpreted, especially by Francisco Suarez, to rest political authority upon the consent of the whole community. Suarez stopped short, however, of calling for representative government, stipulating that where monarchy exists, it claims an authority transferred irrevocably by the originally self-governing community and must be obeyed unless the monarch behaves tyrannically.[63]

Protestants went a good deal further in rationalizing resistance to kings and the replacement of monarchy by parliamentary government. It is hardly an accident that democracy arose first in Protestant-dominated societies or had to be imposed against the objections of religious authorities in predominantly Catholic countries, where, apart from France, it made little headway at first. The acceptance of the compatibility of democratic principles with Christianity, first implicit in Protestantism, was therefore a necessary background to the spread of democracy as a secular ideal.

Along with the ideological influence of Protestantism, Christian practice was also influential in the development of democratic forms of organization, and in this no less important respect Catholic institutions helped lay the groundwork of democracy. "The electoral practices developed in the Christian church during the medieval period." Arthur Monahan has pointed out, "were the forerunners of much of modern western parliamentary practice. The techniques of election by majority—absolute, relative, and qualified—as well as most of the electoral techniques currently in use in civil politics, had their origins in the Church institutions and religious orders of the Middle Ages, rather than in the practices developed in earlier Roman times, which long since had fallen into disuse or been abandoned."[64]

While these techniques were hardly commonplace, they were referred to in canon law and used in the election of church officials in the later middle ages. Almost all earlier elections of popes, bishops and abbots had been by unanimous declaration, on the basis of the Rule of St. Augustine requiring that a community live in perfect harmony and oneness. There were exceptions when majority rule prevailed, such as the election of St. Cornelius to the papacy in 251, Pope Vigilius in 538, and in some reported cases of episcopal elections. Majority rule also prevailed from time to time in important church councils, beginning with the Council of Nicea in 325. In the Benedictine order, St. Benedict provided that an abbot might be chosen without the unanimous consent of the community, provided the electing group had a "better part" (*sanior pars*) "whose individual members were better judges of a candidate or issue than even the major part might be, and who thus were entitled to have their decision accepted." In 1130, similar reasoning was used when Innocent II was named pope with the support of a majority of his clergy; when the result was contested, the election was upheld by the intervention of Bernard of Clairvaux, who, declared Innocent the "more worthy candidate" against a challenge from a minority which claimed to represent the *sanior pars*. In 1179, the Third Lateran Council identified the "better part" with the majority by adopting into canon law the formula "*sanior et maior* [majority] *pars*." The same council introduced the requirement of a two-thirds majority of those present for the election of a pope. This principle was subsequently applied to elections for lesser offices as well. Voting, however, was not necessarily conducted by ballot, open or secret, but often by acclamation, except when there was patent dissatisfaction with this procedure or its outcome. In the thirteenth century, the Dominican Order made the clearest move to the adoption of the principle of majority rule, in such matters as the admission of a friar into an individual convent, the election of officers, including the master general, and the adoption of decisions.[65]

Along with these religious influences, several other ideological forces promoted a renewal of democratic belief in the early modern period of Western history: the revival first of Roman law, then of republicanism, and finally, the comparatively novel development of natural rights/social contract theory.

Roman Law, Consent, and Agency

The earliest of these ideological forces to make an appearance, but the weakest in immediate influence in promoting democracy, was the revival of Roman law by the civil legists who served the temporal rulers and also by the canon lawyers who served the ecclesiastical authorities. Thus Gratian's *Decretum* in the twelfth century asserted the principle that laws to be valid must in some way rest on the consent of the whole people. The Roman maxim *quod omnes tangit ab omnibus tractari et approbari debet* (what touches all must be approved by all), which appeared in the Justinian Code of 531, where it is applied to private law, was explicitly cited by Gratian and often repeated by later authorities.[66] The same principle had been invoked earlier by Bernard of Clairvaux in aid of a group of clergy attempting to wrest episcopal election from the control of lay rulers. The nineteenth century English historian Bishop Stubbs put such importance on this principle that he took its presence in the royal writ of Edward I directing the calling of parliament in 1295 as "conclusive evidence that this gathering marked the beginning of the English parliamentary system."[67] More typically, the principle was cited in support of the belief that feudalism rested upon voluntary agreement, but was not accompanied by or made manifest in any form of representation. The principle was understood to mean only that the interest of all parties must be taken into account, but not that this interest must be expressed in consensual form, whether directly, or by representatives. But it did significantly affect legal procedure, "guaranteeing that at a minimum every individual affected by a matter under litigation had a right to be summoned to and heard in any court exercising jurisdiction over the matter at issue."[68]

The principle that one person might stand for another, and thus represent him, arose as the medieval lawyers reworked other principles of Roman law, notably those of the corporation or *universitas* and the proctor or *procurator*. Once it came to be accepted that a group or corporate entity might be considered a fictive legal person, that corporation could be understood as the legal personification of its members and the bearer of their interests. The proctor was understood as an individual able to function in place of another. Both ideas enabled agents to represent corporations and individuals in courts and assemblies from the thirteenth century onward. The convening of general church councils embodied a principle of representation of the whole community which also prefigures and influenced—especially through the conciliarist movement of the late middle ages—the rise of modern democracy.[69]

The Republican Revival

The rebirth of republicanism gained important support when Renaissance humanists rediscovered and refurbished the classical legacy. The Renaissance republic was, Bouwsma has observed, the antithesis of the *respublica christiana*. The tone of Giovanni Botero's eulogy of Venice and Genoa is completely different from the earlier Christian disparagement of the Roman republic:

> From good government derive all those good qualities in subjects that belong to civil and virtuous life, every means for doing good things, all the arts of peace and war, of acquiring and saving, all polite customs, all noble manners, every honored form of politeness. For this reason free cities of great size surpass those that are subject to princes, at once in magnificence of buildings and in beauty of streets and squares, in multitude of people, in variety of arts, in refinement of manners, and own every kind of polity and humanity. Venice and Genoa prove it, and Florence and Siena did so in their time.[70]

The new secular ideal centered on the human capacity for virtue—understood both in the pagan sense of manliness and the Christian sense of goodness—rather than on incorrigible human sinfulness and incapacity. Humanistic rationalism was skeptical not with respect to the capacity for virtue, which was a function of will and could be nurtured by education and good laws, but toward the power of unaided reason, as the theologians had used it, to grasp the absolute structure of creation and the hierarchical order of the universe. In effect this very skepticism broke the great chain of being that made submission and subordination necessary to the very order of the universe. The capacity for virtue was enough to entitle all human beings to determine their own destiny, and the need in civic life for prosperity required a variety of talents and callings and an openness to study and discovery. The independence of the republican state from control by religious authorities was the *sine qua non* and primary expression of liberty. Whether the state should be ruled by a prince or people became, in the humanistic mind of Niccolò Machiavelli, a function of the degree of virtue in society, but that it should be the home of liberty was taken for granted.

The influence of republican ideology spread as feudalism was being dismantled by the rise of the nation-state under the aegis of absolute monarchy.

At first, however, republicanism seemed too closely tied to a small-scale, communitarian perspective to serve by itself as an alternative to monarchy in the era of the nation-state and the incipient market economy. Federalism was embraced by republicans as an answer to the need for larger associations, and it was to play a very important role in promoting republicanism as a practical option.

As a practical alternative to monarchy, the new outlook took shape in calls for the supremacy of parliament and in demands for the substitution of the rule of law and constitutionalism for the arbitrary power of the monarch. In the process both ecclesiastical and secular institutions experimented with schemes of representation that are properly understood as forerunners of modern representation. The idea of representation took root in the medieval concept of the corporation, which came to be understood as a legal fiction in which members were personified by the artificial person of the corporation. In addition, religious and secular deliberative bodies were often composed of elected delegates.[71]

Before Protestantism took hold in the northern regions of Western Europe and brought with it resistance to Catholic monarchs and in some instances a spirit of covenantal egalitarianism, classical republicanism was revived in the city states of Renaissance Italy. A civic consciousness arose in certain of these cities, especially Venice and Florence, deliberately modeled on that of ancient Rome and providing a self-understanding that stood in sharp contrast to feudalism and seemed more appropriate to burgeoning urban and commercial centers. Humanism made the new city dwellers acutely aware of the potential conflict between the Hellenistic view that man was destined to live in society as a citizen among other citizens and the Christian view that he was formed to live in communion with God and the community of the faithful. This conflict might be resolved in aesthetic terms, notably in graphic art and architecture, as the humanist philosophers recast Christian belief to endorse human creativity, especially in the service of religion, but active civic engagement remained a stumbling block until a new ideal of politics took hold. The Renaissance republics were hardly as egalitarian as their eulogists claimed. The rights of citizenship were always restricted; "the people" was understood as the politically competent, a category that did not included the working classes.[72] But fear of despotism engendered a concern for the replacement of monarchy by a constitutional and parliamentary system of government in which citizens, even if not all citizens, could govern the affairs of the city, check the dangers of arbitrary rule and the influence of special interests, and better protect the state from external threats. The doge of Venice may have been described as a "prince," because he represented the sovereignty of the state, but he was very different from other princes because he was subject to the laws of the city and the control of the patricians.[73]

The republican constitution became a model of mixed government, which, with the support of the classical authorities, was thought to be the best guarantor of order.

Writers who reflected the keen concern for civic life, notably Machiavelli and Francesco Guicciardini, sought to fashion a republican ideal of civic virtue coupled with a constitutionalist emphasis on law and restraints on popular authority. By refurbishing an ideal that had been decried as pagan, they revived and transmitted the ancient republican heritage to modern Europeans.[74] In this perspective, Machiavelli's *Discourses on the First Ten Books of Titus Livius*, the work in which he praised the Roman republic for promoting liberty and noted the importance of civic virtue to the defense of the republican form of government, is more important than his more notorious and much more influential book, *The Prince*.

While Machiavelli was convinced that the Roman republic had incorporated the wisdom of the ancients concerning the art of government, as the glorious history of Rome had shown, he was too much the realist not to recognize that the republican form is appropriate only as long as civic spirit is strong. Once a people becomes corrupted, he asserted, a republic will inevitably succumb to monarchy. If the prince were himself "virtuous," not in the Christian but in the Roman sense of civic *virtus*, he might achieve both personal ambition and the civic good, by assuring the security and prosperity of his realm. Machiavelli did not argue, however, that the republican form was inappropriate for large polities: everything depended on whether the people still maintained its civic spirit or was driven by baser concerns. The problem that obsessed him, and many republicans who came after him, was that the very liberty republics inspire also promotes corruption. The loss of civic virtue and its replacement by a shortsighted selfishness dooms the republic. The corruption that set in when Rome expanded and became an empire was a cautionary lesson, one that also suggested the need from time to time of a great reformer, a "legislator" like Solon or Lycurgus, who can rekindle civic virtue by reforming the laws. But Machiavelli was well aware that in such conditions, the opportunity for autocracy presents itself, and that ambitious princes would set out to achieve a very different goal from republics, the goal of self-aggrandizement.

When the republican ideal spread to England, where it was particularly appealing to those who lived outside the royalist strongholds in the cities and universities, it acquired a more pastoral quality. The commonwealth imagined by writers like James Harrington was a society of smallholders, or gentry, which Harrington thought would replace the feudal system with its emphasis on large estates held together through primogeniture. Harrington's utopian vision was not so much that of a Roman republic bent on glory and expansion as of a peaceable kingdom in which families would cultivate the land and live in harmony with each other and the out-side world. This was not a naive view which ruled out all possibility of conflict, but rather one that stressed the need for mechanisms to regulate and resolve the conflicts that would arise from efforts to engross the public domain or from rapacious moves by commercial interests (the most likely source of corruption) that would attempt to monopolize manufactures and wring the surpluses out of the agrarian sector. The "commonwealthmen" who set themselves against the British monarchy and its aristocratic sup-porters and beneficiaries, saw the future society as one in which communi-ties of farmers would manage their own affairs and send representatives to parliaments which would take care of collective business. To prevent the danger of the emergence of a new aristocracy of wealth, Harrington called for an "equal agrarian," a law that would limit disparities in land holding, and for the equalization of the suffrage so that property qualifications would be removed or lowered to a point where smallholders would hold the bal-ance of power. By removing monarchy, they also thought they would re-move the source of expansion and war.

The Puritan Revolt Against Absolutism

The renewal of interest in the classical models of government had a pro-found influence on political life in Western Europe, nowhere more so than in England. As movements for popular sovereignty succeeded in challeng-ing absolutism, especially in Holland and then in England, speculation turned increasingly toward the republican alternative. At the new univer-sity at Leyden, "the youth of the country were instructed in democratic principles."[75] Puritan writers followed John Milton in rejecting the very principle of hereditary monarchy, pronouncing it contrary to natural law and championing the parliamentary cause. In the turmoil of the Puritan Revolution, England came close to adopting a republican constitution. Once the decision had been taken to execute King Charles, and the Roundheads defeated the Cavaliers, there was agitation in the New Model Army for a kind of written constitution, an "Agreement of the People" which would have created a framework for a representative form of government. The earlier Petitions of Right had at least adumbrated a belief in universal prin-ciples of natural rights rather than arbitrary privileges. The proposed Agree-ment of the People declared such matters as freedom of religion, freedom from military impressment, and equality before the law as rights that no government could abridge, and went on to call for the establishment of biennial parliaments to be elected after a redistribution of seats in propor-tion to population. The Putney debates in which the proposals were con-sidered took representative parliamentary government for granted, even though the debates were often spirited on the question of how broad representation should be. Colonel Thomas Rainborough made his famous observation that because "the poorest he that is in England hath a life to live, as the greatest he . . . nothing . . . can convince me, why any man that is born in England ought not to have his voice in election of burgesses." Nor was there anything "in the law of God" indicating that "a lord shall choose twenty burgesses, and a gentleman but two, or a poor man shall choose none . . ."[76] Maximilian Petty, another radical figure in the debates, summarized the Leveller position: "We judge that all inhabitants who have not lost their birthright should have an equal voice in elections."[77] Later theorists like Algernon Sidney, Harrington, and John Trenchard and Thomas Gordon, would advance more secular versions of republicanism, couched as advocacy of the commonwealth, the anglicized form of republic,[78] but the refusal of Oliver Cromwell and the Independents to endorse Leveller radicalism during the Puritan revolution and the bad example of Cromwell's own rule dealt the republican campaign a setback from which it never recovered. After Cromwell's protectorate was ended, the restoration of monarchy quelled republican agitation and made the focus of reform the Whig effort to limit monarchy by transferring power to an elected parliament. The republican movement reflected in the writings of the English "commonwealthmen" had a more revolutionary effect elsewhere, especially when it was reinforced by the development of natural rights-social contract theory.

5

Individual Autonomy: Liberal Democracy

All eyes are opened, or opening, to the rights of man. The general spread of the light of science has already laid open to every view the palpable truth, that the mass of mankind has not been born with saddles on their backs, nor a favored few booted and spurred, ready to ride them legitimately, by the grace of God.

—Thomas Jefferson[1]

Alongside the republican revival there emerged a more individualistic philosophy of life, coupled with a more atomistic social and economic order. This new individualism found expression in the political theories of natural rights and the social contract which inspired and rationalized campaigns for a form of government and society that came to be called liberal democracy. The emphasis of liberal democracy is on the autonomy of the individual rather than on either communal or plural autonomy. The paramount concern of liberal democrats is therefore how to protect the rights of the individual from abridgement or interference by majorities or coercive social groups. In their zeal to protect individual rights, liberal democrats have sometimes turned a blind eye to inequities due to class and status rather than governmental coercion. In the United States, where liberal ideology was reinforced by relatively widespread property ownership, liberal democracy took firm root, though it almost foundered on the reef of slavery and has endured constant conflict between extremist tendencies to egalitarian populism on the one hand and plutocracy on the other. In Europe and elsewhere, experiments in liberal democracy often disintegrated under the pressures of class and ethnic conflict.

The general movement toward democracy in western Europe was the product of many forces, including especially the shift from a self-sufficient agricultural economy toward a more complex and balanced market economy involving an increasing emphasis upon trade and manufacturing. Alongside the economic changes, and in part as a product of them, came major changes in social structure and values. The rise of the market economy created a new system of economic relationships and with them a new social order. Gradually, the hold of the more organic hierarchy typical of feudalism and the village was weakened by the creation of a more urbanized social system in which at first craft guilds and merchant companies and smaller holders of landed property joined forces to compete for power against the feudal nobility and absolute monarchs. In England, the struggle for power was centered in the House of Commons, erupting in civil war in the 1640s and leading to the constitutional crisis of 1689 in which the throne was declared vacant because James II was accused of "breaking the original contract between King and people."[2] Out of this "Glorious Revolution" fully representative government gradually evolved, though not without struggle. On the continent, a new hierarchy of economic classes based on the possession of capital as well as land rose like an ominous shadow over the old estate system until, in the French Revolution, the old regime was shattered in France and afterward in other countries caught up in the wake produced by the French Revolution. As entrepreneurial capitalism took hold, the old bonds of fealty were replaced by new ones forged by what Thomas Carlyle called "the cash nexus." Sir Henry Maine summed up the transition in the famous formula, "from status to contract."

There was more to this transformation than a change in economic relationships alone. Protestant individualism and Enlightenment skepticism also eroded the traditional social order. A new secular political philosophy arose to provide a common platform for movements of reform and revolution. Alongside the revival of republicanism, a more individualistic theory of society arose, based at first on the conception of the state of nature and the social contract, and embodying a belief in natural rights and/or the "general will" as its moral foundation. As a theoretical ideal, modern democracy resulted from the synthesis of a restated republicanism with natural rights-social contract-free market thinking, later to be called liberalism. This new political doctrine, expounded in its most popular form by John Locke and Jean-Jacques Rousseau, became the basis for parliamentary government in Britain and revolutions in France and the United States which established republican governments founded upon respect for universal human rights. Although the liberal underpinnings at first restrained the tendency toward democracy, by limiting the suffrage to those who met property qualifications, they ultimately made democracy seem natural and appropriate by making universal rights the foundation of the hypothetical social contract by which alone governments were to be considered legitimate. The outcome was the most prevalent modern form of democracy, blending majoritarian representative government with constitutional restraints designed to protect individual rights. The formula took hold in a number of countries, but efforts to apply it in less hospitable conditions often failed. Even where democratic constitutions were adopted, economic hardship, sometimes coupled with defeat in war, led to the overthrow of democracy in favor of various forms of autocracy.

Where democratization was most successful, support for democracy as an ideal and for representative government as its practical expression grew among the three distinct socioeconomic groups produced by the development of the market economy: the middle class of urban property owners or bourgeoisie, the craftsmen and industrial workers, and the farming populace, whether peasants or independent farmers. Property owners embraced republicanism as an opportunity to wrest power from the landed aristocracy and keep it from the propertyless. Natural rights liberalism at first served this campaign for a limited reform by protecting the right of property from political abridgement. Urban workers also rallied to the republican cause, but where it succeeded, they demanded the extension of the suffrage and where it did not, they divided into factions pursuing political reform, anarcho-syndicalist "direct action," and revolutionary conspiracies. Peasants often resisted republicanism at first because it seemed to promote the interests of the urban populace at their expense and to embody a new commercial and individualistic ethos in conflict with their traditional values. They were apt to vent their frustrations in populism until republicanism became democratic enough to afford them access to power. The net result, over many decades and in a number of countries, mainly in Western Europe and North America, was the transformation of republicanism into the more inclusive and egalitarian form of democracy. This transformation was accompanied by a political restructuring. New economic and status elites formed conservative parties—paradoxically often relying, like the Thatcherite Tories of modern times, on classical liberal ideology. These parties aimed to withstand, limit, and modify democratic tendencies. More progressive liberal and social democratic parties sought to enhance those tendencies by broadening the suffrage, providing mass education, and otherwise promoting the interests of the populace. The populist parties found themselves drawn in both directions and sometimes also toward anarchism.

Republicanism and then democracy inspired and rationalized reform and revolution throughout Europe and in North America directed against absolutism and in favor of popular sovereignty and guarantees of "natural rights." These efforts met with mixed success. In some cases, monarchy was abolished in favor of parliamentary systems based on a limited suffrage and codes protecting fundamental rights, in others monarchs were forced to share power with parliaments, and in still others absolute rulers were able to cling to power until World War I proved their undoing. In all cases, the new social systems that emerged to support the structures of government were riven by class and/or racial, religious, and ethnic conflicts reflected in the political parties that emerged to organize elections. Internal divisions were often held in check by nationalistic ideologies that contrasted starkly with the universalistic principles of natural rights. The result was that the early experiments with democracy often became a struggle against forces that threatened to undermine them.

The Whigs and Natural Rights

The English Whigs were responsible for creating political conditions in which natural rights-liberalism could first take hold. When Whig agitation led to the installation of the House of Orange in 1688, Britain entered a period of constitutional monarchy in which the power of Parliament was greatly increased at the expense of the royal prerogative. As the intellectual collaborator of the Whig leader, the Earl of Shaftesbury, John Locke formulated the rationale of the grand compromise between traditional monarchism and the new parliamentarianism.[3] The first of Locke's celebrated *Two Treatises on Government* attacked the argument for patriarchalism advanced by Sir Robert Filmer in an effort to provide a rationale for monarchy more persuasive than divine right. The second set forth "the true original" of political power, which he argued could be ascertained by imagining a state of nature prior to civil society (or society with government), using the style of analysis earlier used by Thomas Hobbes. Unlike Hobbes, however, Locke argued that individuals in such a state of nature had rights to liberty and property as well as to life, the sole right Hobbes had seen as arising out of nature rather than convention. To secure those natural rights (which Locke sometimes asserted could all be summed up under the head of "property") and thereby escape the "inconveniences" of the state of nature (a rather milder formula than Hobbes's view of it as a "war of all against all"), Locke hypothesized that individuals would enter into a social contract to respect each other's rights and create a government which would make the enjoyment of those rights more secure. Contrary to Hobbes, who made the grant of power to the sovereign irrevocable, Locke provided that the power granted to the legislature, as the seat of government, would be subject to recall by the contractors whenever those in power forfeited their trust by violating the rights of the contractors or usurping their ultimate authority to determine the form of government. Locke's theory not only denied that any government had authority not subject to popular consent, but also effectively undermined the case for absolute monarchy by making the legislature the fiduciary instrument of the contractors.

"Thus we are *born Free*, as we are born Rational; not that we have actually the exercise of either: Age that brings one, brings with it the other too."[4] On the basis of this bold assertion, Locke presented a fundamentally new and different foundation for society. Although he too had the agrarian bias of many republicans, reflected in his famous view of property as the result of a mixing of one's sweat with the soil, Locke provided a rationale for social organization which was based both on philosophic reasoning and on the Protestant version of Christian social teachings. He thus brought out the secular implications of a reformed Christianity, stressing that natural law created an equality of natural rights. Natural law had earlier been used primarily as a way of emphasizing obligations, rather than the rights that individuals might claim against interference from others or from governments. Locke portrayed society as a collection of atomistic individuals each endowed by their Creator with enough rationality to understand the moral law and its corollaries, which he declared to be natural rights. In a state of nature, people would use their God-given talents to secure themselves by taking from nature what they needed for subsistence, but would be prohibited by natural law from taking from nature more than was necessary for their own sustenance. Because they would lack a common judge to decide disputes, and might be blinded to the dictates of the moral law by self-interest and passion, this condition was bound to be precarious and full of "inconveniences," so much so that a Hobbesian state of war might ensue. To avoid these inconveniences, Locke reasoned, they would join in a social compact consisting of an exchange of promises, or a set of mutual obligations, to respect each other's natural rights. In order to assure that the terms of the compact were kept, the contractors would also agree to establish a fiduciary instrument of government, a legislature that would be bound by the terms of the compact.

The members of the legislature would be elected by the compactors, "in proportion to the assistance they provide the public," a formula by which Locke seems to have meant in proportion to taxation, even though his notion of the social compact made the compactors equal without regard to property ownership. In this respect, he may well have been trying to soften the more radical egalitarian implications of his own theory, so as to provide greater influence to owners of property. This reading is consistent with his oft-cited claim that by the introduction of money, "outside the bounds of the social compact," men had tacitly agreed to a way of circumventing the natural law limitations on "infinite appropriation" with the result that they had consented "to a disproportionate and unequal Possession of the Earth . . ."[5] Both considerations have often been taken to mean that although Locke begins with an equality among the individual compactors, he ends with a formula for government which is biased toward the wealthy. Locke undoubtedly shared the fear of the masses of both Whigs and royalists, even though he argued that rational capacity was universal, but it is too simple to suppose that he was merely trying to protect wealth. Locke saw wealth as the product of the application of reason and industry and its possession as a sign of both. Wealth was also a sign of independence: a household servant would be subordinate to the master of the house and could not have the same independence as a freeholder. Those without some minimal property of their own could not be expected to use the franchise to exercise independent judgment. If the right of property was the corner-stone of all liberty, it was not immune to regulation in accord with natural law limits, for the establishment of civil society does not nullify the opera-tion of these limits: "The Obligations of the Law of Nature, cease not in Society, but only in many Cases are drawn closer . . . the Law of Nature stands as an Eternal Rule to all Men, *Legislators* as well as others. The *Rules* that they make for other Mens Actions, must, as well as their own and other Mens Actions, be conformable to the Law of Nature, *i.e.*, to the Will of God, of which there is a Declaration, and the *fundamental Law of Nature* being *the preservation of Mankind*, no Humane Sanction can be good, or valid against it."[6]

In emphasizing the continuing relevance of the law of nature in society, Locke established the basis for legislative regulation of the inequality of possessions that resulted from the introduction of money outside the bounds of the social compact. "For," as he notes in the discussion of prop-erty, "in governments the Laws regulate the right of property, and the pos-session of land is determined by positive constitutions."[7] In a society in which land is scarce, and in which employment is industrial rather than simply agrarian, it is at least consistent with Locke's notion of the natural law limits that governments should act to assure equal opportunity, even if this should require restrictions on property ownership and redistribu-tion of wealth. Locke himself may not have foreseen that the welfare state and the managed economy are both legitimate emanations of his own theory, but the theory certainly provides for this reading as it does for the more conventional liberal gloss. He believed that government ought to direct the economy and assure that idleness is avoided. The modern-day split between unreconstructed classical liberals, who see the need for a weak government in order to preserve the liberty of the individual, and the pro-gressive or welfare-state liberals who see the need for a positive state to regulate the economic market and assure full employment, reflects a ten-sion already apparent in Locke's theory.

Rousseau's Variant

Rousseau made this division within liberalism apparent in his rework-ing of social contract theory. As a moral theorist Rousseau differs from Locke in sharing with David Hume and Adam Smith the view that the foundation of morality does not lie in a rational determination of what the law of nature requires. "Reason," Hume observed, "being cool and dispas-sionate, is no motive to action, and directs only the impulse received from appetite or inclination, by showing us the means of attaining happiness or avoiding misery."[8] As our natural impulses, he thought, were directed by sentiments of utility, so public morality favors actions that promote public utility while condemning those that disserve it. With Adam Smith, Hume also believed that the foundation of morality lay in the human capacity for sympathy.[9] Rousseau too contended that natural compassion can become the basis of civic morality and therefore of what he described as the general will. Unlike Locke, he was suspicious of the corrupting power of reason and more confident of the purity of natural compassion. Consequently, he gave less importance to the natural law discovered by reason as the source of natural rights and instead emphasized the sense of both rights and duties that would emerge from the social compact as the expression of universal or general will.

From this difference in moral theory arises another difference affecting the rights individuals may claim. Locke's interpretation of natural rights specifies the rights to life, liberty, and property, whereas, for Rousseau, the rights the compactors would enjoy would be whatever rights they unanimously agree upon. Although Rousseau supposed everyone would agree that individuals should have the right to own property, he also thought the compactors would want to limit disparities of property ownership so as to avoid the corrupting influences of great inequality. Nor did Rousseau champion an absolute right of freedom of expression. In order to prevent free speech from corrupting morals, he approved of censorship of the arts, notably the drama, and presumably would also have allowed censorship of other forms of expression having deleterious influence.

Rousseau's unwillingness to make rights corollaries of natural law and as such prior to civic enactment, and his readiness to permit these rights to be restricted for the social good, has led many to criticize his theory as dangerous to liberty. It seems to provide a warrant for collective interference with individual liberty (even though Rousseau sought to avoid such interference by requiring unanimous consent to the social compact) by some committee of public safety which claims to be protecting the public good. Nevertheless, Rousseau has deservedly been hailed for the contribution he made to the theory of democracy by showing that liberty requires self-government. As A. P. D'Entrèves explains, expounding Rousseau's view: "Liberty in the positive sense is in fact nothing else than self-government, autonomy. It cannot be realized except when the power which commands is the self-same power of him who obeys. The achievement of liberty in the State is therefore conditional on the sovereignty of the 'general will.' 'Subjects' become 'citizens' only in as far as they share in that sovereignty and partake of the general will. Their complete surrender to the State, to the 'country' (*la patrie*), secures them 'against all personal dependence.'"[10]

Rousseau was not in favor of direct self-government, as distinct from the direct exercise of sovereignty. Even though he put great emphasis on the exercise of citizenship, as a means by which people could exchange natural liberty for civil or moral liberty, he thought it appropriate and necessary that the political rights of citizens be restricted to the establishing of basic law, and to the choice of the form of government and of those who should exercise power. He may be considered a democrat to the extent that democracy means popular sovereignty, or "legislative rule by the whole body of citizens,"[11] but he did not favor active self-government (or the possession of executive power) by the citizenry. He feared that by taking an active role in government, citizens would lose the general perspectives which enable them to pursue the common good in basic law, and instead succumb to the corrupting force of self-interest. In the strict sense of the word, he therefore argued, "there has never been a true democracy and there never will be. It is contrary to the natural order that the greater number should govern and the smaller number be governed." It is inconceivable that the people would sit permanently in an assembly to deal with public affairs or that they could successfully delegate their power to commissions. As a form of government, he believed, democracy presupposed conditions difficult to maintain: a very small state, in which each citizen may know all the others, a great simplicity of manners and morals, a large degree of equality in social rank and wealth, and little or no luxury.[12] Instead, he stipulated that the people as sovereign must establish the basic law and confer the power to govern on a prince or a small number of magistrates whom they name and whom they may periodically remove from office. There is some ground for supposing that he also thought society would remain perpetually dependent on the "lawgiver," a human deus ex machina like Moses or Lycurgus who would give the law to a people and in so doing bring them out of the state of nature into a civil society and who remains needed to prevent them from relapsing.[13]

Unlike Locke, who endorses representative government as the agency by which the social contract is transformed into a system of civil government, Rousseau is caught on the horns of a dilemma. He laments the loss of ancient participatory democracy but assails the election of representatives, as well as the substitution of taxation for direct social engagement,[14] as signals of the death of citizenship. But he proposes no alternative except a Genevan model which he knows is suitable only for small communities and which is any case in reality oligarchical.

The Impact of Natural Rights/Social Contract Theory

The general impact of this profound reworking of political theory, largely in England and France but elsewhere as well, was to remove the ideological justification for absolute monarchy and prepare the ground for representative democracy. In all its forms, natural-rights/social contract theory posited an original equality of rights among all citizens and denied the legitimacy of the claim of royal families to a right to rule based on original consent or descent rather than continuing consent. In this respect, it differed from republican theory which relied on a more general belief in popular sovereignty emphasizing the need for civic virtue on the part of the populace. The liberalism that emerged from a combination of natural rights-social contract thinking and *laissez-faire* economics allowed for restrictions of suffrage on the rationale that property ownership was evidence of the capacity for civic virtue whereas poverty was a sign of incapacity. The independent yeoman farmer was thought to be the most likely to be uncorrupted by self-interest, but even republican theorists were likely to accept the need for a natural aristocracy in providing leadership and an exemplary commitment to the public good. Whereas Locke argued exclusively on grounds of natural right and social contract, other theorists, notably Algernon Sidney, combined the two strands.[15]

Monarchy initially survived the challenge, but its power almost everywhere was steadily attenuated. Even though for some time to come the British prime minister would be accountable to the monarch as well as to Parliament, more and more the dependence of the monarchy on the taxes that only Parliament could impose effectively led to a transfer of power. As extra-parliamentary parties developed and the suffrage was extended, England pursued a gradual evolution to democracy. But the assault on monarchy launched in England, and reinforced both by the Puritan revolution and the settlement of 1688, set the stage for a more radical challenge in the American and French revolutions.

The Democratic Revolutions and the Rise of Representative Parliamentary Government

Especially in the light of the work of modern historians, it is widely though not unanimously accepted that the French Revolution was more a social revolution than the American,[16] and also that the American Revolution was the more successful in laying a foundation for stable democratic government because of its liberal character. The American colonists were rebelling in the first instance against imperial control rather than against the British system of government, which was in any case a mixture of royal and parliamentary rule. They initially demanded only a degree of representation which the remoteness of parliament made a practical difficulty. Only when both the monarch and the parliament of England denied them an opportunity for an alternative in the form of limited self-government (such as Canada later received in becoming a dominion) did they reject colonial status and monarchy along with it. Gordon S. Wood has argued that the American Revolution was nevertheless a "radical revolution" in that it transformed a colonial society suffused with age-old distinctions of rank, notably the separation of gentlemen from commoners, and such residues of patriarchal feudalism as primogeniture and entail, into "the most egalitarian nation in the history of the world. . ."[17] In the larger sense of the word "revolution," this interpretation is well-founded. As an historical event, however, the French Revolution represented a still more abrupt rupture with the past. British monarchy had long ceased to be absolute and British beliefs in the liberty of the subject were if anything better realized on the colonial frontier, with its widespread property ownership and sense of self-reliance, than in the motherland. By contrast, the people of France had long accepted the prescriptive right of absolute monarchy and the privileges of the *noblesse* and now suddenly rejected both.

Despite the differences, both instances represent a similar tendency away from what remained of feudalism and the absolutism which had arisen out of it and in the direction of a new form of social, economic, and political organization. The societies that emerged were at first largely agrarian, but with more of the land worked by peasants in the French case and by farmers (both tenants and freeholders) in the American, and with a growing urban market economy managed by a property-owning middle class drawing upon the wage labor of skilled and unskilled workers. The people of France were divided by class and region, and united temporarily only by Napoleonic nationalism. A democratic regime only emerged during the Third Republic, almost a century after the Revolution. The United States too suffered a civil war, due to sectional conflict and even more to a near-fatal constitutional compromise over slavery. From the start, however, the American constitution reflected a consensus on liberal principles that was to make the triumph of democracy all but inevitable once the trauma due to slavery was overcome.

In France, François Furet contends, the Revolution took over an empty space, or rather proliferated within civil society, a once powerless sphere of life. In sum, the Revolution "mobilized society and disarmed the State."[18] It was at the same time the embodiment of the idea "that history is shaped by human action rather than by the combination of existing institutions and forces."[19] France had been a kingdom of subjects; now it was a nation of citizens. A new ideology was created, based on the belief that equality must be achieved in every sphere of life; all personal problems and all moral and political matters became political. The Revolution thus invented democratic politics. It was the origin of the belief in the people as something more than an aggregate of individuals. The novelty of the Revolution was that it marked the creation of democratic politics, rather than the transformation of the social order. The insistence on the general will made intermediary institutions objects of suspicion, as devices that stood between the people and government.

Patrice Higonnet's comparison of the French and American revolution, drawing on the analysis of the American liberal tradition by Louis Hartz, takes Furet's analysis considerably further by highlighting the differences between the two democratic revolutions. Higonnet notes that there is a certain overlap to begin with in that many of the same people figured in both events, including the Marquis de Lafayette, Thomas Paine, even Jefferson, "the most Parisian of the Virginia philosophes." Both revolutions, moreover, stood for the same principles—popular sovereignty, nationalism, the rights of man, no taxation without representation, republicanism, and suspicion of established religion. Several French institutions and concepts had American precedents, including the convention, federalism, a written constitution, political clubs, even the Committee of Public Safety, as well as paper money, loyalty oaths, and the Declaration of the Rights of Man.[20] Nevertheless, as he also points out, the two revolutions proceeded very differently, the French to turmoil, terror, and the temporary restoration of monarchy, the American to the establishment of a workable constitution. The rhetoric of revolutionary violence was expressed in the American Revolution, and may even have helped inspire the willingness to use violence in the French Revolution. Jefferson, in a letter written from Paris in 1787, noted that "the tree of liberty must be refreshed from time to time with the blood of patriots and tyrants." Later, at the trial of Louis XVI, Bertrand Barère argued similarly that "the tree of liberty can only grow if watered by the blood of kings."[21] The difference was that the French actually did kill not only the king and his wife but a great many others, making it seem that democracy and terror were somehow linked, whereas there was no reign of terror in America. The contrast between what happened in France and in America is striking. French democracy suffered at the hands both of its partisans and of those who cited the excesses of the Revolution in justifying a restoration of monarchy and aristocracy. The United States also experienced a milder conservative backlash against Daniel Shays' rebellion and the Whiskey rebellion, which were cited by the Federalists to justify the need for a government strong enough to cope with the rebelliousness of the poor, but they could hardly propose as a cure the re-establishment of monarchy and the privileges of aristocracy. The two countries also differed decisively on the question of the degree of centralization of power in the central government. The framers of the American constitution deliberately did not create a strongly centralized government, whereas France became the scene of a regime even more absolutist than the Bourbon monarchy when Napoleon took control of the revolution.

On other scores, it is too easy to exaggerate or oversimplify differences. It would be wrong to say, for example, that in France democracy came to be associated with the violence and terror of the Revolution, whereas in

the United States it took an altogether peaceful course. Canadian historians have often pointed out that the use of violence by the American colonists against Britain set a pattern repeated in later history, especially on the
frontier, in sharp contrast to the peaceful Canadian settlement of the west.[22]
The cruel behavior of Americans toward the native Indian population during westward expansion may have been partly a continuation of the tradition of militant self-defense bred by the legend of the Minutemen, as Davy
Crockett emulated the men of Lexington. American democratization involved far less internal conflict because the social injustice of slavery was
overlooked and allowed to fester. When South Carolina seceded, the citizens of Charleston went to the City Hall to sign a declaration of independence modeled on the original. In that sense, the revolution produced an
anarchic propensity for secession as well as a willingness to resort to violence in defense of liberty, in the spirit of Patrick Henry. In the aftermath of
the civil war, the vigilantism of the Ku Klux Klan was probably also rooted
in the guerilla tactics of the Sons of Revolution, whose harassment of
Redcoats and loyalists was taken as a precedent.

What is most striking in the comparison, Higonnet argues, is that while
both revolutions gave birth to systems designed to express the importance
of individualism, they took different courses not only because of the different behavior of their leading actors, but also because of deep differences in
the social conditions that preceded the revolutions. The basic difference is
that feudalism left a residue of corporatism in France, whereas in America
the absence of so significant a feudal past left the field to liberalism. Democracy took hold more easily in America because it was easier to establish on a foundation of liberal individualism than on that of feudal
corporatism. In America, Tocqueville had pointed out, European feudalism had not been fully transplanted, and individualism had taken root
instead, supported by the relative absence of primogeniture and by widespread property ownership. Civil society became strong and the state comparatively weak. In France, feudal corporatism remained a powerful obstacle which the democratic revolution sought to remove. The effort to
smash the corporations led to the emergence of a strong state and a weak
civil society. Guilds which restricted individual liberty were abolished by
the Le Chapelier law of 1791, which made "liberal individualism, defined
in terms of property rights, the first law of the land."[23] No such complete
upheaval was needed in the United States. The French revolutionaries set
out to destroy institutions that might separate the citizen from the nation
and to institutionalize the rule of the "general will."[24] The role of the state
was at first sharply restricted to allow for a *laissez-faire* economy, but after
only a few years, these policies were reversed and the role of the state was
dramatically broadened, as wages and prices were set by law, due process
was suspended, and other developments put in place which foreshadowed

dictatorship. The American revolution, by contrast, produced a system of checks and balances and federalism which deliberately weakened government and created the conditions for a self-interested individualism to produce a dynamic capitalism. Instead of adopting the idea of the general will to promote a unitary state, the Americans set out to build space for pluralism and individualism and created a liberal democracy. The reason, Higonnet argues, lies in the antecedent structure of the two societies. In the American colonies, what began as an effort to rekindle republican civic virtue ended by creating a new individualism more suited to free-wheeling capitalism. In France, the elite was to a large extent converted to ideals of individualism and the institutional apparatus of corporatism had decayed, but the mass of the population was still attached to older communitarian values.

The American Revolution also entailed a profound social transformation, but one that was accomplished more peacefully. As in France, the republican transition from subject to citizen meant in the first instance that Americans came to believe that they had suddenly gained an equal share in political sovereignty. "Subject is derived," David Ramsay, a South Carolina physician and historian explained in 1779, "from the Latin words, *sub* and *jacio*, and means one who is under the power of another; but a citizen is one of a mass of free people, who, collectively, possess sovereignty. Subjects look up to a master, but citizens are so far equal, that none have hereditary rights superior to others."[25] As a republican constitution was adopted protecting this equality of rights, civil as well as political, republicanism shaded into liberalism.

Although this revolution occurred in a region in which religious concerns had been uppermost in several of the earliest settlements, by the time of the Revolution, secular concerns had become more influential. American republican sentiment reflected Puritan covenentalism, but by 1776, the religious background was overshadowed by explicitly secular concerns and conceptions. The economy encouraged an individualistic materialism that religious sentiment deplored, and spokesmen like Jefferson in the Declaration of Independence and Thomas Paine in his revolutionary pamphleteering moved consciousness away from Christian concerns to those of natural-rights/social contract theory.

As Hartz pointed out, following Tocqueville, the single most important consideration in understanding the development of American ideology is the absence of a significant degree of feudalism. As a result, class consciousness could not develop among Americans, who saw themselves as Lockean individualists. The effort to find an alternative to monarchy first inspired Americans to think along the lines of the English radical Whigs. Republican sentiment enabled them to see the need first for redress of grievances and then, when no redress was granted, to insist on independence.[26] In rationalizing their claim, they drew upon the republican views popular among radical Whigs in England, who frequently invoked the example of classical popular government. "Give me liberty or give me death" was a line burgled by Patrick Henry from Addison's Roman drama, *Cato*, written in 1713.[27]

Because of the weakness of colonial feudalism, and therefore of a strong sense of corporate identity that might have inhibited individualism, the early influence of Whig republicanism was eventually eclipsed by that of natural rights liberalism. The roots of the American receptivity to liberalism lay not only in Protestantism and Enlightenment rationalism but also in the strong reaction against British mercantilism that set in among American merchants. Trade ensured the growth of New England, which set the tone for the new country. Even in the early 1770s, one-third of Boston's adult males were part owners of some merchant vessel. As early as the 1680s, individualism had become the cornerstone of New England's economic life. Experiments in communal agriculture were abandoned. The communities themselves broke up, as individuals struck out on their own, moving where land was available. The European guild and peasant commune were nowhere to be found. Corporations and estates had been a central feature of French life for so long that even after they were formally abolished they continued to exert an influence. Guilds were not created in America for several reasons. Colonial artisans reasoned they would do better economically and perhaps socially in a free market where they could move about and sell their labor as they wished; wages in America were high and general starvation unknown, so guilds were not needed to provide relief for the poor; colonials and their authorities may have reasoned that the desirable control over quality which the guilds provided would be offset by undesirable coalitions among them to demand higher wages.[28]

Thus, already by the end of the seventeenth century, the American colonies exhibited a distinctly individualistic value system. Unlike Europe, where *Gemeinschaft* yielded to individualism and individualism produced a class-conflict-ridden *Gesellschaft*, in America a sense of community (expressed in local pride and patriotism) was blended with a sense of individuality. Americans clung to a sense of community even as they embraced a frenetic capitalism. Agriculture, the economic preoccupation of most of the population, along with incipient manufacturing, began to be oriented toward a market system of exchange. The American farmer was not a peasant aiming to support the family on a self-sufficient manor. America was resolutely capitalist; everything was bought and sold, including human beings. This capitalism did not produce a rigid system of classes and of conflicts among them both because Americans were not as inured to class distinctions as Europeans were and because a general prosperity muted such distinctions and the tensions they aroused. Immigrants arrived from

Europe destitute and were grateful that in America they too could prosper. Urban wages were high and artisans became property owners. The high cost of labor was a goad to the perpetuation of slavery and led to the elimination of indentured servitude for whites. American agricultural productivity rose steadily. Americans ate better than Europeans and grew taller. The opening of the west was also a factor in preventing the formation of classes.

In France, a population surplus became a politically volatile underclass; in America, opportunity beckoned to immigrants who were for the most part too eager to settle down and take advantage of the opportunities to become independent farmers to take part in agitation. Ethnicity also acted to dampen class solidarity: whereas in Paris the *sans culottes* had a shared experience of belonging to a single grouping, in America ethnic variation served as a cross-cutting cleavage. By 1790, 20 percent of whites in America were not of British origin at all; the others came from different sub-communities. As a result, the poor never became a coherent class. Race was another fragmenting force, pitting poor whites against poor blacks. Religion too made for social fragmentation along other than class lines.[29]

Hartz argues that because feudalism disposed Europeans to think of themselves as belonging to classes, those who subsequently became wage earning workers acquired a sense of class identity enabling them to stigmatize the owners of capital on whom they were dependent as class enemies. In America, the relative weakness of feudalism made it less likely that class consciousness would succeed status consciousness. American workers developed neither a strong sense of class solidarity nor the hatred for an upper class of capitalists that went with a sense of proletarian solidarity.[30] Before and during the Revolution, Americans were devoted to liberal individualism. Afterward, American workingmen were therefore more likely to respond to calls for the "pure and simple" unionism advocated by leaders like Samuel Gompers than to the politicized and class-based unionism that was far more successful in Europe. Whatever social and political radicalism the experience of revolution produced faded when independence was won and the leaders of the Revolution settled down to the task of building governments, which they constructed on more conservative principles. The framers of the American constitution deliberately set about weakening the power of government, while creating a non-elective Supreme Court to hold popular majorities in check, in order to prevent what even Jefferson called "an elective despotism."[31] The French meanwhile proceeded to strengthen the powers of the central government. For Americans, the purpose of the state was to defend the rights of individual citizens against the state. This individualism led to a redefinition of the classical ideal of civic virtue. It "more often referred to a private quality, a man's capacity to look out for himself and his dependents—almost the opposite of classical virtue," as Joyce O. Appleby has put it.[32]

The Spread of Democracy

Both the French and the American example spurred imitation. The last four decades of the eighteenth century have been described by the historian R. R. Palmer as "the age of the democratic revolution." Even before the outbreak in France, there were major efforts to overthrow monarchy in Scandinavia and the Hapsburg empire. The success of the French revolution sparked and reinforced democratic tendencies elsewhere. Edmund Burke, the most articulate opponent of the French Revolution in England, was so fearful that democracy would come there next, whether by invasion or uprising, that he gave orders before his death that his remains be secretly buried so they could not be dug up and desecrated by revolutionaries. Revolutions inspired by the French precedent broke out in Ireland, the Netherlands, and Switzerland in 1798, in the major cities of Italy in the same year and the two years just before it. In Poland in 1794 Thaddeus Kosciusko, a Polish hero of the American Revolution, led an abortive uprising in his homeland. In Greece, in 1797, delegates from Athens, Crete, Macedonia, and other Greek territories met in secret to plan an uprising against the Ottomans, hoping to receive military assistance from the French army. Similar conspiracies were discovered or suspected in many other places, including Latin America, southern Africa, and Siberia. These movements were suppressed almost everywhere, but they left a residue which had a considerable long-term effect.[33] In 1830, Belgium won independence from Holland and adopted a constitution under which it became a parliamentary monarchy. In 1848 the revolutionary spirit of 1789 echoed throughout Europe, again inspired by events in Paris. In Hungary a group led by Lajos Kossuth issued a declaration of independence modeled after that adopted by the United States. Again, the old order was restored, but the second half of the nineteenth century witnessed many moves toward democratization, including Argentina's adoption of a constitution on the American model in 1853 and the introduction of parliamentary checks on absolutism in many European countries. At various times in the nineteenth century, other Latin American countries, including Mexico, Venezuela, and Brazil, adopted constitutions following the precedent of the United States.[34]

Parties and Class

The major difference between developments in the United States and in virtually all the other countries in which republicanism and democracy were taking root is that in most of these others representative government became a focus for class conflict. Plural autonomy, in other words, was more salient a political force than communal and individual autonomy, and something very much like the Roman struggle of the orders took modern form.[35] In England, the House of Commons became, in Maurice

Duverger's words, "The Trojan Horse of Plutodemocracy." The initial victory of the European bourgeoisie was short-lived because after 1848 the propertied class faced a new enemy in the industrial proletariat. In both Europe and America, but especially in Europe, the triumph of Western-style democracy required the dampening of class conflict. For that reason, political parties were frowned upon, because it was feared that they would result in polarization. Although political parties existed and organized campaigns for elections to parliaments, in some countries it was forbidden until 1914 to allude to them in parliament. "There were only deputies, who were separated from one another and, in theory, independent."[36] The word "party" had originally denoted a faction established around important personalities—like the party of Brutus or Caesar in Rome. True parties came into being only when parliaments appeared, as organizations of groups in parliament; they became national phenomena as the suffrage was extended and they were used to organize mass electoral campaigns. The first parties were "electoral committees" formed in each district to sponsor candidates which often survive the elections. Those committees sharing similar views united in national organizations, nominating a central committee. In Britain this central committee was at first tantamount to the parliamentary group of each party, but eventually the parliamentary group came to share control with the constituency organizations.

As the suffrage was extended, the parties came to be primarily class-based, though with platforms reflecting internal splits and efforts to attract voters from other camps. The first true modern parties, the British Whigs and Tories, were both established by aristocrats: the Whigs were more liberal and republican in sentiment whereas the Tories were attached to the throne and the traditional order. As the Whigs became the Liberals of the nineteenth century, they gained the support of urban wage earners at first, until the emergence of the British Labor Party ; the Tories drew popular support from small farmers suspicious both of liberal capitalists and socialists, and tried to win over the working class by contrasting paternalistic "Tory democracy" with the Liberals' dogmatic attachment to *laissez-faire* economics. In Scandinavia a liberal agrarian party emerged, making the conflict in that country three-sided rather than two-sided. In various countries, religious and ethnic conflicts were superimposed on the class-based party system, and ideological splits further complicated party alignments. Middle class parties sometimes split between moderates and radicals; aristocratic parties sometimes split between legitimists and ultraconservatives. Threatened by the rise of socialism, especially when mass labor parties made their appearance, the aristocracy and middle class made common cause. The labor parties became the focus for the organization of the working class and of efforts to circumvent the repressive techniques used by the bourgeois-controlled state by gaining control over the state. The politicization of the socialist movement compromised its revolutionary hopes, however, as the socialist parties were coopted by the democratic system and induced to make alliances and accept moderate reforms.

At the end of the first World War, this system of party-mediated representative government seemed to have emerged as the political victor. "The rulers in business suits in Paris, London, and Washington," Duverger observes, "had conquered the rulers in uniform in Berlin and Vienna."[37] Parliamentary institutions were extended to other countries and even internationalized in the League of Nations. But appearances were deceptive and the victory proved short-lived. In Central Europe, liberal institutions were grafted onto to economically underdeveloped and largely agrarian societies and did not take. There de facto dictatorships were soon established, except for Czechoslovakia, which had a heavily industrialized region, and with it an electorate as committed to the parliamentary process as those in Western Europe. The obstacles to economic reconstruction in the 1920s and then in the Great Depression battered and destroyed newly-minted democratic regimes. The fascist movements that came to power in the 1920s and 1930s were responses to the fear of anarchy and socialism.

The American situation was different from the outset and remained so, mainly because the social structure was different. The American parties did not represent classes, and therefore had fluid constituencies and only marginal and sometimes very changeable differences from each other. The rivalry between the American parties had to do not so much with ideology as with sectional interests, tariffs, bimetallism, and similar policy issues. Whatever strength and persistence the parties had was due less to social support and ideological commitment than to the spoils system, which provided the patronage that held them together as systems for office seeking. For this reason, parties played even more of an institutional role in the United States than in Europe, creating powerful "machines" to distribute patronage and organize the vote. By the end of the nineteenth century, the excesses and corruption of the machines and the bosses aroused the anger of the voters and led to the progressive reforms, such as the direct primary, intended to take power out of the hands of the bosses and return it to the "grass roots." The parties survived these reforms in part because they were more necessary to the operation of the democratic system than the progressives recognized, but also because immigration and the expansion of the functions of government gave them a continued lease on life. The Democratic Party in particular became the party of the immigrants and workingmen, as well of southern whites with bitter memories of the Republican role in the Civil War and Reconstruction. The Republican Party attracted more affluent, rural, and assimilated elements of the population. The assimilation of many of the immigrants, coupled with the rise of the welfare state, undermined the power of the big city machines, however, and resulted in a shift of political power to the suburbs from which the Republicans were the principal beneficiaries.

Duverger argues that liberal democracy produced an inherently contradictory social system: political equality was established by suppressing the privileges of the aristocracy, but the economic inequality allowed to develop led to the rise of a new aristocracy, the "plutocracy." American progressives and European radicals might battle on behalf of the little man against what Justice Louis D. Brandeis called "the curse of bigness," and might alleviate the plight of the poor, but they could not overthrow the system itself. The plutocracy was not a coherent oligarchy, but neither was it the anarchic jumble of pluralistic groupings that liberal writers claim it was. In Duverger's view, modern democratic governments remain the instrument of the ruling class, but they maintain control through an intermediary class of politicians, civil servants, and media professionals. This intermediate class formulates and implements policies reflecting the interests of the dominant social groups, using a mixture of the coercive power of the state and propaganda to shape public opinion. The machinery of candidate selection makes it possible to control elections; since the candidates require large campaign war chests, those who control wealth use it to control the selection of candidates and their behavior in office.

Whatever criticisms may be addressed to this analysis of the contemporary situation, it is very helpful in understanding the recent past. In particular, it explains why the broad movement to establish democracy that emerged following the democratic revolutions of the late eighteenth century did not fulfill the expectations of those who saw it as a means to achieve greater social and economic equality, and also why this disillusionment created fertile grounds for antidemocratic appeals. Universal suffrage had turned out to be a means by which a propertied oligarchy preserved stability. Democracy survived only where enough voters feared that upheaval would only make things worse and voted for candidates and parties committed to preserving the status quo. Where economic conditions became so bad, especially in the wake of the chaos resulting from the first World War, that any alternative seemed preferable to the status quo, more and more people were willing to take a chance on another system. The age of democracy that had dawned with such bright hopes in the republican revival seemed to have produced a new form of inequality. The way was open for a backlash against democracy and in favor of alternatives that promised a better life by other means.

6

Backlash: Criticism and the Rise of Modern Autocracy

Fascism attacks the whole complex of democratic ideologies and rejects them both in their theoretical premises and in their applications . . . Fascism denies that the majority, through the mere fact of being a majority, can rule human societies; it denies that this majority can rule by means of a periodical consultation; it affirms the irremediable, fruitful and beneficent inequality of men, who cannot be levelled by such a mechanical and extrinsic fact as universal suffrage.

—Benito Mussolini[1]

The emergence of popular government in the late eighteenth and early nineteenth centuries rekindled the opposition to democracy that had first surfaced among the upper classes in ancient Greece and Rome. This time, however, the more radical criticisms helped foster disastrous twentieth century experiments with authoritarian and totalitarian alternatives.

Certain of the complaints, like those of John Ruskin,[2] reflected nostalgia for a vanishing old social order; others, the apprehensions of liberals and conservatives who were the dominant political actors in the nations undergoing democratization. Liberals feared that a full enfranchisement of the working class would threaten private property and, more broadly, the ideal of individual liberty. The antidotes they proposed were constitutional guarantees for property rights and the obligations of contract, restriction of the suffrage to property owners, extra votes for the better educated, and a judiciary impervious to pressure from majorities. Conservatives, who were particularly appalled by the violence and radical levelling of the French Revolution, saw democracy as the upshot of a belief in equality rooted in envy and conducive to despotism. Some of the critics, like John Stuart Mill, James Fitzjames Stephen, and Henry Maine in England, and Alexis de Tocqueville and the *"Doctrinaires"*—François Guizot, Pierre Paul Royer-Collard, and Benjamin Constant—in France,[3] were either sympathetic or resigned to democracy, but anxious to ward off what they feared were its excesses. Others, notably Thomas Carlyle and Friedrich Nietzsche, were contemptuous and implacably hostile.

As debate proceeded, a variety of new doctrines and theories were advanced that went beyond criticism to propose alternatives to democracy. On the right, these alternatives drew upon a variety of anti-egalitarian sentiments and theories: intense nationalism, often coupled with imperialism; racism, usually confused with ethnocentrism and nationalism; elitism, often associated with hero-worship; Social Darwinism, sometimes linked with eugenics; and the theory of mass society. On the left, socialists either too impatient to wait for socialism to triumph at the ballot box or disdainful of democracy argued that the transition from capitalism could be accomplished only by violent revolution and the provisional installation of a "dictatorship of the proletariat." On both extremes, autocratic alternatives gained favor.

The search for a rightist alternative had early support among the titled nobility, who were losing their privileges almost everywhere as the economic base of their landed estates was eroded by industrialization. The new industrial "plutocrats" at first saw the landed aristocrats as rivals, but came to share with them an interest in preserving the right to property. For both groups, nationalism and racism had the popular emotional appeal needed to counter both democracy and socialism. Instead of having to argue only for the preservation of hierarchy or for free enterprise, they could frame the debate in terms of these populistic sentiments, using them to check demands for expansion of the suffrage or economic redistribution. In the hands of ambitious demagogues, nationalism and racism acquired an even more potent and sinister role, serving as rationales for the rejection of limited popular government and for the suppression of labor agitation. Buttressed by theories of mass society and elitism, these criticisms undermined popular support for democracy and helped pave the way for authoritarian and totalitarian alternatives.

J. S. Mill's Liberal Critique

John Stuart Mill was typical of many liberals in being favorable to democracy in principle but leery of it in practice. His father, James Mill, had been converted to representative government when he became convinced of the truth of Jeremy Bentham's Utilitarianism. Bentham had asserted that because all human beings by nature sought to pursue pleasure and avoid pain, the only appropriate scheme of government would be one which would enable all citizens to pursue happiness. But since direct government by the entire community was impractical, and since kings and aristocrats would be guided by their own self-interest, the senior Mill concluded that representative government was the only practical way to assure that legislation would conform to the will of the community.[4]

Mill *fils* agreed with his father's conclusions even though he was troubled about the implications for the liberty of the individual of the egalitarian premise of Utilitarianism. The appearance of the first volume of Tocqueville's *Democracy in America* in 1835 gave him a foil with which to express his doubts about the effects of democracy on liberty and to begin to rethink the principles of representative government.[5] Although well aware that the inequalities of property were "greater than in any former period of history," he saw that the momentum of history lay with democracy: "If America has been said to prove, that, in an extensive country, a popular government may exist, England seems destined to afford the proof, that, after a certain stage in civilization, it must: for as soon as the numerically stronger have the same advantages, in means of combination and celerity of movement, as the smaller number, they are the masters; and except by their permission, no government can any longer exist."[6]

But Mill did not accept Tocqueville's view that democracy must inevitably mean majority rule. In practice, he observed, it had so far brought rule by the middle class, especially in the United States, because "America is *all* middle class; the whole people being in a condition, both as to education and pecuniary means, corresponding to the middle class here."[7] He saw Tocqueville's warning against a tyranny of the majority as a useful counter against his father's a priori argument in favor of equal and universal suffrage. He knew that this warning had a Tory ring to it and would be exploited by Conservative politicians like Robert Peel, but he refused to dismiss it on that account. He took note of Tocqueville's finding that Americans often overlooked the candidates best qualified to hold office, not only because they were incapable of discriminating merit, but out of indifference and out of jealousy of those who were better educated and more successful. Rapid turnover, moreover, produces instability and prevents statesmanship from becoming a profession:

> There is no body of persons educated for public business pursuing it as their occupation, and who transmit from one to another the results of their experience. There are no traditions, no science or art of public affairs. A functionary knows little, and cares less, about the principles on which his predecessor has acted; and his successor thinks as little about his. Public transactions are therefore conducted with a reasonable share, indeed, of the common sense and common information which are general in a democratic community, but with little benefit from specific study and experience; without consistent system, long-sighted views, or persevering pursuit of distant objects.[8]

Mill worried that the middle-class character of American democracy was not a reliable safeguard because the middle class might be intolerant of individual idiosyncrasy and religious nonconformity. The American Protestants who burned an Ursuline convent were aware that no jury could be found ready to convict them. Rule by the working class would be no better. A working class majority might well interfere with the right of contract and pass laws on mistaken principles of political economy such as those that allow for a minimum wage or a tax on the introduction of machinery.[9]

In later works, especially *On Liberty* and *Considerations on Representative Government*, Mill reiterated and elaborated these concerns and proposed remedies. In *On Liberty* he argued that freedom of thought was the prerequisite of all progress in promoting the general welfare, that the majority cannot be justified in interfering with the liberty of the individual if that liberty is "self-regarding," and that contrary to the prevailing view, the cultivation of individuality is what ennobles humanity: without the creative minority "human life would become a stagnant pool."[10] In *Representative Government* his deepest concern was Platonic in its emphasis on the importance of giving power to those would use it most wisely: "A representative constitution is a means of bringing the general standard of intelligence and honesty existing in the community, and the individual intellect and virtue of its wisest members, more directly to bear on government . . ."[11] The other main danger he saw was that a majoritarian government would produce "class legislation." But he also pointed out that mere exercise of the suffrage did not guarantee that the people as a whole would actually govern themselves or that legislation would promote their best interests. In reality, the people who influenced political outcomes were those who were active, not all who were citizens. Because representatives are not the same as those they represent, they are likely to try to substitute their own judgments for those of their constituents. The remedies he proposed were proportional representation, to nullify the dangers of an overbearing majoritarianism; weighted voting, to allow the educated greater influence; and widespread participation in government, if only in local affairs, in order to assure that everyone has some experience of self-government. In general, as Dennis F. Thompson suggests, Mill's aim was to propose a system of representative government combining competence and participation.[12]

Carlyle and Nietzsche: The Attack On Egalitarianism

Both Thomas Carlyle and Friedrich Nietzsche spoke for those in the nineteenth century who were repelled by the tendencies toward materialism and mediocrity which they believed had been unleashed by the triumph of egalitarianism. The very universe, they thundered in response, echoing the traditional view, is inconceivable without hierarchy. Civilization rests on the achievements of superior individuals—Carlyle's hero and Nietzsche's "overman." Both had nothing but contempt for the mass of mankind, whom they considered an untutored rabble driven by the base promptings of appetite and envy. Both were more bombastic than empirical in their assault, and neither can be said to have propounded a political doctrine that offered an alternative to democracy.

The Calvinist Carlyle denounced liberalism and democracy alike for putting far more emphasis on human rights than on human duties. Parliaments, he contended, were fit only to advise sovereigns, not to command or replace them. Hectoring the aristocracy as a pack of idlers who had neglected their duty to rule, he described the French Revolution as "the open violent Rebellion and Victory, of disimprisoned Anarchy against corrupt worn-out Authority."[13] He also denounced the "dismal science" of economics, with its doctrine of laissez-faire, for focussing human activity only on the achievement of material gain and reducing all human relationships to those of the "cash nexus." His attacks on Manchester economics and the new "Aristocracy of the Moneybag,"[14] coupled with a demand that government take paternalistic care of the laboring classes, won him the plaudits of socialists while earning him the grudging respect of the upper classes for also rejecting socialism. The closest he came to advocating a form of government was to express confidence that only the sort of mysterious "election" by which civilization produced such great men as Mohammed and Luther, and not the mechanical process of democracy, could produce authentic leadership. He spent thirteen years writing a six-volume biography of Frederick the Great, evidently in the belief that Frederick was the closest to a genuine hero-leader the modern age might produce.[15]

Nietzsche was a far more complex and subtle thinker than Carlyle, but he shared with him a contempt for mediocrity and an admiration of those who rise above it by force of will. He saw Western civilization as having been degraded by a revolt against nobility of character. The result had been the triumph of a "slave morality" grounded in resentment of superiors promulgated in Judaism and triumphant in Christianity. Although he was not the political anti-Semite he has sometimes been made out to be, he sought to expose what he thought was the fallacy of the ideal of human spiritual equality central to Judaism and Christianity and in so doing helped nurture the cruder popular view, influential upon Hitler, that the Jews had fostered democracy, with its denial of the belief in heroism and the natural superiority of the Aryan race.[16] Walter Kaufmann has well identified the difference between Carlyle and Nietzsche: "Carlyle, as a historian, finds that great men make history, that society depends on hero-worship, and that without heroes there can be only anarchy which he abhors. For Nietzsche, the overman does not have instrumental value for the maintenance of society: he is valuable in himself because he embodies the state of being for which all of us long; he has the only ultimate value there is; and society is censured insofar as it insists on conformity and impedes his development."[17] Indeed, Nietzsche's ideal of the overman was that of the self-reliant creator, who could tame the "wild dogs" of impulse and express the "will to power" by creating his own values, rather in the way Freud's creative individual would sublimate instinctual drives and achieve self-mastery. In Nietzsche's case, the ideal has a generally aesthetic rather than political character; only "where the state *ends*," Zarathustra proclaims, "can meaningful humanity begin."[18]

Nietzsche's contempt for egalitarianism and for democracy as its political expression had an impact in the twentieth century which was more than aesthetic, however, even among sophisticated readers. In the early decades of the century, before the rise of totalitarianism led to renewed appreciation for democracy, it found an echo in the thinking of such critics as the philosopher George Santayana and the writer H. L. Mencken. Convinced that belief in the governing capacities of ordinary people—"the ignoble conglomerate beneath"—contradicted the naturalness of inequality, Santayana called for a "timocratic" order in which only proven leaders would rule."[19] Mencken, a kind of newsroom Nietzschean, gave vent to a characteristically splenetic contempt for democracy:

> Everywhere its fundamental axioms are accepted: (*a*) that the great masses of men have an inalienable right, born of the very nature of things, to govern themselves, and (*b*) that they are competent to do it. Are they occasionally detected in gross and lamentable imbecilities? Then it is only because they are misinformed by those who would exploit them; the remedy is more education. Are they, at times, seen to be a trifle naughty, even swinish? Then it is only a natural reaction against the oppression they suffer: the remedy is to deliver them. The central aim of all the Christian governments of to-day, in theory if not in fact, is to further their liberation, to augment their power, to drive ever larger and larger pipes into the great reservoir of their natural wisdom. That government is called good which responds most quickly and accurately to their desires and ideas. That is called bad which conditions their omnipotence and puts a question mark after their omniscience.[20]

Nationalism and Imperialism

While such criticisms and denunciations of democracy had the effect of eroding respect for popular government and its philosophic foundations, other political forces had an even more corrosive effect. Among these were the chauvinistic versions of nationalism that spread like a fever in the nineteenth century and often found an outlet in imperialism. The word "nation" entered the language of politics in the age of Enlightenment when it was used to designate the amalgamation of previously often hostile duchies, principalities, and counties by centralizing monarchs. Voltaire, Maurice Cranston points out, thought that it was "the historic achievement of successive French kings to end the anarchy and knit together all these different communities into one *patrie*, royal subjects united by common allegiance and taught to feel a common identity, thus acquiring a consciousness of being French . . . . The Kingdom of France was seen by Voltaire as being transformed from the territory subject to the French crown into the society of people brought together under that crown; in making a civil society the kings had made a nation."[21]

Nationalism had arisen in Europe in the late Middle Ages when the universalism of the Holy Roman Empire lost its hold and people in various communities began to emphasize parochial bonds. Instead of relying solely on Latin, they put more emphasis, in literature and documentation, on the "vulgar tongues." They began to feel a consciousness of belonging to social groupings greater than their families and estates but less inclusive than the *corpus Christianum*. The new feelings are evident in Machiavelli's Italian patriotism. Even though he prides himself on being a Florentine, he issues his famous exhortation to the Medici to unify Italy, drive out the foreigners, and reveal the greatness of which the country is capable. As Machiavelli saw, patriotism could be a potent instrument of unification if it encouraged people to subordinate some of the pride of origin and family that made them antagonists and weakened their resistance to foreign invaders.

As the feudal system was undermined and replaced by a notion of common citizenship, nationalism reinforced the sense of group solidarity. In the constitutional and democratic state, nationalism seemed even more "natural" than in feudal or autocratic conditions because it reflected the popular character of the system and gave cultural reinforcement to political identity. In the absence of a strong sense of nationhood, democracy cannot take hold. Homogeneous groups inhabiting adjoining or the same territory will be unwilling to join together to form a single overarching polity with authority over all, whether the polity is majoritarian or consensual, unitary or federal. Apart from confederation, only an autocratic regime, like that of the Hapsburgs in Austria or of Tito in Yugoslavia, can keep a multi-national state from falling apart. Although well aware that sentiments of nationality arose from feelings of identity of various kinds, Mill treated the question politically, as though it were synonymous with statehood and represented a collective expression of the right of self-determination: "Where the sentiment of nationality exists in any force, there is a *prima facie* case for uniting all the members of the nationality under the same government, and a government to themselves apart. This is merely saying that the question of government ought to be decided by the governed."[22] Giuseppe Mazzini became a champion of such a liberal nationalism, his famous image that of different nations as the fingers of the hand, separate, but working in harmony for the greater good.

Kept separate from the political structure of the state, nationalism can be apolitical; but it is an inherently volatile force which can become a particularly emotional political force. To champions of particular forms of nationalism, the doctrine usually connotes a cultural rather than a political bond, and one that sharply distinguishes one society from another. To belong to a nation—a term that has sometimes been used synonymously with race—is to speak a certain language, or one of its dialects, to be part of a community, usually territorially defined, in which not only language but custom, legends, and mores were shared. Often, it also means to belong to a particular ethnic group and to share one religious affiliation. In some instances, nationality is a form of bonding that enables societies riven by religious conflict to achieve a sense of secular unity. In the aftermath of the Reformation, nationality was sometimes divorced from acceptance of the dominant confession, but where a national church was established non-adherents could be accused of disloyalty to the state and barred from public office. Rising secular nationalism, based more upon romantic notions of language, culture, and ethnicity, restored some of the cohesion lost due to religious dissolution. The nation-state amalgamated cultural or sub-national entities in one political framework allowing for cultural differentiation or enforcing the hegemony of a dominant culture.

Nationalism has thus been a potent force for social integration, but in nineteenth and twentieth century Europe it was also often used to promote xenophobia. Nationalism could serve as a counter-force to democracy because it resembled democracy in its populistic appeal but did not necessarily require respect for democratic norms, institutions, or procedures. It therefore acquired a deceptive similarity to democracy, as an expression of self-determination but without the foundation in universal human rights which could moderate its parochial thrust. For those opposed to democracy, it served as a convenient foil, especially because it stood squarely against the universalism of the belief in human rights. The French reactionary Joseph de Maistre said he knew no universal men, but only Frenchmen, Italians, etc. From the rejection of universal human rights, it is a short step to the reintroduction of other distinctions with domestic bearing. One of these was the distinction drawn by French reactionaries between the "legal nation" and the "real" nation (*le pays légal et le pays réel*)—the nation founded by equal citizenship and language and the one based on common descent. This distinction allowed another one even more exclusive, which was the claim that the aristocracy was the bedrock of the real nation. By encouraging this sort of nationalism, reactionaries used patriotic sentiments to extend the life and appeal of aristocracy. The German nationalist, Arthur Moeller van den Bruck, whose book *Das Dritte Reich* (1922) came to be regarded as a prophecy of the rise of the Nazi state, praised inequality as the necessary basis of national greatness and railed against liberalism as the sponsor of democracy, weakness, and materialism.[23] Joined with and reinforced by imperialism, nationalism became a rationale not only for differentiating one's own society from others, but for asserting superiority over and a right to dominate supposedly inferior societies. Germany's destiny, according to Moeller, was to become synonymous with Europe and to amalgamate kindred peoples into a grander and more powerful *Gesamtdeutschland* or integral Germany.[24]

Racism and Ethnocentrism

Intense and integral nationalism shaded into racism. Race thinking had begun rather innocently in the eighteenth century, inspired by the travel literature resulting from European exploration of other continents. On the basis of the reports of travelers and missionaries, some eighteenth-century theorists fashioned the myth of the noble savage—the idea that there was something noble, pure, and beautiful about the life of uncivilized peoples, compared to the corrupting influence of civilization. It may be thought of as a secularized reworking of the myth of paradise and the expulsion from paradise. Most Enlightenment theorists took a very different view, arguing that civilization, founded on the progress of reason and science, was vastly superior to the life of savages, who were the extant examples of the barbarism Europeans had exhibited while they too still labored under the yoke of superstition and ignorance. By the late eighteenth century, when the idea of progress took hold, the notion that became popular among intellectuals was a combination of these two views. Humanity, it was thought, took various forms, as far as pigmentation was concerned, but in natural capacity all peoples were essentially alike. The savages were simply people at an early stage of development, before the progress of reason transformed them; the duty of the enlightened was to help these unfortunates to see the light and share in the benefits of civilization. But as Europeans began to colonize other continents and to subdue the inhabitants, most imperialists and colonizers took a very different view, justifying their domination either on the basis of the right of the superior to rule the inferior or on the ground that they were moral benefactors, spreading Christianity, assuming "the white man's burden," or undertaking what the French referred to as their *mission civilisatrice*. Sometimes imperialism took a nakedly antidemocratic form, but sometimes it took a democratic guise, as when it was advocated as a way of raising less advanced peoples to a level at which they would be capable of governing themselves.[25]

Race become a subject of interest because European scientists of all sorts had become absorbed in making classifications, often the first stage of scientific activity. Carl Linnaeus, the great biological classifier, turned his attention to the subject for this reason. So did Georges Louis Comte de Buffon, the French naturalist, and Johann Friedrich Blumenbach, the German anatomist. Blumenbach also set about measuring skulls, to see whether he could arrive at a criterion for classifying members of different races. Theorists speculated that there might be a correlation between the position of the head on the spinal column—the angle at which it rested—and ambition for power. This inquiry had some of the character of later racism, but it did not produce any credible evidence that whole groups were different in intellectual capacity. There were hints of what was to come in the work of anatomists and physiologists, some of whom concentrated on the shape of the head, dividing humanity into round heads and oblongs. By the early decades of the nineteenth century, Europeans were fascinated with the subject that became known as phrenology—literally the science of the mind, but actually the effort to prove that the shape of the cranium revealed what went on inside because different faculties were located in different regions. People began to talk learnedly of the mental and psychological differences between dolicocephalic and brachycephalic—long skulls and broad skulls. Some more respectable doctors of medicine and physiologists contended that quite apart from the shape of the head, there were indeed differences of constitution, contrary to the Enlightenment arguments of philosophers like John Locke, Claude A. Helvétius, and Paul Henri Dietrich d'Holbach. The French physiologist Marie François Xavier Bichat suggested that there are three types of people, based on the different emphasis of common functions in their physical constitution, the brain, motor, and sensory. Bichat was among those Napoleon stigmatized as mere *idéologues*, giving the term "ideology" the pejorative connotation it still often carries.

Although it was pseudo-scientific, this research tended to cast doubt on the assumptions of democracy. The Enlightenment view of human beings as fundamentally the same was being challenged by supposedly more scientific theories which promoted a belief in inequality. Locke, Helvétius, and Holbach had argued that because the mind was a *tabula rasa* or blank slate, it could be shaped by education and environment; education would be a great equalizer, breaking the social barrier between the literate and the illiterate, the well-informed and the ignorant. The new theory suggested that mental differences were innate and ineradicable. Other theorists attacked the idea that people were isolated and atomistic, as social contract theory and liberalism seemed to require. Henri de Saint-Simon and Charles Fourier, for example, thought that people must be thought of not so much as discreet individuals but as members of distinct groupings or classes. Among socialists, eighteenth century egalitarian individualism was being overthrown by a fixation on class struggle as the motor of historical change; among conservatives and some liberals it was challenged by a more amorphous blend of nationalism and the belief that competition and inequality were necessary to life and progress.

The writer who enjoyed the dubious distinction of being the first to put forward an influential theory of the role of race in history was Count Arthur de Gobineau, a French nobleman exiled after the revolution who returned to pursue a career as a writer and diplomat and maintained a lengthy correspondence with Tocqueville, his friend and patron. As Tocqueville predicted, Gobineau's four-volume *Essay on the Inequality of the Human Races* had only a lukewarm reception in France but was well received in Germany, if only because it popularized the belief that the Germans were a master race. This idea had been advanced earlier by other writers who saw the history of France as a history of two competing groups—Germanic invaders and indigenous "Gaules." The French nobility was presumably descended from these Germanic invaders and the mass of inhabitants from the conquered Gaules.[26]

Influenced by the romantic novels of Henri Stendhal and Victor Hugo, Gobineau saw himself as a bold iconoclast who would destroy the myth of human equality. As they satirized middle class morality and admired adventurous spirits like their respective fictional protagonists, Julien Sorel and Jean Valjean, so Gobineau set out to overthrow the conventional belief in the universality of mankind and its supposed progress. Humanity, he insisted, was sharply divided by race, and, far from world history being progressive, it was actually a process of degeneration. "We are at the end of European society . . . ," he wrote to a correspondent toward the end of his life, in 1882, "Its present state represents its death agony."[27] He attributed the decline to the adulteration of the blood of the white race responsible for European civilization by that of the dark race of uncivilized Africa.

In support of his thesis, Gobineau set out to show that mankind was divided into three different racial groupings—white, black, and yellow—and that each of them had different traits of character: the white nobility, the yellow fertility and stability, the black sensuality and the artistic temperament. Although he insisted that he was simply describing objective differences, he also contended that the variations showed that the races were not equals. The racist implications emerge blatantly in his descriptive caricatures. The "negroid variety is the lowest," he wrote, "and stands at the foot of the ladder . . . the animal character stamped on the form of his pelvis imposes his destiny from the moment of birth . . . All foods are good to him, nothing disgusts him, nothing repels him. What he desires is to eat, to eat to excess, furiously; no carrion is too revolting to be swallowed by him." The yellow race "has little physical energy, and is inclined to apathy," is practical but uninventive, though superior to the black race. About the white race Gobineau could barely restrain his superlatives: "These are gifted with reflective energy . . . [and] have a feeling for utility, but in a sense far wider and higher, more courageous, more ideal, than the yellow races, . . . greater physical power, an extraordinary instinct for order, . . . a remarkable, and even extreme, love of liberty . . ."[28]

The French nobility, he thought, was a fragment of the Aryans, the most superior subset of the white race, thought to be mentioned in Sanskrit legends as fair conquerors who had come to Europe from India, but the lower strata of the French people were of a different, mongrel order. They "form an abyss over which civilization is suspended," he wrote,[29] antici- pating Nietzsche's description of the overman in *Thus Spake Zarathustra* as a rope stretched across an abyss. Gobineau saw the aristocracy as the upholder of European civilization and the peasants as its enemy within. However beneficial intermarriage might be for the lower races, it was di- sastrous for the superior. Once the blood of a "race of princes" is adulter- ated, the result can only be "a confusion which, like that of Babel, ends in utter impotence, and leads societies down to an abyss of nothingness for which there is no remedy."[30]

Could anything be done to stop the decline? Presumably, the only rem- edy was to maintain racial purity in the superior white race. Democracy stood for racial mixing. "When the majority of citizens have mixed blood flowing in their veins, they erect into a universal and absolute truth what is only true for themselves, and feel it their duty to assert that all men are equal." The egalitarian doctrines of democracy are therefore the poisonous lies of people of mixed race. To be sure, Gobineau noted, some of this is hypocritical. The Americans, for example, profess to be believe in equality but then they turn around and claim superiority for Anglo-Saxons over Indians and the Negroes they enslave. Gobineau scoffed at the idea that all people had the same intellectual capacities, using the standard racist argu- ment that one only had to compare what they had achieved to see the dif- ferences. On the notion that the immigrants to democratic America would merge into a new, stronger hybrid stock, Gobineau heaped even more scorn:

> They are a very mixed assortment of the most degenerate races of olden-day Europe. They are the flotsam of all ages: Irish, crossbred Germans and French, and Italians of even more doubtful stock. The intermixture of all these deca- dent ethnic varieties will inevitably give birth to further ethnic chaos. This chaos is in no way unexpected or new; it will produce no combination which has not already been, or cannot be, realized on our continent. Nothing pro- ductive can result from it, and even when the ethnic combinations resulting from infinite unions between Germans, Irish, Italians, French and Anglo-Sax- ons join in the south with blood there composed of Indian, Negro, Spanish and Portuguese essence, it is quite unimaginable that anything could result from such horrible confusion but an incoherent juxtaposition of the most deca- dent kinds of people.[31]

Tocqueville was appalled by Gobineau's work and after some diplo- matic evasion he told him so bluntly: "Evidently Christianity wishes to make all men brothers and equals. Your doctrine makes them cousins at best whose common father is very far away in the heavens; to you down here there are only victims and vanquished, masters and slaves, due to their different birthrights."[32] Nor would he accept the implication of Gobineau's arguments to the effect that democracy was a uniquely grave threat to liberty and order:

> I have always said that it is more difficult to stabilize and to maintain liberty in our new democratic societies than in certain aristocratic societies of the past. But I shall never dare to think it is impossible . . . No, I shall not believe that this human race, which is at the head of all visible creation, has become the bastardized flock of sheep which you say it is, and that nothing remains but to deliver it without future and without hope to a small number of shepherds who, after all, are not better animals than we are, the human sheep, and who indeed are often worse. You will forgive me when I have less confidence in you than in the goodness and justice of God.[33]

Gobineau's ideas had a powerful if somewhat delayed impact. He was not widely read but he was admired by influential people, notably in Germany where a cult grew up around his work numbering among its devotees the composer Richard Wagner. From their point of view, all that was wrong with Gobineau was that he was too pessimistic, too preoccupied with decline and not enough with renewal. But racism had to be given a more proximate focus. It was only a short intellectual step to a still looser ethnocentrism identifying certain European groups as superior to others or lumping all Europeans into a single homogeneous group in danger of infiltration from inferior peoples moving northward from Africa and the Middle East. For French racists, of course, it was more comfortable to think of all white Europeans as one blood line, but others identified the Nordic races as the true aristocracy. The racism espoused by Hitler blended race with ethnicity, relying on the notion of the Aryan or Germanic race, a term borrowed from philologists, who had identified the roots of most European languages as "Indo-European" or "Indo-Germanic," leading to speculation that Europeans were descended from a conquering group of Aryans from India. Aristocratic nationalism, coupled with ethnocentric racism, became a weapon in the anti-democratic arsenal of ideas, an arsenal used by demagogues promoting new forms of elitism even more effectively than it had been by aristocrats.[34]

Although each national version of racism had its own particular notion of superiors and inferiors, one European people was readily identifiable as a racial enemy within—the Jews. They were vulnerable on several counts. Religious hostility toward Jews was long-standing and universal among followers of all Christian faiths. Judaeophobia had arisen and been maintained by the church authorities and theologians, who promulgated "the teaching of contempt" for Judaism.[35] Throughout the Middle Ages

Jews had been turned into a pariah people, made to wear different dress, including the yellow badge, a stigma borrowed by church authorities (after it had been introduced by an Islamic caliph in the ninth century[36]) and sanctioned by Saint Thomas Aquinas. Forced to live apart in ghettos, forbidden to own land and engage in farming or professions, Jews were allowed to became money lenders while this activity was forbidden to Christians, thus fostering the stereotype embodied in Shakespeare's Shylock while conveniently permitting Jewish financiers to serve a vital economic function. Jewish settlements were viciously attacked during the crusades, as the crusaders stopped off to massacre Jews before doing battle against the infidels. Jewish communities had been uprooted and expelled from England and Spain, after bloody persecutions and forced conversions. Suddenly, thanks to the Enlightenment and the democratic revolutions, they were emancipated in much of Western Europe and began to use long-suppressed talents in ways that made them seem aggressive and too successful. The immigration of poor east European Jews into Germany reinforced old hatreds, leading so prominent a personage as the historian Heinrich von Treitschke to observe ominously, "The Jews are our misfortune."[37] The mid-nineteenth century literary critic Paul de Lagarde went even further, declaring the Jews to be a terrible misfortune for all Europe's peoples and comparing them with vermin, for which the only remedy was extermination.[38]

The fixation on the new role of Jews made it seem as though they were the principal beneficiaries of democratization. Emancipated from all the special disabilities long imposed upon them, they had become equal citizens, with the same rights as others, including the right to practice their religion, to hold property in land, and to pursue any vocation. They thus came to seem the bearers and representatives of modernism and *ipso facto*, in the minds of those who feared dispossession, a threat to all that was traditional. On this account, as well as because of entrenched religious hostility, anti-Semitism became a focal point of racism, and the Jews became a prime target for reactions against democratization. In France, during the Dreyfus affair, the nation became divided between the republican Dreyfusards led by Émile Zola and Georges Clemenceau, and the reactionary anti-Dreyfusards, led by leading figures in the army and the church and rabid anti-Semites like Edouard Drumont. His appallingly venomous and popular diatribe, *La France Juive*, claimed that France was being taken over by its 500,000 Jewish citizens, exaggerating even their number, actually less than 100,000.[39] In Austria, where the Jewish community had became an anomalous "supranational people" in a multi-national state, the parliamentary politician Georg von Schönerer rallied pan-German nationalists with "diatribes against finance Jews, Northern Railway Jews, Jew peddlers, press Jews, Jew swindlers and the like," and Karl Lueger became mayor of Vienna after abandoning an earlier commitment to liberalism and democracy in favor of the same combination of nationalism and anti-Semitism.[40]

Belief in the importance of racial distinctions and in racial superiority became more and more prominent. Houston Stewart Chamberlain, who walked in Gobineau's footsteps but took his argument further, urged Europeans to do more than merely lament racial degeneration. An Englishman enthralled by everything German, who admired Richard Wagner and later married his daughter, he wrote a book on *Lohengrin*, and then, in 1899, a two-volume opus entitled *Foundations of the 19th Century*. Here he goes beyond Gobineau's effort to classify races and lament the decline of civilization by contending that the question to be resolved in the twentieth century is which race would triumph, the Teuton or the Jewish. According to Chamberlain, these were the only two pure races in Europe, and they represented two very different ways of life struggling against each other, only one of which can prevail. In a strangely perverse fashion, indicating both the insecurity and projective character of the impulse behind racism, Chamberlain makes the Jews a model for emulation. Out of the midst of the "Chaos of Peoples," he writes, "towers, like a sharply defined rock amid the formless ocean, one single people, a numerically insignificant people—the Jews. This one race has established as its guiding principle the purity of the blood; it alone possesses, therefore, physiognomy and character." But the Jews are threatening, alien infiltrators, carriers of a debilitating rationalism and materialism. The Teuton, who presumably represents will and spirituality, is "the soul of our civilization;" the real dawn of history would begin when "the Teuton with his masterful hand lays his grip upon the legacy of antiquity."[41]

To Chamberlain, pessimism was unwarranted because a noble race does not decline from its original purity; it only grows more noble. What is important is "consciousness of the possession of race." "The man who belongs to a distinct, pure race, never loses the sense of it . . . Race lifts a man above himself; it endows him with extraordinary—I might almost say supernatural—powers, so entirely does it distinguish him from the individual who springs from the chaotic jumble of peoples drawn from all parts of the world."[42] As with thoroughbred animals, superior races must be bred by "artificial selection." Miscegenation can lead only to the deterioration of the superior race.[43]

Chamberlain's work, though a dense and lengthy excursion through European history, was reprinted twenty-four times. It was considered highly respectable by German conservatives and was popular among German young people before, during, and after World War II.[44] It was directly influential on the thinking of the Nazi ideologist, Alfred Rosenberg, who entitled his book on the party's program *The Myth of the Twentieth Century*.

A Baltic emigré who became well known for his favorable commentaries on the Czarist forgery, *The Protocols of the Elders of Zion*, and for elaborating the need for *lebensraum* as the rationale for German expansion to the east, Rosenberg was said to have prepared extracts from Chamberlain's work for Hitler's study.[45]

Hitler paid respect to Chamberlain and to the rest of the Wagnerite circle, though he came to anti-Semitism directly, especially through his exposure to the agitation against the Jews in Vienna and in Germany after World War I. He made use of Judaeophobia to fashion a notion of the German *Volk* mixing race consciousness with a concept of nationality as cultural identity—one that in effect truncated and polemicized the view of history as the history of folk cultures popularized earlier by Johann Gottfried von Herder.[46] In so doing, he could draw on anti-Semitic feeling to nurture contempt for democracy (as a form of government that had presumably enabled the Jews to win control) and encourage Germans to believe that despite their defeat in World War I, they were a potential master race which could rise up to conquer the world by following him. The obverse of anti-Semitism was the campaign for racial purification. Once Nazi Germany had won the war, Hitler planned to make the elite SS (from *Schutzstaffel*, literally "guard detachment") the bearer of racial purity through the special breeding programs already introduced.[47]

Elitism

Racism was reinforced by a doctrine that came to be called elitism and was also claimed to have "scientific" credence. Elitism arose when the traditional belief in aristocracy—the rule of those of noble descent—was reshaped into a naturalistic and sociological theory. In the largely Protestant countries, the Calvinist doctrine of predestination reworked the traditional understanding of aristocracy to single out the religiously elect, supposedly identifiable by the signs of economic success. In the late nineteenth century, elitism emerged as the secular belief that societies are always governed, despite appearances, by small and usually closed groups reflecting a dominant social force.

Though he did not use the term, the first exponent of the existence of such political elites was Gaetano Mosca, who thought that all societies are governed by a *classe politica* or political class. He is often paired with Vilfredo Pareto, who introduced the idea of the "circulation of elites"—the process by which new elites succeeded older ones.[48] Mosca did not like the use of the word "elite," which Pareto had made popular, because it implied that the political class had intellectual and moral superiority. Mosca asserted only that the political or governmental class has the capacities needed to rule, the skills a society needs at a particular time, whether these be military, priestly or commercial.

Mosca set forth his thesis in part to refute Marx's contention that it was possible to conceive of a future in which there would be no classes and hence no ruling class. Mosca's argument was that a political class was inevitable in every society, and therefore that the Marxist vision of a classless, leaderless utopia was an illusion. The truth is, Mosca argued, that government is always in the hands of a minority which has the characteristics of a coherent group or class:

> In all societies—from societies that are very meagerly developed and have barely attained the dawnings of civilization, down to the most advanced and powerful societies—two classes of people appear—a class that rules and a class that is ruled. The first class, always the less numerous, performs all political functions, monopolizes power and enjoys the advantages that power brings, whereas the second, the more numerous class, is directed and controlled by the first, in a manner that is now more or less legal, now more or less arbitrary and violent, and supplies the first, in appearance at least, with material means of subsistence and with the instrumentalities that are essential to the vitality of the political organism.[49]

By implication, then, there can be no democratic government, and in the strictest sense no monarchy either, because presumably rule by a single individual is a facade for oligarchy. The dominant group, or elite, preserves itself because it absorbs the "social forces" of the time, co-opting potential enemies from among the masses. In every period of history, some functional characteristic determines the basis of membership in the elite. In a primitive society it is the ability to fight and hunt, in feudal times, control of land. In modern times, the middle class emerges, its leaders comprising those who master the tasks of industry and capital accumulation. Thus, each set of social forces tends to assert itself at different stages of history and furnishes the political class. If there is a plurality of social forces, the political class will do well to reflect the society's diversity. In order to gain support, the ruling class uses a "political formula"—a myth or ideology which rationalizes its rule. Pareto spoke of these ideologies as "derivations," by which he meant what are now referred to as rationalizations. The political formula is important, Mosca thought, because it is in human nature to find it easier to submit to an abstract principle than to some human being, who rules because he is fit to do so. Democratic beliefs are designed to lull the masses into accepting rule by the political class. The members of this class face a challenge whenever social forces change and a new group of leaders embodying some unassimilated social force tries to take power. They must either co-opt that new leadership or risk being replaced by it.

Parliamentary government is therefore in effect government by political parties; the question of who governs really turns on the question of who controls the parties. According to the political formula, those who run the parties are supposed to take their orders from the voters. The truth is that "the representative is not elected by the voters but, as a rule, has himself elected by them," or rather that "his friends have him elected."[50] Voters are compelled first of all to choose whether to abstain or to vote for one of the candidates likely to win. The candidate is only a candidate because he is supported by those with money and influence; the voters are forced to choose among those chosen by the political class. Thus, in a so-called democracy, it is those who can organize and deliver voting blocs who hold real power. Mosca does not have in mind only party bosses, but the industrialists who support them financially. He was also not very impressed with the caliber of members of the Italian Chamber of Deputies, who he found were invariably mediocrities. The result is that parliamentary government is weak government, representing an abdication of power on the part of the state.

Although Mosca never retracted his analysis, he did grow to appreciate parliamentary democracy more than he had at first. Later he developed his concept of "juridical defense," by which he meant a system of law that restrained power holders and protected people in their rights, including the right of property.[51] He thought such a system was preferable to rule by a government with absolute power. A liberal political class, because it adopted the principle of juridical defense, was much to be preferred to an absolutist class. While he continued to believed that the political class was necessary to all societies, he added that in parliamentary democracies this class was constantly being renewed from below, in the process fulfilling a representative function, albeit one too weak to provide a government strong enough to control the free market economy.

Mosca's personal trajectory offers a poignant commentary on the consequences of commitments to radical critiques which lead to dangerous experiments. Before composing the final version of his theory, *Elementi di Scienza Politica*, he had presented his thesis in *Teorica dei governi e governo parlamentare*. Once he experienced the rise of Italian fascism, he realized that there was a profound difference between parliamentary systems, with their free elections and protections for liberty and systems in which a single party monopolizes power. He therefore modified the theory, without fully abandoning it, regretting that he had contributed to the disparagement of representative government:

> Fifty years ago the author of this volume opened his career as a writer with a book which was a book of his youth but which he does not disown. In it, he sought to lay bare some of the untruths that lie embedded in certain assumptions of the representative system, and some of the defects of parliamentarism. Today advancing years have made him more cautious in judgment and, he might venture to say, more balanced. His conclusions at any rate are deeply

pondered. As he looks closely and dispassionately at the conditions that pre-vail in many European nations and especially in his own country, Italy, he feels impelled to urge the rising generation to restore and conserve the politi-cal system which it inherited from its fathers.[52]

Roberto Michels is often considered a co-contributor to elite thinking because of his influential formulation of the "iron law of oligarchy."[53] Michels arrived at this law by examining the record of the European move-ment that was supposed to be the most egalitarian or democratic in its objectives—the socialist movement—and discovering that even there in-equality was inescapable. The reason was partly the belief in charismatic authority that Max Weber stressed but even more the need for oligarchy in any organization set to achieve some particular set of goals. This finding seemed so inescapable that even those who professed to be democratic theorists tried to adopt it, notably Walter Lippmann and Joseph Schumpeter.[54] Both developed theories which acknowledged the need for oligarchy and argued that the role of the people should be restricted to choosing their leaders so as not to have unrealistic expectations about what democracy could accomplish. This has been called the theory of "demo-cratic elitism" by Peter Bachrach, who has criticized it as essentially un-democratic because it reduces the role of the ordinary citizen to that of a manipulated spectator.[55]

Social Darwinism

Adding to the onslaught of anti-democratic ideas was Social Darwin-ism, the belief that emerged in the 1860s after the publication and growing popularity of Darwin's work on natural selection. In the interpretation of Herbert Spencer and the other apostles, including the American apostle of *laissez-faire*, William Graham Sumner, Social Darwinism was taken to mean that far from being all equal by nature, some people, like some animals and some species, are "fitter" to succeed in the struggle for survival that seemed to be both natural and, in the logic of the social Darwinist, progres-sive. It was Spencer, not Darwin, who coined the phrase "the survival of the fittest," and it was he who created Social Darwinism, the doctrine that said there was an analogue in society to the evolutionary process based on natural selection in nature. Social Darwinism combined traditional laissez-faire arguments with the new naturalism and the new belief in evolution to produce a potent counter-argument to the liberal and socialist belief in progress based either on human rights or collectivization. It dovetailed with a belief in the superior individual, already popularized in Carlyle's hero-worship. Coupled with the movement for eugenics, based on the work of Darwin's cousin, Francis Galton, it too cast doubt on the egalitarian assump-tions of the democratic ideal.

Social Darwinism had an appeal which undercut the supposedly senti-
mental rather than scientific egalitarianism of democracy. In the United
States in particular, it seemed a perfect counterpart to the belief in the self-
made man, the successful entrepreneur to be immortalized in the Horatio
Alger stories, the robber baron of whom tycoons like Jay Gould, John D.
Rockefeller, and Andrew Carnegie were the prototypes. Apart from the
curious influence he exerted through Beatrice Webb in persuading Fabian
Socialists of the need for managerialism, Spencer was far more influential
in the United States than in his native England.[56]

Forebodings of "Mass Society"

Belief in the inevitability of elites helped inspire forebodings of the rise
of "mass society," another development in social theory sharply critical of
democracy and also promoted as a scientific finding. The various versions
of the theory expounded in the nineteenth and early twentieth centuries
revolve around the view that the appearance of the masses—large groups
of people inhabiting urban environments, generally cut adrift from old roots
and inhibitions, and governed by irrational impulses apt to produce sheepish conformity—is the central defining feature of modern history. The new
mass society does not allow either for the rational individualism which
enabled liberals to embrace democracy or for the proletarian class consciousness which accompanied the socialist version, but promotes an irrational crowd psychology which must turn democracy either into anarchy
or, more likely, into a despotism. While open to criticism on many scores,
the theories deserve attention because they preceded, influenced, and in
some respects predicted the rise of totalitarianism.

Whereas Marxists had referred to the masses with a sense of expectation and even reverence, the theorists of mass society did so with a combination of disdain and fear. Gustave Le Bon's description of the rise of the
masses in 1896 is typical:

> Scarcely a century ago the traditional policy of European States and the ri-
> valries of sovereigns were the principal factors that shaped events. The opin-
> ion of the masses scarcely counted, and most frequently did not count at all.
> To-day it is the traditions which used to obtain in politics, and the individual
> tendencies and rivalries of rulers which do not count; while, on the contrary,
> the voice of the masses has become preponderant. It is this voice that dictates
> their conduct to kings, whose endeavour is to take note of its utterances. The
> destinies of nations are elaborated at present in the heart of the masses, and
> no longer in the councils of princes.[57]

Le Bon and the other theorists of mass society all tend to argue that
democratization, coupled with industrialization and urbanization, produces results very different from the idealized visions of the democratic

philosophers. Liberals counted on democracy to transform ignorant peasants into independent yeoman farmers, governing themselves as Locke, Rousseau, and Jefferson envisioned, whether directly in small communities or through representatives in larger societies. In the socialist version, it was supposed to transform ordinary factory workers, or wage slaves, into conscious, self-determining agents of their own destiny. They were supposed to serve on worker councils and in labor parties, meanwhile educating themselves so as to be able to understand the economic order. Thus Lenin's slogan, "All power to the soviets"—the councils of workers' and soldiers' deputies—and the designation "Union of Soviet Socialist Republics." Power was supposedly to flow upward in accordance with the theory of "democratic centralism." The theorists of mass society contend that what actually happens when democracy is introduced is that the newly emancipated common people do not think and act as rational individuals but as an irrational mob.

For these theorists, mass society is a phenomenon in which individuals lose the sense of special identity which restrains them in class societies. Both the nuclear and extended family tend to dissolve and lose their powerful role. So do the estates and classes into which people were once born without hope of escape. The newly emancipated masses cannot support their liberty. They cannot achieve autonomy and they are hardly as rational as democratic theory supposes. Instead, they are dominated by irrational fears and desires and find security in conformity, not in being independent or different. They form an amorphous mass which can be mobilized by demagogues and tyrants. The old religious myths which gave people security and consolation in times of distress must now compete with more apocalyptic myths, myths that promise the new insecure masses utopia here on earth. Instead of religious messianism, there is political messianism. Similarly, the new creeds promise them revenge against their enemies in the here and now, not just in the hereafter. To make up for their own sense of powerlessness, the masses want an all-powerful state. They want the security of knowing that they are part of some group or group cause that goes beyond themselves, something in which they can find the identity that was lost when the old pre-modern society disappeared. They crave the sense of power they cannot have as separate individuals. They worship authority and appreciate order much more than personal liberty; its members are driven by envy rather than self-respect. They hate everything that reminds them of their inferiority and impotence. They want to bring everything down to their own common level. They demand a mass culture. Its crude appeals to the senses replace traditional folk culture and make high culture the preserve of the aristocrat and highbrow intellectual, for whom they have only contempt. The masses are ripe for manipulation by unscrupulous leaders, usually not from the elite but from the same low ranks as they, leaders who know how to simplify things for them, how to appeal to their emotions, their ethnic chauvinism, who can promise to give them revenge against their supposed enemies and fill their heads with visions of a better world.

When the masses were not marching in armies on the battlefields, they were trooping to the polls, insisting that they were wiser than their supposed betters. Suddenly, it seemed that a new phenomenon had been unleashed which threatened to plunge European civilization into precipitous decline. In the democratic nations a new tyranny would arise of which Napoleon was a foretaste. Despots would rise to power with the support of the masses. Once in power, they would employ the techniques of control made possible by science and mass psychology to turn these masses into robots or worker ants, ready to do whatever the state required of them. Some of these theorists of mass society did not live to see the rise of totalitarian regimes in Europe, but the appearance of these regimes later made them seem prophetic. Not that the theorists of mass society would have been happy to see their prophecies fulfilled. They were themselves usually great believers in eighteenth century ideals of reason and liberty, but not in democracy. Late in the century and early in the twentieth, a flood of writing sought to uncover the psychology of "mass man." Several writers produced popular versions of this theme, including Le Bon, Wilfred Trotter, and Sigmund Freud.[58]

Authoritarianism

These currents in the realm of ideas and ideology served to reinforce skepticism about republican government and democratic values not only among the privileged and well educated, but perhaps ironically also among many of those in the lower strata stigmatized as herd-like masses incapable of self-government. Peasant farmers in particular often resisted the appeals of liberal and socialist parties committed to parliamentary government and social reform and rallied instead both to more traditional conservative parties and to new fascist movements and populist tax-protest parties like the Poujadists in France. But racism directed at internal minorities, nationalism in support of imperialist adventurism, and arguments for order and strong leadership to overcome threats of anarchy and civil war attracted people from all segments of the population to rightist movements. The newer right-wing movements were especially appealing to those fearful of modernization and angry and resentful for other reasons, such as economic hardships. Except in a relatively small number of countries where parliamentary democracy became well established, much of the political history of the twentieth century is dominated by efforts to install and maintain authoritarian regimes, including absolute monarchy (as in the sheikdoms of the Persian Gulf) and, more often, replacements for this older form of autocracy.

All non-democratic systems of government have been labeled "authoritarian" on the ground that they tend to be built upon exclusive control or dominance by a single party, in contrast to the pluralistic, multi-party systems characteristic of political democracy.[59] Psychologists have also attempted to define an "authoritarian personality" as a set of attitudes typical of those who reject democratic values in favor of ethnocentric beliefs and who crave autocratic leadership.[60] The term is also used, as it is here, in a more limited sense, to refer to regimes which, while also autocratic, do not aim to control society so completely as do totalitarian regimes. An authoritarian regime, in this understanding, is one in which political authority is concentrated in a dictator or ruling group (whether a dynastic family, a tightly-controlled party, or a junta) which does not submit itself to free competitive elections. Often such a regime is established by a coup d'état and must rely heavily on the allegiance of the military leadership, which is often the source of counter coups which replace one set of authoritarian leaders with another. The regime usually draws support from powerful groups in civil society, such as churches, large landowners, and other business interests. It may allow for a significant degree of liberty of action and expression, provided no groups or expressions of opinion threaten its rule. Since the regime controls the apparatus of the state, it is likely to exercise considerable control over private activities, including economic activities, so much so that in some forms it becomes corporatist, in the sense that private enterprises and associations, including trade unions, become effectively if not formally agents of the state. In order to preserve its power, it will establish systems of internal security which intimidate potential dissent and are allowed to engage in acts of state terror against conspirators and rebels. The difference between such authoritarian regimes and those that set out to become totalitarian—in the sense that they seek to remove any distinction between the state and civil society and to create a totally state-controlled society—is therefore a difference of degree.

In this more limited sense of the term, the regimes of Spain under Franco, Portugal under Salazar, Greece under the rule of the colonels, and many Latin American, Asian, Middle Eastern and African regimes of this century would be classed as authoritarian. These regimes vary from dictatorial (Spain) to oligarchic (Greece), bureaucratic (Mexico), and populistic (Argentina under Peron, 1945-55, 1973-76). The societies in which they emerge differ even more widely in socioeconomic and cultural terms. But most have in common certain key characteristics. They are usually marked by a relatively low level of economic development, a high concentration of wealth and wide disparity of income, a weakly developed civil society, and a high degree of illiteracy. These socioeconomic conditions are usually reinforced by a civic culture that puts a premium on obedience to authority rather than self-assertion and on unity rather than pluralism. Under these conditions, those with privileges to protect are anxious to support governments that will preserve the status quo, especially when it is threatened by civil war and revolutionary movements, while those who suffer from the status quo are too weak and disorganized to mount effective political challenges, except by joining guerrilla movements which can usually be suppressed. In other cases, however, such as Argentina in the 1930s and the Gulf states in recent times, authoritarianism has emerged in comparatively wealthy states undergoing economic modernization, for reasons that seem to have to do more with such factors as the social composition of the population and cultural traditions than with the degree of economic modernization per se.[61]

Changes in these authoritarian regimes have come about in various ways and for a variety of reasons (to be more fully discussed in chapter ten). In some cases, measures of political liberalization, such as restricted elections intended to strengthen support for the regime among the privileged, turn out to introduce opportunities for the development of opposition. Initial economic development enlarges the ranks of the middle class and professionals and strengthens trade unions, and sustained economic development requires the cooperation of all segments of the population. In other cases, reactions against the oppressiveness of authoritarian rule promote democratic protest and demands for free elections. These demands are often partly inspired by the example of other freer and more prosperous societies, brought into even the remotest villages by film and television. But for most of the twentieth century, authoritarianism served as a barrier to democracy rather than as an agent of transition; only recently has it come under serious challenge, especially in southern Europe, Latin America, and Asia.

Totalitarianism—The Most Radical Antithesis

Totalitarian movements achieved extraordinary success in the first half of the twentieth century. The most prominent were those that came to power in Nazi Germany, the Soviet Union under Stalin, China under Mao Zedong, and Fascist Italy. Although the immediate impetus in the European cases was the clash between extremes of right and left catalyzed by economic and psychological problems resulting from World War I, the standard anti-democratic themes provided rationales for right-wing dictatorship, and the association of democracy with capitalism served revolutionaries on the left as an excuse for a "dictatorship of the proletariat."

These movements were to a considerable extent the outgrowth of the anti-democratic backlash of the nineteenth century. Racism was most conspicuous in Nazi ideology in the form of anti-Semitism. The Nazi ideologist Alfred Rosenberg and Hitler himself claimed that the fate of Europe would rest on the outcome of the struggle between the Aryan and the Semite. On September 3, 1939, when Britain honored its commitment to Poland and declared war against Germany, Hitler explained the British decision to the German people as the result of a Jewish democratic plot: "Our Jewish democratic global enemy has succeeded in placing the English people in a state of war with Germany."[62] He had earlier warned in the Reichstag that if war came, he would hold the Jews responsible and make them pay. Tragically, he remained true to his word, so much so that the extermination campaign was allowed to proceed even though it hurt the German war effort by killing potential slave laborers and using freight cars to transport the victims even up to the last days of the war. In his final testament, written as Soviet troops were closing in on his Berlin bunker, Hitler ended as he had begun, blaming the war on "international Jewry" and its agents.

When racism plays so important a part in an ideology, the likelihood is that it is the expression of some deeper need for an enemy against whom to focus popular resentment. Important as it is to recognize the depth of the influence of anti-Semitism on Hitler's thinking, it is plausible to suppose that if there had been no Jews, he would have found some other target against which to focus popular hatred. He made clear that after he had eliminated the Jews, he would take steps to subdue and remove, if not eliminate, the other supposed European *"Untermenschen"* (literally, gangsters or thugs), notably the Slavs. The Nazi example shows that racism can serve a function for the enemies of democracy as a way of dividing the opposition and winning support for a repudiation of the ideal of human rights that lay behind the emancipation and toleration of groups previously discriminated against, such as the Jews. Nationalism of the highly chauvinistic sort was certainly a factor in promoting right-wing totalitarianism , but explicit racism was a prominent factor only in the Nazi case. It played only a minor role in the rise of Italian fascism (a movement in which some Jews early on played prominent roles) and none in the rise of Spanish fascism.

Nazism was part of a broader European tendency to embrace fascism, a word that came from the Italian term for combat groups, *fasci di combattimento*. Those who belonged to these combat groups were called the *Fascisti*. *Fascismo* in Italy also had a strong connotation of togetherness. The Nationalist Party associated the term with the old Roman symbol of authority, the fasces, or rods, which were tied together and used to chastise offenders. The Fascists borrowed this usage from the Nationalists because they wanted to associate themselves with the glory of Rome. Italian fascism encouraged nationalist fervor largely for the sake of justifying militaristic unity and imperial expansion into Africa. There was more than an element of racism in this national chauvinism as in other forms of imperialism, but Italian fascism was promoted by its adherents more in nationalistic than racial terms.

Another strand of anti-democratic thought, elitism, was important to Italian fascism, partly because it was a homegrown belief, but also because it seemed to justify the overthrow of the parliamentary system. If parliamentary democracy was an illusion, according to the best political sociologists, then why fight to save it? And why become a socialist if socialism too would produce elitism despite its egalitarian pretensions? Mussolini was very explicit in repudiating democracy for elitism. Democracy, he claimed in 1922, had been utterly discredited in the nineteenth century; the twentieth would belong to fascism as the rule of the few best:

> The immense historical importance of the Great War lies in the fact that this democratic war par excellence, which was supposed to achieve its immortal principles for all nations and classes—shades of Wilson's famous fourteen points and the sad, sad, decline of the Prophet!—this democratic war, then, ushers in the century of anti-democracy. The chief epithet of democracy is *all*, a word which has completely filled the nineteenth century. The time has come to say: the few and the *elite*. Democracy is on its last legs in every country in the world; in some of them, as in Russia, it was murdered; in others it is falling prey to increasingly obvious decadence. It may be that in the nineteenth century, capitalism needed democracy; today it has no such need. The War was revolutionary in the sense that it liquidated—in rivers of blood— the century of democracy, the century of majority, of numbers, of quantity.[63]

Fascism would replace democracy because democracy rests on the fallacious belief in human equality and majority rule, which is actually a myth: "By democratic regimes we mean those in which from time to time the people is given the illusion of being sovereign, while true effective sovereignty lies in other, perhaps irresponsible and secret, forces."[64]

The totalitarian experiments of the twentieth century both drew upon and seemed to vindicate the theories of mass society. If, as the theorists claimed, human psychology was governed by instinct and emotion, and if, especially under modern conditions, individuals freed from previous forms of social organization could not sustain their independence but would form an amorphous mass craving a leader, democracy could not be sustained. Only dictatorship could enforced discipline, respond to the craving for order and authority, and provide a secular myth to inspire sacrifice.

The phenomenon of totalitarianism has taken a variety of forms, but all the manifestations have in common the complete rejection of democracy and everything it stands for. Sometimes propagandists of the various forms seem not to reject democracy entirely, as when they emphasize the solidarity and popular character of the regime. Hitler called his doctrine *völkisch* or popular. The east European dictatorships called themselves "people's democracies," presumably to distinguish them from regimes that were formally democratic but were actually controlled by plutocracies. Giovanni Gentile, the philosopher of Italian fascism, claimed that the Fascist state "is a popular state, and in this state, the democratic state *par excellence.*"[65] But Gentile was too intelligent not to realize he was engaging in a semantic charade, a cynical tribute that vice pays to virtue by adopting its name while denying its substance. The term totalitarianism arose in Italy, possibly having come from the French, though the French dictionaries are eager to give the credit to Italy. Benito Mussolini first used the word in public in 1925 in a speech attacking the remnants of opposition in the Italian Chamber of Deputies, speaking of *"la nostra feroce volontà totalitaria"* ("our fierce totalitarian will"). He did not invent the word, however, that dubious honor belonging to Gentile, who early that year had spoken of fascism as "a total conception of life." Opponents of fascism used the term as a pejorative to describe the dictatorial and dishonest practices of the fascists. Mussolini came to like the word and used it regularly, proudly describing the Italian state as *lo stato totalitario.* He and Gentile collaborated in writing an official exposition of fascist doctrine and the word appears in the two sections of the document, the first describing the fascist movement, the second the government pursued by the Fascist Party.[66]

In Germany, the word also appeared but did not stick. In 1931 Carl Schmitt—a political theorist sometimes considered the equivalent in the early period of Nazism for Gentile—discussed the National Socialist idea of the totalitarian state, but Hitler was not comfortable with the term, preferring *Autorität*, a word with a more traditional and satisfying ring for Germans. In the Soviet Union, the word was applied only to fascist regimes, never to the Soviet state, which was depicted as the penultimate stage in the emancipation of the proletariat, to reach final fulfillment in the passage to communism. In English usage, the word "totalitarian" has caught on to some extent and is usually understood to refer to doctrines or regimes which aim at being all embracing, or at wiping out the distinction between the public and the private, the state and civil society. A totalitarian ideology is usually defined as a political doctrine which its adherents embrace completely and which in turn embraces them completely. It leaves no room for competing ideologies and the state it rationalizes aims to control the whole of social life.[67]

Mussolini made the denial of individual rights explicit in defining fascism: "The world seen through Fascism is not this material world which appears on the surface, in which man is an individual separated from all others and standing by himself, and in which he is governed by a natural law that makes him instinctively live a life of selfish and momentary pleasure."[68] Having begun his political life as a socialist, Mussolini in effect borrowed the socialist critique of liberal democracy as a system of belief that aims to rationalize selfish hedonism. He was equally clear in defining the Fascist alternative: "The man of Fascism is an individual who is nation and fatherland, which is a moral law, binding together individuals and the generations into a tradition and a mission, suppressing the instinct for a life enclosed within the brief round of pleasure in order to restore within duty a higher life free from the limits of time and space: a life in which the individual, through the denial of himself, through the sacrifice of his own private interests, through death itself, realizes that completely spiritual existence in which his value as a man lies."[69]

This is the essence of the difference between democracy and totalitarianism in caricatured form. If democracy requires respect for human dignity and freedom, totalitarianism compels its subjects to surrender freedom and become instruments of some larger whole. In order to maintain as complete a control as possible, the totalitarian state inevitably becomes a police state relying on state terror. Its police organs, like the Gestapo and the KGB, become all pervasive, and rely on the threat of imprisonment and execution, as well as torture, to suppress dissent and opposition. State terror becomes a standard practice. Opposition is kept from developing by the very pervasiveness of the security forces, by the encouragement of informers, and by the climate of fear that inevitably results when people do not know whether they will be overhead in their own homes, turned in by a neighbor or their own son in the Hitler Youth for some off-hand remark, and when they know that the punishment will be much worse than social disapproval or the equivalent of a slap on the wrist. In totalitarian countries defense lawyers represent the state, not the individual, and are apt to demand a higher penalty than the prosecutor asks for.

To the same end of acquiring absolute control, the regime stamps out all opposition, and uses education and culture as propaganda tools to create new attitudes and standards of behavior incorporating its values and deprecating alternatives. Mussolini was especially frank about this requirement:

> [Fascism] is not simply a mechanism which limits the spheres of the supposed liberties of the individual. It is the form, the inner standard and the discipline of the whole person; it saturates the will as well as the intelligence. Its principle, the central inspiration of the human personality living in the civil community, pierces into the depths and makes its home in the heart of the man of action as well as of the thinker, of the artist as well as of the scientist: it is the soul of the soul.[70]

This intention of remodelling society means in practice that the totalitarian state puts enormous emphasis on the control of information and the media of communication and entertainment. The aim is to purge all the old corrupt ideas and install only the new "pure" thoughts that reflect the aims of the state. Hitler entrusted this task to Joseph Goebbels, his propaganda minister, the man who invented the idea that one should never bother with small lies; the bigger the lie, he said, the harder it is to deny it and therefore the more readily it will be believed. Goebbels made sure that the only films shown in German theaters inculcated the Nazi message, that politically unreliable actors and directors were sent packing, that art the Nazis considered degenerate was banned, that books they disliked were removed from libraries and burned in bonfires set by Hitler Youth. The Nazi authorities even put on a "degenerate art" exhibit including works by outstanding artists that backfired because it proved to be the most popular art exhibit in the regime's history. Hitler pressed the radio manufacturers to come up with a cheap model that everyone could afford. They produced a *Volksempfänger* or "people's receiver" that sold for seventy-six marks (then about thirty dollars) and another that sold for half as much that could receive only domestic broadcasts. Seventy percent of German homes acquired a radio and Hitler made very effective use of it. Radio loudspeakers were installed in factories and beer halls and work was halted when an important program was broadcast. Every neighborhood had radio wardens who made sure people listened only to the right broadcasts and reported their reactions.[71]

The Soviet rulers were if anything even keener on using propaganda to rear the "new socialist man." To this end they mandated the rewriting of history in accordance with the party line, the censorship of books and magazines, attacks on religion as the opiate of the masses, the jamming of foreign broadcasts, etc. The most insidious result was that intellectuals began practicing self-censorship, conforming their views to what they knew or hoped would be acceptable in order not to run afoul of the censors.

Uniforms are very much favored in totalitarian regimes, as are gymnastic extravaganzas and marching, all of them designed to give people a sense of being parts of a large and perfectly organized society. The Italians introduced the fascist salute, modeled after the old Roman salute, and Hitler liked it and produced his version. The dramatic new swastika which he designed into the Nazi flag had the same function. Old songs are put aside and new ones introduced, like the catchy Nazi "*Horst Wessel Lied*," with its bloodthirsty anti-Semitic lyrics, or like the equally tuneful Italian song, "*Giovanezza*," which competed with the socialists' "*Internationale*" and "*Biandèra Rossa*" and celebrated the youthful appeal of the movement. In Spain, the communists had the better songs; Franco's Falange was not as much given to rousing militancy but was much more a party of order, allied with the Church and opposed to everything modern, whether liberal, socialist, or anarchist.

In order to consolidate power and maintain it, the totalitarian regime sets out to coordinate all sectors of society to serve the purposes enunciated by the state. The leadership is not interested in allowing people to do as they please but rather in imposing discipline and the will to serve the state. Mussolini promised he would restore discipline and make the trains run on time. Hitler put the unemployed to work building *Autobahnen* and armaments, lifting Germany out of the depression by forced draft, enrolling young people in the Hitler Youth and the *Bund Deutsche Mädchen*. The regime was careful to give people a sense that life was much better under the new order. Hitler approved plans for Dr. Ferdinand Porsche to design the Volkswagen, a car that was to enable the masses to make use of the autobahns they were building. In the Spartan tradition, everyone ate one dinner a month together — the *eintopf* (one-pot) meal, a barley soup which in its very lumpiness gave people a physical taste of the solidarity of the social bond.[72]

The Soviet and Chinese Communists emphasized the unity of class. Everyone was to feel a bond of proletarian solidarity. All other social classes were the enemies of the revolution, and someone who was descended from aristocrats or bourgeois merchants was automatically suspect when he applied for admission to school or for a job. "We recognize nothing private," Lenin told young Communists in 1920. "Our morality is entirely subordinate to the interests of the class struggle of the proletariat . . . We do not believe in eternal morality."[73] The new socialist man would feel solidarity with the proletariat of other countries, in line with Marx's slogan, "Workers of the world unite, you have nothing to lose but your chains."

The effort to create a totalitarian state requires active campaigns to assure that virtually every aspect of thought and behavior and all social institutions are made to serve the purposes of the state, by whatever means are available, including both conditioning and ruthless coercion. The Nazi *Gleichshaltung*, whereby everything from religion and education to sporting activities was subordinated to state purposes had its parallel in the Bolshevik effort to forge a "new Soviet man" by directing schooling, providing anti-religious propaganda, and making sporting activities and entertainment functions of the state subordinated to its ends.

The very importance of a unitary mission in such societies makes it likely that they will be aggressive in wanting to spread their control over others or in helping others, as they see it, to liberate themselves and join their fraternity. Gabriele d'Annunzio, the poetic nationalist who helped prepare the ground for Fascism by appealing to the emotions of the people and by leading military campaigns for Italian expansion, said: "Civilization is nothing but the glory of incessant struggle. When man is no longer a wolf for other men, a nation will and always must be a lioness to other nations . . . Let us assert it and exalt it. Italy is great and wishes to become greater."[74]

Filippo Marinetti, the poet leader of the group called the Futurists which captured the spirit of fascism in the early years, said: "We want to glorify war—the only cure for the world—militarism, patriotism, the destructive gesture of the anarchists, the beautiful ideas which kill, and contempt for woman . . . We want to demolish museums and libraries, fight morality, feminism, and all opportunist and utilitarian cowardice . . . Standing on the world's summit we launch once again our insolent challenge to the stars!"[75] The Fascist state, he declared, must be "a power that makes its will felt abroad, making it known and respected, in other words, demonstrating the fact of its universality in all the necessary directions of its development. It is consequently organization and expansion . . . Thus it can be likened to the human will which knows no limits to its development and realizes itself in testing its own limitlessness."[76] In a pointed repudiation of Kant's prophecy of perpetual peace, Mussolini adopted Marinetti's glorification of war as an essential tenet of fascism: "[Fascism] believes neither in the possibility nor in the utility of perpetual peace. It repudiates the doctrine of Pacifism—born of a renunciation of the struggle and an act of cowardice in the face of sacrifice. War alone brings up to their highest tension all human energies and puts the stamp of nobility upon the peoples who have the courage to meet it . . . It is education for combat, the acceptance of the risks which it brings; it is a new way of life for Italy . . . [The Fascist] looks on life as duty, ascent, conquest . . ."[77]

Totalitarianism in Retrospect

There are similarities as well as differences in the ways totalitarian systems arose in Europe. They all appeared in conditions of chaos, but the conditions were somewhat different. Bolshevism came to power largely as a result of the defeat of the czarist regime in World War I. In the chaos that resulted, it was able to take advantage of general discontent, especially in the army, and ally with other larger groups to seize power. Once power had been taken away from the czar and a provisional government formed, which set out to be democratic, the Bolsheviks seized control of it by force and suspended the parliament and installed their own dictatorship of the proletariat. They consolidated their power by ruthlessly suppressing all opposition and purging their own ranks. Stalin proceeded on the calamitous collectivization of agriculture, causing the deaths by violence or starvation of at least fifteen million citizens, and erected a regime based on purges, terror, and propaganda. Under the same Marxian inspiration, the Maoist movement gained power in China, after the country had been racked by invasion, and proceeded to install another version of a single-party dictatorship bent on total control.

Similarly, Mussolini's movement came to power as an indirect result of the turmoil that followed World War I. Although Italy was one of the victors, many Italians felt cheated out of their share of the spoils. A sense of indignant nationalism created the preconditions for the rise of fascism. Fear that socialism would arise out of the turmoil among a populace not attached to liberalism also helped generate support. The parliamentary system was weak and uncertain, the constitutional role of monarchy unclear. But Mussolini had dismal success in parliamentary elections and took power by seizing it after vicious street fighting between Socialists and Fascists, when the Fascists finally staged a March on Rome in 1922—a march in which he waited for word that the coup had succeeded so that he could arrive by train when he knew it was safe to do so.

In Germany, too, Hitler started his campaign by appealing to other World War I veterans to repudiate the harsh terms imposed by the Versailles treaty. When the great depression arose in Germany, his appeal gained force. In 1932, shortly before Hitler came to power, there were six million people unemployed in Germany as a result of the depression, and only two million of these were covered by unemployment insurance. The previous runaway inflation had wiped out people's savings so they had no cushion to fall back on. It was easy to blame the government, especially since Germany did not have a long tradition of parliamentary democracy. Before 1918 Germany had had a strong monarchy, buttressed by a deep-rooted authoritarian tradition in every institution, from the family to the church and the academy. The Weimar regime could easily be depicted as having been foisted on the country by the victors. Conservative forces supported the Nazis out of fear of Bolshevism. Communists and Socialists controlled the trade unions; a brief communist revolution had seized power after the war in Bavaria; and there had also been a socialist elected to the leadership of the Weimar regime. There was fighting in the streets between the forces of left and right that the government was virtually powerless to stop.

But Hitler did not come to power by a revolution against the Weimar regime. When he did attempt a coup, in the 1920s, his effort was thwarted and he was jailed, although it was altogether too comfortable a jail because the authorities were sympathetic to war veterans like Hitler, allowing him to write *Mein Kampf*, the autobiographical manifesto that was to win him popular support. He eventually came to power by winning enough votes in general elections to force the other parties to deal him in. They expected to be able to manipulate him, especially when the new president, the war hero Field Marshal Paul von Hindenburg was the one who appointed him chancellor. Hitler outfoxed his conservative allies, making use of his new respectability to win even more votes.

Nazi sentiment was strong even in the universities. In 1927 the student organizations voted by 77 percent to ban non-Aryans from membership.[78] By 1931, Hitler's support in the universities was twice what it was in the country generally, a sobering reminder that academics are hardly immune to irrational enthusiasms. The leading German philosopher, Martin Heidegger, became a member of the Nazi Party and, as a reward, the rector of Freiburg University. When the Nazis came to power the intellectuals and students who were not forced to emigrate cooperated with the propaganda ministry to gather the books that Goebbels ordered consigned to bonfires in public ceremonies—books by such authors as Heinrich Heine, Thomas Mann, Jack London, and Albert Einstein.

In 1930, when many Germans still underestimated him, Hitler received 6.4 million votes or 34.3 percent of the vote, which gave him 107 deputies and made the Nazis the second largest party in the parliament. In March 1933, he and his nationalist allies won 51 percent of the vote, though his own party still fell short of an absolute majority, with 44 percent of the votes. When he had enough support, he proceeded to crush democracy altogether. That was the last free election Germany had during the Third Reich.

In Spain, as in Germany, the republic was also a recent phenomenon, and Francisco Franco, as an army general, was able to win support from the church and the old nobility and take advantage of the divisions within the republican ranks. His cause was also aided by the refusal of the liberal democracies to come to the aid of the republic, leaving only the Soviet Union to supply arms to the loyalists while Hitler and Mussolini used the Spanish civil war as an opportunity to rehearse for what was to come. The Spanish case was different in other respects as well. Some of the forces on the republican side were intensely anticlerical and carried out atrocities against the churches and the clergy. Others were so intent on revolution that even during the war they were more interested in seizing farms and industries than in uniting with other loyalists to stop the fascists. The republican government was indecisive in opposing the army mutiny, and it was weakened too by its own failure to introduce the kind of social legislation that could have kept workers from giving greater loyalty to syndicates led by anarchists and communists.

Although he shared the ideology of fascism, Franco's efforts to remake Spain were less thoroughgoing than those of either Mussolini or Hitler. He did not set out initially to impose some new order so much as to restore an old order. Still, once he and his Falange took over, with the help of fascist movements elsewhere, their behavior resembled that of other similar movements and might have done so even more had Franco not been wise enough to keep Spain neutral in the war and had Germany and Italy not been defeated. As it was, Spanish fascism could keep control and pass it to the monarchy which allowed itself to be constitutionalized so that Spain could join the rest of the Europe.

To assess the strengths and weaknesses of these movements, it is important to appreciate that they had their strongest appeal when democracy seemed unworkable but also that they themselves exhibited potentially fatal flaws. Their positive appeal was the promise of unity and order. Once in power, the force and terror they were willing to use in order to maintain themselves made resistance difficult or impossible. Because totalitarian regimes are dictatorial, however, they are vulnerable to weakening and collapse once the dictator dies or is deposed. Spanish fascism effectively died with Franco, although by then it had become distinctly unfashionable in Europe and Spaniards were anxious to become part of western Europe to gain economic advantages. Franco permitted technocrats to start modernizing the economy, but the regime itself could not be tampered with while Franco was alive. The Soviet Union began to disintegrate in the aftermath of the death of Stalin. Hitler's thousand-year *Reich* also died with him, as did the imperial dreams of his ally, Mussolini. Hitler's *Götterdämmerung* was brought about by his insatiable appetite for expansion. In a sense, this is the fatal flaw of totalitarianism: the dictators it nurtures are tempted to overreach themselves. Hitler insisted on going to war when his generals thought the country was still not ready. When he proved right at first, they could not resist him when he decided on a disastrous two-front war. The Soviet rulers also overreached themselves by acquiring an empire they could not sustain, and by building a state-controlled economy too inefficient to produce the goods they promised. But the regime could not be overthrown from within, and began to change only because the leadership itself decided it had to be reformed it they were to retain power. The problem faced by totalitarian regimes when the leadership feels a need to remove and replace the prevailing dictator is an inherent weakness. The Soviet party leaders learned this lesson when Nikita Khruschev told the twentieth party congress not only some of the truth about the crimes committed by Stalin, but also of how powerless the party hierarchy was in trying to oust him.

The revelation of these grave defects, coupled with the devastation resulting from the rise of Nazism, and the subsequent disillusionment with Soviet and Maoist-style socialism has produced a profound and widespread revulsion against totalitarianism. Even cynics convinced of the weaknesses of democracy have had second thoughts about the wisdom of experimenting with alternatives. The post-war contrast between the stability, freedom, and prosperity achieved in democratic societies and the stagnation and repressiveness of most autocracies has sparked a new and broad interest in democracy.

Theory

7

Modern Democracy: Compound Autonomy

In sharp contrast to the autocratic alternatives, democracy aims to empower all citizens in equal measure. However short of this aim actual democracies may fall, it is this goal—the goal of autonomy—that characterizes them most centrally in both normative and empirical terms. The analysis of modern democracy must therefore begin with the analysis of the meaning of autonomy and of the means by which it is realized. From this preliminary analysis certain requisites follow: 1) the moral ideal of individual autonomy; 2) a civic culture appropriate to democracy; 3) the coexistence in demarcated spheres of civil society and public government; and 4) a system of popular, constitutional government based primarily on elective representation but also on direct participation.

Compound Autonomy

Modern democracy may be thought of as a compound of the three variant forms of autonomy: communal, plural, and individual. Communal autonomy finds expression in patriotism, national self-determination, and in the acceptance of an overriding sense of the common good or the public interest as a standard of loyalty. Plural autonomy takes form in the organization of sub-groups of citizens based on shared affinities of identity, interest, and belief. Individual autonomy consists both of the right of citizens to be left alone to pursue ends of their own choosing and of their right to arrive at their own political judgments and act upon those judgements with full independence. Each form of autonomy has its own strengths and weaknesses, from the point of view of social harmony, political stability, and the balance of liberty. All modern democracies give expression to the compound, but in different measure, and there is likely to be disagreement as to the proper balance among the variants. Claims on behalf of each form of autonomy lead to constant tension, as the rights of individuals and groups must be weighed against the civic good. The coexistence of the variants, however, allows for a mix of personal, group, and corporate creativity and interaction that gives democracy its special character and distinguishes it most fundamentally from all forms of autocracy.

The compound autonomy of democracy exhibits itself in norms, institutions, and procedures. Normatively, democracy is grounded in the belief in the moral autonomy of the individual. This normative belief is enshrined in the belief in universal human rights and inculcated in norms of conduct often referred to as the democratic civic culture. The institutional structure consists in the coexistence of civil society and public government. In civil society, groups form associations to achieve separate ends—voluntary associations which may be freely entered and freely dissolved. Privately held resources allow for the independence of media and interest groups. Public government enables citizens to unite to achieve common ends and to protect the rights of individuals. Under modern conditions, representative government is more practical than direct democracy, but participatory democracy remains important in promoting citizen involvement. Representative government may be either presidential/congressional or parliamentary. Political parties mediate between the two spheres, enabling interest groups to influence public policy but compelling them to strike bargains and take account of larger social concerns, and providing opportunities for citizens with multiple and cross-cutting identities and interests to join in choosing candidates and to find common ground on the issues. The media of communications allow for access to information and the debate of public issues. Procedural democracy, especially in the form of voting and elections, keeps public government responsive, but the various types of electoral systems reflect differing views of the emphasis that should be placed on the variant forms of autonomy. This chapter will review these dimensions and variations in order to provide an ideal-typical description of modern democracy.

The Normative Foundation: Kantian Rational Justice

The question of whether and how a normative foundation of democracy can be established is a subject of continuing discussion and debate. Some philosophers argue for a reliance on natural law and its corollary, natural rights, others for Utilitarianism, a few, such as Hume and Rousseau, on the common capacity for moral sentiment and empathy. Still others contend that in view of the ineluctable disagreement over ultimate values, democracy must rest on agreements over the procedures by which decisions can be reached by reasoning and deliberation. Immanuel Kant's moral theory offers a strong philosophical case for the view that the democratic premise of universal moral autonomy is best grounded on the common human capacity for rational judgment, as it is given effect by the motive force of will in a context of social interdependence.

Kant sought a foundation for social contract theory that removed the need to rely either on natural law or moral sentiment. In effect, he argued that by reason alone it can be shown that moral conduct must be defined as adherence to maxims capable of being practiced universally. Human beings are capable of moral autonomy because they are capable of reason. They achieve moral autonomy when they follow the maxims reason dictates—the "categorical imperative," rather than the "heteronomous" influences of interest, desire, or external compulsion. Thus, while the freedom characteristic of human beings makes it possible for them to will whatever they choose, that freedom only becomes autonomous when it is used to regulate behavior in accordance with the dictates of reason. When it is autonomous, as Ernst Cassirer explains,

> the will submits to no other rule than that which it has itself set up as a universal norm and proposed to itself. Wherever this form is achieved, wherever individual desire and wish know themselves to be participants in and subject to a law valid for all ethical subjects without exception, and where on the other hand they affirm that this law is their own, then and only then are we in the realm of ethical questions . . . The concept of such a rational being, which must be regarded as legislating universally by all maxims of its will so as to judge itself and its actions from this perspective, leads directly to the correlative conception of a community of rational beings in a "realm of ends." If all rational beings stand under the law so that, in constituting their personhood, they are in relation with the moral individuality of others, and so that they demand the fundamental worth which they thus grant themselves from every other subject and acknowledge it in all other subjects, from this there springs a "systematic union of rational beings through common objective laws."[1]

Kant advanced his view of autonomy in several works, especially the *Foundations of the Metaphysics of Morals*, but also in his "Essay on Theory and Practice," a critique of Hobbesian social contract theory, and an essay expounding a philosophy of history, "Idea for a Universal History with Cosmopolitan Intent."

In the *Foundations* he follows Rousseau in emphasizing will rather than reason as the foundation of moral action, but he assigns the reasoning faculty the critical role of formulating rules and taking account of consequences. His basic assumption is that nature does nothing without a purpose, and therefore that in providing each of us with a will of our own, nature gives us the means to achieve our well being or happiness. Reason alone would not have been sufficient for this purpose because reason by itself does not provide springs of action. Reason enables us to contemplate what happiness requires and what our will is like, but it cannot actually move us to act in such a way as to bring about our fulfillment; that is the function of the will. On its negative side, reason may induce us to saddle ourselves with excessive wants. Even when it leads to scientific breakthroughs, each breakthrough opens another application which encourages us to want to do or to need something new. While many of the advances contribute to human welfare, the judgment of what constitutes happiness and well being is not the function of reason alone, and action, while it must be informed by reason, is not directly a function of reason. The basis for the achievement of happiness must therefore be the will, which is served by reason as its guide and instrument.

But if the will is to be good as well as a guide to happiness, it must be governed by what Kant refers to as "law in general." This is the fundamental principle that leads him to formulate his justly celebrated "categorical imperative": "I should never act in such a way that I could not also will that my maxim should be a universal law."[2] This formula amounts to a restatement of the moral theory advanced by Rousseau and indicates why Kant thought of Rousseau as "the Newton of the moral world" and kept a bust of him as the only ornament of his simple study.[3] Rousseau had argued that morality arises from the human impulse to compassion or sympathy. Kant refers to this impulse as will or good will and sees it as the source of law in general. The test of whether a given rule is just or lawful is whether it embodies the idea that what is in the interest of one is in the interest of all. Rousseau believed that a maxim which passed this test could be considered an expression of the general will; Kant's categorical imperative involves exactly the same consideration. It represents an objective principle or a command of reason but can be discerned better by "ordinary reason" than by philosophy because, Kant observed, philosophy always proposes a multitude of considerations foreign to the immediate question of right and wrong. Morality is therefore something ordinary thinking people can come to by the exercise of will informed by reason.[4] Another way to put Kant's view of morality is to observe, as William A. Galston does, that "for Kant, virtue cannot even be defined without reference to all men or all rational beings; it is intrinsically social. . . Kant's rational being cannot act without considering the totality of human beings. Every man acts alone, but for all men."[5]

To explain and vindicate his belief in the categorical imperative, Kant offers a number of examples. Someone who despairs of life might be inclined to commit suicide, but if he inquires whether his action could become a general rule, he would be compelled to recognize that the result would be the destruction of life. Since the nature that creates life and permits its reproduction cannot logically wish its destruction, suicide cannot be considered a general law of nature. Similarly, borrowers should not borrow money knowing they cannot repay it because if everyone were to behave in this way, no one would believe anyone's promise to repay a loan and the confidence necessary to any system of credit would disappear. By asking what is necessary to maintain human life and social intercourse, we can presumably learn what our duties are and by implication what rights we must respect in others: "The will is thought of as a faculty of determining itself to action in accordance with the conception of certain laws. Such a faculty can be found only in rational beings. That which serves the will as the objective ground of its self-determination is an end, and if it is given by reason alone, it must hold alike for all rational beings."[6]

The practical upshot is expressed in another of Kant's celebrated formulas applying the categorical imperative: "Act so that you treat humanity, whether in your own person or in that of another, always as an end and never as a means only." We may therefore not transgress the life, liberty, or property of another, because to do so would be to use others as means not ends, whereas "as rational beings, they must always be esteemed at the same time as ends."[7] The crimes against humanity that Hannah Arendt had so much in mind when she called for a new construction of universal human rights[8] would clearly be proscribed.

For Kant, however, unlike traditional religious philosophers, or philosophers relying on transcendental sanctions, people who fulfill these duties do so not because they follow the commands of some higher power but because they recognize the force of the categorical imperative and live accordingly. They are, in his understanding of the term, autonomous rather than "heteronomous"—not subject to contingent and empirical influences but to the dictates of pure universal reason; and there is no contradiction between their individual autonomy and that of all others.

Kant was well aware that these metaphysical foundations have implications for society and politics. The civic state, he writes in his polemic against Hobbes, must be based on certain a priori principles:

1. The freedom of each member of society as a man.
2. The equality of each member with every other as a subject.
3. The autonomy of each member of a commonwealth as a citizen.[9]

These conditions are the only ones consistent with the rational principle on which it is possible to conceive of human beings entering into a social compact. In advancing this argument Kant recapitulates the essential belief in autonomy introduced in ancient Greece, but in the idiom of rational philosophy and of the natural rights of the individual. He recognizes the right of property, as do other natural rights/social contract theorists, but criticizes systems of government that give more voting weight to large property owners than to small. He denounces in no uncertain terms the notion that people are so unworthy of consideration that their rights need not be respected and that they need some supreme leader to control them. If that notion were to be accepted, he points out, it would follow that people have the right to resort to force as much as any leader has such a right. But where force prevails, there can be no law and no legal constitution because a legal constitution requires respect for human rights.

In the essay on philosophic history, he makes clear that the drive for human autonomy is a force of nature itself, because the supreme objective of nature is "the development of all the faculties of man by his own effort." For this objective to be attained, competition or antagonism is necessary. Social life must therefore be arranged so as to allow both freedom under external laws and irresistible force to contain antagonism and channel it into constructive paths. As Rousseau had proposed a just civic constitution, to be followed by the creation of a federal union of civic commonwealths, so Kant too foresaw an eventual federation of republics. He did not believe it would come about by an act of will, however, but rather as the outcome of the experience of conflict: "Man wants concord but nature knows better what is good for his kind; nature wants discord."[10] Through the hard experience of conflict, people would eventually recognize the need for federal union as the way to make peace secure. Kant refused to believe that God could create a social universe destined forever to experience destructive conflict; His will must have been to create an order of struggle so that out of travail would come a higher order. In this way, Kant refined the natural rights argument and shaped it into a case for republican government and world federalism.[11]

Complementing Kantian Rational Morality with Utilitarian Self-Interest

Kant's brilliant formulation does not operate automatically, however, when human beings interact politically. As Kantian actors enter into a social contract, they presumably legislate in accordance with the categorical imperative and experience an autonomy which is at once individual and collective. Unfortunately, the very freedom of the will that Kant posits also explains why individuals may choose not to be autonomous in his sense. Even apart from complaints that Kant had enunciated a purely formal morality (unwarranted in view of his examples of specific maxims) or that by making reason the sole foundation of morality he deprived it of support from revelation or emotion, his formulation is open to the criticism that it does not provide an alternative for those who may be unwilling to follow the harsh dictates of duty when they can have no assurance that others will do so. This failure in turn opens the possibility for a coercion in the name of an unrecognized rationality. Wrongly applied, Kant's theory can provide a spurious validity, as Isaiah Berlin has warned, for despots who find Kant's "counsel of perfection" an excuse for imposing on recalcitrant subjects despotic laws they claim to be the embodiment of reason :

> If I am a legislator or ruler, I must assume that if the law I impose is rational (and I can only consult my own reason) it will automatically be approved by all the members of my society so far as they are rational beings. For if they disapprove, they must, *pro tanto*, be irrational; then they will need to be repressed by reason: whether their own or mine cannot matter, for the pronouncements of reason must be the same in all minds. I issue my orders and if you resist, take it upon myself to repress the irrational element in you which opposes reason.[12]

To guard against the need to rely too much on duty and altruism and against the danger of the misapplication of the Kantian standard, autonomy as conceived by Utilitarians is a useful complement. R. M. Hare has advanced the unconventional thesis that Kant's theory can be interpreted "in a way that allows him—perhaps even requires him—to be one kind of utilitarian." He admits that Kant's puritanical upbringing imbued him with certain moral values (about capital punishment, suicide, and even lying) which no Utilitarian would be likely to endorse. But he argues that both Kant and Utilitarians—at least those who subscribe to "rational-will utilitarianism"—agree that "we should do what will conduce to satisfying people's rational preferences or wills-for-ends—ends of which happiness is the sum."[13] Without necessarily accepting this highly unconventional view of Kant as a Utilitarian, we may recognize a profound affinity between Kantian and Utilitarian ethics in one critical respect. This is that Utilitarianism also requires a form of autonomy in its twin cardinal assumptions that all human beings aim at happiness and that all are their own best judges of what conduces to pleasure and pain.

For those who reject social contract theory and Kantian ethics, Utilitarianism provides an alternative which supports the same conclusion. Utilitarianism is fundamentally democratic in requiring that each individual count for one and "none for more than one" and that government be designed to permit all to advance their interests in the summing up process by which the happiness of all is determined. Beginning with David Hume and Jeremy Bentham, the Utilitarian analysis rejected natural rights theory and reliance on a social contract and put forth instead a theory of human conduct and morality based on the universality of the natural impulses to seek pleasure and avoid pain. From this premise, the Benthamite Philosophical Radicals deduced that society ought to respect rights—understood not as metaphysical abstractions but as socially useful rules. Because there is no explicit recognition for a right of liberty in Utilitarian doctrine, John Stuart Mill sought to show that it is essential to happiness and progress. Although the absence of a specific commitment to liberty in Utilitarianism remains troubling, its very individualism makes Mill's argument plausible even without the other more debatable arguments he adduces in clarifying the Utilitarian view of pleasure or happiness. Frederick Rosen argues that Bentham's belief in the importance of security implies a recognition of the need for liberty, which Bentham defined as a branch of security.[14] As to democracy, although Bentham at first thought that some enlightened despot could use the "felicific calculus" to reform the legal code to achieve the Utilitarian goal of the greatest good of the greatest number, he soon realized that it would be far better to rely on a representative legislature to register the preferences of individuals than on the caprice of a single absolute ruler.

Different as they are, the Kantian and Utilitarian formulations can be brought together, resulting in a strengthened concept of autonomy. By relying on interests rather than right, the Utilitarian is admittedly open to Kant's objection that he has succumbed to heteronomous influences and introduced relativistic criteria, insofar as the happiness of each individual is affected by varying standards of pleasure. But this objection can be met, at least to some extent, by pointing out that some interests are more fundamental than others and that the shared assumption of independence and free will requires in both cases that human beings be treated only as ends and never as means. With this important qualification, the greatest happiness principle need not lead either to the sacrifice of liberty for security or happiness or the imposition of a single standard of happiness. Utilitarianism may be thought of as a potentially complementary alternative to Kantian ethics which involves a similar premise of individual autonomy in the sense that each person "legislates" a mode of conduct for himself based on a recognition that what he wills cannot fairly interfere with the same opportunity exercised by all others. The main practical difference is that while for Kant the ends are all given a priori in the form of maxims, for the Utilitarian they require a felicific calculus to determine how each individual's pursuit of happiness can be reconciled with that of all others.

With this in mind, it is perhaps possible to appreciate more fully what the philosopher John Rawls has attempted to do in developing his understanding of "justice as fairness" as a basis for democracy.[15] In effect he has combined Kantian and Utilitarian principles: to imagine contractors ignorant of their self-interest and guided solely by reason (Kant's "noumenal" selves) but anxious at the same time to protect their actual or empirical self-interest whatever it might be. Thus, they would seek to assure not only that all would enjoy equal liberty but also an equal share of "primary goods" and a distribution of wealth that would satisfy the interests of the "least advantaged" while providing an incentive to the "most advantaged" to use their talents to the common benefit. Whereas Locke would have rewarded the diligent and industrious by allowing them to acquire property within the limits of natural law, and Kant would have relied on the categorical imperative to require us to use our talents, Rawls, in the spirit of Bentham, opts for material incentives tied to the general welfare. By appreciating the synthesis he attempts, it is also possible to understand why he sees the moral imperative decided upon by the contractors as hypothetical rather than categorical: it follows from their wish to protect their interests and to benefit from social cooperation, not from a priori reasoning alone.

A synthesis of Kantianism and Utilitarianism makes it unnecessary to rely upon a putative moral sense that may in reality be shaped by antidemocratic and parochial cultural values. The criticism that the formalism of the Kantian emphasis on duty leads to willingness to obey any authority is unwarranted, provided that the categorical imperative is understood in the terms in which he defined it. But an exclusive emphasis on duty presupposes a willingness to subordinate private interests to the general good that may not always be strong enough to be relied upon. If it can be buttressed with a sense of self-interest "properly understood," in Tocqueville's sense, to make self-interest and public interest interdependent, autonomy will be the stronger.

The Interconnection of Autonomy and Democracy

The capacity for moral autonomy, then, is the ability to make a number of important and related judgments and to act upon them: to distinguish right from wrong or just from unjust, to appreciate the likely consequences of an action, and to regulate one's own behavior accordingly. Because moral autonomy requires liberty—liberty to become informed, to exercise choice, to will an action and carry it out—liberty is the fundamental human right, presupposing the right to life itself. Modern democracy is the form of social organization and government in which that right is protected and expressed as a matter of basic principle.

This recognition of autonomy does not imply that liberty is a right for everyone to do as he or she pleases, regardless of effects upon others, or that all moral values are relative to individual judgment. It implies only that people mature enough to be responsible for their actions and adequately educated in the use of their faculties should enjoy the opportunity to set their own rules and determine their own destinies, both in making judgments of a personal nature and in cooperating with fellow citizens to set rules for social interaction. The equality of rights implies an equality of obligation to respect the moral autonomy of all other citizens forming a community in which mutual undertakings can have legal as well as moral force. Democratic liberty is therefore reciprocal and universal rather than a right of anyone to do anything that might provide any sort of gratification.

The notion that democracy can do without a concept of autonomy altogether, however, is very dubious. To argue that substantive ideals are adventitious to democracy, which should be defined purely in procedural terms,[16] is to chase one's own tail. If democratic procedure is defined, as it must be, to include free discussion and debate, uncontrolled access to information, and the right of citizens to cast votes with the same weight as others, then procedural democracy is inherently substantive. The procedures, in other words, follow logically from moral principles.

Some democratic theorists have rejected the principle of autonomy because they identify it with an impractical form of constant direct democracy or with a subordination of the individual to the state, but others have come to appreciate its validity as a basic principle realized both on the private sphere of life and in representative government. Giovanni Sartori seems to reject the belief in autonomy as a foundation for democracy because he identifies it with the small community of the ancient *polis* and (like Isaiah Berlin) with the distorted notion of "true freedom" used to rationalize coercion by modern dictatorial regimes.[17] Robert A. Dahl, however, observes that "to be morally autonomous *is* to be self-governing in the domain of morally relevant choices" and that "because the democratic process maximizes the feasible scope of self-determination for those who are subject to collective decisions . . . it also maximally respects the moral autonomy of all who are subject to its laws."[18] Sartori's objection may be more semantic than substantive, because he seems to define autonomy not as self-government in a broad sense but more narrowly as constant and direct participation in the making of all laws. Dahl's broader view of moral autonomy makes it compatible with representative government, which Sartori also favors.

Other analysts are strongly convinced of the importance of autonomy to democracy. J. Roland Pennock observes that "the supreme value that democracy places on individual autonomy, thriving, and all that contributes to a person's well-being, is fundamental. Without autonomy the individual is degraded. An individual capable of autonomous behavior, and aware of that fact, possesses something of great intrinsic value. It is good in and of itself."[19] "Liberal democracy," Geraint Parry and Michael Moran write, "is grounded upon the autonomy of the individual.[20] Joseph Raz sees "the autonomy-based doctrine of freedom" as the moral basis of state action in three particular respects:

First, its primary concern is the promotion and protection of positive freedom which is understood as the capacity for autonomy, consisting of the availability of an adequate range of options, and of the mental abilities necessary for an autonomous life. *Second*, the state has the duty not merely to prevent denial of freedom, but also to promote it by creating the conditions for autonomy. *Third*, one may not pursue any goal by means which infringe people's autonomy unless such action is justified by the need to protect the autonomy of those people or of others.[21]

In modern usage, then, autonomy connotes a social system in which individuals experience both a guarantee of individual rights, which enables them to be self-governing in areas where majority rule may not intrude, and the opportunity to take part as equal citizens in representative self-government.[22] It can obtain on the individual level, when we regulate our conduct toward other individuals, or when we aim at achieving a degree of self-sufficiency and self-fulfillment in some narrow domain, such as a métier. It can also come into play on a collective level within a variety of social sub-units, such as the family, the work unit, the professional or vocational association, religious, ethnic, and cultural affinity groups, etc. It expresses itself as well when we identify ourselves with the concerns of people in other societies or with humanity in general. Autonomy, in other words, is not a concept exhausted by the categories of individual and society or citizen and state. It is a concept of self-regulation in many dimensions.

The ideal of autonomy is not restricted to the level of the solitary individual because, as thinkers from Plato and Aristotle onward have also recognized, human beings are inherently gregarious and in need of society. Biologically and psychologically, they are incapable of achieving autonomy, even in the limited sense of the ability to survive without assistance, for years after leaving the womb. Even as adults, they depend upon others and owe all others with whom they enter into relationships of mutual benefit a due regard for their right to the same degree of autonomy they claim for themselves. Once fully formed, however, they become autonomous not just in the sense that they can survive outside the womb, but that they can achieve a degree of independence and self-direction which of all animals only human beings are capable.

The historical evidence that democracy is a viable social and political system shows that a high degree of autonomy can be achieved in communities of virtually any size, provided that social and political structure allows for a degree of differentiation that balances centralization and devolution of authority. In order to assure that the moral autonomy of all individuals is respected, a basic code of human rights must be considered the cornerstone of all government, or, in other words, the limit of state authority. Within this framework, the play of interests should determine policy.

Democracy is therefore not simply a matter of popular government, direct and indirect, by the citizens of a given society. Without respect for human rights, popular government is not democracy in the modern sense of the term, because it does not aim at promoting autonomy in the individual as well as in the collectivity of citizens. Majorities unconstrained by respect for the rights of individuals and minorities can become as tyrannical toward dissidents as any dictator. Because it is an effort to promote autonomy, democracy requires respect for the right of individuals to govern themselves in their personal lives and in their political life—the life they must lead in common with other citizens. It requires cooperation in the pursuit of social goals. This cooperation cannot be achieved without at least some degree of active participation by all citizens in the management of their own and public affairs. Democracy is a process by which separate claims for autonomy are accommodated and mediated. The philosopher John Dewey described it well:

> Democracy is much broader than a special political form, a method of conducting government, of making laws and carrying on governmental administration by means of popular suffrage and elected officers. It is that, of course. But it is something broader and deeper than that. The political and governmental phase of democracy is a means, the best means so far found, for realizing ends that lie in the wide domain of human personality. It is, as we often say, though perhaps without appreciating all that is involved in the saying, a way of life, social and individual. The keynote of democracy as a way of life may be expressed, it seems to me, as the necessity for the participation of every mature human being in formation of the values that regulate the living of men together: which is necessary from the standpoint of both the general social welfare and the full development of human personality.[23]

Many important corollaries, in the form of requisite institutions and practices, follow from this basic definition. Inevitably, problems arise in drawing limits and working out the applications of the principle of autonomy in the political as well as the civil sphere. Particularly hard questions arise when what is at stake is public regulation of individual decisions affecting such profound choices as giving birth and taking one's own life. The right of a woman to abort a fetus she carries is often said to contradict the right of the fetus to be born. The contention that a fetus has any human rights rests on the controversial assumption that an embryo, even before it reaches the stage of viability outside the womb, is already a living person. A less difficult but still troubling question is whether individuals may claim a right to die, or in other words, to take their own lives, directly or with assistance. Here, since no harm is entailed to another human being or, as in the case of a fetus, to a potential human being, it is easier to argue that individuals of sound mind who find their lives not worth living should have the right to terminate their own existence under conditions that allow them dignity. But these issues are controversial just because they arise from the same common substrate of human rights. The serious difficulties of application should not obscure the common philosophical root of democracy in the principle of autonomy.[24]

The Civic Culture

To promote responsible and effective citizenship, democratic societies require a strong underlying "civic culture" embodying the democratic norm.[25] Autocracies are buttressed by cultural attitudes calling for veneration of authority and disparaging individualism and dissent. A democratic civic culture inculcates respect for human rights and for habits of compromise, combined with political activism or a sense of "efficacy." Benjamin Barber has rightly described civic cultures of this sort as the basis of "strong democracy."[26] If the civic culture is weak, the representative system will readily lend itself to the abuse of power by officeholders, and to a cynicism among the governed that leads them to attempt to evade the legal process and either resign themselves to unaccountable rule or conspire against it. If it is strong, politicians learn that to develop successful careers, they must show themselves to be skillful at accommodating diverse interests and groups and solicitous of public trust, and citizens take initiatives to make their wishes known and promote common causes. To the extent that representatives and unelected officials know they will be held accountable by the voters, they will be less beholden to views and interests which do not coincide with those of their constituents. In an admirably designed study of why some Italian regional governments are more successful than others, Robert Putnam and his collaborators have found that differences in civic culture are a major explanatory variable: "Some regions of Italy, we discover, are blessed with vibrant networks and norms of civic engagement, while others are cursed with vertically structured politics, a social life of fragmentation and isolation, and a culture of distrust. These differences in civic life turn out to play a key role in explaining institutional success."[27]

The civic culture requires an atmosphere of trust, but it also promotes a readiness to enter into public debate and take positions on matters of principle and policy. Freedom of expression and assembly are the primary means by which citizens may influence outcomes by shaping public opinion, but the staging of protests and demonstrations to call attention to grievances and concerns is not necessarily subversive of democracy. Even some degree of civil disobedience—refusal to obey the law on grounds of conscience or principle in order to challenge a law and express dissent—is usually tolerated because of the commitment to respect autonomy and a critical spirit. If rioting and civil disobedience become commonplace, however, even when political remedies are available for discontent, the civic culture is undermined and stability is threatened.

Civil Society

As an acknowledged relatively separate sphere of activity, civil society arose in the effort to limit the power of absolute monarchy. The democratic revolution sweeping over the West, Tocqueville observed, was the expression of a centuries-long tendency which "extends far beyond political mores and laws, exercising dominion over civil society as much as over the government; it creates opinions, gives birth to feelings, suggests customs, and modifies whatever it does not create."[28] Benjamin Constant put the point even more compellingly, by contrasting ancient or communitarian liberty with modern individual liberty. To the ancient Greeks and Romans, he pointed out, liberty meant the opportunity, indeed the duty, to submerge individuality in the collectivity, even to sacrifice their lives for the preservation and glory of the *polis* or *civitas*:

> You find among them almost none of the enjoyments which . . . form part of the liberty of the moderns. All private actions were submitted to a severe surveillance. No importance was given to individual independence, neither in relation to opinions, nor to labour, nor, above all, to religion. The right to choose one's religious affiliation, a right which we regard as one of the most precious, would have seemed to the ancients a crime and a sacrilege. In the domains which seem to us the most useful, the authority of the social body interposed itself and obstructed the will of individuals. Among the Spartans, Therpandrus could not add a string to his lyre without causing offence to the ephors. In the most domestic of relations the public authority again intervened. The young Lacademonian could not visit his new bride freely. In Rome, the censors cast a searching eye over family life. The laws regulated customs, and as customs touch on everything, there was hardly anything that the laws did not regulate.[29]

"Thus," Constant concluded, "among the ancients the individual, almost always sovereign in public affairs, was a slave in all his private relations. As a citizen, he decided on peace and war; as a private individual, he was constrained, watched and repressed in all his private movements . . ."[30]

The one partial exception to the rule, Constant noted, had been Athens, and the reason was that in Athens commerce was a significant activity. As a result, individuals were given greater latitude in their private dealings than elsewhere. In this respect, Athens was a forerunner of the democracies of the future because modern republics would be even more devoted to commerce, both domestic and international. Indeed, it was the rise of commerce that would make the republican form increasingly necessary. So long as war is the primary focus of social organization, the subordination of the individual is inevitable, because armies demand hierarchy, regimentation, and collective discipline. A society devoted to commerce has different needs. Trade requires entrepreneurs and independent producers, consumers and brokers. To the extent that commerce replaces war, individual liberty therefore becomes more possible and more necessary. Constant was confident that the industrial revolution would replace warfare with commerce as the normal state of affairs because experience would show even the most ambitious individual that commercial exchange is a "milder and surer means of engaging the interest of others to agree to what suits his own."[31] In the era of the commercial republic, civil society and not the public sector would be the most important sphere of liberty; government would become indirect and representative, and its functions would be limited so that it could not encroach on the rights of the individual or cripple economic efficiency by interfering with exchange.

Within civil society, democratic ideals exert an influence over "private government"—the modes of decision making and regulation that prevail in organized groups independent of the state or public sector. Until recently, the term "government" was usually reserved for institutions in the public sector, but there is good reason to extend it to apply to private associations, from the most informally organized, like the family and other kinship groupings, to the most formally organized, like the business corporation, the church, the professional association and trade union, and universities, whether they are completely private or relatively autonomous under public sponsorship.[32]

A civil society may exist alongside an undemocratic political order, but its existence must be precarious because it depends upon privileges allowed by those who rule rather than on rights guaranteed by basic or constitutional law and systems of law allowing for appeal against government actions. The personal liberty that civil society provides must be uncertain so long as it is not protected and reinforced by political democracy.

Civil society is the principal source and bastion of plural autonomy. This pluralism is evident in the variety of relatively autonomous groupings that is characteristic of democratic civil societies, ranging from the family (both the traditional nuclear form and varieties that depart from the traditional form) to religious, ethnic, and religious groups, business corporations, schools and universities, trade unions and professions, and civic associations. Democracy encourages the proliferation of such associations because it does not give preference to social establishments of any kind. The very mobility and uncertainty that democracy produces, moreover, leads to a search for multiple secondary identities rather than only those determined by birth, prolonged residence in a single place, and lifetime employment with a single employer.

The two spheres must exist in symbiosis, even though there is bound to be tension between them. The institutions of civil society enable individuals to pursue a variety of purposes, some of which, like religious beliefs and practices, may be at variance with those of other citizens, without

requiring majority approval or disapproval or allowing government interference. In a host of ways, these institutions also act as a buffer against the
expansion of the state's power and sphere of action. A market economy
allows individuals and interest groups to exchange goods and services and
promote their own welfare without depending on a bureaucratic and potentially paternalistic system of economic organization. Well-regulated
market systems provide more scope and encouragement for initiative and
innovation than monopolistic state enterprise and a "command economy."
The signals of demand and supply, transmitted and mediated by decisions
to invest and buy, assure a more finely-tuned and flexible system of exchange than any centrally organized effort at micro-management could
achieve, thus promoting efficiency and prosperity as well as liberty. Civil
society allows independent media of communication to provide uncen-
sored reports on political events, expose wrongdoing by government officials, and enable commentators and citizens to express views on public
issues without fear of being deprived of a livelihood. It also encourages
citizens to band together to promote differing notions of the public good,
assuring a marketplace of ideas as well as of goods and services.

The danger, as James Madison appreciated, is that the very opportunity
civil society provides for the expression of plural autonomy sometimes
enables groups with special interests to gain more influence over public
policy than their numerical size would otherwise justify. Insofar as the electoral process depends on private resources, politicians can ill afford to ignore the interests of campaign contributors; indeed they may cultivate those
contributors to such an extent that they become their agents rather than
representatives of the constituencies that elect them. The large private corporation and business associations become political actors capable of ex-
erting considerable and sometimes disproportionate influence upon public policy.[33] Plural autonomy is often in tension with individual and communal autonomy, not only with respect to the role of business corporations but with respect to that of trade unions, professional associations,
and many other interest or pressure groups.

Corruption is a problem in all systems, but corruption by money is an
especially acute problem in democracies because of the very existence of
civil society. The corrupting influence of money in politics is a problem in
all democracies, as recent experience has shown in countries as different as
Japan, India, Brazil, and Italy. It is all but inherent in systems of government like the American where, in order to prevent overcentralization, the
constitution deliberately creates a system with diffuse and multiple authorities and where candidates for office must raise their own funds rather
than depend on party organizations. "In totalitarian societies," Daniel Bell
has pointed out, "corruption is the arbitrary use of power. There is no rule
of law. The decrees of the dictator, or the party, override everything else.

There are no checks and balances from institutions or competing groups; and few appeals against verdicts from the top. In a democracy, on the other hand, corruption is money. The politicians needs to be elected, and modern campaigns are costly. Businesses seeking contracts will bribe officials to win a job, or politicians will demand money to award contracts."[34]

Because civil society presupposes the existence of private property and a market economy, it cannot survive under full-blown socialism. Karl Marx took a very different and much more critical view of the advent of civil society than did Tocqueville and Constant. For him, it represented the triumph of the bourgeoisie, the property-owning class that stood to profit most from the existence of an untrammeled market economy. To emphasize the role of this class, he popularized the French translation of civil society as bourgeois society. For Marx, the liberty celebrated by liberals like Constant amounted to the liberty of economic exchange, and civil society was the arena of class conflict. If the workers succeeded, whether through the ballot box or by direct action against capital, the state would remain an instrument of civil society, but one that would serve the needs of workers rather than the owners of capital. The interim "dictatorship of the proletariat" would wipe out lingering resistance to socialization of the means of production and pave the way for the advent of communism. The state as an organ of repression would "wither away" and be replaced by a managerial regime which would plan the economy and regulate the distribution of income in accordance with socialist ideals.

The Marxian formula left unclear what was to happen to the separation between state and civil society after the revolution, and the actual experience of socialist societies has been varied. Even in societies where democratic socialist parties have gained considerable influence, economic activity remains largely in private hands. Democratic socialist governments have ameliorated the harmful effects of market economies while aiming to maintain productive and internationally competitive. They have been no less committed than those formed by other parties to protecting the right to vote in free, competitive elections, including the right to privatize nationalized industries, and have not interfered in non-economic affairs. In the Soviet Union and Maoist China, however, "bourgeois democracy" was rejected and democracy revamped to mean permanent one-party rule and the suppression of civil liberties.

Actual experience does not show that all forms of socialism are incompatible with democracy. Everything depends on the degree to which the authority of the state is expanded over civil society. A completely socialized economy in which all means of production are publicly owned or closely controlled must greatly enlarge the scope of state activity at the expense of civil society. All major media of communications, as well as churches, schools, and universities, would be hard pressed to survive without state subsidies. These subsidies would inevitably have strings attached. Workers and professionals would be too dependent on the state to strike because all strikes would become strikes against the public welfare rather than against some private entity. The scope of the state could, in theory, be limited, and private institutions could survive on support from individual contributions and payments, but the likelihood is that once all economic activities were absorbed into the public sector, the independence of other activities would be hard to sustain. As Dahl observes, "a centrally directed command economy would provide political leaders with access to such powerful resources for persuasion, manipulation, and coercion as to make democracy extremely unlikely in the long term, no matter whether firms were collectively or privately owned. The only feasible alternative is some kind of market economy."[35]

In modern democracies, however, the once seemingly irreconcilable difference of opinion over the character and the role of civil society vis à vis the state has been considerably compromised in recent times by the rise of the managed economy and the welfare state. Governments have come to perform a host of regulatory functions: preventing the growth of inefficient monopolies; protecting the right of workers to bargain collectively, imposing taxes in support of social insurance and income transfer projects; monitoring economic activities affecting the public interest (in the name of such goals as national security, full employment, and environmental protection); and intervening to promote growth and stability by fiscal and monetary policy. In the process, government policies sometimes reflect the distribution of wealth in civil society, but democracy allows electoral majorities to mobilize effective political resources against economic interests. Social Democrats continue to agitate for more egalitarian distribution of wealth and for greater political management of the economy,[36] whereas classical liberals and libertarians warn that such encroachment violates liberty and undermines efficiency.[37] But all democratic governments hew to a middle path in one variation or another.

Demarcating Public and Private

The question of how to demarcate the division of functions and responsibilities between the state or public sector and civil society gives rise to constant friction, but the principle at stake is fairly clear: the collectivity, embodied in the government or the state, should deal with issues of common concern; all other matters should be left to the determination of individuals and their civil associations. Dennis C. Mueller puts the distinction empirically, in the economics-influenced language of rational choice theory, "Police protection is purchased invariably collectively, cups and saucers privately."[38] Even this distinction between security and personal activity can be fuzzy in practice because security is not invariably purchased collectively. In the United States, James Q. Wilson points out, "private security firms have more employees than do municipal police forces."[39] Individuals who put locks on their doors and bars on their windows are also purchasing security privately. But the generalization certainly holds for most instances. Even self-described libertarians concede that people in a state of nature would end up conferring the function of providing security upon a single monopolistic collective organization, in accordance with Max Weber's classic definition of the state as the territorial organization with a legitimate monopoly of the means of coercion.[40]

There are democratic grounds for public intervention in otherwise private relations. Basic rights, both civil and political, require legal protection, and only public governments can provide such protection. Public authority must protect the rights of individuals against infractions by other individuals and associations, such as corporations, professional associations, and trade unions. For this reason, the administration of civil and criminal justice is a major function of public authority.

Public authority in a democracy must also prevent denials of equal opportunity for employment by public contractors or in admission to public schools (as well as private institutions which benefit from public subsidy). Discrimination in the provision of publicly sponsored or assisted opportunities, whether on grounds of race, religion, gender, or other irrelevant criteria, denies individuals the right to autonomy in civil society. As a moral matter, the democratic norm should also apply to employers and schools not dependent upon public assistance, but public authority to enforce equality of opportunity is limited, and the right of free association may permit groups of like-minded people to establish exclusive criteria for membership. To require churches to admit non-believers or medical associations to admit unlicensed physicians would be absurd and hardly a requirement of democracy. More troubling but nevertheless permissible under the right to freedom of association is discrimination practiced by voluntary associations, such as clubs, fraternities and sororities, which accept only those members who fit exclusive criteria or are proposed and accepted by members. In a gray area is discrimination by voluntary associations which has the effect of denying those excluded equal opportunity to do business or engage in a profession—as is arguably the case when women are excluded from "service" organizations in which businessmen socialize.

The public sector must also provide protection for those incapable of exercising their civil rights, such as children and the disabled. In democracies, the law properly requires that all children receive schooling, because some minimal level of education is necessary to the exercise of autonomy. The taxpayers may therefore properly be called upon to underwrite education, whether or not they have children who benefit from public provision of education. Compulsory education, even though it may interfere with the civil rights of parents, is justifiable as a guarantee of the rights of children against irresponsible guardians. Interference with parental liberty is also warranted when medical treatment is required for children of parents whose religious convictions bar such treatment, although in such cases the courts must weigh the rights of parents to practice their religion against the right of children to be protected from neglect or maltreatment.

Whenever the rights and interests of others are adversely affected by the behavior of individuals, public authority may limit and override the liberty of individuals. Measures to protect public health, such as quarantines and compulsory vaccination, are therefore justifiable, even when they interfere with religious and personal liberty, although vaccination can provide significant protection even when administered to most, but not all, of the population. The public authority may also mandate the use of safety devices (such as automobile seat belts and helmets for motor cycle drivers) because accidents and injuries are costly to the public and not merely to those injured because of their own negligence.

Gray areas appear when public health standards seem to dictate not just campaigns to educate and persuade people to the danger of practices injurious to their health, such as cigaret smoking, but prohibition, again on grounds of cost to the public. In such cases, John Stuart Mill's well known distinction between self-regarding and other-regarding acts is hard to apply. Taxation of tobacco consumption can be justified, up to a point, by the costs to society from illnesses due to smoking. Full legal proscription would deny liberty and generate an illicit trade, as it did with liquor in the United States during the "noble experiment" of prohibition. Banning smoking in confined spaces is justifiable because it has been shown that non-smokers can be injured by "passive smoking." The case for the use of taxation to make special assessments of smokers, however, is difficult to distinguish from the case for similar taxes of other consumer items which may be deleterious to health and safety, from fattening foods to automobiles.

Still less defensible are efforts to legislate moral restrictions on behavior that does not affect the interests of others but is considered an affront to widely held moral standards. Strictly from the point of view of democratic theory, for which the sole moral consideration is moral autonomy, legislation ruling out polygamy or polyandry or consensual adult sexual activities is unjustifiable except insofar as any of these practices can be said to be coercive in effect even though not in theory. Restrictions may be justified on other grounds, however, such as the tendency of some forms of behavior to promote attitudes disrespectful of the rights of others and of human dignity.

An intellectually influential and challenging way of thinking about the character of political democracy has been advanced by the "rational choice" school of analysis. This approach, which derives from Utilitarianism and welfare economics, posits that individuals are self-interested and rational, and examines their behavior in two spheres, the economic and the political, or the marketplace and the electoral system. In the economic sphere individuals engage in exchanges for mutual benefit; in the political they cooperate and compete in determining the allocation of public benefits. Whereas market activity aims to achieve "private goods"—ones that may be enjoyed by some individuals but not all—public activity is aimed at achieving "public goods"—ones the benefits of which are either indivisible or widely shared. An example of a private good is the salary paid to an employee by a private company. Examples of public goods are the clean air and water necessary for all and the security people enjoy because armies protect borders from invaders and police patrol neighborhoods against criminals. Economists often argue that whereas the marketplace is the most efficient system of exchange for private transactions, it is unsuitable for the allocation of public goods and for the rectification of "externalities"—adverse effects on third parties from private transactions. Thus, government action is called for under two conditions: whenever there is a need (1) to provide "public goods to all individuals collectively" and (2) to induce individuals "to modify the selfish pursuit of their own goals in order to take account of the unintended external effects of their actions on others."[41] Economic theory also makes clear, as Wilson explains succinctly, "that government (that is, an institution wielding coercive powers) must compel us to pay for national defense or clean air because the market will not supply these things. The reason is simple: Since everybody will benefit from national defense or clean air if anyone in particular benefits, no one has any incentive to pay for these things voluntarily. We would all be free riders because none of us feasibly could be excluded from these benefits if he or she refused to pay."[42]

It is not as clear, however, whether certain goods, such as housing and education, are best left to the individual and the marketplace (with or without public subsidy) or are best purchased collectively. Some advocates of the superiority of private to public enterprise suggest that public schools and prisons be privatized along with railroads, the postal service, and other functions often considered to require public monopoly. But regardless of the particular list of functions that should be reserved for government, the rationale suggested by rational choice theory is that services that cannot be efficiently provided by the market should be provided collectively. Many actual functions performed by governments would not pass so strict a test because in many the distinction between public and private goods is hard to discern. A bridge or dam built in a particular locality as a result of "pork barrel politics"—that is, the interplay of special interests—serves a public function even though it is also a "divisible" good. Defense expenditures of general benefit also provide special (or "divisible") benefits to defense contractors and the localities in which they are sited; in such cases, the public good and private goods are intertwined and rational choice theory does not offer a clear criterion for disentangling them. Sometimes, far from serving the public welfare, governments "create private benefits, not public goods, at collective cost," as when public regulation results in cartels and monopolies that draw higher "rents" than consumers would have to pay in an unregulated, competitive market.[43]

The theory is persuasive in identifying the rationale for public government, but it also points to serious problems of implementation. The root of these problems is the consideration that whereas private transactions seem to assure that individuals will pursue their interests and achieve them freely, the same is not necessarily the case in the political process. One potential reason is the "free rider problem," which arises because services provided as collective goods are enjoyed by all, including those who do not pay for them. A classic example arises in labor relations when nonmembers receive the benefit of a higher wage negotiated by a union even though they pay no dues to the union. Free ridership is also a problem in the public sector. A conscientious objector gains security even though he does not serve in the armed forces. Those who pay no taxes get many of the same benefits as those who do pay. In such cases, there is an incentive to "defect" rather than cooperate (in the terminology used in the well-known example of the prisoners' dilemma). Similarly, those who do not vote enjoy whatever benefits government may provide to all. The tendency to shirk responsibility or pay only minimal attention to public business is an expression of the free-rider problem.

Representative Government and Participatory Democracy

In large, heterogeneous societies, a primarily representative form of government is the only practical form of political democracy. Whether representation is understood as virtual or mandatory, it enables citizens to delegate specific authority to accountable officers—legislative, executive, and in some cases judicial—for limited periods, and enables these agents in turn to appoint non-elected administrative and judicial officials. In some democratic systems, a popular constituent authority determines the basic or constitutional law within which representatives make statutory law; in others the constitutional authority is assigned to parliaments. Bicameralism allows representation by state or province to balance representation based on national population as well as differentiation in function and authority. Representative systems may be variously classified as presidential and parliamentary, "Westminster" and consensual, though many actual examples are of mixed character.

Virtual and mandatory representation amount to variations on a common theme. In campaigning for election to Parliament from the city of Bristol, Edmund Burke presented the case for virtual representation. The representative, he argued, should be expected to judge what is in the best interest of constituents and to act on their behalf, without having to ask their opinions in advance. The "mandatory" view holds that as the voter is a principal and the representative an agent, representatives should follow the will and instruction of voters as faithfully as possible.[44] Effective and accountable representation requires a combination of both views. No mandate can anticipate all the issues that will arise or specify the details of legislation, and elected representatives must take some account of the interests of those who supported other candidates and of those outside the constituency who will be affected by legislation. Analytically and practically, however, there is difference between a form of representation that aims to act as a surrogate for public opinion, and even to instruct the electorate as to how its interests are best served, and one that seeks to ascertain and implement the public will.

Fair, frequent, and competitive elections are indispensable to the operation of representative government. The electoral process enables voters to hold the government of the day responsible for its stewardship. When all citizens have an equal voice in choosing accountable representatives in such elections, they can expect those they elect to office to be their agents, not their masters. Where democratic values prevail, only governments so established may properly claim to be legitimate. To improve the prospects that elections will produce coherent and accountable governments, independent, competitive, and well-organized political parties are necessary. Political parties are indispensable because by nominating candidates for office, conducting election campaigns, and coordinating the work of government and opposition, they enable voters to choose representatives whose views they can readily identify and hold accountable for their conduct in office.

Electoral systems differ, however, and the differences also embody other differing assumptions about the nature of representation. Bentham's formula, "Everyone to count for one and none for more than one," is generally accepted as a necessary condition for representation to be considered democratic, though schemes of weighted voting have sometimes been proposed. There are different views, however, of how the electors should be grouped into districts, whether elections should be designed so as to yield plurality/majority results or proportional representation (PR), and whether, as in single-member district systems, representatives should represent all voters in particular districts, or as in PR systems, segments of the electorate, either regional or national. Districts coterminous with the territorial boundaries of political sub-units, such as states or provinces and cities, provide representation of coherent regional interests. Districts composed of less coherent but compact territorial segments are usually justified as a way of avoiding extremes in the numbers represented in districts. The single-member district is often said to provide the most focussed form of representation for all voters, not just those who supported the winning candidate, but critics argue that the system effectively deprives those who support losing candidates of effective representation. Districting, especially when it is segmental, is open to partisan manipulation aimed at producing safe seats, a practice known in the United States as "gerrymandering." The name was suggested in 1812 by an editor after the artist Gilbert Stuart gave an odd-looking district drawn during the administration of Elbridge Gerry, a Massachusetts governor, the features of a salamander.[45]

PR systems distribute legislative seats in accordance with the relative size of the vote for the candidates of each party that surpasses a minimal threshold. PR districts may be national or regional, but must be multi-member. As a general rule, the higher the district magnitude (defined by the number of seats to be won in each district), the larger the assembly, and the lower the threshold, the more proportional will be the outcome of an election. The rationale for PR is the view that it provides the fairest form of representation because all significant groupings are represented according to their numerical strength; the rationale for majoritarian and plurality elections is that voters should be encouraged to form and support large amalgamated parties so as to reduce the prospect that minority parties can exercise vetoes over majorities and to improve the chance that elected governments will not be composed of coalitions not chosen by the voters but arranged among the parties. In theory, if not always in practice, amalgamated parties in essentially two-party systems must be pluralistic in membership and appeal in order to attract members and voters with varying identities and interests. When amalgamated parties fail to provide enough such opportunities, or when a sizeable fraction of the electorate supports minority parties unable to achieve seats in single-member district plurality elections, demands are likely to be expressed for introducing PR.

Direct participation complements representation, and may be achieved by referenda, direct communication with representatives, party politics, nomination and election campaigns, various forms of local government, including the jury system, and campaigns for particular causes and policies. These opportunities encourage citizens to take an active part in public affairs, combating tendencies toward apathy and feelings of political impotence and frustration. Pericles was perhaps the first to point out the importance of active citizenship in a democracy: "We do not say that a man who takes no interest in politics is a man who minds his own business; we say that he has no business here at all."[46] John Stuart Mill, even as he advocated indirect democracy, also emphasized the importance of personal involvement, pointing out that the opportunity for participation tends to raise the political sophistication of the ordinary citizen and make him more sensitive to the public weal: "He is called upon, while so engaged, to weigh interests not his own; to be guided, in case of conflicting claims, by another rule than his private partialities; to apply, at very turn, principles and maxims which have for their reason of existence the general good . . . He is made to feel himself one of the public, and whatever is their interest to be his interest. Where this school of public spirit does not exist, scarcely any sense is entertained that private persons, in no eminent social situation, owe any duties to society, except to obey the laws and submit to the government."[47]

Over-reliance on referenda, however, risks undermining the benefits of the representative process by tempting politicians to avoid dealing with controversial questions and tempting voters to suppose, sometimes with results that do not pass judicial scrutiny, that they can draft better legislation than their representatives. Citizen assemblies convened to deliberate on public issues and candidates[48] or to mobilize support for particular causes also serve a critical educational function, both for those who take part in them and for politicians, by articulating the views of well-informed constituents. Public opinion surveys are also useful in sampling the views of the electorate between elections, though they are notoriously sensitive to the form in which the questions are posed, do not always discriminate between well-informed and poorly-informed responses, and offer citizens a chance to vent frustrations without having to make the practical choices they must make when voting. Effective use of the mass media, not only for speeches, press conferences, and the broadcasting of legislative debates and committee hearings, but also for interactive "town hall" meetings and mass media call-in programs, further strengthens the communication between voter and representative vital to democratic government.

Representative government, thus modified to provide opportunities for direct communication and participation, may not meet the most demanding criteria for collective self-government as well as direct democracy, but it has proven to be a workable approach to the democratic ideal in large societies in which direct democracy is impractical. Once well established, it also promotes stability, because the opportunity to influence or change government in parliamentary votes and regular elections makes unnecessary and unjustifiable attempts to do so by conspiracy, coups d'état, or revolution. The opportunity to "throw the rascals out" is a far less destabilizing safety valve for popular discontent than riots or civil disobedience. Freedom of speech, press, and assembly provides a legitimate outlet for criticism and dissent and allows those opposed to prevailing policy to drum up support for reform. Because no group or party can plausibly claim to have been denied an opportunity to make its case, and because a party that fails to win one election can hope to win the next, the process inspires a willingness to accept defeat once "the people have spoken." Those who do not prevail but hope to do so in the future form a "loyal opposition." Those unable or unwilling to entertain such a hope may insist that "the system" is somehow rigged against them, but the claim is bound to ring hollow if the electoral process is fair and open. In view of the difficulties that often attend transitions of power in other systems, the acceptance of the result of an election has a simple majesty about it that commands respect and contrasts sharply with experience in other systems.

Direct democracy enables citizens to decide for themselves whether to adopt or change laws and, in jury trials, to apply the laws in particular cases. It may be experienced in town meetings, in local zoning review hearings, and partially (because no participation in public deliberation is required), in referenda and plebiscites. Switzerland and Italy provide for referenda and initiatives on national questions, and other parliamentary systems sometimes use them in matters considered constitutional, such as the recent debates over European federation. In some states of the United States, the constitution allows referenda on state issues.

While direct democracy is most suitable only for relatively small constituencies, it can also be practiced in some forms within larger, representative systems. Among the best-known modern examples of direct democracy is the eighteenth century New England town meeting, which survives in attenuated form.[49] The use of juries is another example, except that juries, being selected rather than impanelled at random, are to some extent representative bodies. Referenda can also be considered examples of direct democracy, except that because they do not entail the deliberation that goes on in a legislature or a jury, they are a form of direct legislation that resembles plebiscitary democracy.

For good reasons, direct democracy is often thought impractical and even dangerous in large and complex societies. In large societies it is impractical to assemble all citizens in one place. Even in Athens, where direct democracy was the norm, the Pnyx was not large enough to hold more than a fraction of the eligible citizenry.[50] In complex modern societies, moreover, citizens are preoccupied by the many demands entailed by the more immediate exercise of autonomy in civil society. Many may also be poorly informed and otherwise not well qualified to decide policy questions. When confronted with a choice on a referendum or an initiative, they may therefore be inclined not to try to decide the issue for themselves but to employ "information shortcuts" such as the opinion of friends, political parties, and newspaper editorialists, or the endorsements of notables and interested groups.[51] Although such short-cuts may enable them to cast votes roughly in accordance with their interests, this form of direct popular legislation lacks the opportunities for deliberation and amendment that the representative process allows. Judges schooled in the nuances of the law are better qualified than lay juries to try cases in which the interpretation of law, rather than findings of fact, is at issue. When constitutional questions are at issue, courts with the power of judicial review serve as surrogates for the sovereign people. Given these realities, a constitutional government—one in which the basic laws reflect common interests and are subject to revision by large majorities—coupled with a system of accountable representatives and appointees, may well be a more sensible expression of democracy than would be a constant effort to decide every issue by public referendum, even if that were practical (as it may become in the era of interactive electronic communication).

The question of whether representative or direct democracy is the better form turns not only on technical practicality but on competence under conditions of complexity, "information overload," and specialization. Prospective advances in interactive telecommunications may make it feasible to achieve direct "electronic democracy"[52] in the form of instant referenda on public issues, but these are hardly any more desirable than ordinary referenda, which have proven to be gross instruments of decision-making in states like California, where a commission formed to study the use of the initiative identified serious deficiencies: the propositions put to the voters are frequently too long and complex and beyond the capacity of many voters to understand; the initiative is inflexible, making amendment impossible even when flaws are identified; proponents with either-or propositions discourage legislators from working out compromises that might obviate the need for expensive electoral campaigns; constitutional amendments, once enacted, are extremely hard to repeal; counter-initiatives can readily be used to confuse voters; media campaigns disseminate incorrect or deceptive information; court decisions eventually disqualify some and leave others standing; and money plays too important a role in initiative qualification and campaigns.[53]

Some degree of participation is critical, however, because without it citizens lose the incentive to understand social issues and cannot cast their votes intelligently. Direct participation is possible even in large, complex societies, through the use of citizen advisory committees, via the jury system, political parties and election campaigning, on local school boards and zoning boards, and in the many other ways in which citizens make it their business to keep abreast of the public business and make their views felt. Direct democracy is important even in primarily representative systems because the more remote citizens come to be and feel from the business of government, the more they are inclined to regard laws that restrict their freedom or impose taxation as nuisances imposed upon them and the more the government is likely to function as an overlord rather than a fiduciary instrument.[54] In extreme circumstances, ostensibly democratic systems can become effectively oligarchical, and many citizens, once they come to feel powerless and alienated from "their own" government, can feel so betrayed and resentful that they will refuse to perform civic duties.

The trouble with indirect democracy, of course, is that it opens the possibility that representatives will either usurp power or exercise it by public default. Critics of representation like Rousseau have often warned that whenever citizens delegate authority they put a master over themselves and that in electing new representatives, they merely exchange one master for another. But these critics neglect the role of elections in signalling voter approval and disapproval.

Whatever its deficiencies measured against direct democracy, representative government has advantages that make it not only necessary but desirable. Democracies benefit from leadership and the surrogate function that politicians perform when they examine legislation and debate policy questions on behalf of the electorate. When the representative system works well, able and dedicated politicians who win public confidence are re-elected and advanced to higher office. They perform a vital function in articulating the various shadings of public opinion, drafting rules by which the public business is best conducted, and scrutinizing the conduct of unelected officials. Although the bargaining and accommodation that effective politicians must practice, both within and among partisan groupings, is often criticized, it is essential to the democratic process. "To get along you have to go along" is sometimes an excuse for political weakness, but it is also a truism that points to the need for cooperation and compromise.

Term limits may be advisable to limit the advantages of incumbency and make representatives more responsive to their constituents, but strong counter-arguments can be made against them. By removing the hope of re-election, they remove a key incentive for accountability in the representative's final term, except for those who may seek election to other offices. They deny the right of voters to select whatever candidate they prefer. They deprive the government as well as the representative's constituents of the benefits in policy expertise and parliamentary skills the representative acquires and tend to discourage commitment to a political career.

Representative government allows for a presidential form of executive, in which the president is directly elected and accountable to the electorate, and a cabinet-parliamentary system in which the prime minister is chosen by the president and subject to dismissal by parliament and in which the prime minister and the other ministers are responsible to parliament. The result is sometimes, as in recent French experience, that a president is compelled to "co-habit" with a prime minister from a different party. Constitutions provide for a presidential executive in a number of countries, notably

Chile, Costa Rica, France, the Philippines, the Russian Federation, the United States, Uruguay, and Venezuela.

With Latin American experience in mind, Juan Linz has argued that a presidential form of executive power is often dangerous to democracy because it vests so much power in the presidency that incumbents readily make themselves dictators or must be removed from office by coups d'état. Especially where the electorate is fragmented, he contends, a system in which the executive is accountable to parliament is more likely to be durable and acceptable.[55] In agreement with Linz, Arturo Valenzuela attributes the success of presidentialism in the United States to several peculiar factors: the role of the Supreme Court as an arbiter between the two other separate branches, the tradition of civil control over the military, the importance of the states as a counterweight to the national government, and, above all, the fact that the American two-party system has often resulted in the election of a president whose party has a majority in the Congress. In Latin America, by contrast, only six of thirty-three presidents elected in recent years have succeeded in maintaining parliamentary majorities over their term of office. When gridlock prevents them from being able to govern, presidents in these circumstances must either accept the paralysis of their office or try to assume control in violation of the constitution, usually with the help of the military.[56]

Other analysts have suggested that special factors account for the Latin American experience and that the parliamentary system is also problematic. Donald L. Horowitz has pointed out that in Africa and Asia, parliamentary systems often break down because they do not permit the decisiveness necessary to maintain stable democratic government.[57] Seymour Martin Lipset adds other examples of the collapse of democratic parliamentarism—Spain in the inter-war period, Portugal, Greece, Italy, Austria, Germany and most of Eastern Europe—and notes that in other cases presidentialism has brought stability. He argues that weakness of presidentialism in Latin America is more a function of political culture and economic factors than constitutional structure: the more enduring democratic systems have been those of Protestant and wealthier countries, whereas Latin American countries are Catholic in religion and beset by problems of development. A cultural tendency toward authoritarianism coupled with discord due to economic disparities presumably invests presidents with greater power and invites their overthrow when they fail to fulfill expectations.[58]

Apart from the question of whether one form of executive authority is in itself more apt to promote stability than the other, the two systems work differently. In a presidential system, the terms of office for the executive are not affected by votes in the legislature, and in other respects as well the two branches are more independent of each other than in a parliamentary system. As Lipset points out, a prime minister with a parliamentary majority has more power to enact his program than an American president, who must persuade a majority in both houses of Congress (including members of the president's own party) to support the legislation proposed by the executive. In a parliamentary system, the representatives in the majority know that if they should desert their leader, the parliament may be dissolved and they would have to be renominated and reelected. (In some systems, however, cabinets may simply be reformed after losing a vote in parliament.) As a result, party discipline is strong. In a separately elected assembly, members of the party controlling the executive are free to debate issues and take sides without fearing that they may bring down the government, and party discipline is weak. In presidential systems, the executive is apt to be weaker than the prime ministership because the president must depend on the agreement of the assembly.[59] But this weakness is counterbalanced by the dependence of the party in control of the executive on the president's popularity (the "coattail effect") and the ability of the president to act as the only directly elected national leader and appeal directly to the electorate to put pressure on representatives to support the executive program.

Different issues are posed by the accountability of civil servants or bureaucrats. Since their mandate is presumably limited to the implementation of laws established by elected representatives, this should in theory be less of a problem than holding the representatives responsible. In practice, however, authority is delegated to civil servants in many cases or assumed by them by default, with the result that rule-making by agencies often has a quasi-legislative, quasi-executive character. From the point of view of the citizen who must deal with the civil service, moreover, it can be an impenetrable, Kafka-esque castle. The contest between the taxpayer and the tax collector becomes unequal if, for example, the taxpayer is forced to contemplate legal action against a government agency which can deploy its legal resources at public expense. Another serious problem is that agencies may be captured by those they are presumably established to regulate. When this happens, the public interest is distorted in favor of private interests. The process may involve blatant manipulation, but it may also arise from the fact that regulators are often drawn from the industries they must regulate and from sociological conditioning that members of the agency experience. They become protectors of "their" industry and are loathe to regulate it if regulation would mean interfering with its functioning. (The role of the former United States Atomic Energy Commission as both promoter and regulator of nuclear power is a striking example, but it is repeated in numerous other areas, albeit less starkly.)

Inevitably, the movement of highly placed officials from private industries to government agencies and back (the so-called "revolving door" problem) also poses questions of accountability. Studies have shown that in the United States a great many military officers retire to take jobs with defense contractors. Military officers therefore have an interest not only in cultivating good relations with their opposite numbers in industry and in providing contracts that keep these companies in business. The same problem arises in the case of lawyers and business executives who move from government service into jobs in the private sector. Legislation has been adopted to address such conflicts of interest by barring high officials from having dealings with any agency in which they worked for some time after leaving it, but to some extent the problem is unavoidable so long as government agencies seek to recruit the most experienced and able people in the areas of business to be regulated.

A more basic problem inherent in all bureaucratic organization arises from the fact that bureaucracy by its very nature aims to establish and adhere to rules. These rules may not always suit particular cases well but are necessary for efficiency and to avoid favoritism. Intervention by representatives systems may impede the rationality and equity of bureaucracy but it also enables citizens to challenge unfair and officious behavior by bureaucrats. To avoid undue influence but allow flexibility, an office like that of the Swedish ombudsman is useful (somewhat the way the Roman tribune represented the *plebs*). The threat of intervention by representative officials is a potent tool against bureaucratic abuse because agencies are aware that representatives can question an agency's budget requests and investigate its performance.

Accountability can also extend to institutions of civil society when they perform services for governments. When a private contractor or another entity, such as a university, receives public subsidy, whether in the form of a contract or grant, or tax forgiveness, it becomes accountable for its use of public funds. This accountability can entail compliance with rules and regulations in the performance of its functions, in managing public funds. and in complying with public standards in its employment policies. A delicate balance must be struck between requiring accountability and encouraging autonomy on the part of private institutions doing work considered of value for public purposes (such as universities and defense industries). Allowing private firms to escape scrutiny or the rigorous test of the market by negotiating contracts rather than submitting competitive sealed bids may be necessary in advanced military projects, where outcomes are uncertain, but it comes at a price in accountability.

The Role of Political Parties

In themselves, elections are not enough to assure effective representative government. The single most important additional element to the electoral process is the existence of competitive political parties. Such parties are indispensable in organizing elections and providing voters with a way to identify and discriminate among the candidates by ideological and policy orientation. Where party discipline is strong, the party can enforce adhesion to the views of at least the fraction of the electorate that supports its candidates. Where it is weak, representatives are not only more independent of party control but more susceptible to the influence of organized interest groups, both local and national. This influence may well divert the representative from his proper role, except insofar as other organized interest groups exert countervailing force and enable the representative to take a more balanced stand. In general, however, a representative form of government with weak political parties tends to give more weight to the structure of interest groups than to the aggregate will of voters.

Parties perform a function analogous to that of entrepreneurs in the marketplace. They solicit and collect the "investment capital" needed to sell their wares—candidates for office and party platforms—to the voters. Their goal is to achieve and hold office, presumably in order to accomplish public purposes. To do so they must formulate policies that will appeal to enough voters and change their policies when necessary to win elections. Incumbent parties defend their record in office; challengers criticize their record. All parties must develop policy options that will appeal to a significant bloc of electors. Economic or class issues are one common axis of political appeal, and to the extent that wealthier voters are more apt to exercise their franchise and give greater financial support to candidates and parties, concern for their interests will offset any tendency for politicians to cater to more numerous, less wealthy voters. The parties must also formulate policies designed to appeal to ethnic and other groups concerned with particular interests.

Alternation in office among rival parties is a salutary, though not a necessary feature of representative government. Competitive parties are most effective in offering credible alternatives when there is a serious prospect that they will gain at least a share of executive power. Systems in which there is at least a real possibility of alternation among governing parties also tend to minimize, even though they cannot altogether prevent, abuses (in the form of patronage and cover-ups of scandals) which are all but inevitable if one party holds power for great periods.

Even a well-designed democratic system, complete with strong political parties, cannot avoid serious problems with both representative and direct forms of self-government. In view of the fragmentation of public opinion on many issues, achieving consensus is often difficult. When those who execute policy have operative authority that goes beyond delegated bounds, maintaining accountability can also be very difficult. Representative democracy functions poorly in conditions of widespread apathy, ignorance, and incompetence. Although party competition assures that politicians will be responsive to the will of voters, it cannot guarantee that consensus will be achieved or that popular control over public officials will be maintained. Regular elections are nevertheless the most effective means by which citizens can control the actions of their governments. Not surprisingly, the mode of election is therefore open to considerable debate and variation.

8

The Individual and the Group: Voting and Elections

The choice of leaders and policies by voting—in fair, competitive constituency elections and representative assemblies—is the single most common procedural characteristic of democratic polities. Some generalizations can readily be ventured. Thus, in representative constituency elections the secrecy of the ballot protects the integrity of the process, whereas in parliamentary voting openness assures accountability. Otherwise, however, questions concerning the voting act and the choice among electoral systems pose hard theoretical questions. Why should an individual citizen take the trouble to vote? Is majority rule feasible when there are multiple alternatives and fragmented electorates making the choices? Which is preferable, from the point of view of democratic theory: majority/plurality voting or proportional representation? Should elections be thought of as efforts to aggregate individual and group preferences or should they be structured so as to promote stable government even at the cost of representativeness? How, finally, are representatives best held accountable to their constituents?

Rationality and the Act of Voting

If citizens are assumed to be rational calculators, why they should vote at all in large constituencies is a puzzle, inasmuch as individual votes make little difference to the outcome. For the same reason, why should they even take the trouble to become informed about the issues and the candidates? If voting is to be understood according to the same principles of economic rationality as market exchanges, it should presumably be engaged in only when the voter can reasonably expect to benefit. "Every rational man decides whether to vote," Anthony Downs has observed, "just as he makes all other decisions: if the returns outweigh the costs, he votes; if not, he abstains."[1] Presumably, the voter "compares the utility income he would

189

receive were each party in office"[2] and votes for the party whose success is most likely to benefit him." But Downs recognizes that an individual vote cannot be decisive because "it is lost in a sea of other votes."[3] For many voters, he concludes, the decision to take the trouble to go to the polls probably reflects a "sense of social responsibility relatively independent of their own short-run gains and losses" informed by a long-term interest in the survival of the system.[4] From the perspective of rational choice theory, the decision to vote is "typically irrational," although it confers intrinsic emotional benefits, such as "affirming allegiance to the political system" and "affirming a partisan preference."[5] Raymond Wolfinger has criticized this sort of analysis, as it applies to American voting, for paying insufficient attention to the question of why people register to vote, given that a high proportion of those who register do vote in general elections. The leading factor in accounting for the tendency to register, factoring out other considerations such as the difficulty of changing registration because of mobility, is level of education, suggesting that the decision to vote is more a function of a general appreciation of the desirability of electoral participation than it is of a specific utility calculation.[6]

However the decision to vote is accounted for, the choice exercised through the vote is assumed to be a rational act, provided the voter obtains adequate information to make possible a rational choice. If information about the issues and the candidates is made easily accessible through campaigning, the voting decision will be relatively rational and "affordable," in the sense that voters will find it sufficiently in their interest to acquire the information needed to make a choice. What constitutes adequate information is problematic. Candidates and parties are bound to want to structure and package information in ways that enhance their appeal to voters, even if that requires making vague statements of position to avoid alienating voters, misrepresenting the views of opponents, and emphasizing negative or "attack" advertising that avoids positive or substantive statements. Public commissions and private watchdog agencies set up to promote campaign fairness can have some influence, but their findings often appear too late to influence the outcome of an election. The most effective antidote is an intelligent and skeptical voter able and willing to filter the messages by personal "reality checks."

Since it would be impracticable to require unanimity, elections for representatives must be decided by majority, plurality, or by allocating seats in proportion to votes. The idea that the individual can be said to retain freedom while submitting to a legislature composed by any of these criteria is one that anarchists and libertarians reject, but it is nevertheless compatible with the democratic belief in moral autonomy insofar as legislative authority is limited by guarantees of individual rights and inasmuch as collective self-government is a form of moral autonomy.[7]

Even in the best of circumstances, however, the exercise of the suffrage puts a burden on voters. In a two-party system, the ideal rational voter must "(1) examine all phases of government action to find out where the two parties would behave differently, (2) discover how each difference would affect his utility income, and (3) aggregate the differences in utility and arrive at a net figure which shows by how much one party would be better than the other."[8] In a multi-party system with PR, voters face a less daunting challenge, because they can be content to register preferences, but they too must consider the consequences of their vote for the composition of the government and the likelihood that their vote will not simply state a preference but satisfy their expectations measured in terms of "utility" benefits. Uncertainty and lack of information prevent even the most intelligent and well-informed voter from behaving in precisely this fashion. Voters may try to make estimates of their "utility income" from government policies, but they may not measure utility solely by personal advantage.

Rational choice theory is open to criticism in supposing that political behavior is necessarily as self-interested as economic behavior. As the republican theorists suggested, democratic citizens may be motivated by considerations of "civic virtue" or a sense of patriotism. They may support long-term environmental goals, for example, even if they are not likely to benefit from them, except in the form of intangible satisfaction. They will sometimes go to war for their country, even if they risk their lives in doing so. Even if they are not motivated by self-denying altruism, they may be prompted by a sense of collective interest. They may recognize, for example, that an increase in taxes is necessary for the general welfare even though the increase will be more costly to them as individual taxpayers than it may be directly beneficial. Similarly, they may support laws requiring greater fuel efficiency in automobiles out of concern for the nation's energy independence or fear of the "greenhouse effect" on global climate even though they may prefer to drive more powerful, less fuel-efficient cars. Such decisions are hardly irrational, and they suggest once again that autonomy should not be thought of merely as a synonym for self-interested individualism; autonomy may take the form of identification with a group or association or cause thought to be of equal or greater concern than immediate self-interest.

Thus, a recent study of American voters shows that contrary to earlier findings, voter attitudes are often determined by general perceptions rather than specific interests. Government employees are not more supportive than others of public expenditures. The economically discontented are not more supportive than others of tax and spending cuts, though they have been shown to be more opposed than others to specific measures likely to affect their jobs. Women do not support women's issues more than men do. There is no greater support among the elderly for Social Security or Medicare spending than among the general population.[9] Nor is this pattern of behavior a reflection of disparities in information. Studies have shown that "the best informed were actually the least self-interested in three of four issue areas, but the differences were trivial."[10]

Problems in Ascertaining Majority Will

The adoption of representative government results not only from the impracticability of assembling all citizens to govern themselves—which modern means of interactive communication may make more practical— but also from the understanding that voters may not be in a good position to deliberate issues or draft legislation; at any rate, not as good a position as when they make decisions in many private transactions. The voters are therefore well advised to elect representatives who reflect their views in general but who will be better able (if only because they are paid to devote time to the study of the issues) to make informed judgments. Nor should the process be understood simply as one in which voters' preferences are neatly reflected and aggregated by their elected representatives. Rational choice theory oversimplifies in positing that legislative choices can be reduced to fixed preferences. The deliberative process in legislatures often involves the revision of the language and provisions of bills to take account of the sensitivities and objections of affected groups. These efforts inevitably alter pre-existing preference patterns. Voters and their representatives start with maximalist objectives, but the give and take of the legislative and electoral process often compels legislators to modify preferences in order to achieve passage of legislation that is at least minimally satisfactory. The major potential distorting influence therefore arises not so much from the difficulty of ascertaining the public will as from the influence of campaign financing and the corruption of the legislative process by those seeking political favoritism. The insulation of the representative process from both forms of improper influence is vital to the protection of democratic norms.

Bismarck's famous remark that neither legislation nor sausage making is for the squeamish remains apt. Whether political decisions are made directly or indirectly, it is hard if not impossible to ascertain the "general will," for various reasons, even apart from fraudulent electoral practices. These include:

Intransitivity, or the problem of cyclical majorities. Even if the constituency voter and the representative are well informed, they cannot escape the "disequilibrium" which occurs when voter preferences cannot be amalgamated into a single option preferred by a majority. This so-called paradox of voting was discovered in the eighteenth century by the Marquis de Condorcet and has been elaborated in the twentieth by Kenneth J. Arrow in the form of his "impossibility theorem."[11] Arrow developed a number of criteria that would have to be met by a voting system if it would always be certain to reflect the preferences of a majority and found that none could be designed—hence his theorem. The criteria are that voting be rational, in the sense that the voter's preferences are ordered and transitive (if x is preferred to y and y to z then x is preferred to z); that the voting system be such that it can cope with every possible configuration of individual preferences; that the aggregate result should be consistent with voter preferences; that the ranking of options depends on individual rankings of the pair and is not affected by rankings of either preference against others; and that there is no individual whose preferences always become society's regardless of everyone else's preferences. Arrow's theorem, which is generally accepted, holds that there is no logical method for ascertaining the choice of the majority under these conditions when votes are distributed among more than two preferences. Peter H. Aranson offers a clear illustration of the paradox:

Simple example of intransitive social preference.

Voter	First choice	Second choice	Third choice
1	A	B	C
2	B	C	A
3	C	A	B

As Aranson explains,

Suppose that an electorate of three voters—1, 2, and 3—casts pairwise votes for three motions—A, B, and C—and that three voters have individual preference orders as depicted in Table 1. In a vote between motions A and B, voters 1 and 3 vote for A over B; voter 2 votes for B; and therefore A defeats B by a vote of 2 to 1. In a vote between B and C, 1 and 2 vote for B; 3 votes for C; so B defeats C by the same margin. But in a vote between A and C, 2 and 3 vote for C; 1 votes for A; so C defeats A by the same margin. Hence the "social-preference" relation is
     A>B>C>A
where ">" reads "is preferred to."[12]

Because this paradox cannot be overcome by any system of voting,[13] there can be no assurance that the outcome of votes involving more than two options will reflect the preferences of the voters.

In view of this difficulty, William Riker argues that the populist model of democracy is clearly inferior to the "liberal" model of representative government. According to what he describes as the populist model, elected surrogates must reflect the popular will in a clear, consistent, and meaningful manner. The Arrow paradox makes that impossible. In the liberal model, voters can reject "candidates or officials who have offended so many voters that they cannot win an election." Although he admits that this is a "negative ideal" of representative government, Riker contends that in view of the paradox of voting, it is a more realistic way to ascertain popular preferences than the populist model.[14] One problem with this alternative, however, is that elections for candidates invariably pose more than one policy choice and require voters to indicate preferences among candidates, not just policies, and among parties and party leaders.

The Arrow paradox is more appropriately applied to legislative deliberation than to popular elections, where the choice is either between two leading candidates or, under PR, where several candidates may win election. It suggests that in theory no single amalgamated social welfare function (more commonly thought of as the public interest) can always be ascertained by voting. It also suggests that an assembly president or chair can manipulate the agenda by controlling the order in which propositions are voted on so as to bring about a preferred outcome. As Aranson explains, "if he most prefers C, he can set A against B in the first vote, and the winner, A, against C, which then wins by a two-to-one vote in the second vote. More generally, by bringing up his most preferred alternative last, against the winner of the previous vote, he ensures the alternative's victory."[15]

Other considerations operative in general elections and in deliberative assemblies can also affect the outcome of voting in ways that present serious complications for the effort to ascertain majority will:

Strategic Voting. Individuals and blocs of voters may vote in favor of motions or candidates they do not really prefer in order to force a choice between alternatives that will give the advantage to an option they do prefer but which would not otherwise be chosen by a majority. In an "open primary," for example, voters from Party A can vote in Party B's primary in order to defeat a candidate who would pose a stronger challenge to Party A in the election. While this particular practice can be eliminated by changing the rules governing participation in primary elections to prevent voting by other than party members, similar tactics may be used in legislative proceedings where they cannot easily be ruled out. A parliamentary voting bloc can throw its support behind a measure which it does not favor in order to defeat an alternative it likes even less, so as to make its own preferred alternative more acceptable.

Skewed Willingness or Ability to Bear Information Costs. For decisions to reflect the actual interests of the parties, they must all possess the requisite information. Since information is costly to acquire, those with only a weak interest at stake may be unwilling to pay for it. Even if the interest is strong, the voter in a large constituency knows that one vote will have too little effect on the outcome to warrant the expenditure of time and effort necessary to become well enough informed.

Agenda Control by Strategically Placed Groups. Those who control the agenda determine whether an issue reaches a vote and in what form it does so. Legislative committees, like the United States House of Representatives Rules Committee, act as "gatekeepers" in authorizing consideration of bills and assigning priority. By controlling the strategic "gates," interest groups are sometimes able to prevent consideration of some measures and shape those that reach the floor.

"Log-Rolling." Vote trading may enable those with special interests to prevail in cases where their interest is salient enough for them to be willing to trade support on issues where they do not have as intense an interest.

Concentration of Resources to Affect Salient Issues. Those for whom an issue is particularly salient are often more willing than others to devote resources to the pursuit of their objective. When these resources are funds for electoral campaigns, and money is a factor in elections, the result can easily distort the outcome of the process so that the views of the majority are shaped by the views of organized minorities. In electoral systems in which representatives are dependent on private financial support, they may pledge their votes to gain support or at the very least offer contributors special opportunities to press their views, especially on issues not particularly salient for a significant group of their constituents.

Amalgamation of Choices in Elections. Voting in elections compels voters to amalgamate their preferences. When the voting is not on ballot propositions, but on candidates, voters are compelled to combine preferences on issues, that is, to vote for the candidate whose stand comes closest to theirs on issues they consider especially important, but not necessarily on all issues. When an issue is only vaguely articulated in an election campaign, moreover, successful candidates are free to interpret their electoral mandate as they wish, and they can easily argue that changing circumstances have rendered campaign promises obsolete.

Enforced Moderation or Rhetorical Vagueness? In plurality systems, the electoral process forces the candidates to tailor their positions so as to appeal to marginal voters. They must therefore avoid taking extreme positions which could lose them votes of people apt to cluster in the middle. Although it might seem that this system encourages the candidates to develop positions which will appeal to a majority of voters, they are often advised by campaign strategists to address the most controversial issues only in the form of banal generalizations and to draw attention away from the major issues likely to be on the governmental agenda by focusing instead on emotional issues and symbolic and psychological appeals (such as, for example, "to get this country moving again"). By defining issue positions in detail, they are usually warned that they risk alienating some voters and providing opponents with materials that can be taken out of context and used against them.

Single-Issue Voting. When some voters become obsessed with a single issue (as in the controversies over abortion and gun control in the United States), politicians find themselves in a particularly ticklish position because elections may turn on that one issue while the rest of the candidate's stands are ignored. That issue, moreover, may be one over which the candidate will have the least influence (if, as in the case of abortion in the United States, the question is a constitutional one apt to be resolved mainly in the courts).

The Effects of Personality and "Packaging." In selecting among candidates, voters take personality and campaign style into account and not just the issues or party affiliation. Voters can also be persuaded to vote more on the basis of emotions than reason when the issues are presented in a highly emotional way (as in the notorious television commercials on the treatment of criminals in the 1988 American presidential election). Personality, style, and behavior on the campaign trail may sometimes signal a candidate's principles and policy views.[16] But under modern conditions, when marketing techniques are used to discover consumer preferences via such devices as "focus groups," and candidates are "packaged" and advertised like consumer products, the opportunity for manipulation is increased, and personality and style become even less reliable indices.

The Possibility of "Minority Rule." In Australia, where voters are fined for failure to vote, rates of electoral participation are predictably higher than elsewhere. In most democratic countries, a sizeable fraction of the electorate abstains. Where the rate of abstention is high, winning candidates and parties often reflect the votes of a minority of citizens even in two-party contests. In multi-party-elections in plurality systems, the winner is even more likely to be chosen by a minority of the voters. Even when there is a run-off election, the winner may not be the first choice of the largest number of voters. The result is that political leaders and cabinets may lack the mandate or the sense of legitimacy they need to act decisively and expect public support. In parliamentary systems with proportional representation, coalitions of minority parties are frequent, raising the question of whether the government can claim to reflect the will of a majority of the electorate.[17]

In theory, there are ways of dealing with some of these difficulties, though the remedies are problematic. Voters can communicate their wishes to the representatives in public opinion surveys or in constituency polls. To the extent that the representative takes such polls seriously, any deviation between his views and that of the electorate will tend to be diminished.

Polling is, however, notoriously dependent on the way the questions are framed, and public sentiment may fluctuate. Political leadership sometimes requires politicians to take unpopular positions and hope that the results will vindicate them. The party organization usually provides a common platform which has been hammered out in convention and which serves to inform voters of the positions candidates for office will support, thus relieving them of the need to inquire into the views of each candidate. But if party discipline is weak, the party platform is not binding on those elected to office, and in such cases it may promise far more than can be delivered.

Electoral Systems: Plurality/Majority versus PR

Although they cannot overcome all of the theoretical and practical difficulties that make it difficult to ascertain the public will and make it the constant guide of public policy, electoral systems are critical to the functioning of representative government because they are the most explicit and decisive form for ascertaining the public will.[18]

When the electoral system is perceived to be fair, outcomes of the political process are more likely than otherwise to be accepted as legitimate. But the choice of electoral system has an indirect effect on the number and type of political parties, as well as on their cohesiveness or internal discipline. The type of electoral system influences the tendency toward cabinet coalitions and the efficiency and stability of the system of government. The variation in electoral systems reflects different notions of what fairness requires as well as of how political parties should be structured and of the degree of unity in government that is advisable for efficiency and stability.

Although there are many conceivable electoral systems, two types predominate, one known as "winner take all" or "first past the post," the other involving various forms of proportional representation. The winner-take-all type usually allows for election by plurality, though in some cases, such as the election to the presidency and National Assembly in France, winning candidates must have an absolute majority, and a run-off is held if no candidate gains a majority in the first round. In addition to France, Poland, Portugal, Austria, Brazil, Chile, Peru, and Finland also require run-off elections in the event that candidates for the presidency do not receive a majority in the first round. Under PR, votes are cast either for party lists (sometimes allowing indications of preference among candidates) or by rank-ordering individual candidates, a technique known as the Single Transferable Vote (STV). Under the list system, in use in Belgium, Italy, Luxembourg, Spain, the Netherlands, Israel, and partly in Germany, voters indicate a preference for one party list over others, sometimes with the option of indicating favored candidates. Votes are proportionally allocated to the parties, with the result that all those on the lists who receive more than the required minimum are elected. Various mathematical formulas are used to allocate seats.[19] In STV systems, used for elections to the Dail in the Irish Republic and for the Australian Senate, voters rank order the candidates to indicate their preferences. All candidates who receive the necessary quota of votes—first preferences plus lower preferences transferred from already elected or eliminated candidates—are elected.

A variation on PR, sometimes considered a form of semi-proportional representation, is "cumulative voting," whereby voters are allowed to cast all their votes in a multi-member district election for one candidate or divide them among two or more candidates. This technique improves the chances for strongly favored candidates. It was used for elections to the lower house of the Illinois state legislature for more than a century, until it was abandoned when the size of house membership was reduced as an economy measure. It had been adopted as a bipartisan compromise aimed at assuring the election of some Democrats from the preponderantly Republican southern part of the state and some Republicans from preponderantly Democratic Chicago districts. It has lately been proposed as part of a reform proposal which would establish multi-member congressional elections in the United States in order to assure minority group representation.

Some electoral systems allow for the formal linking of party systems, a technique known by its French name, *apparentement*. Although voters vote for one of the parties, the votes are initially combined in the allocation of seats as though they were for one party; the seats are subsequently divided between the two parties. This has the effect of counteracting any tendency, even in PR systems, to overrepresent larger parties. This technique was first adopted in France with the aim of enhancing the electoral prospects of smaller centrist parties.[20] Switzerland and Luxembourg use another technique, called *panachage*, which also helps small parties. Voters have as many votes as there are seats for the district, and they may distribute these among two or more parties.

The difference in the assumptions on which the two most commonly used systems rest is marked though complex. The plurality/majority system reflects two basic assumptions: 1) the aims of democracy are best served by electing a single representative (whether a president, a congressional representative, or a member of parliament) to serve an entire constituency; and 2) governments formed or dominated by a single party govern most effectively and can best be held accountable because they have less need than under PR to enter into broad coalitions which give minority parties the power to frustrate majority will. Preference for the plurality/majority system emphasizes legislative and executive efficiency and coherence as well as accountability. The PR system reflects two different assumptions: 1) for the sake of fairness, significant groups should be able to elect representatives in proportion to their electoral strength; 2) legislatures are deliberative assemblies in which the diversity of opinions and interests should be represented as fully as possible.[21] Proponents of PR criticize plurality election not only because it deprives significant minorities of a chance to elect representatives but also because it can result in the violation of the democratic principle of majority rule when more votes are cast against than for a winning candidate. The possible need for coalition government in PR elections is thought by its advocates to be a virtue, not a defect. If executive power-sharing through coalition government is made necessary by the results of an election, that is considered a desirable outcome because a less proportional result would impose policy outcomes either not favored by a majority or opposed by significant minorities. In practice, both options are not always consistently pursued, and both are open to criticism on various scores.

The plurality/majority system is used in the United Kingdom, in countries influenced by British practice, including the United States, Canada, Australia, New Zealand, and India, and for presidential elections in several other countries. In the United States, however, the constitutional provision for divided government, expressed in the separation of the legislative, executive, and judicial branches, tends to defeat one of the purposes of plurality/majority electoral systems by inviting "gridlock" rather than one-party government.

Most other democratic countries use PR, though some combine the two types. The German system is a notable and often admired example of a hybrid system. The voter has two votes. One is exercised to select among individual candidates for each electoral district; the other is cast for a party. Half the seats in the Bundestag are elected on a winner-take-all basis in single-member districts. The other half are allocated to the parties on a regional list basis. The result is that seats are allocated among the parties in close proportion to the vote, but voters are also assured that their particular district will be represented by a candidate chosen by a district plurality. In 1993, Italy adopted a new electoral system under which voters also have two votes. In this case, however, three-quarters of the seats in the lower house of its parliament are held by candidates elected in single-member districts, while the remainder are distributed according to the second, party vote.

Until the 1993 election, Japan used a system of semi-proportional representation involving a single non-transferable vote (SNTV) in elections for the lower house. Each voter had one vote in each multi-member district, and candidates receiving the most votes were elected. This system made it relatively easy for minority parties to gain some degree of representation, but it also opened opportunities for major party candidates to win more than one seat in each district. In 1993, the Japanese Parliament voted to change the electoral laws to eliminate multi-member districts and elect half the members of the lower house by PR, half by plurality election.

Two forms do not fit within either type. One is designed to assure some representation for designated minority groups, as in New Zealand, which has several districts in which only Maoris can vote, and India, which has a large number of districts in which only members of so-called scheduled castes and tribes can be candidates. The other is the alternative vote system used for elections to the Australian House of Representatives. In this system, the voter lists the candidates in order of preference. A candidate must obtain a majority to be elected, but if no candidate has a majority of first preferences, the candidate with the lowest number of first preferences is eliminated, and his or her second choices are allocated to the remaining candidates. The process continues until one candidate achieves an overall majority, thus assuring that the candidate selected is the one relatively more favored.

Debate over the merits of the two most widely used systems has been intense but inconclusive for more than a century. Those favoring the plurality/majority type tend to stress its tendency to produce two large and usually centrist parties, one of which forms the government, the other the opposition. The result is said to be more accountable and decisive government than is provided by PR systems, which encourage the proliferation of smaller parties and may lead to unstable cabinet coalitions. "The single member plurality system has been defended," two students of the British electoral system have noted, "not on the grounds that it produces a fair result, but rather that it encourages the electorate to choose between alternative governments and that it encourages governments to be responsive to the wishes of the electorate."[22] Downs argues that parties in a two-party system "deliberately change their platforms so that they resemble each other," thus encouraging centrist programs, although that he admits that a two-party democracy "cannot provide stable and effective government unless there is a large measure of ideological consensus among its citizens."[23]

Partisans of PR see it as a fairer mode of representation because it reflects all the shadings of electoral opinion and allows representation to electoral minorities as well as majorities. They also contend that it produces governments with greater legitimacy than plurality elections. If PR leads to coalition governments, they contend, it is because electoral diversity demands it. The need to form and maintain governing coalitions induces the parties to negotiate compromises and avoid the adversarial divisiveness of two-party systems, whereas a single party in control of the government can adopt radical measures that do not have strong popular support. They also note that plurality/majority elections frequently result in the election of governments with the support of less than a majority of voters and that in PR systems fewer votes are "wasted" either on

losing candidates or on candidates who have enough votes to win without them.[24] A British Labor Party reform group has criticized the plurality
system on just this ground: "Most votes in Britain are wasted at a General
Election. In 1987, although 10 million voted Labour, only three million
were needed to elect 229 Labour MPs. The other seven million were either
wasted on a losing candidate or were used to boost the majorities of winning candidates."[25] Many of the losing votes were in the south, where
Labor's strength is relatively weak, and therefore produced many fewer
Labor seats than in Scotland, where Labor is relatively stronger.

Plurality system defenders counter that for large parties, losses in one
region are compensated by gains in others, and that PR saddles voters
with coalition governments they have not chosen, formed by "horse trading" among the parties. To say that votes are wasted in a plurality/major-
ity election is therefore in their view to beg the question, since it is in the
nature of such elections to produce only one winner. Adopting PR, moreover, does not necessarily enable minority groups to exert greater influence, inasmuch as such groups may only succeed in causing political paralysis and weakening the power of government to protect the interests of
minorities.

Another difference between the two electoral systems is in the number
of representatives chosen to represent each electoral district. Plurality/ma-
jority elections are typically (though not necessarily) held in single-member districts. (Thus, in the United States, one representative is elected from
each congressional district, but two senators are elected from each state.)
PR systems require multi-member constituencies or treat the entire polity
(as in the case of the Netherlands and Israel) as one electoral district. Advocates of the single member district argue that it makes the representative
more solicitous of a majority of the voters in the districts. A single member
chosen to represent an entire district must take account of the will of a
majority if he or she is to be reelected; those who hold one of several seats
will be most solicitous of the smaller group of constituents on whom their
reelection depends. Proponents of PR counter that multi-member districts
offer fairer representation. The higher the district magnitude, the more proportional the representation.[26]

PR was first adopted by Denmark in 1856 for the election of over half
the members of its national legislature. In 1859 Thomas Hare's *The Election
of Representatives* urged its adoption in England, and a year later John Stuart
Mill gave it his influential endorsement in his *Considerations on Representative Government*. It was advanced in order to meet the objection that plurality elections effectively deny representation to minorities. Mill argued that
the most important minority that might be denied representation is the
educated segment whose participation he was anxious to have because he
feared the power of less well-educated and working class electorates in an

extended suffrage. The very reason for having a representative government, he argued, is that it is "a means of bringing the general standard of intelligence and honesty existing in the community, and the individual intellect and virtue of its wisest members, more directly to bear upon the government, and investing them with greater influence on it, than they would have under any other mode of organization."[27] PR, he thought, would help assure that educated citizens, even if they should be in a minority, would have a voice in government. But this rationale for PR has been less important in promoting adoption than the concern for more complete representation, particularly in societies with intensely felt cleavages, whether economic, religious, linguistic and cultural, ethnic, or ideological.

Many European and Latin American countries adopted PR, especially between 1900 and 1925. In the aftermath of the fall of democratic regimes in the 1930s, notably the Weimar Republic in Germany, it was held responsible for promoting weak executives and enabling anti-democratic splinter parties to use the electoral process to subvert democracy.[28] To meet these weaknesses, countries with PR have often adopted threshold requirements which have the effect of making PR less perfectly proportional but also less encouraging to splinter and extremist parties. In Europe, the thresholds range from the Netherlands' .67 percent to Germany's 5 percent and Turkey's 10 percent. In the absence of thresholds, small district magnitudes have a similar effect in discouraging splinter-groups.[29] If only a small number of candidates can be elected from each district, weak parties are likely to be less successful than in districts with many seats.

Critics of plurality/majority elections often point out that it not only overrepresents large parties but is also biased in favor of parties with strong regional support and against those with broader support. In the 1987 general election, the British Conservatives, with 42.3 percent of the vote, won 376 seats in the House of Commons, a majority of ninety-eight over all other parties, not an unusual result. (Since the 1930s, no British government has been elected with more than 50 percent of the vote.[30]) In 1992, Bill Clinton won a majority of electoral votes, and therefore became the American president, although he received just over 40 percent of the popular vote. In the 1983 elections, the British Alliance parties polled only 2 percent less of the popular vote than the Labor Party but ended up with 29 percent fewer seats because their votes were spread rather than concentrated.[31]

In order to address the difficulties of plurality voting, a British Labor Party working group recommended in 1993 that the party consider proposing a reform of the electoral laws for the House of Commons which would maintain the single-member constituency but substitute for "first-past-the-post" a modified alternative vote system. A majority of the committee favored the "Supplementary Vote" scheme devised by a Labor MP, Dale Campbell Savours, whereby voters would be given the opportunity to vote for a first and second choice (rather than rank all candidates, as in the unmodified version of alternative voting). Any candidate with more than 50 percent of the vote would be elected. Otherwise, the second votes for any but the two leading candidates would be assigned to them. This reform would have the effect, in the view of the majority, of "limiting the imbalance between votes and seats that has characterised many election results in Britain." A minority of the working group favored a "mixed member" system, whereby about 500 MPs would be chosen in individual constituencies, and another 150, divided equally among ten regions, would be elected on the basis of party votes. This recommendation resembles the German system for the Bundestag, except that it does not give the voter two votes or result in an equal division between constituency and party seats. The fifteen additional members in each region would be the unsuccessful candidates with the highest percentage of votes from parties which win at least one constituency. The aim would be to minimize regional imbalances in parliamentary representation and bring the number of seats received by the parties closer to the proportion of votes they receive.[32] David Butler, a leading student of British general elections, has warned that the Supplementary Vote proposal might have the unintended consequence of fracturing the vote for the current three major parties, by encouraging their wings to compete with each other for seats. In some scenarios, he suggests, this would produce outcomes in which second preferences would lead to distributions of seats even less proportional to votes than those that would result from votes for unified parties under plurality voting or the mixed member option. It would also have the defect of "wasting" first preference votes for candidates who finish a close third.[33]

Deficiencies such as the Labor Party working group found with plurality voting seem to strengthen the case for PR, whereby results are more closely reflective of voting patterns. Richard Rose's Index of Proportionality, which measures deviations between party votes and seats won clearly shows, as might be expected, that PR produces higher proportionality than plurality/majority voting,[34] but the difference is a matter of degree rather than kind.

PR has both strengths and weaknesses. Advocates of PR argue that it is especially desirable for societies with relatively diversified electorates and that it allows for new tendencies, such as those associated with environmentalism or regional autonomy, to achieve a political role commensurate with public support. In newly democratic societies, where the electorate tends to be fragmented, PR has often been considered the more appropriate system. Critics point out that PR often produces coalition governments which are sometimes unstable and in which small parties have a pivotal role. The case of the Free Democratic Party in Germany is a case in point. Although it has often won only enough votes to surpass the exclusion threshold, the FDP has been part of governing coalitions since 1969, and in 1982 it brought about a change in government not determined in an election, simply by shifting its support from the Social Democrats to the Christian Democrats. (Proponents of PR contend that the FDP has played a useful role in German politics by dampening the ideological conflict between the two major parties. But the electoral system allows for the emergence of more ideological parties, including the Greens and right-wing extremists, which might not have the same moderating effect.) In some instances, coalitions become so beholden to small parties that the effect is to produce majority rule skewed by minority veto, at least on the issues of major concern to the small parties, and sometimes on larger issues.

Israel is an interesting example of the potential weaknesses of PR, though it is by no means typical. Israel's experience demonstrates both the compelling case for PR under conditions of electoral fragmentation and that the reliance on PR can result in fractious and unstable coalition governments. Israel's political divisions make it difficult for a government to maintain power whenever a decision must be made that threatens to unravel a fragile coalition. The majority party or alliance in the coalition must often in effect pay blackmail to minority factions (such as religious groups concerned more with subsidies for education and control over marriages than with foreign and economic policy) to stay in power and carry out its electoral mandate. In the first period of the country's history, when a party with strong support (*Mapai*) could choose its coalition partners from a wide array of small parties, PR was not as debilitating. But when the situation changed in the 1980s to one in which one-party dominance was replaced by competition between two equally well-supported groupings (the *Maarach* or Alignment and *Likud*), neither of which could win a majority of seats in the Knesset, the balance of power shifted to small parties mainly concerned with single issues—notably the religious parties—which used their leverage to extract concessions from both of the major parties.[35] Splinter parties can be discouraged by building in a threshold requirement, like the 5 percent minimum required in Germany. In Israel the threshold has been raised from 1 percent to 1.5 percent.

In Israel's case, the PR system is a relic of the pre-state period in which Zionism was a movement with many fractious wings that needed to be accommodated. It remains to be seen whether the adoption of a PR system at an early stage, when it seems more appropriate, tends to make replacing it difficult at a later stage when it is no longer so desirable. If the system were changed, even if only by significantly raising the threshold, religious interests would have an incentive to pursue their concerns within rather than outside the major parties, depriving them of their ability to enter government coalitions but not of all opportunity to exert an influence.

PR is now in use in a majority of countries which have been democracies since 1950. It has also been made a requirement for elections to the European parliament in all the member states. A number of countries (including Germany, Italy, and the Scandinavian countries) use a two-tier system with much larger districts at the national level and smaller districts at the local level. Following the Germany precedent, in the December 1993 Russian elections, half of the 450 delegates elected to the lower house were chosen in constituencies, half from party lists.

The mixed systems tend to confirm Arend Lijphart's suggestion[36] that from an empirical perspective democratic regimes are of two different types, which he calls Westminster (or majoritarian) and consensual (sometimes also consociational), though many are hybrids. The Westminster type, so called because of its British origins, reflects an individualistic social system in which there may well be group cleavages, such as class divisions, but no attempt to assure that such cleavages are necessarily reflected in the executive branch of government. The expectation is that with the possibility of an alternation in power, any significant group that finds itself a minority in one election may come to power in another. Majority rule is not thought to pose a threat to the corporate interests of minority groups. Typically, Westminster systems are based on plurality elections in single-member districts. Representatives (and presidents, in the other version of a majoritarian system) are chosen on the first-past-the-post or winner-take-all principle. Governments are formed by the party or coalition with a majority in parliament.

The consensual type, of which Switzerland is one of the few consistent examples, is usually designed to suit fragmented or segmented societies in which there are sharp cleavages, especially due to differences of language, culture, ethnicity, and/or religion. The intention is to guarantee minority groups a degree of autonomy and corporate representation. Elections are by PR. To mitigate tensions and promote social harmony, power-sharing in a "grand coalition" is required rather than majority or plurality rule. In Switzerland, the result is a cabinet in which seats are allocated according to the 2:2:2:1 "magic formula," an arrangement whereby two seats are held by each of the three largest parties and one goes to a medium-sized party. Since the parties vary along religious as well as socioeconomic lines, the cultural and regional groupings have roughly proportional representation in the cabinet. Lijphart suggests that in pure form the two types exhibit quite different characteristics:

Westminster	**Consensual**
1. Concentration of executive power	Executive power-sharing (grand coalition) in one-party bare majority cabinets

Westminster	Consensual
2. Fusion of executive and legislative	Separation of powers
3. Asymmetric bicameralism	Balanced bicameralism, minority representation
4. Two-party system	Multi-party system
5. One-dimensional party system	Multi-dimensional party system
6. Plurality elections	Proportional Representation
7. Unitary, centralized government	Federalism and decentralization
8. Unwritten constitution, parliamentary sovereignty	Written constitution, minority rights
9. Parliamentary government/ no referendum	Referendum

Except for countries like Switzerland and Belgium, however, where language cleavages are major considerations, most countries that display elements of the consensual type—like the United States—rely just as heavily if not more on elements of the Westminster type. Where the major cleavages are cross-cutting rather than one-dimensional, the majority-plurality system is more appropriate. The consensual type may be advisable for societies split into coherent fragments, but it tends to freeze differences in place rather than encourage groups divided by ethnicity, language, religion, and/or region to join amalgamated parties united by other affinities, such as ideology and economic interest.

Lijphart has argued that in the case of South Africa, power-sharing among self-selected groupings offers the best prospect for a democratic solution, and the interim constitution adopted in 1993 follows this approach. It remains to be seen whether this interim arrangement will be retained or replaced by a majoritarian/plurality formula in the permanent constitution. Donald L. Horowitz, while agreeing that PR may be the most appropriate electoral system for the South African legislature, contends that the use of the alternative vote might give the various groups an incentive to cooperate by pooling votes. He also points out that a president elected by a coalition of ethnic groups is likely to be more effective and to pursue a more comprehensive program than a power-sharing coalition cabinet. Such a coalition executive elected in Northern Ireland in the 1960s under a power-sharing formula was not successful in promoting compromise reforms between Protestant "unionists" and Roman Catholics demanding Irish unification. Citing experience elsewhere, including India and Malaysia, Horowitz contends that executives elected by groups induced to form coalitions will be more likely to transcend their own ethnic affiliations than cabinets representing these different groups.[37]

As Lijphart's comparative examination shows persuasively, however, even mainly majoritarian systems are apt to have consensual elements. The danger posed by these arrangements is that they may tend to harden differences by entrenching them in the constitution and creating constituencies and political leadership with a vested interest in their survival. Along with respect for individual and communal autonomy, however, democratic systems must also allow for pluralistic forms of autonomy.

Both majoritarian and pluralistic tendencies are reflected in and reinforced by electoral laws. In the 1940s, Maurice Duverger suggested that experience with electoral systems seemed to indicate the operation of a social scientific law: plurality/majority elections tend to produce two-party systems and stable governments; PR tends to produce multi-party systems and less stable coalition government.[38] Whether the electoral laws reflect social and political divisions or engender or help perpetuate such divisions has long been controversial.[39] An intermediate view holds that electoral laws and social cleavages interact.[40] Giovanni Sartori has reformulated Duverger's "laws" as "tendency laws": 1) "Plural formulas facilitate (are facilitating conditions of) a two-party format, and conversely, obstruct (are an obstructive condition of) multipartyism," and 2) "PR formulas facilitate multipartyism and are, conversely, hardly conducive to two-partyism."[41] The plurality/majority system tends to encourage the development of a two-party (or sometimes two and a half-party) system, in which the parties are coalitions of groups that would be likely to field separate parties in a PR system. The two-party system induces those who might otherwise prefer to form or support other minor parties to work within either of the two major parties. Where the direct primary is used, dissidents from the "mainstream" of the parties and "single-issue" candidates may try to achieve the nomination of one of the two major parties, but they have difficulty contesting elections as third parties. The requirement of an electoral majority tends to discourage smaller parties, except that where run-off elections are provided for, smaller parties may hope to influence the outcome in the second round by doing well enough in the first to deny success to larger parties. The requirement of a plurality is also a deterrent to smaller parties, though a lesser one, inasmuch as a party that can muster only a third of the vote can win if votes are evenly split among several candidates. A comparison of sixty-nine electoral systems using either plurality or PR systems has shown that "only plurality succeeds in creating a two-party system, by reducing the average effective number of about three elective parties to one with two parliamentary parties."[42]

Other Options and Issues

In theory, constituents could communicate their views to politicians in ways other than voting for one or a small number of candidates and their parties. They could be asked to engage in approval voting, veto voting, or point voting.

In approval voting, invented by Steven Brams, voters are not restricted to voting for just one candidate. Instead they can vote for, or approve of, as many candidates or as few as they like. The winner is the candidate approved of by most voters. This avoids the difficulty posed by the election of a minority-approved candidate in a field of more than two.[43] This system has not yet been used, but in the 1990 parliamentary elections in several of the republics formed from the Soviet Union voters were asked to strike out the names of candidates of which they disapproved, a technique similar to approval voting.

Another technique hardly ever used but favored by many students of the theory of voting is the one discovered by Condorcet and named for him. In this system, voters are always asked to choose between pairs of candidates. If there are three candidates, voters are asked to choose between A and B, A and C, and B and C. In this way, the outcome is sure to represent the choice of a majority. The trouble with this proposal is the same as in the Arrow paradox. As Condorcet himself recognized, it is possible that there may be no winner. The Condorcet technique is shunned not only because of this defect (which is unlikely to apply in practice) but also because it is considered difficult for voters to understand and hard to administer, especially where there are more than three candidates. With modern computers, however, it could be easily managed. All the voters have to do is to rank order the candidates (as in STV and the alternative vote), and the computer can readily determine the outcome of pairwise preferences.

Voting by veto may be used in choosing among policy alternatives. The voters, whether in a legislative assembly or a referendum, are presented with a series of policy options, including one favoring the status quo. Each voter unhappy with the status quo is asked to remove one policy option plus the one favoring the status quo.[44] By using this procedure, voting on issues avoids the problem of strategic voting and the problem that arises when a particular motion fails and a scramble sets in to develop an alternative.

Voting by points enables voters to demonstrate the intensity of their support for particular alternatives, leading to outcomes that provide a weighted sum of preferences.[45] While theoretically possible, this system has never been tried.

Other factors also affect the electoral process and through it the character of the representative system. The size or "magnitude" of the electoral district, measured by the number of representatives elected in it, affects the viability of smaller parties. As a rule, the larger the district magnitude, the easier it is for smaller parties to elect representatives. Relatively small single-member districts, like those in the United Kingdom, tend to penalize smaller parties by giving them less representation than their votes might achieve if many representatives were elected from each district. Where a majority is required for election, multi-member districts make the outcomes especially disproportional and favorable to the larger parties. The larger the district, however, the more attenuated is the link between representative and voter. The most extreme cases are those of Holland and Israel, where representatives are elected in a single at-large election. Malapportionment is said to exist when districts are of significantly different population size. Japan's Liberal Democratic Party is notorious for having created and maintained a system of districting in which the votes of rural voters have effectively had more weight than those of urban voters less firmly attached to the LDP.

Simultaneous election for the legislature and the national executive, as in the American case, is thought to reinforce the effect of the plurality formula in producing a two-party system. Since the vote for the president is nation-wide, smaller parties are likely to be handicapped in achieving nominations and campaigning in all states.

Representation and Accountability

Representative government is, as John Stuart Mill emphasized, a relationship between the people and their deputies. It raises some of the same problems of accountability as the relationship familiar in legal reasoning between a principal and an agent. The problem of maintaining accountability is one that arises on various levels of democratic government and differs according to the nature of functions and relationships. It arises not only in the relationship of electors to representatives, but also with respect to the relationship between representatives and appointed officials and between the public government and agencies in the private sector (such as universities and private corporations) subsidized with public funds or serving as government contractors.

Although impeachment and criminal prosecution are used in particular instances of misconduct, periodic elections are the main general method by which representatives are held accountable by those they represent. In terms of accountability, strong parties are preferable to evanescent movement parties because they must be concerned with their long-term survival. The voters may reward and punish parties even when they cannot always do so with respect to particular politicians, who may simply choose to retire. Similarly, a parliamentary government without a division of power between executive and legislature offers the voters a better opportunity to hold representatives accountable than a system of divided power like the American that inevitably leads one party to blame the other for anything that voters might find offensive. But representatives are often expected to perform so many different functions (including services for constituents) and cast votes on so many different issues that voters cannot easily hold representatives accountable except in cases where they act scandalously or cast a clearly unpopular vote.

9

Federalism: Devolution and Cooperation

Especially in large and regionally diverse societies, representative democracy is often modified and supplemented by federalism—a term with two different connotations, both of which play hob with the notion of sovereignty. In one usage, federalism connotes a type of association more exactly called confederal, in which each of the units retains complete sovereignty; in the other, it connotes a shared authority between a central government and affiliated states or provinces. This authority may take the form of coordinate sovereignty (whereby the central and affiliated units have authority over the same functions). In the more usual case, it entails a constitutional devolution of specific functions of local bearing to the affiliated units, while more general responsibilities, such as for security and foreign relations, are reserved for the central government. In either form, federalism is not inherent in democracy but has long been recognized as an arrangement of great value to democracy. It minimizes difficulties of size, enhances opportunities for popular participation in government, and limits the potential for the abuse of power by the central government by creating other countervailing governments. By itself, federalism does not always succeed in containing fissiparous tendencies, as is evident from the American Civil War, the recent collapse of the Soviet and Yugoslav federations, and the separatist movements in Canada and other federal countries. In tandem with representative government, however, it improves prospects for stability and can help promote peaceful dissolution when unity cannot be maintained.

Federalism operates at various levels of government. At the lowest level, it takes the form of metropolitan government, associating cities and unincorporated areas and allowing a strong political pyramid to be created using neighborhoods as building blocks. Metropolitan government facilitates regional planning while also allowing for local differentiation and control.

At the national level, federalism can exert direct influence if the legislature is structured to allow for regional representation. Otherwise, it permits a distribution of power which makes government less remote and more sensitive to local needs. Internationally, federalism permits nation-states to retain control over matters considered vital to national interest and identity while cooperating in matters in which it is advantageous to coordinate policy and share burdens. Especially on the international level, defining the areas of separate jurisdiction and "subsidiarity" is bound to be difficult. In the case of the European Union, the creation of a federal system is elevating onto an international level the domestic conflicts on these issues between classical liberals and social democrats and, ironically, reviving nationalist passions. But the benefits of association and cooperation, coupled with advances in communication and travel, will likely promote continuing integration.

Federalism in Modern History

Interest in federalism arose with the revival of republicanism in modern times when theorists and statesmen alike reasoned that if republics must be small to be viable and to avoid the dangers of overcentralization, confederation or federation with some degree of consolidation would enable them to avoid the dangers of weakness due to small size. This concern was reflected in the adoption of federal constitutions by a number of republics, notably Switzerland and the United States. The American civil war showed that federalism could not overcome deep-seated conflict, especially when the conflict arises over core values of democracy. In the nineteenth century there was also interest in federalism in Latin America, but it did not take hold. The Venezuelan and Mexican experiments failed to produce real devolution. In Argentina, the *federales* and *unitarios* were locked in conflict. Brazil, with its centralized monarchy, was the most stable Latin American country in the century. Then, as now, background conditions seem to have been influential in determining whether federalism would be adopted. In the United States, federalism followed successful colonial experience with local self-government. In Spanish America, the failure of the *cabildos* or town councils may have inhibited the adoption of federalism.[1]

In Europe, the picture was mixed in the nineteenth century. In France, where the regions had been bastions of resistance to the Revolution, centralization was considered necessary to assure that republicanism would not be subverted. In Spain, however, federalism found favor among republicans. The Spanish Republican Party, founded in the middle of the nineteenth century, was federalist from the outset, and Francisco Pi y Margall, its major theoretician and the first president of the republic, saw Spanish federal republicanism as part of a wider revival of Western republicanism. Pi, who was also influenced by the anarchist writings of Pierre Joseph Proudhon and by Hegelian dialectics, went so far as to argue that nations as they existed and were emerging were "false nations" created by wars and secret diplomacy, more the products of monarchical fiat than "natural" nationhood or popular will. Federalism, he believed, would encourage the emergence of more homogeneous self-determining republics whose alliances would remove the grounds for war and thus lead to peaceful co-existence. Pi pointed to the changes underway in Austria-Hungary and Germany as evidence of the universality of federalism, though these were hardly good examples of the real thing.[2]

The Benefits of Federalism for Democracy

The same considerations that make federalism seem essential to republicanism also apply to democracy. Without a way of breaking up the units of government and devolving authority to the local level, democratic government must be remote from most citizens, and large constituencies must be content with only administrative functions but little or no political life of their own. Without federalism, large-scale democracy invites an overcentralization in which bureaucratized central governments can fashion clumsy "one-size fits all" policies. With federalism, democracy becomes a rich if often tension-ridden process of give and take in which localities must bargain with each other, in which local government becomes a stepping stone for careers in national politics, and in which the central authority must take local concerns into account. Federalism in its various forms gives citizens a greater opportunity to scrutinize the workings of government in terms that are likely to be most familiar, and even to become engaged themselves in local elections and local issues. A federated state in which some authority is devolved to regional entities allows for variations in policies and practices designed to take account of different circumstances and values. It allows the units to serve as laboratories of experiment in which measures may be tried out and if successful later adopted by others or by the national government. It enables regions with ethnic or linguistic minorities to achieve a plural autonomy which, while it falls short of full sovereignty, at least provides the opportunity for cultural survival. Federalism also has the distinct advantage over separate sovereignty for such regions of allowing those not in the ethnic majority to retain their rights as members of a larger community. It also avoids the prospects of boundary disputes which claims of sovereignty make almost inevitable. Autonomy in a federal arrangement is constitutionally guaranteed to Quebec, Catalonia, and the two linguistic communities of Belgium; France, which is otherwise a unitary state, also grants autonomy to Corsica.

Such federal arrangements can serve as useful models for newly democratized states. Some of the hostilities that have arisen as a result of the break-up of the Soviet Union might have been muted if most if not all of the successor states had accepted a stronger form of federation than the tenuous unification provided for in the Confederation of Independent States. In 1993 Russia itself adopted a federal constitution acknowledging the identity of eighty-nine constituent entities comprising republics, territories, provinces, federal cities (Moscow and St. Petersburg), and autonomous provinces and regions. The upper chamber of the bicameral Federal Assembly, the Council of the Federation, consists of 178 deputies elected from the constituent units. While Russian is established as the state language of the Federation, republics are given the right to certify the use of their own state languages as well. Many of the most important functions are allocated to the federal government, and federal law is given precedence over local law. Certain functions, however, including education, the protection of the rights of members of minority groups, the use of natural resources, and the protection of the environment, are assigned jointly to federal and regional authorities.[3]

It is worth bearing in mind, however, that federalism has not been adopted only in ethnically or culturally diverse societies. Most federal systems, Murray Forsyth has pointed out, "were not constructed with a view to reconciling different ethnic demands."[4] Federalism has usually been adopted in societies notable for relative ethnic, racial, and linguistic homogeneity. The thirteen cantons of the old Swiss Confederation were originally associated in the fourteenth century by people of Germanic stock; not until 1815 were the subordinate French- and Italian-speaking communities given equal status with the other cantons and the Swiss union transformed into a multi-lingual compact. The American federal system was adopted by people who shared a common descent and a common language. The same is true for the German *Bund* of the nineteenth century (as it is of the Federal Republic of today) as well as the Dutch United Provinces and the Commonwealth of Australia. In these instances, federal arrangements were adopted because they seemed to be a good way of achieving the benefits of larger size without losing the opportunity for maintaining government close to the people.

The first federation to be formed to accommodate ethnic and cultural differences was the Canadian in 1867. The British North America Act simultaneously united several previously separated provinces and divided one of them, Canada, into Upper and Lower Canada, or southern Ontario and Quebec. "Most of the English-speaking Fathers of Confederation from Canada and the Maritime colonies," Donald Smiley has pointed out, "would have preferred a unitary system—in the language of the day a 'legislative union'—but the French-Canadian Conservatives were unwilling to agree to any political settlement which would have placed those powers they deemed necessary to the integrity of their cultural and linguistic community in the hands of the majority in the new Dominion."[5] Belgium, India, and Spain subsequently also adopted federal arrangements to accommodate cultural and linguistic diversity. By itself, territorial federalism may not fully meet the need to protect ethnic and linguistic diversity, unless it is accompanied by other arrangements for power-sharing affecting the central government. The danger posed by these arrangements is that they may tend to harden differences by entrenching them in the constitution and creating constituencies and political leadership with a vested interest in their survival.

Four Different Cases in Point

Both the concern for a balance of centralization and decentralization and respect for pluralistic autonomy have made federalism more and more appealing. The systems actually adopted show considerable variation.

1. *The United States*. American federalism was originally designed to satisfy the concern of the states in the union to preserve a measure of the independence they had won in shedding their colonial status. Before long, it became especially important to the southern states, which sought to preserve slavery under the banner of "states' rights." In the aftermath of the American Civil War, when slavery was outlawed, federalism atrophied as the authority of central government was expanded to allow for greater economic integration. Because of concern with the growth of the central government, however, federalism has experienced a revival of interest, manifested in such slogans as "the new federalism" and "cooperative federalism," which symbolize efforts to promote administrative cooperation in matters where jurisdiction is coordinate, such as welfare, education, housing, transportation, and environmental protection. The national government sets the standards and provides conditional grants; the states develop plans to spend the money and they manage the programs, subject to national government scrutiny. Nevertheless, the American model is one in which the locus of authority is in the central government and the original jurisdiction of the states is limited to certain areas specified in the constitution, notably education, and to others in effect devolved by the national authority. It is in effect a system of federation in which the central government is the dominant partner but in which certain functions are either fully or partly devolved upon the states. A good example is the current debate over the right to abortion. While the national Supreme Court has given constitutional status to a woman's right to have an abortion, the Court has lately ruled that the states may regulate the exercise of that right. Further courts with members opposed to the previous decision could overrule it and give the entire authority to the states. But the American constitutional system is so fluid that Congress could provide statutory protection to the right to abortion, and the Courts could conceivably bow to the will of the national legislature rather than that of the state legislatures.

2. *Canada.* Created in 1867 and reconstituted just over a century later when the constitution was patriated, the Canadian federation was specifically designed not to take account of the regional character of a sprawling country but to try to overcome tensions between two founding communities which a Canadian writer has described as "two solitudes." Although the arrangement has been a constant source of tension, it has so far survived, suggesting that French Canadians have found it beneficial to be a part of a a larger country so long as they can enjoy enough autonomy to protect their cultural survival and economic interests. The Canadian system, Alain Gagnon suggests, "has been successful, not so much in resolving conflict as in managing it, and striking a flexible balance between the divergent views of the initial bargain." The system allows for swings between central and local power and for an "asymmetrical federalism" to take account of Quebec's special place in confederation.[6]

Canada has been particularly effective in working out institutions and policies (such as unconditional federal grants to the provinces) that give political reality to the formal framework of federalism by maintaining strong provincial governments with fairly well-defined responsibilities. Ironically, however, the effort to go from pragmatic arrangements to formal agreement has proved extremely difficult. A painstaking effort to hammer out an accord in the form of an amendment to the constitution, known as the Meech Lake accord, which was designed to meet Quebec's conditions for remaining within confederation, came close to being accepted but failed. When the Supreme Court of Canada ruled in 1988 that Quebec's French-only sign law violated Canada's Charter of Human Rights, public opinion in English-speaking Canada turned against the accord and its centerpiece, a clause recognizing Quebec as a "distinct society." Quebecers have often expressed discomfort with the terms of confederation, and came very close to rejecting them altogether in a 1995 referendum. It remains possible, however, that constitutional recognition of Quebec's "special status" may prove more acceptable to its Francophone majority than a struggle for separate sovereignty—in view of the boundary conflicts, minority status issues, and economic uncertainties that peaceful separation would entail. Separatists sometimes argue that Quebec can have the best of both worlds, by adopting a compromise formula for "sovereignty-association," but opponents have warned that the province's adoption of such a formula would spell the end of confederation. The underlying question, Peter H. Russell has stressed, is whether Canadians can become "a single sovereign people"[7] or must remain a composite nation, at best a mosaic, at worst a badly divided polity. The question may never actually be resolved, if the recent mood of "constitutional fatigue" holds; more likely, as Russell suggests, it will be suspended by a recognition that Canada, like many other modern nations, must live with its diversity and may be the better for doing so.[8]

3. *Belgium*.[9] Belgium provides an example of a very different tendency, leading away from centralization toward a diffusion of authority. Belgium was initially created during the fifteenth and sixteenth centuries when the Dukes of Burgundy succeeded in uniting French-speaking with Dutch-speaking provinces under their personal rule. The present nine provinces are the successors of the old principalities that formed the Burgundian state and subsequently fell under Spanish, Hapsburg, and French republican and imperial rule before becoming the independent kingdom of Belgium. When the provinces were taken over by the French in the 1790s, the occupying forces imposed both a Jacobin centralization and a policy of Frenchification so as to ensure that annexation to France would be taken for granted. Steps were even taken to ban the Dutch language. From then until 1970, the Belgian state remained strongly centralist. Change came about because of growing Flemish militancy. After independence in 1830, the French-speaking ruling groups who prevailed throughout the country imposed their language as the only official tongue. But because its population consisted of a majority of Dutch-speaking Flemings (now estimated at 5.5 million) and a smaller number of Francophones (now estimated at 3.25 million), as well as German speakers (now estimated to number 70,000), there was great dissatisfaction with the effort to impose French language and culture. A Flemish movement developed in the nineteenth century which sought to restore the status of Dutch in the country as part of an effort to revive Flemish culture. The tensions generated led to a series of changes in the law of the state affecting the public status of the two major languages which culminated in the adoption of a federal system. Two homogeneous cultural communities were given constitutional recognition in 1970, and four linguistic regions were recognized which could be altered or reshaped only by a law passed by a specially qualified majority. In 1980, a new political agreement, the so-called Community Pact, was agreed to and confirmed by most of the parties to the negotiation for a new government; a draft law embodying the principles was tabled but lapsed due to the dissolution of Parliament. In 1987, the constitutional reform entered its last stage when it received approval by both houses of parliament and the King.

Under this latest agreement, Belgium is to be divided both territorially and culturally, into regions, language areas, and three (linguistic) communities. Certain powers are to be conferred exclusively to the national government, others are to be exercised by the regional governments, either exclusively or concurrently, and by the linguistic community councils. The

House of Representatives is to continue to represent the nation, but the Senate is to be structured so that it represents communities and/or regions. There are to be three community organizations to manage the respective affairs of the Flemings, the French, and the German speakers. The members of these councils are to consist of directly elected members of the relevant language group in the Senate. The regional councils consist of members of the relevant language groups directly elected in the provinces in which the language is spoken. The three communities are to have full powers over education with the exception of matters relating to a "Schools Act"—an agreement among the political parties to maintain a financial balance between the state network and the Catholic network. The present Court of Arbitration is to be transformed into a Constitutional Court with the task of ensuring the observance of the constitution. The functions of the community councils are to manage cultural affairs, except for music, which is recognized as a national function, "personalized" matters, including health provision and health insurance, and welfare policy. The regional institutions are to have competence in such non-cultural areas as environment, housing, water and energy policy.[10] The aim is to confer explicit powers on the communities and regions, and by implication to give all residual powers to the central government, but since there are apparently overlapping responsibilities entailed, and since the taxing power is national, there is bound to be disagreement over the exact division of authority.

4. *Spain: "The State of the Autonomies."* When Spain became a short-lived republic, from 1873 to 1876, it also became a federal state. This experiment proved to be a disastrous failure, but with the recreation of the republic in 1931 and lately with the return to constitutional monarchy, the federal concept has been revived, with great emphasis on providing regional autonomy. Pi y Margall, the theorist of the first Spanish republic, argued, as Alistair Hennessy recounts, that the Spanish liberal state "was an artificial creation, the heir of Bourbon and French Revolutionary inspired centralization both of which were alien to the essence of the national spirit in which loyalty to the *'patria chica'* (the 'little fatherland') eclipsed wider loyalties."[11] In fact, the Spanish monarchs had permitted the Basques, Navarrese, Aragonese, and Catalans, as well as Castilian towns, to maintain separate legal codes (*fueros*) to win their support. After the Napoleonic invasion, the central state collapsed and Spain became, as Pi pointed out, virtually a federal republic. The Bourbon restoration could not restore the legitimacy of the monarchical state, and the Liberal revolution of 1820 mounted the first of a series of challenges that eventually led to the overthrow of monarchy. The Liberals were opposed to federalism, because they were anxious to break the political stranglehold of rule by local elites and the clientelism (*caciquismo*) they practiced to assure their control. But there was grassroots support for federalism not just from the

notables but also from members of the professional middle class, who could hope to find employment in the local governments, and from lawyers who could expect to make a living mediating between the units of government. Pi's federalism was also built on naive foundations insofar as it ignored these conflicts and sought to impose a rationalist Hegelian scheme that took no account of economic inequalities among the regions or of tensions between Catholic belief and secular liberalism, neither of which could be satisfied by a patchwork nationhood with different ways of life. Even more serious as a danger to federalism was the development of peripheral capitalism in Catalonia and the Basque provinces, which threatened the view that no region should predominate. Regionalism burgeoned into nationalism and threatened Pi's conception of federalism. Indeed, it is industrial progress in the Basque country and Catalonia which, more perhaps than ideology, has propelled demands for autonomy and total independence. The Second Republic tried to meet the demand by maintaining a unitary state but allowing any republic which wished it a right of autonomy well short of independence; Catalonia was the only province to claim the right before the Civil War.

Franco's authoritarian centralist policy sought to crush all but folkloric expressions of regionalism, including the use of languages other than Spanish, and to inculcate Spanish patriotism through the schools and the state-run media. A reaction in favor of decentralization was inevitable, and it has taken effect under the constitutional monarchy. The end of the Franco dictatorship led to a reopening of tensions between Spanish and peripheral nationalisms, and the present two-tier system of autonomous communities is the result.

The latest scheme provides autonomous status to seventeen regions. The Constitution of 1978 allows for a two-tier solution allowing for degrees of autonomy. While asserting the "indissoluble unity" of "the Spanish nation," the constitution guarantees the right to autonomy of the nationalities and regions. A distinction is made between the historical nationalities (Catalonia, the Basque provinces, and Galicia) and those regions which in the past had not articulated demands for autonomy, but in order to avoid resentment on the part of regions whose people might resent the fact that some of the regions were able to extort concessions, the constitution recognizes two levels of autonomy. Catalonia, the Basque provinces, Galicia and Andalusia are explicitly granted autonomy under one article, Article 151, while the eleven other regions are given eligibility for autonomy, under another provision, Article 143, after a period of five years in which at least two-thirds of the local provincial councils show a clear majority in favor. The powers vary, depending upon which article they are granted under, and also upon political agreements to be struck by the levels of government and decisions of the Constitutional Court. Originally, it was not intended that the communities established under Article 143 should achieve the same degree of autonomy as those authorized under Article 153.[12]

In 1983, seventeen autonomous communities came into existence. Each has a regional legislative assembly consisting of a single chamber (whereas the central parliament is bicameral, to allow for both direct popular and regional representation, except that representation to the Senate is primarily from the provinces rather than the autonomous communities; 25 percent of the representatives are appointed by the parliaments of the autonomous communities). The leader of the parliamentary majority party or coalition becomes president of the autonomous community and governs with a cabinet of ministers. Each community has a High Court of Justice which resolves disputes of a regional nature, but in the final instance each of these courts is answerable to the national Supreme Court of Justice.[13] The effort by Catalonians and Basques to use autonomy as a way of limiting the authority of the central government to national security, foreign affairs, and the control of currency, led to a reaction on the part of Spanish nationalist forces which culminated in the negotiation of compromise amendments. The main difference between the two tiers of autonomy is that the most autonomous provinces have explicitly recognized control over education, but the opportunity is available for all provinces to claim the same degree of control. The central state is empowered to plan the country's overall economy and has the primary power to raise taxes. The autonomous communities can also levy taxes, but only to the extent that this power is delegated to them by the central state. Only a small fraction of Spanish taxation is in fact levied by the communities. The national government is specifically empowered by the constitution to allocate revenues in such a way as to alleviate regional disparities.

Whether Spain actually becomes a highly decentralized state or merely one with the potential for becoming so remains to be seen. Something may depend upon the attitude of the military leadership. The military ideology under Franco was that the military had saved the state not only from communism but also from political fragmentation. The greatest threat to the stability of the present arrangement lies in the Basque provinces. The aim of the most radical terrorist groups seems to be to provoke a military coup and thus win acceptance for Basque nationalism. But a military coup could conceivably move Spain back toward centralization with respect to the provinces that remained part of the country, even assuming that the military would be prepared to recognize Basque independence. Hennessy's wise observation offers food for thought on the vexing question of the future of Spain as a nation and of the ties between Spaniards and the rest of Europe:

The gap between Spain and Europe has narrowed so that both share the same inanities, enjoy comparable freedoms, suffer from similar problems—terrorism, pollution, drug abuse—both share similar tastes arising from the homogenising tendencies of mass culture. As social and geographical mobility increase as a consequence of these tendencies it may be argued that the desire to find recognizable identity in more restricted loyalties and the urge to recapture a vanishing sense of community increases. It may be too early to speak of a disappearance of the national community and the emergence of a nation of small communities comprising small, participatory groups such as family, ethnic and voluntary associations, but if trends in the United States are a reliable indication the time when Spain will be a federation of smaller communities enjoying Pi y Margall's sense of "unity in variety" may not be that far off.[14]

Sovereignty Versus Autonomy Under Federalism

These notable examples, as well as others that might be cited, suggest that federalism is a viable technique for dealing with the problems posed for modern democracies both by size and by territorially-based ethnic cleavages. For both reasons, federalism may be emerging as an alternative to the more rigid concept of the sovereign state. "In the modern world," Reinhard Bendix observed, "the state is the dominant political institution."[15] This generalization still holds, but it can no longer be said to be as robust as it once was. Although the state remains the matrix of domestic and international politics, pressures toward internal devolution and external interdependence are giving new life to alternatives to sovereign statehood. During the Cold War, the disparity of power in the era of nuclear weapons and intercontinental delivery systems led to a bipolar confrontation between two more or less hegemonic alliances led by two "superpowers"—a development representing a *de facto* compromise of independent state sovereignty. In the same period, economic relations as well were characterized as hegemonic, and their stability was thought to be a function of the control exercised by the two superpowers as hegemons over their respective alliances. Domestic frictions in multi-lingual, multi-religious, and multi-ethnic states have caused serious internal divisions, in some cases leading to partition, in others to persisting civil war and separatist terrorism, and in still others to the adoption of territorial federalism. The end of the Cold War has led to the resurgence of nationalism and sub-nationalism in eastern and central Europe. Meanwhile, at both regional and global levels, a growing sense of the reality of interdependence has arisen, due to many factors. These include the concern for collective security, the advantages of freer trade in a "globalized" economy, the rise of giant transnational corporations, the newly felt need for concerted ecological policy, as well as the impact of cultural homogenization, migrations, and vastly improved communication. While some of these developments evoke demands for micro-states, others make the whole notion of separate statehood seem anachronistic.

In view of these developments, the question deserves to be raised of whether the notion of sovereign statehood as the *sine qua non* of modern politics retains its descriptive and normative validity. While the sovereign state arose for compelling historical reasons, recent developments are making it less and less appropriate and an obstacle to further progress in resolving or at least stabilizing domestic and international conflicts. At least in some cases and in some respects, the alternative of autonomy under federalism is more appropriate and a more flexible instrument of accommodation.

Many modern analysts have pointed out that federalism has already become an alternative to state sovereignty in a number of countries, including the United States, Canada, Australia, and West Germany, and that ethnic and territorial conflicts elsewhere can best be addressed by adopting proposals for autonomy rather than by creating mini-states.[16] Ivo Duchacek has emphasized the association between federalism and democracy, noting that federalism is "a territorial expression of the core creed of democracy . . ."[17] As belief in the ideal of democracy spreads, more and more countries can be expected to adopt it as a domestic expedient and to become more open to it internationally.

But there is bound to be resistance to the call to abandon a notion that has become ingrained and that seems, however mistakenly, to promise stability because it connotes certainty about the locus of ultimate authority. The very word "sovereign" has long carried an aura of assurance that often turns out to be illusory. Under the pressure of domestic tensions or of external dependency, all that seems so solid can easily melt away, leaving both authority and power either fragmented or controlled from without. By contrast, federalism is a continuing exercise in living with uncertainty. This very flexibility, however, is its strength. As a "co-ordinate division of powers" between a general authority and regional authorities,[18] modern federalism has the advantage of allowing for a blend of interdependence and autonomy that statehood and sovereignty do not readily permit. This blending makes it increasingly appealing under modern conditions.

The case for sovereignty was first made four centuries ago in the vacuum caused by the final collapse of the Holy Roman Empire, when the struggles that ensued for control of the emerging nation states of Europe erupted in dynastic and civil wars. In view of the threats posed by religious schism and by efforts to protect the traditional rights of the hereditary nobility and medieval constitutional authorities like the *parlements*, the French "Legists" of the middle decades of the sixteenth century had a plausible case for locating *imperium* in monarchy. If royal authority had not been endowed with supreme and indivisible rule, anarchy and civil war would have been unavoidable. Writing at the height of the Huguenot revolt in 1576, even moderate constitutionalists like Jean Bodin became converted to their cause.[19]

The concept of sovereignty was directly associated with the acceptance of the validity of the territorial state as the primary unit of government. The state was assumed to be the highest practical unit of government, much as the *polis* had been assumed to be the highest possible unit of government by the ancient Greeks. Bodin made the idea of sovereignty a central consideration in an attempt to settle the question of how, not necessarily by whom, the territorial state must be organized for the sake of order. "The question that he asked, in other words," Julian Franklin has observed, "was what prerogatives a political authority must hold exclusively if it is not to acknowledge a superior or equal in its territory."[20] There must be, Bodin answered, a single concentrated focus of power and authority which is both "absolute and perpetual."[21] It is "not limited either in power, or in function, or in length of time."[22] As the source of law, the sovereign must be, in the phrase he made well known, *legibus solutus*, or not subject to law. In view of the fact that rule was exercised by princes, it was a short step to a confusion of sovereignty with their rule, and Bodin took it: "Since there is nothing greater on earth, after God, than sovereign princes, and since they have been established by Him as His lieutenants for commanding other men, we need to be precise about their status [*qualité*] so that we may respect and revere their majesty in complete obedience, and do them honor in our thoughts and in our speech. Contempt for one's sovereign prince is contempt toward God, of whom he is the earthly image. That is why God, speaking to Samuel, from whom the people had demanded a different prince, said, 'It is me they have wronged.'"[23]

As Bodin acknowledged, however, sovereignty did not require or necessarily imply absolute monarchy. The authority of the monarch might be constrained by moral law and by customary law, including the law of succession, and by the subjects' right of property. In some circumstances sovereignty might belong to the assembly of the people, though Bodin was quick to add that it would be unwise to allow "deliberation on affairs" to popular assemblies, effectively making the only institutional alternative to monarchy an assembly of gentlemen such as the Venetian Great Council.[24]

Precisely because the ideas of the state and of sovereignty proved to be even more adaptable than Bodin supposed, they survived attack over several centuries and came to be recognized as serving indispensable purposes, both for legal theory and for political practice. The state, in Max Weber's canonical phrase, came to be defined as that body possessing the legitimate monopoly of the means of physical coercion in a given territory. Sovereignty, in the thinking not just of John Austin and later positivists but of international lawyers as well, was understood to be both the source of the legal sanctions governing the use of physical coercion and an attribute which serves as the basis for the recognition of the state by other "sovereign states."

Criticisms of Sovereignty and Its Defense

The notion of sovereignty was attacked almost from the outset on two particular grounds: 1) some commonwealths were said to have mixed constitutions and therefore to defy the rule that all states must have an indivisible sovereign; 2) because absolute monarchy seemed all too convenient an expression of sovereignty, the idea was at first considered incompatible with parliamentary government and the liberty of the individual. Both attacks were fended off but they left the case for sovereignty weakened, opening the way for efforts to dispense with it altogether.

Bodin himself was well aware of the first objection, but he contended that it was based on a mistaken view that systems of government could function successfully without an ultimate source of power and authority. He noted that commonwealths in which kings consult the estates of the realm were said to have mixed forms of government in which there was no locus of sovereignty. He disposed of these cases by pointing out that the kings of England, France, and Spain often imposed laws without asking the consent of the estates. He faced a more formidable challenge in rejecting this objection as it applied to Rome, inasmuch as such venerable authorities as Polybius and Cicero had attributed Rome's republican perfection to its mixed constitution. He dismissed this case too, by denying that republican Rome in fact had a mixed constitution. The Senate had the power to deliberate and to decree, he contended, but the ultimate power to order rested with the people of Rome, in accordance with the ancient Roman saying, *Imperium in magistratibus, auctoritatem in Senatu, potestatem in plebe, maiestatem in populo* ("Command in the magistrates, authority in the Senate, power in the commons, and sovereignty in the people").[25]

Bodin's dismissal of Rome's mixed constitution was either disingenuous or a result of a failure to appreciate the realities of shared power. His aim after all was to identify sovereignty as a real exercise of power, not as some remote or metaphysical source of authority that might express itself in tacit consent to whatever actual rulers did. He was determined to show that wherever power was exercised, it always emanated directly from some single indivisible source. This way of formulating the question strongly suggested that sovereignty required absolute monarchy. That very effort to make sovereignty absolute yet limited provoked a second objection which Bodin did not address. His claim that the sovereign could tax subjects was inconsistent with his implied admission that subjects could not be taxed without their consent (lest the restrictions on the taking of their property be transgressed). This inconsistency had little consequence at first, but ultimately became a ground for resistance by revolutionaries bent on transferring sovereignty from the king to the people.

The first theorists of sovereignty were hardly in favor of that sort of transfer. Although Bodin acknowledged that sovereignty might reside in the people, as in the case of the Roman Republic, he would not have considered it legitimate or conducive to good order for subjects to deprive their kings of sovereignty or hold them accountable for their exercise of power. Monarchs held their titles on the presupposition that sovereignty had been irrevocably conferred. Similarly, when Thomas Hobbes continued the work Bodin had begun, he could describe his task as the definition of the "rights of states, and duties of subjects."[26] Like Bodin, he was particularly anxious to show that the insistence on liberty of conscience by dissenting religious sects was a recipe for anarchy. He too was preoccupied with the need to establish the principles by which political communities could be protected against the uncertainties and internal weakness due to conflicting claims of authority, especially those between *regnum* and *sacerdotium* that had riven Europe since the investiture controversy of the eleventh century.

Perhaps because they did not appreciate the degree to which the concern with the right of property would become a metaphor for the larger concern with the liberty of the subject and a justification for revolution, neither Bodin nor Hobbes saw it as a serious threat to sovereignty. Hobbes gave reassurance that subjects would enjoy liberty in those things "by the laws praetermitted,"[27] but argued that obedience to the sovereign was the *sine qua non* of security—the necessary basis for any liberty at all on the part of the subject.

Popular Sovereignty

Nevertheless, in developing the notion of the social contract, Hobbes opened the door to a restatement of the classical notion of the popular basis of sovereignty. Even Legists implied that the authority the king exercised could be understood in two ways, either as *majestas* or *regnum*, recognizing a distinction between the authority the king exercised on behalf of the state and the authority he exercised in his own personal right. Roman political theory had assumed that the authority of the emperor had ultimately been conferred by the people. The Legists were reluctant to make this explicit, but some early modern theorists, especially Johannes Althusius, made it very explicit by defining the social pact as a pact among the ("consociational") groups that compose society.

By so doing, Althusius took Bodin's concept of sovereignty, as Carl J. Friedrich pointed out, "and in a most ingenious fashion . . . made the organized community, that is the 'people,' the sovereign."[28] Althusius did not go so far as to propose that popular sovereignty be institutionalized by a revival of republicanism. Instead he attempted to counter Bodin's elevation of monarchical power by arguing that sovereignty should be exercised by the estates and corporations. This effort was doomed to fail because it amounted to a wistful attempt to reconstitute medieval society at a time when the state was emerging out of the pressures to overcome the fragmentation of society into hierarchical corporate segments. The centralization of power in the hands of absolute monarchs reinforced apprehensions such as those of Althusius and continued to make medieval corporatism look more and more attractive. Thus, Montesquieu pointed out that in preventing a concentration of power, "intermediary powers" had preserved liberty. Like Althusius, he too vainly proposed that the role of the estates be revived.

Later champions of republican and parliamentary government, including John Locke, sought to change the language of politics altogether so as to eliminate any need to define the state or locate sovereignty. Locke wrote not of the state but of "civil government" and avoided any reference to sovereignty. Locke's insistence that rights were natural and that political power originated in an effort to protect these rights both rationalized and encouraged efforts to restrict the power claimed in the name of sovereignty. Jean-Jacques Rousseau's version of the social contract had an equally momentous effect in promoting the belief in popular sovereignty. Locke's argument that authority originates with the formation of civil society and is given to a representative and accountable legislature as a fiduciary responsibility was readily assimilated to the idea of popular sovereignty. Rousseau was much more explicit in calling for popular sovereignty because he saw no need to restrict it by natural law. As Maurice Cranston has noted, Rousseau agreed with Hobbes "that sovereignty must be absolute or nothing, but he could not bring himself to accept Hobbes' notion that men must choose between being governed and being free."[29] The *Social Contract* was his answer to Hobbes in the sense that he revised the concept of sovereignty to make it apply to the entire body of citizens acting in their capacity as citizens rather than subjects, cooperating to express their common or general will. They could thus be governed and free (or self-determining) at the same time.

The constitution of the Fourth French Republic, adopted in 1946, made Rousseau's identification of democracy with sovereignty explicit: "National sovereignty belongs to the French people. No section of the people nor any individual may assume its exercise." And, in an echo of the Declaration of the Rights of Man, the Constitution adds, "The principle of all sovereignty rests essentially in the nation. No body and no individual may exercise authority unless it emanates expressly from the nation."[30] In this form it seems to protect the individual liberty guaranteed by the Declaration; in principle, however, and disassociated from such a declaration, popular sovereignty becomes a recipe for a tyranny of the majority.

That danger appeared to be a real one not just to opponents of the French Revolution but even to some participants in the American revolution. As Tocqueville remarked, "The dogma of the sovereignty of the people came out from the township and took possession of the government; every class enlisted in its cause; the war was fought and victory obtained in its name; it became the law of laws."[31] Tocqueville learned the phrase "tyranny of the majority" from the Whigs (or former Federalists) he met in America, and made it the focus of his anxieties for the future of American democracy.

Sovereignty Confounded: The American Case

These fears were misplaced, however, because the framers of the American Constitution were not at all enamored of popular sovereignty. The first American constitution, the Articles of Confederation, left sovereignty more in the hands of the constituent states than of the new federal government. The final version made sovereignty all but impossible to find in the American constitution. Formal sovereignty presumably inhered in the constituent authority that had created and could amend the constitution, but amendment was deliberately made cumbersome, and operative sovereignty was parcelled out among the three branches of the federal government and the states. In *Federalist* 46, Madison sought to deny that the constitution had divided sovereignty between two levels of government and thereby created the dread problem of *imperium in imperio*, but he could only claim in rebuttal that both the federal and state governments are "substantially dependent on the great body of the citizens of the United States" and who are therefore the locus of sovereignty. Both the states and the national government were merely "agents and trustees of the people."[32] The authority of the central government was expressly conferred in the written constitution and limited by the specification of enumerated rights which the government was forbidden to deny. Even the ever-insightful Tocqueville failed to appreciate the degree to which the dogma of popular sovereignty had been vitiated in its implementation. "The people, he observed, reign over the American political world as God rules over the universe. It is the cause and end of all things; everything rises out of it and is absorbed back into it."[33] Given the care with which the framers of the American Constitution hedged and restricted popular sovereignty, they may better be understood to have sought to avoid establishing any but an ultimate locus for sovereignty. They knew well that Blackstone had put sovereignty in the king, lords and commons of England, and therefore effectively in Parliament, and they sought instead to put it in no agency of government.

The Survival of State Sovereignty

Elsewhere, partisans of the French revolution readily associated sovereignty with monarchy and condemned them indiscriminately. But the demand for liberty did not succeed in overthrowing the felt need for a fixed authority which was so well met by the concept of sovereignty. Prudent monarchs agreed to respect the customary, common law, or natural rights of their subjects and to share their authority with parliaments. From the petitions of right in the seventeenth century to the various bills of rights in the eighteenth, legal challenges and enactments resulted in the limitation of the power of the sovereign, first in England and then elsewhere, as the example spread.

In the nineteenth century, anarchists like Pierre-Joseph Proudhon renewed the attack on both the state and sovereignty, and in the early decades of this century, the anarchists were joined by a more respectable chorus of pluralists (such as the younger Harold Laski, G.D.H. Cole, J. N. Figgis, and Léon Duguit), who denied that "the omnicompetent state" could require the exclusive or ultimate loyalty of all "subjects" without competing for their affections against other associations such as churches and trade unions. These challenges too were successfully rebuffed.

The sovereign state survived these attacks because civil discord and the persistence of war made its existence the *sine qua non* of order, just as its earliest advocates had argued. Liberals sought to remove the threat of state despotism and the dangers to liberty of popular sovereignty by constitutionalizing the authority of the state so that it could not infringe upon basic rights. But everywhere, the state grew more and more "institutionalized" as the exclusive framework for public law and government, territorial security, and economic management.

This domestic institutionalization was reinforced by the failure to achieve a degree of supranational organization capable of overriding state sovereignty. "Idealists" imagined a world under international law in which sovereignty and statehood were respected and "realists" defined the international system as anarchic, making states the principal actors in it and sovereignty, wherever it was actually enforced, the mark of statehood.

The birth of the modern state system, of which theorists like Bodin and Hobbes may be said to have been the midwives, was momentous for Europe and afterward for the rest of the world. The Peace of Westphalia in 1648 created the modern system of international relations, a system in which many states, each sovereign in its own territory, coexist as equals without subordination to any higher authority. The system rests on international law and the balance of power—"a law," Leo Gross has observed, "operating between rather than above states, and a power operating between rather than above states . . ."[34] Before then, the imperial system that had more or less united medieval Europe had formed one of four great imperial systems in the world, the others being those of the Asian Han, Kushan, and Parthian kingdoms.[35] The transformation of this empire in the West into an order of independent states was eventually to affect these other empires as well. As the new European states undertook great efforts of exploration and expansion, they spread ideas of nationalism which challenged the remnants of the other empires. World War I led to the defeat of the newer Ottoman empire. The European powers created new empires of their own but eventually lost them. Waves of de-colonization in Africa, Asia, and the Middle East, made the system of independent sovereign states universal, even though in some cases the state systems remained fragile and poorly institutionalized.

In the decades and centuries that followed, this system has been extended to virtually the whole of the world. The end of imperialism left the state as the predominant political organization in regions where it was a foreign imposition upon tribal and personalistic forms of rule. Balance of power strategies first created alliances in which dependent states forsook formal sovereignty in order to enjoy subvention and protection from richer and more powerful states. Potentially the most far-reaching change has been the creation of international organizations, first the League of Nations and later the United Nations, designed to provide a measure of collective security without challenging the principle of national sovereignty.

Modern Tendencies: The Challenge to State Sovereignty

The rise and persistence of anomalous mixed systems of government like that of the United States of America, in which power is deliberately divided and federated, began to put both related concepts of the state and sovereignty in question. If the Swiss Confederacy could be dismissed as a small and marginal aberration, the example of the United States could not be so readily ignored; and as early as 1793, in a landmark opinion of the Supreme Court (*Chisholm v. Georgia*) Justice Wilson noted pointedly that "to the Constitution of the United States the term sovereignty is totally unknown."

More recently, the controversy over sovereignty was renewed, less for political than for intellectual reasons, but without leading to rejection. Concern for the clarification of political language led S. I. Benn and R. S. Peters to initiate the modern discussion by remarking that sovereignty "is an ambiguous word, and the theories associated with it are complex and often puzzling." Benn delineated six different meanings of the term and found them so lacking in coherence and empirical relevance as to make a "strong case for giving up so Protean a word."[37] The ambiguity that Benn and Peters had in mind was mainly the expression of the conflict between de jure and de facto interpretations. As they point out, the claim to exercise supreme legal authority is not necessarily or always coincident with the ability to enforce obedience to that authority, whether by consent or coercion.[38] Indeed, diplomacy has often been bedeviled by the question of whether or not to consider de facto sovereignty the basis of de jure sovereignty, also known diplomatically as "legitimacy." This ambiguity is a secondary effect of the ambiguous character of the modern state, to suit which the term sovereignty was designed. The theorists of the state begged the question of whether the order designated as sovereign was legitimate—or in other words whether it was acceptable to those whose lives and liberties were being ordered.

In the decade of the 1960s, F. H. Hinsley and A. P. d'Entrèves separately answered this complaint and made persuasive cases for retaining the term. Sovereignty, Hinsley argued, reflects the important effort to convert power into authority and thereby set limits to the exercise of coercion by the state.[39] While admitting that increasing social complexity has made it harder to locate sovereignty and even brought the existence of a single sovereign authority into question, he concluded that because of the persistence of statehood, sovereignty remained an indispensable notion.[40] D'Entrèves took a similar line, pointing out that the late medieval jurists who first "invented" sovereignty sought, under Roman influence, to make law the authoritative expression of supreme power, defining sovereignty as both the foremost attribute of a plurality of states and the basis of their justification.[41] Rather than abandon the notion of sovereignty as obsolete in a world of fragmented and interdependent states, d'Entrèves warned that it remained necessary in order to reduce friction and prevent civil wars in unstable states with "mixed constitutions"[42] and to restrain the exercise of force in political organizations aiming to transcend the state: "Surely all the delicate mechanisms by which the power of the Nation-State has been brought under control may equally be needed if the World-State ever comes into being."[43] With good reason and strong support, W. J. Stankiewicz therefore concluded in 1969 in an introduction to book of essays called *In Defense of Sovereignty* that for its all ambiguities, sovereignty remains a vitally needed concept because it provides a unifying theory in which the interests and purposes of any political order can be defined and made the basis of the exercise of power and of the obligation of those subject to it to respect that exercise of power.[44]

As persuasive as these arguments were in supporting retention of traditional usage, empirical developments continued to bring it into question. As the Cold War approached freezing point, a more or less bipolar universe was said to have come into existence in which many legally sovereign states had become subordinate in military and economic respects to two "hegemonic" superpowers, the United States of America and the Soviet Union. A "balance of terror" resulting from the possession by both sides of nuclear weapons and intercontinental delivery systems was said to have imposed "hegemonic stability" in a formally anarchic world of independent sovereign states.[45]

Once again, however, empirical developments appeared at first to have rescued sovereignty from impending oblivion and even vindicated it. No sooner had a thaw in relations between the two superpowers loosened the ties binding the Western alliance and all but destroyed them among the satellites and subordinated nationalities of the Soviet bloc, than previously suppressed feelings of national and sub-national independence have come to the fore. In the former Soviet Union, these feelings have produced a political implosion. Throughout eastern Europe, the same feelings have been reasserted, and the loosening of the Moscow's grip has led to the reunification of Germany and the division of Yugoslavia, the latter formerly held together by fear of the Soviet Union and by what was widely but erroneously thought during the time of "Titoism" to be a fervent nationalism overriding religious and ethnic loyalties. Czechoslovakia, newly restored to the independence it was given at Versailles, almost immediately split into two separate sovereign states. Similar fissiparous tendencies are at work elsewhere in the world and could lead to the breakup of other ethnically, religiously, and/or linguistically diverse states, including Iraq and Lebanon and possibly even Spain and Canada. The multinational (or transnational) entities, moreover, have not proven altogether immune to state authority, as the negotiation of agreements on monetary policy, tariffs and trade makes plain.

This latest turn of events is apt to provide only a temporary reprieve. Although recent developments seem to suggest that whatever sovereignty may mean, belief in it is becoming more, not less pronounced, countervailing forces make its prospects uncertain. It is by no means clear, for example, that either the large states that will remain intact or the smaller new states to emerge from the current process of disintegration can possibly become as fully sovereign as the nation-states of Europe sought to become when the concept of sovereignty first emerged in the sixteenth and seventeenth centuries. If sovereignty requires not only recognition of legal control over a certain defined territory but also military and economic independence and, no less critically, a separate sense of cultural identity, it may become harder and harder to find in the modern world. Modern technologies of all sorts, from space surveillance satellites to transportation and communications systems, make geographical and physical frontiers much more permeable than they were when oceans, rivers, mountains, and man-made walls promised isolation and protection. Economic growth and stability require the concerting of monetary and trade policies and often the assistance of global lending agencies; a growing cultural homogeneity is eroding folk cultures and creating a global mass culture. The intermingling of peoples, products, and ideas, especially among the most economically advanced countries, makes insular nationalism hard to sustain despite its emotional appeal. The need to adopt formal and informal systems of cooperation for the sake of security (such as NATO) and economic exchange (such as the Common Market and now the European Union) has not abated with the end of the Cold War. In addition, there are signs of a growing recognition of the need to protect both human rights and environmental health and safety. As a result of all of these forces, de jure and de facto systems of federalism are being adopted that limit if they do not altogether replace sovereignty.

Today, however, it is not just the experience of one or two countries, whether small or large, that is shaking the foundations of the state and sovereignty. The threats are arising from both centrifugal and centripetal forces which are being felt in different ways and in different degrees in many parts of the world. The centrifugal forces appear most visibly in renewed national and sub-national claims for independence or at least special status. Some of these have arisen in the wake of the Cold War, as the grip of Soviet imperialism has been loosened, and are now apparent in the former territories of Soviet Union and in several of its erstwhile satellites in eastern Europe. These developments do not necessarily show that statehood and sovereignty are obsolete; on the contrary, they entail demands for the proliferation of statehood and sovereignty rather than for their abolition. But in doing so they call traditional claims of both statehood and sovereignty into question and raise the problem of an almost infinite regression of both statehood and sovereignty. As some ethnic and cultural minorities form new states, they are apt to assert their sense of liberation and national identity in ways that seem threatening to citizens who constitute a minority within these states, like the twenty-five million ethnic Russians living in the newly independent states of the former Soviet Union. In the most notorious case, that of Yugoslavia, the Muslim minority has become the victim of efforts of expulsion and even genocide described as "ethnic cleansing." Such groups are bound to feel that they can protect themselves only by seceding and achieving their own statehood or at least acquiring specially protected status. As a result, the nations of eastern and central Europe may break apart still further, forming states out of little more than territorial enclaves. The resulting patchwork of real and aspiring separate national states could well prove highly unstable. Similar centrifugal tendencies are also appearing elsewhere, as the quest to preserve traditional identities from cultural homogenization arouses passions in Spain, Canada, and in newly decolonized nations in the Middle East, Africa, and Asia. These pressures are putting new strains on the ability of the state to uphold the claim to exclusive control over "its own" territory, and they suggest a need in many cases to reconstitute both statehood and sovereignty to make them less "either/or" choices and more opportunities to accommodate diversity under federal systems allowing a significant degree of autonomy.

The centripetal forces come from growing economic interdependence, from progress in communications which promotes cultural universalization, from the need to achieve protection against the increasing lethality and range of modern weaponry, and lately from a growing perception of planetary solidarity induced by threats to the environment that cannot be dealt with except through concerted action. Transnational organizations like the Universal Postal Union, trade regimes for coffee and other commodities, and quasi-cartels like OPEC have been seen as harbingers of a new functional transnationalism that is moving the world "beyond the nation state."[46] Similarly, the rise of the transnational corporation is said to have put "sovereignty at bay."[47] The United Nations, even though its charter acknowledges the principle of state sovereignty and its very existence and effectiveness depend on the willingness of independent states to pay its bills and supply its peacekeeping forces, nevertheless represents a step toward an unprecedented form of international government in which the privileges and immunities of state sovereignty are subject to abridgement in the name of collective security and human rights. The federative arrangements of the European Union, while still highly controversial and uncertain in character and extent, also presuppose some sacrifice of traditional independence.

Federalism and Autonomy

Taken together, these trends make imperative a reexamination of the reliance on statehood and sovereignty as the *sine qua non* of political organization. More positively, they support the desirability of resurrecting a concept even older than sovereignty—the concept of autonomy which, coupled with federalism, provides an alternative to statehood and sovereignty yielding the benefits of integration while preserving individual and collective liberty.

In the modern world, sovereignty is unlikely to disappear,[48] but it will have to co-exist with new forms of government in which mechanisms of federalism will provide for more limited forms of self-determination by states and subordinate entities. These forms of self-determination are best described as forms of autonomy rather than sovereignty. As has been pointed out earlier, the ancient ideal of *autonomia* began as a recognition of the relative independence of one *polis* from another.[49] It was initially transformed by natural rights/social contract theory from a corporate to an individual ideal, but nationalism has again made it a corporate ideal as well. If corporate *autonomia* is to be a viable and peaceful ideal, however, the autonomous entities, whether they are sovereign or only semi-sovereign states, must become associated in federations which will recognize and protect their right to autonomy while requiring measures to protect common interests and fundamental human rights.

It would be too simple, even in some respects altogether wrong, to say that in view of both the international integration and domestic disintegration now occurring or in prospect, sovereignty is already an obsolete notion. Even domestic disintegration, as in the case of the former Soviet Union, only leads in the short run to the multiplication of sovereignties, not to their elimination. Formally or legally, and in power-political terms as well, the nation-state remains the central actor. But the new ties which have lately developed among nation-states, such as those that are reflected in the United Nations, the European Union, NATO, and the Organization of American States, have begun to introduce a significant degree of federalism and interdependence. These changes still fall far short of visionary dreams, but they complicate the old picture of the political world as a collection of isolated and independent sovereignties.

If sub-national conflicts are to be addressed successfully, experiments will need to be made with systems of political autonomy that fall well short of traditional sovereignty but derive strength from federalism. As Daniel J. Elazar has remarked, "The homogeneous nation-state embracing a population of individual citizens undivided by permanent group ties, which was the goal of the sovereignty movement as it grew out of the European context, has simply not been achieved, nor is it likely to be in the foreseeable future."[50] Autonomy under federalism offers a constructive alternative. The Spanish reform is a shining example. A similar scheme of autonomy might have made more sense than complete independence for many peoples of the former Soviet Union and the other east European states. Even in well established states, such as Canada, France and the United Kingdom, demands for autonomy are being made on behalf of linguistic, cultural, or regional groupings. Some form of communal or plural autonomy will surely have to be granted to both the Greek and Turkish communities of Cyprus if that troubled island is to become more tranquil. An arrangement for autonomy (under formal Argentine sovereignty) might have been an acceptable enough solution in the Falklands/Malvinas controversy to have averted war. The residents of Hong Kong would surely prefer autonomy to full absorption into China. It may also be the only practical basis for resolving the claims of Kurds and Palestinians. The creation of a fully independent Kurdistan would require the extremely unlikely agreement of several countries—Turkey, Syria, and Iran as well as Iraq—to lop off parts of their territory. Autonomy within Iraq may be more feasible, especially if the United Nations continues to play a supervisory role. Such an arrangement might also set a precedent for addressing the status of Kurds in the other countries of the region. Fully sovereign Palestinian statehood would pose difficulties for both Israel and Jordan, both of which would have reason to fear irredentism from Palestinian Arabs who have claims on the territory of both states and who constitute a majority of the population of Jordan and a sizeable minority of that of Israel. This difficulty could be alleviated by federation, either between Jordan and an autonomous Palestinian entity, or between Israel, Jordan and the new entity, perhaps as part of a larger Middle Eastern community of states. Many other conflicts (including those involving the Catholics and Protestants of Northern Ireland and mainland and Taiwanese Chinese) might also profitably be addressed by solutions entailing autonomy within either bi-national or uni-national federation.

Federalism is thus a highly useful adjunct to democracy. Pressures on sovereignty from within and without could have beneficial effects in promoting liberty, if devolution is balanced with protection of individual rights. Although sovereignty once threatened to deny the liberty of the individual, the compromise later worked out in the creation of constitutional democracies has served well to protect domestic liberty and even helped create a global demand for human rights by showing that liberty and order are not incompatible. There can be no guarantee that domestic devolution will be equally respectful of individual liberty, especially when it is done to placate sub-nationalist demands. Forbidding English-speaking Quebecers from displaying English-only signs on their shops does not enhance individual liberty. International association, on the other hand, could promote prospects for individual liberty if it leads to the adoption of uniform codes of human rights and establishes mechanisms like the European Court to which individuals can appeal against their own states. Not only do such associations promote a wider consensus on human rights, but they also allow for greater personal mobility and diversify and multiply the structure of authority in ways that may well enhance opportunities for dissent and redress. In a democratic age, all politics must be conceived of as a form of power sharing involving both individual citizens and groups, as well as different levels and agencies of government. In an increasingly interdependent age, it must also be understood to involve relationships, perhaps even rights and obligations, that transcend territorial boundaries.

Practice

10

Democratization: Perils of the Passage

By any standard, the spread of *belief* in democracy since World War II, especially in the most recent period, is impressive, but the difficulties often experienced in putting the belief into practice cast a cautionary shadow over prospects for worldwide democratization. Successful democratization requires a transformation not only in governmental institutions and practices, but also in social and economic structure, institutions, behavior, and values. This broad and deep restructuring is most likely to be accomplished in societies in which levels of education and standards of living are relatively high to begin with and in which democratization raises them further. The transition to democracy is much harder to achieve in societies in which most people are poor, illiterate, and sharply divided by group identities and loyalties. In such settings, efforts of restructuring are likely to arouse resistance among the privileged and powerful before the benefits for the mass of the people become tangible enough to mobilize their countervailing support. During periods of change, entrenched elites— whether bureaucratic, military, economic, or ecclesiastical—can undermine reforms and sometimes make and unmake governments. If reforms are implemented gradually, resistance from the privileged can be muted, but only at the cost of disappointing the expectations of the impoverished. If radical economic reform is attempted, however, it may impose short-term economic hardships upon those least able to bear them. Those factions able to influence the transition will try to protect their own interests by structuring constitutional and electoral laws and using state offices and patronage to shield themselves from opposition and accountability. The problem of achieving a successful transition is often compounded by regional and ethnic rivalries and by appeals to nationalism. Cultural traditions are sometimes said to be threatened by efforts to modernize the society and integrate it into the international economy. Small wonder, then, that efforts of democratization often founder and sometimes only lead to autocratic reactions.

Waves and Reverse Waves

The modern transition to democracy, Samuel P. Huntington has pointed out, has occurred in three waves, each of the first two followed by a reverse wave. The first occurred between 1826 and 1926, ending in often disastrous experiments in Wilsonian self-determination on the part of ill-prepared fragments of dissolved empires; the second, from 1943 to 1962, when the defeat of fascism revived the fortunes of democracy in areas that did not fall under the control of the Soviet Union; the third began in 1974 and is continuing, at least in part because the economic success of market-oriented democracies has made it seem that prosperity requires democratization. In the first, over thirty countries established at least minimally democratic institutions on a national scale. In the second, shorter wave, twelve more succeeded in adopting democracy, or at least in moving significantly toward doing so, while several others made tentative efforts which were short-lived.[1] The third wave began at the periphery of Western Europe, in Portugal and Spain in the west and Greece and Turkey in the east, spread to Latin America and Asia (notably to South Korea and the Philippines) and has had its largest impact in the fifteen former constituents of the Soviet Union and its central European satellites. In all, some thirty more countries have been added to the roster during this third wave, bringing the total to about seventy. By 1994, 114 of the world's 191 states were listed by Freedom House as formally democratic, representing 45 percent of the world's population, though thirty-seven of the newer additions were only "partly free," so much so that some would be more likely to be considered autocratic.[2] The move toward democracy seems well entrenched, but with significant exceptions and the possibility of another reverse wave.

Preconditions and Requisites

In view of the manifold problems that may arise in the transition, and of the different paths it may take, analysts have often recognized the futility of adopting a single universally applicable formula to account for democratization. Nevertheless, some generalizations seem to hold well. Certain preconditions and structural requisites have often been identified as favorable to success, and success is measured by parameters which will be familiar from the previous discussion of the theory of representative democracy. Democracy is likely to be adopted, and to survive, in societies with relatively high levels of literacy and education and with widespread well being—or at least a widespread expectation of economic growth.[3] Some degree of inequality inevitably accompanies the creation of a market economy, and even extreme inequality may be politically tolerable in stable democracies, so long as the general level of well being is relatively high and rising. It is critically important, however, that economic development not be so devoted to capital accumulation as to ignore the need to improve general living standards.[4] Ethnic, religious, racial, and linguistic conflicts must be contained within a framework of common identity allowing for pluralism and preventing attempts by one group to dominate or exclude others. The military establishment must be willing to accept civilian rule. Religious institutions must not be in a position to prevent secular authority from functioning autonomously and enforcing religious toleration. The associations of civil society must not be so dependent upon the state as to be incapable of nurturing habits of self-reliance and entering into coalitions with other associations to achieve common ends. A civic culture must take hold in which bargaining, negotiation, and compromise are accepted as basic norms of civil and political life and in which respect for the popular will allows peaceful alternation in power as a result of free competitive elections. Political parties must provide structured opportunities for the emergence of political leaders and for groups of voters at all levels to influence public policy and hold representatives accountable.

As these preconditions and requisites are achieved, they become pragmatic bulwarks. In the stable democracies, the state or public sector coexists with civil society, a complex network of quasi-autonomous groupings not controlled by the state. An active civil society checks the tendency of the state to become so "omnicompetent" as to threaten liberty. Interest groups interact to influence and control the public agenda. Political parties serve as intermediaries between the state and civil society, articulating choices among leaderships and policies, and organizing both the government and its loyal opposition. An effective government, capable of implementing laws, regulating the economy, protecting security, and providing social welfare, checks the tendency of powerful groups to run roughshod over the public interest and prevents extremists from taking public conflicts out of the legislature and into the streets. The democratic state itself is made subject to constitutional restraints on the exercise of power. It may also be federalized to allow for the devolution of authority and power. Political activity centers on the competition of freely organized political parties and interest groups appealing for public support in free elections and parliamentary proceedings.

Under the best circumstances, each of the preconditions and requisites reinforces the others. Voting becomes more meaningful as people become better educated and informed. The media come to enjoy freedom to report the news and provide a forum for debate, even when doing so puts the government or powerful social forces in a bad light. Out of the experience of being able to influence government policy, citizens come to accept the norms of the civic culture, which serve as a basis for political activism and of willingness to work within the system. The key measure of the civic culture is the feeling of efficacy on the part of the citizen—the belief that votes matter, that governments are by and large accountable, that the process is one through which redress may realistically be sought for grievances. As this culture takes hold, ethnic and racial tensions are likely to be muted. Sub-group loyalties enter into the give and take of pluralistic politics or are deliberately taken into account in formalized power-sharing arrangements, but they no longer serve effectively as rallying points for separatism and opposition to the existing government and constitution. The civic culture relies on and works through democratic institutions of government, including a representative parliament elected in free and regular elections, a multi-party system with alternation in power, a judicial system protective of the rights of individuals and minority groups even against the power of the state, and a civil service accountable to the parliament and free at least of rampant corruption. As confidence in the accountability of government grows, the executive branch can be given greater authority without arousing fears of a return to autocracy. Where this confluence of factors is in place, democracy can be said to be stable and well-established; where one or another element is missing or weak, it remains fragile.

The Need for Civil Society

The growth or creation of a civil society is essential if the transition to political democracy is to take hold, for the reasons Philippe Schmitter has emphasized:

> The root hypothesis is that for an effective and enduring challenge to authoritarian rule to be mounted, and for political democracy to become and remain an alternative mode of political domination, a country must possess a civil society in which certain community and group identities exist independent of the state and in which certain types of self-constituted units are capable of acting autonomously in defense of their own interests and ideals. Moreover, these identities and interests must not only be dispersed throughout the country, they must also be capable of being concentrated when the occasion demands, that is, they must be organized for coherent collective action. In democracies, such participation is accomplished in large part consensually through political parties which compete to win electoral majorities, ally with others in dominant coalitions, or enter into consociational arrangements. Underneath these "superstructural" expressions of territorial and partisan representation lies a particular social configuration—"a historic bloc" to use Antonio Gramsci's expression—that orients the direction of change, provides the dominant ideology, and organizes the distribution of benefits.[5]

It was with just this understanding in mind that the intellectuals who sought to undermine the totalitarian regimes of eastern Europe worked for the creation of a civil society. In effect they turned the logic of Antonio

Gramsci against the socialist state. Gramsci had proposed that the best way to counter the power of the bourgeoisie was to destroy the pervasive hegemony its control of the state allowed it to exercise over civil society. By gaining control of the trade unions, the means of communication, and the schools and universities, socialists might weaken this hegemony and prepare the ground for a political takeover. The dissidents of central and eastern Europe sought to build the institutions of civil society in order to weaken the hegemony of the state and prepare a foundation for a transition to democracy and a free-market economy. One of the major institutions of civil society in eastern Europe was the church, whose relative independence from the state and opposition to its ideology made it a rallying point even for those with primarily secular concerns. In Poland the movement for a free trade union, Solidarity, was a further expression of the same principle, more directly confrontational because it challenged the effort of the state to control labor organization. Clubs for free intellectual exchange like Civic Forum in Czechoslovakia and Charter 77 in Hungary were similarly designed to get around censorship, provide watchdog agencies to protest violations of human rights, and otherwise provide a more or less allowable gathering place for dissidents. Unofficial and sometimes illegal publications, like the *samizdat* of the Soviet Union, represented a form of free expression that also helped created the framework of a civil society.

In the absence of a free economic market, these efforts could not succeed in modifying state control over the primary sources of wealth and social control, nor could they, with the significant exception of Solidarity and to a lesser extent the churches, provide a mass base for a political opposition. The edifice of totalitarian communism in eastern Europe may have been weakened by the effort to create civil society, but it was toppled as a result of its own structural weaknesses, which revealed its economic inefficiency and its tendency to create a privileged and protected political elite. The effort to replace statism by democracy will require the development of civil societies where they have been deliberately suppressed. As the Russian historian, Yuri N. Afanasyev, has observed, "The main reason the Russian people have not escaped totalitarian systems, before or since 1917, has been the lack of a civil society. The state monopolized every activity, and no autonomous society existed apart from its all-pervasive scope."[6] Efforts of reform must therefore aim not only at privatizing many of the economic enterprises controlled by the state, but also at removing state control from other associations and institutions.

The transition to democracy in Spain offers a valuable case study of the role of civil society in enabling a transition to democracy. As Victor M. Perez-Diaz points out, the recent transition was achieved in good measure because during the Franco period the institutions of civil society were permitted to prepare the ground. Civil society and the state sector are bound together because the same individuals function in both spheres with the same set of values: "They may be citizens *only* because they are autonomous agents, and they may be autonomous vis-à-vis the state *only* because the state has a limited power to enter these agents' reserved domain."[7] The public sector and civil society "constitute a system of cooperation and competition among a very large number of autonomous agents" which allows for "a relatively high degree of self-coordination."[8] The state confronts civil society both in a coercive mode and as a purveyor of services. In the former, the state protects external and internal peace; in the latter, it helps society to attain prosperity, social integration, and a sense of collective identity. To the extent that the state is successful in performing these functions, it will be considered legitimate and will enjoy a high degree of loyalty on the part of citizens, quite apart from the obedience it is capable of imposing by means of its monopoly of the means of physical coercion. To the extent that they become dissatisfied, citizens will withdraw their allegiance and focus it instead on agencies of civil society. The state cannot be successful, however, without engaging in bargaining with the associations of civil society: "Thus, the state rulers of liberal capitalist societies need the concourse of socioeconomic elites (such as businessmen and labor leaders) to deliver the modicum of prosperity (economic growth and social integration) on which their substantive legitimacy depends; they need the concourse of territorial elites to articulate a sense of collective identity for the entire community; and they also need the cooperation of the cultural elites to persuade people of the legitimacy (both formal and substantive) of their rule."[9]

This analysis, in stressing the role of territorial elites, conforms best to Spanish experience and to that of other states in which territorial divisions are also cultural and ethnic divisions, but suitably revised to stress diverse economic or cultural interests, the analysis holds true more broadly. A democratic society is one in which the state or public sector co-exists with a relatively autonomous civil society. Political parties and the media of communication serve as channels by which political leaders can mobilize support within civil society and by which the interest groups in civil society can make their views known and felt.

Modes of Transition

It is easier, however, to describe the end points by which democratization can be determined to have been successfully achieved than to prescribe the route by which they may be reached. If anything is striking about the process of transition, it is how different, in retrospect, are the courses by which it has occurred and how much strife they all entail. Although a typology risks making the distinctions sharper than they are in reality, at least five different historical routes may be discerned:

1. *Revolution.* In France, and to some extent abortively earlier in England, democratization had its beginnings in a rebellion against absolute monarchy. In the United States it came about as a by-product of a revolution for national independence, but after a longer period of habituation to limited self-government. In Latin America as well, between the 1770s and 1830s, colonial rebellions occurred against the imperial rule of Spain and at the same time against monarchy and in favor of republican government. In these cases, however, efforts to consolidate democracy after the revolutions either suffered severe setbacks or succeeded only gradually.

2. *Evolution.* In Britain, the Low Countries and Scandinavia, democracy has come about as a result of evolution from monarchy and oligarchy, an evolution influenced by its success elsewhere and by demands for inclusion by groups deliberately marginalized or denied the franchise. In Brazil, too, a constitutional monarchy installed upon Portugal's grant of independence gave way to an oligarchical, corporatist republic and then to military dictatorship, and only recently, after a period of liberalization—known as the *abertura* or opening—to what appears to be a movement to a democratic system. The same evolutionary process has been attempted, so far with little success, in the decolonized states of Africa.

3. *External imposition.* In modern Germany and Japan, democratic constitutions were imposed by the victors after World War II. In Austria, an occupation authority composed of the four victorious powers presided over the reinstatement of the 1920 constitution and the establishment of an elected government, until Austria was declared independent in 1955.[10] In Italy, the democratic constitution was revived as a result of an indigenous insurgency against the Fascist regime reinforced by the Allied expulsion of German forces and by postwar assistance under the Marshall Plan.[11]

4. *Transformation from above.* Democracy has sometimes been installed by an oligarchical elite, often after a coup d'état, either civil or military, sometimes in an effort to stave off a more radical alternative. The case of Spain is often cited as an example of transformation from above. The Spanish transition took place after the death of Franco in 1975, when King Juan Carlos took decisive action to establish parliamentary government.

5. *Mixed modes.* The Greek transition in 1974 is an example of mixed modes of transition. It followed the decision of a regime of colonels which had lasted only seven years, and had begun by proclaiming itself an instrument of the transition to parliamentary democracy, to turn power over to a civilian government. But the downfall of the junta was in considerable part due to the enlargement, as a result of economic growth, of a middle class which demanded greater political participation.[12] Venezuelan democratization was initiated between 1945 and 1948 under the aegis of a civil-military junta which replaced a dictatorship and encouraged popular organization and electoral participation, but the reforms provoked a reaction which resulted in a military coup, followed by a restoration of democracy a decade later as a result of popular demonstrations and street fighting. In Chile, the coup that suspended democracy ended when the military regime allowed elections to be held and abided by the unexpected outcome. In Argentina, the most recent effort of democratization resulted from a military defeat in the Falklands/Malvinas War when the ruling military junta was forced out of office. Most efforts of democratization in eastern Europe following the collapse of communism—the major exception being the fall of the Ceaucescu regime in Romania as a result of popular unrest—are also examples of the same mixture of modes, in these cases occurring as a result of changes introduced by the Communist leaderships in response to popular discontent and perceptions of impending collapse.

While some efforts of democratization by these various routes have been successful, in other instances, where the preconditions have been weak and turmoil has allowed opposition movements to gather strength, democratization has been attempted and failed, as in Weimar Germany and in the parliamentary experiment that was cut short by the Bolshevik coup in Russia.

Dimensions of Transition

In the world as a whole, democracy is still the form of government only of a minority of states. It has been adopted, however, in almost all of those considered to be the most advanced by the usual measures of economic and social well being and has become a standard for emulation in less developed countries. Despite exceptions like the oil-rich dynasties of the Persian Gulf and the unusual case of Singapore, which has some of the trappings of democracy but is in the most important respects autocratic, the belief has grown strong that because self-government is linked to prosperity, democracy and market economies work in tandem. The difficulties arise from several sources: the resistance of entrenched dynasties, elites, and privileged classes; the persistence of ethnic, religious, and racial tensions; and difficulty in establishing viable and growing economic systems that allow for competition and inequality but also provide benefits for all. Resistance to democratization arises from all three sources, but in different degrees in different settings. Reversals remain possible for reasons not hard to discern from recent experience. The transition to democracy is acutely influenced by several dimensional factors: economic, social structural, and ideological.

1. *Economic.* The clamor for freedom and popular self-government arouses expectations of economic improvement. Where relatively open market economies must be created to replace state ownership or relatively protected economies, dislocations, hardships, and corruption are inevitable, and antidemocratic forces may succeed in capitalizing on

discontent. Subsidies for consumer goods must be eliminated to promote market efficiency, and rising prices for these commodities work great hardship on most consumers, especially elderly pensioners and those in low-wage employments. Jobs in relatively inefficient industries are often at risk, and wages cannot rise to match prices because of the labor surplus. As uncompetitive producers lose once-controlled markets, displaced employees cannot easily find new jobs. Trade unions, freed from the repressive controls and cooptation that often forced them into acquiescence, find themselves under pressure from their members to protest policies instituted by democratic governments they have helped install.

Meanwhile, the breakdown of autocratic systems of control often leads to increased corruption, as racketeering that would previously have been more effectively suppressed become more brazen and as a new emphasis on profit-making attracts extortion and protection rings connected to newly established private businesses. Some highly placed managers in state enterprises use their positions to take advantage of opportunities opened by privatization, provoking public anger and cynicism. Others engage in bureaucratic resistance to privatization or take advantage of disappointment and anxiety by re-making themselves into populist opponents of economic "shock therapy." Foreign investors are confronted by a tangle of red tape, inadequate infrastructure, and sheer inexperience. If enough workers and consumers are disappointed and unwilling to wait patiently for improvement, they may not support democratically elected leaders or tolerate the delay and compromise democratic procedures require. Stephan Haggard and Robert R. Kaufman have summed up the various ways "backsliding" from democracy can occur if the state cannot manage the economic transition well enough to allay discontent:

> A general erosion of faith in the capacity of democratic governments to manage the economy would increase the appeal of authoritarian "solutions" to the economic crisis, not only among elites but among the public at large. The erosion of support for democratic institutions would lead to the election of leaders or parties with plebiscitarian or openly authoritarian ambitions, or reduce the perceived costs to the military of intervening. Economic decline might also reverse democratization more indirectly by leading to an increase in crime, strikes, riots, and other forms of civil violence and to the polarization of groups at opposite ends of the political spectrum. Such social unrest and political polarization provide the classic justification for military intervention.[13]

2. *Social Structural.* In periods of transition, when political institutions are weak, military organizations may exploit their pivotal role by supporting or undertaking coups. Those accustomed to intervening in politics and

unwilling to give up traditional prerogatives may take advantage of instability to prevent the new system from taking hold. Other groups and actors inexperienced with democratic processes and motivated by personal ambitions and short-term interests, may cause political stalemate. In drafting constitutions and electoral rules, all parties are bound to try to protect their particular interests, in the process inspiring cynicism about the extent to which formally democratic systems enable the people rather than the best organized interests to rule. The need to break stalemates and override factionalism tempts leaders to behave undemocratically, setting a bad precedent at the very least, and installing autocracy at the worst. In societies sharply divided by ethnic, racial, linguistic, or religious cleavages, struggles for dominance also may prevent cooperation and undermine efforts to create amalgamating institutions.

3. *Ideological.* The process of political opening releases previously pent-up forces, especially ethnic, religious, and nationalistic tensions, that engender ideological conflicts in a context in which democratic constitutional constraints on struggles for power are still only weakly institutionalized. Where democratic norms are not traditional, those who lose elections may not accept defeat gracefully. Radicals of various persuasions, ranging from Maoists like *Sendero Luminoso* ("Shining Path") in Peru to the rightist *Pamyat* ("Memory") movement in Russia, seek to exacerbate the difficulties by mobilizing mass opposition and in some instances resorting to terror to intimidate the regime and expose its weakness. Some of these difficulties of transition can be eased by foreign aid from democratic countries, but the coincidence of the collapse of communism in central and eastern Europe and of authoritarianism elsewhere with a global recession has reduced the ability of the Western democracies to come to the rescue. So far, however, these difficulties have led only to a few reversals, which is strong testimony to the strength of belief in democratic principles and of the hopes associated with the transition.

Consolidation in Western Europe

Although the global balance sheet of democratization is mixed, in Western Europe it seems to be in strong condition, thanks in no small measure to the success of the economic recovery after World War II made possible by American economic aid. Forebodings for the future of democracy inspired by turmoil in the late 1960s and early 1970s have largely been dissipated as democratic principles have come to be widely accepted. In 1974, the German Socialist leader, Willy Brandt, had grimly warned that "Western Europe has only twenty or thirty more years of democracy left in it; after that it will slide, engineless and rudderless, under the surrounding sea of dictatorship, and whether this dictation comes from a politburo or a junta will not make that much difference."[14] In part because committed democrats like Brandt struggled against the threat they perceived, it did not materialize. The challenge to democracy represented by the strength of the Communist parties, notably in France and Italy, disappeared in the 1980s. First the parties themselves became "Euro-communist," a euphemism for the acceptance of democratic norms. Then their popular support plummeted due to growing disenchantment with the Soviet model of both government and economic management. Under the Fifth Republic, France is governed by a mixed presidential-parliamentary system that provides a degree of strength and stability missing under the earlier constitutions. In the politically stable and economically successful Nordic countries (Denmark, Finland, Iceland, Sweden and Norway), democracy remains the unquestioned norm. It is equally well established in the Benelux countries (Belgium, Netherlands, Luxembourg), and in the other smaller countries of Western Europe, Austria, Ireland, and Malta. It prevails in Greece, Turkey, Spain, and Portugal, if not yet as firmly as in the other democratic states of Europe.

Italian democracy remains precariously in place despite a fragmented electorate and regional tensions. The Italian experience is among those where it has become apparent that successful democratization requires competitive parties and alternation in power. For forty years, a single party, the Christian Democrats, survived challenges by adroitly controlling shifting coalitions and using patronage on a massive scale. Because the public sector has played such a large role in the country's economic development, accounting for a quarter of gross domestic product, the patronage often amounted to corruption. Ties to the Mafia are alleged to have helped deliver the Christian Democratic vote in the south.[15] The courageous role of the judiciary in exposing these scandals, and the public reaction to the revelations, drove the party from power. It remains to be seen whether the dominance of the Christian Democrats will be replaced by alternation between a party of the left and a party of the right, or whether the fragmentation of the electorate into ideological and regional blocs will continue to produce unstable coalition government. Given earlier Italian history, it is conceivable that instability could again strengthen the appeal of extremist movements.

Germany, forced by the defeat of the Third Reich to resume the democratic path taken after the first World War, shows few signs of retreating or of deviating from that path. Its absorption of the formerly separate east German state that was a sham democracy has been far more costly than anticipated, but the resulting economic difficulties have in no way weakened support for Germany's democratic system of government. The country's electoral system and its federalism have become models for emulation, and support for the moderate parties is far greater than for right-wing extremists.

Spain, since the death of Franco, and Portugal, after Salazar, have undergone transformations to democracy coupled with a general weakening of opposition forces which had previously made democracy seem unlikely in Iberia. Especially in Spain, the growth of the middle class, the strengthening of civil society, and the adoption of federalism appear to be establishing a strong foundation for the survival of democracy. To the extent that the European Union succeeds in promoting greater economic and political integration and that living standards in both countries continue to improve, the prospects that they will remain democratic are good.

Despite the remarkable progress of democratization in Western Europe, it would be premature to suppose that democracy faces no remaining challenges there. The most obvious danger comes from the persistent viruses of xenophobic nationalism, sub-nationalism, and religious antagonism. Ethnic and cultural tensions remain salient in Northern Ireland, in Brittany, in the Basque country of Spain, between Flemings and Walloons in Belgium, between Muslim Arab immigrants and ultra-nationalists in France, and in Germany between natives and both guest-workers and recent immigrants. Even in the United Kingdom, Scottish and Welsh nationalists continue to see themselves as victims of "internal colonialism," and nativist movements have arisen aiming to block further immigration and cultural diversification.[16] In most of these cases the tensions can be ameliorated by assimilation and economic improvement, aided by the mechanisms of devolution and power-sharing, but it would be foolhardy to underestimate the lingering force of group hostility.

The constitutional mechanisms are important as potential solvents for these conflicts because they allow for sub-systemic differentiation and local autonomy. These same mechanisms are now enabling the nations of Western Europe to achieve supranational forms of cooperation while protecting their sovereignty through agreements allowing for "subsidiarity," or national variation from communal norms. The new popularity of federation at the international level could gain the principle more acceptance internally. The more Europeans experience integration and come to think of themselves as Europeans, the more amenable they made to domestic toleration and devolution.

One reason to suppose that the example of continuing European federation will have domestic influence in the member countries is the influence of example on the spread of democracy in the southern regions of Western Europe. The first dramatic success in the spread of democracy in Europe occurred in Greece and Turkey in the east and Spain and Portugal in the west. Even apart from domestic pressures, these states had a keen incentive to follow the example of the northern states. Western Europe was building a common market, and the ticket of admission was adhesion to democracy and the NATO alliance. Rule by dictators and groups of colonels had become distinctly unfashionable and a barrier to acceptance.[17] Besides, the various "economic miracles" achieved in the northern states showed that democracy, rather than being incompatible with economic growth, could be its necessary condition over the long run because it allows for economic regulation in the public interest and the social provision of various safety nets.

Transformation in Central and Eastern Europe

The same phenomenon of imitation, amplified by modern media of communication, helps explain the spread of democratic sentiments in central and eastern Europe. Change in these regions did not come about only because of popular unrest. To be sure, much credit belongs to the courageous dissidents who engaged in literary and religious forms of "antipolitics." They expanded the boundaries of civil society by making the churches in East Germany and Poland, discussion groups like Czechoslovakia's Civic Forum, and in Poland's case, the trade union Solidarity, foci of an alternative vision of the social order.[18] But the notion that change came solely or even primarily as a result of a revolution from below is an exaggeration.[19] Reform in central and eastern Europe came about mainly because the elites in control in effect saw the handwriting on the Berlin Wall. It was those at the top who began to experiment with pragmatic reforms aimed at saving what they could of their ideological commitments and power. Communist Party leaders were forced to recognize that the Stalinist model of development had shown itself to be a recipe for bureaucratic stagnation, in sharp contrast to what was being achieved in countries with free-market economies. The Soviet leadership was not primarily concerned with domestic improvements, however. The major concern was that the ambitious effort of "power projection" had become unsustainable. Reluctantly, they were forced to acknowledge that the economic system upon which they relied had proven to be much less productive and innovative than that of their Western adversaries.

Economic change came first to Yugoslavia and then to Hungary. In Hungary, it seemed for a time that a Communist regime could preside over economic reform that would give more scope to market activity and to some forms of non-state enterprise. From 1956 until the fall of communism in the late 1980s, the ruling Communist Party elite maintained control by means of a tacit bargain with the Hungarian populace. Under this bargain, the ruling elite would preside over a transition to a mixed economy within an eastern Europe that would continue to be dominated by the Soviet Union. As the Soviet Union's hold became weaker and internal opposition stronger, the Hungarian leadership was pressed to approve broader reforms. Political reforms adopted in 1968 stopped short of allowing for multi-candidate and multi-party elections. The next step came in 1983, when multi-candidate elections were decreed for the 352 individual electoral districts. The newly elected parliament proceeded to remove the impediments to real parliamentary government by promulgating individual rights, establishing a constitutional court, and most important for the short run, making the government responsible to parliament. In 1989, these steps were followed by the adoption of a strong parliamentary-weak presidential form of government.[20] When the early economic improvements of "goulash communism" could not be sustained, the regime's leaders lost popular confidence and felt compelled to negotiate constitutional changes with dissident intellectuals.[21] Although both sides anticipated that "reform Communists" would gain the support of a majority of the voters, the first elections removed them from power, without, however, providing any other party with a large enough mandate to govern without a coalition.

The Hungarian transformation proved to be a straw in a wind which soon swept across the whole of central and eastern Europe. In view of what was happening not just in far-off North America and Asia but in neighboring Western Europe, it became obvious that the Marxian alternative to capitalism and the totalitarian alternative to democracy were both bankrupt.

Change finally came to the Soviet Union because the leadership saw that its hold in power was becoming imperilled, in part because of domestic discontent but also because the system was grossly inefficient. Overcentralization relying on force and propaganda had produced a repressive, corrupting social system. Individual initiative was stifled except for those at the top who could manipulate the system for their own benefit. The large and small oppressions experienced in the Soviet Union led many of its people to begin to appreciate, perhaps even to an exaggerated extent, the benefits of the democratic alternative. They came to recognize that democratic and market-oriented systems can release creative energies more effectively than totalitarian systems. Although some were uneasy about giving up a system they knew and had gotten used to for an uncertain future, so many began to chafe at the status quo that the leadership had to think seriously about major changes. In the past, disaffection and dissent were expressed indirectly by various forms of passive and active resistance. Workers worked to rule, treated state property with indifference and cynicism, and built an underground economy. Managers met quotas without worrying about quality control or consumer reactions to their products. Increasingly distrustful of state propaganda, people became expert in reading between the lines of public pronouncements and began to pay more attention to privately printed dissident materials. The struggle that led to the creation of Solidarity in Poland was a struggle not only against the harsh realities of living in the supposed workers' state but at the same time a struggle against the lies that were produced to cover up those realities.[22] Many came to agree with the Yugoslav dissident, Milovan Djilas, that a "new class" had emerged under cover of an ideology of classlessness which took care of its own interests while denying everyone else opportunities for betterment. They now understand that what was at stake was their right to govern their own lives and to have an equal share in electing representatives entrusted with the government of their nations.

A striking change of consciousness began to take hold, foreshadowed in the protest literature of such prominent dissidents as Djilas, Andrei Sakharov, Aleksander Solzhenitsyn, Vaclav Havel, George Konrad, Adam Michnik, Stanislaw Baranczak, and Miklos Haraszti.[23] Die-hard communists clung to the old Leninist faith, but others sought to remake themselves into democratic socialists in the Western European mold, ready to embrace privatization and the market economy coupled with government planning and social welfare. The hold of Leninism over popular consciousness was weakened and broken by a network of interacting fissures. The failure of the system to deliver the economic goods promised in the propaganda of communism was surely one major factor, but another was the revulsion first inspired by the revelations of the crimes of the Stalin era and then reinforced by the later recognition that even in the absence of a cult of personality and a paranoid need for purges, control by oligarchs and bureaucrats could produce stagnation. In retrospect, the last straw may have been the regime's handling of the nuclear reactor disaster at Chernobyl in 1986. At first the authorities tried to cover up as usual, despite the announced policy of *glasnost'* or openness, but eventually the truth began to come out, and the people (especially those in the Ukraine) learned how high a price unaccountable and over-centralized regimes exact. The children of the *nomenklatura* were quietly removed from the Chernobyl region soon after the disaster occurred while other children were allowed to remain, and to take part in the May Day parade, which went on as scheduled. Episodes like this made not only *glasnost'* but democratization seem all the more imperative.

Although the Soviet regime could at least claim a legitimacy that derived from revolution, the other communist regimes were imposed from without, except for Yugoslavia, where it was also imposed from within. Even the Soviet leadership was forced to recognize that the myth of revolutionary legitimacy was wearing thin, and that an electoral sanction was needed if the system were to be reformed. As Mikhail Gorbachev recognized, *perestroika* or restructuring would depend on *glasnost'* and on democratization as well. Gorbachev was reluctant to allow too much democracy, lest the Communist Party lose control, but he recognized that his government needed popular legitimation, so he ended the political monopoly of the Communist Party. The constitution was amended to allow the formation of alternative parties, and contested elections were held for the first time in the history of the Soviet Union. A restructured parliament gave non-Communists at least some role. These were major steps, but they proved too little to overcome the power of the entrenched bureaucracy and aroused opposition from the party *apparatchiks*. Gorbachev himself became the unelected leader of the reform, without a popular mandate.

His decision not to use force to prop up Communist regimes in the satellites was a major turning point. His unravelling of state control was exacerbated by nationalist demands for separation or autonomy. In order to develop support that might serve as a counterweight to opposition from the national centers of power in the bureaucracy, the party, and the military, he tried to establish a network of sympathetic reformers in the constituent republics. But his changes only fed the fires of separatism and provoked a reaction against reform on the part of Russian nationalists. To placate them, he tried to ignore the Baltic demands for separation, but he was unwilling to use force to suppress the separatists. By not acting decisively enough early on to give independence to the Baltic states and to offer autonomy to the Ukraine and the other more integral parts of the Union (which they might well have been content to accept), he precipitated Baltic defection and the subsequent dissolution of the remainder of the Soviet Union. The breakup came in 1991 after Gorbachev survived a coup attempt from a coalition opposed to his reforms but was left at the head of a central government too weak to prevent the disintegration of the union. Russia succeeded the Soviet Union, and Gorbachev was displaced by its first freely elected leader, Boris Yeltsin.

Hungary, Poland, Romania, Bulgaria, the Czech and Slovak republics, and East Germany were all allowed to break free. All these newly liberated societies continued to face economic difficulties in transforming their command economies. In Poland and the Czech Republic, support for the new democratic regime was initially focussed more on charismatic leaders—Lech Walesa in one case, Vaclav Havel in the other—than on parties; in Hungary, where loyalty flows to the parties in the absence of a charismatic leader, the parties and their leaders were vulnerable to public impatience with the failure to achieve tangible economic results.[24] Romania, even after the overthrow of a dictator, suffered from the shadowy remains of Ceaucescu's *Securitate* and his ruling bureaucracy. Bulgaria and Albania too began to grope toward democracy under the guidance of an older political elite.

The transition in eastern Europe involves a number of difficulties, many of which, as Kenneth Jowitt has emphasized, arise as the legacy of so many decades of Leninism.[25] Even as the institutions of centralization and the one-party state are dismantled and replaced, the cultural proclivities they engendered remain, leading to wistful longings for authoritarian leadership. These longings are compounded by the difficulty of transforming a socialist economy into one with a high degree of private ownership and a market system. The need for Western investment is so general in Eastern Europe, moreover, that it cannot possibly be satisfied in short order. Even domestic private investment is inhibited by uncertainty over the ownership of state assets originally taken from private owners. Vested interests allied with the old order are often in a position to resist changes that displace them. The closing of inefficient factories forces people into unemployment under circumstances where new jobs are hard or impossible to find and the safety net is weak. Employees accustomed to perquisites of employment such as housing and special food allocations are understandably reluctant to give them up in view of the hardships and uncertainties that affect the general working population. At the same time, because members of the old *nomenklatura* are often best positioned to take advantage of privatization, they can sometimes make deals for themselves which undermine prospects for competition. The absence of safety nets results in severe hardships for pensioners and the unemployed, arousing resentment of reforms. The weakening of repressive police authority, coupled with inadequate opportunities for legitimate careers, encourages gangsterism and violent robbery.

Despite the difficulties and the hardships of change, the transition to competitive market systems is taking place in Eastern and Central Europe, although at varying pace. In the short-run, at least, ethnic tensions have been even more destabilizing than economic difficulties. The viruses of nationalism and sub-nationalism, exploited by political leaders, threaten several of these new democracies with civil war and dissolution, and in one case, Yugoslavia, the threat has become an actuality. The breakup of Yugoslavia has been a sobering reminder that the loss of totalitarian control can unleash sentiments incompatible with democracy, especially those grounded on age-old identities and hatreds nurtured by the memory of old defeats and atrocities. In societies so divided by ethnic and or religious cleavages, it may be too much to expect that people will think of themselves first of all as individuals and citizens of some transcendent national polity and only secondarily as members of some sub-group, especially when, as in Georgia, independence brings with it an effort to exclude minorities from any role in the new state. The intermixture of populations makes it inevitable that efforts to create homogeneous states will entail "ethnic cleansing," in the euphemism that has come into use in Yugoslavia to describe massacres and expulsions.

Another problem, typical of emerging democracies, is the fracturing of the electorate. When, after a long period of repression, people are offered an opportunity to express their opinions and form political parties, they are apt to take advantage of the opportunity to align themselves into a variety of factions. In Poland, for example, when the hegemonic party system centered on the Communist Party collapsed, the civic movement encapsulated in Solidarity also broke apart. Solidarity's parliamentary representatives created four separate parliamentary clubs in the Sejm. After a presidential election, the followers of a defeated candidate formed another club. All told, fourteen different parliamentary factions emerged in rapid order, and some delegates became independents. A 1990 survey of voters found them divided among twenty parties, with a third to one-half of the voters either in favor of no party or having difficulty choosing one. Solidarity commanded the allegiance of the largest number, but that number fluctuated over several months from a high of 38.7 percent to a low of 15.7 percent. As a result, the electoral laws adopted in 1991 for parliamentary elections embodied proportional representation.[26] In the Russian parliamentary elections in December 1995, over forty parties competed.

In the Russian Federation, opposition both from old-line Communists and nationalists has resulted in the election of parliamentary groups opposed to the economic reform, as well as to the loss of the Russian empire. Deadlock between the Russian parliament and the president, Boris Yeltsin, erupted in a violent confrontation in September 1993 won by the president with the support of the military. In December 1993 he succeeded in gaining the approval of the electorate (but only by a bare majority in an election in which only half the eligible voters took part) for a new constitution which makes the presidency the central locus of power and subordinates all the other institutions of government, parliamentary and local, to the will of the executive.

It remains to be seen whether this constitution will become a step toward authoritarianism rather than democracy. The constitutional provisions have an ominously authoritarian ring. They grant the president control over all executive agencies, not unusual in presidential systems, but to a degree which is highly unusual. Appointments to major administrative offices do not require parliamentary approval. The president is given decree powers limited only by federal law, but these limits are subject to executive control because of the president's power over parliament. The parliament lacks independent power of the purse as well as a credible power of impeachment. Only the government can initiate legislation to change taxes or expenditures. The president can be impeached only by concurrent super-majorities (two-thirds of all members) in both chambers of the parliament supported by separate majorities in the Supreme Court and Constitutional Court. The president need only control a third of the votes in the parliament or half the votes of the two courts (whose members are appointed by the president without the need for parliamentary confirmation). The constitution limits joint meetings of the two chambers of the parliament to occasions when listening to pronouncements, and the president has housed the two chambers in halls distant from each other, thus further ensuring that no opposition leader will emerge who can unite both against the president. The State Duma can vote no confidence in the president, but it does so at its peril, for the constitution allows the president to dissolve that body. The guarantees of civil liberty in the new constitution are impressive, but all that keeps the institutional provisions of the constitution from being altogether undemocratic in effect are the requirement that the president be elected for a four-year term and the provision that the same person may not hold the office for more than two consecutive terms.[27]

Asian Prospects

Asia will undoubtedly prove to be the major testing ground for the hypothesis that economic growth largely generated by market systems cannot be maintained without democratization. The Soviet disintegration has spilled over into the other major bastion of communism, China, with a population now about 1.2 billion, a social order fragmented along urban-rural lines and with fifty-six recognized national minorities comprising 6 percent of the population. China does not yet exhibit the characteristics of a relatively autonomous civil society essential for the development of stable political democracy. Rural residents are grouped in highly integrated and politically controlled village work units. Urban residents are concentrated in work units such as schools and factories operated by nation-wide ministries or similar organizations.[28] This pervasive system of control makes it very difficult for reform movements to develop and challenge the existing system.

The Chinese Communist leadership has sought to suppress demands for political change while unleashing forces promoting a market economy. The ideological purism that sustained the long march and reappeared in the "Cultural Revolution" has given way to a scramble for wealth in which the party and military leadership is as much involved as the rest of society. All that is left of communism is a "market-Leninism"—the belief that disciplined, one-party rule will promote the growth of a market economy whereas democratization will only lead to anarchy and civil war—not to mention the possible ouster from power of the Communist Party. The aim is to emulate Singapore and avoid the undesirable outcome of political reform in the Soviet Union.[29]

The Soviet example did in fact stimulate demands for political reform in China. It was a visit by Gorbachev that catalyzed the student democracy movement, whose protests frightened the Communist gerontocracy into cracking down harshly. The old political system prevails for the time being. As younger leaders take power, they may well be forced to recognize that, as in Taiwan and South Korea—if not in the smaller and therefore more controllable environment of Singapore—sustained economic progress and political legitimacy are interdependent.

Perhaps the fundamental reason political changes can be expected in China over the long run is what Central and East European experience has shown about the incompatibility between over-centralized, over-bureaucratic systems of rule and sustained economic growth. To paraphrase Marx, the Chinese Communist regime's own concern with economic growth may carry the seeds of its own destruction. Marketization and rapid economic growth can certainly be initiated by authoritarian governments, as the Chinese Communist leadership has shown in the post-Mao period, but this very economic growth inevitably generates a civil society that undermines efforts to maintain totalitarian control. A repressive, centralized system may be economically beneficial in the early stages of industrialization and policies aimed at limiting penetration by foreign capital through control of investment and pricing inevitably enhance the power of the government. Just as state-directed mercantilism paved the way for industrialization in Europe, so the social discipline imposed by state-directed socialism in the Soviet Union and China, the authoritarianism of South Korea, Taiwan, Singapore, and Franco Spain in its final, technocratic phase, can focus national energies on economic growth and suppress resistance. Thus, Guillermo O'Donnell has argued, on the basis of Latin American experience, that heavy emphasis on import substitution as a strategy of industrialization led to the emergence of new, stronger, more lasting forms of authoritarianism.[30] At some point, however, too much control becomes counterproductive. Central planners may be good at building dams and piling up armaments, but they are very bad at directing consumer and export-oriented industries which depend on market signals and require entrepreneurs closer to the production process. Peasants and factory workers, moreover, may be more likely to accept such discipline unquestioningly than professionals and white collar workers, whose very skills require an ability to understand, to manipulate data, to communicate, and to make decisions. To expect them to accept dictation is to expect a docility at variance with the culture of professionals and executives. Even to the extent that they can be regimented by bureaucratic systems of management, whether in the public or the private sector, their skills and interests are likely to lead them to want to exercise a political role. As Dahl explained before the collapse of the East European examples of communism, "Because of its inherent requirements, an advanced economy and its supporting social structures automatically distribute political resources and political skills to a vast variety of individuals, groups, and organizations." Because of these all but inevitable consequences of economic modernization, Dahl concluded, some members of the new pluralistic social order "make demands for participating in decisions by means more appropriate to a competitive than to a hegemonic political system."[31] In the case of China, the introduction of a market economy could significantly weaken the regime's present control over the major sources of work and social organization.

These considerations suggest that economic growth could well promote democratization in Asia as elsewhere, but for the time being the record is mixed, and the outcome is far from certain. In China, economic development is leading to a pronounced inequality of income between the booming coastal region and the less transformed interior which could produce tensions that would become explosive during democratization. In view of the dangers of social conflict, it is at least possible that the autocratic model successfully pursued by the ethnic Chinese leaderships of Singapore and Taiwan could prove more appealing than democracy to a new generation of mainland Chinese leaders. But Taiwan has begun to move toward democracy, and Singapore may turn out to be impossible for China to copy because it is sufficiently small and homogeneous to be controlled by a relatively benevolent autocracy. The persistence of autocracy in Indonesia is perhaps a more relevant indication that autocracy can accommodate a market economy.

Elsewhere, the picture is also mixed. Some Asian countries have already experienced a significant degree of democratization, notably South Korea, Taiwan, and the Philippines, though the issue is far from settled in the Philippines because of the strength of the military and the weakness of the economy and family planning. Vietnam remains in control of a Communist oligarchy but there are signs that this ruling elite is embracing the same belief in the need for a market economy as communist leaderships elsewhere have already done. Indonesia is under the control of a dictator who is the heir of a regime created by ruthless slaughter. In Myanmar, formerly Burma, a military oligarchy continues to resist pressures to change in the face of determined and heroic opposition, but economic stagnation may force it to allow some degree of democratization.

The south Asian subcontinent has been rocked by ethnic and religious conflicts which have gravely weakened tendencies toward democracy. Modern India, founded after a partition dictated by religious tensions, is again beset by communal hatreds which have exploded into violence. Elected state governments with a third of the population have been deposed, and the central government has resorted to executive rule with increasing frequency. Sikh militants in the Punjab have risen in rebellion. In Kashmir, separatists aided from Pakistan have waged a guerilla war for several years after the Indian government held rigged elections there. Religiously inspired nationalism among the Hindus who constitute over 80 percent of the population threatens to abrogate constitutional guarantees of religious freedom, posing a serious danger for Muslims, the largest minority, as well for Sikhs and others. Whether this most populous democracy can maintain its constitutional commitment to secular democracy depends in large measure on whether later generations will continue to recognize the lesson of the struggle over partition that "in a diverse, plural society, communal politics can destroy civil society and the state."[32] Although twenty-five years of military rule ended in Pakistan in 1988, Pakistani prime ministers have several times been dismissed by presidents, and the government has been very heavy-handed in interfering in elections and ready to condone and sometimes authorize violations of human rights. Parliamentary government is surviving in Pakistan, but the threat of military intervention remains high and the persistence of poverty is eroding support for democracy while the dependence of the economy on the drug trade is a constant source of political corruption. India and Pakistan have been at war three times since they gained independence from Britain. In Sri Lanka, Tamil separatists have conducted a guerilla war marked by assassinations, ambushes, and terrorism. In Bangladesh, Islamic fundamentalism fueled by anti-Muslim outbursts in India has cast a shadow over efforts to create democracy.[33]

The case of Japan is both anomalous and ambiguous. Japan has been formally democratic since its adoption of a new constitution after World War II, but until the early 1990s, it was a one-party dominant democracy, sustained by patronage and gerrymandering, with a weak parliament. The formal democracy is reflected in a constitutional order based on popular sovereignty, representative institutions, civil liberties, free competitive elections, an active press, and a popular conception of rights (even in a society which had stressed obligations).[34] For many observers, however, the formal constitution is a facade, behind which bureaucratic elements collude with the country's major financial and industrial firms to exercise real power over public policy.[35]

Because of Japan's critical importance to the global economy and its potential role as a military power, the question of its commitment to democracy assumes special importance. Japan is not the only formally democratic country in which one party has been dominant for a considerable period. Denmark, Sweden, Norway, Italy, Mexico, Iceland, Israel, India, and Colombia have had the same experience, though unlike Japan many of these countries have also experienced alternation and coalition government. T. J. Pempel has identified four dimensions of single-party dominance: a political party is dominant in number in the sense that it wins more seats than its opponents; it holds a dominant bargaining position, whether or not it has an absolute majority; it is dominant chronologically, or over a substantial period of time; and it must be dominant governmentally, in the sense that it controls the public agenda and maintains a preeminent standing with the electorate. Japan, as he points out, was a clear-cut case in which all four dimensions were met.[36] Japan's Liberal Democratic Party held sway in both houses of parliament, designating all prime ministers and most cabinet officials, from 1955 to 1993, when a coalition government came to power.

Although the predominance of a single party is not in principle incompatible with democracy, inasmuch as the electorate has the opportunity to choose other leadership in free elections, one-party dominance tends to produce a weak form of democracy. The longer one party holds a virtual monopoly of power, the more it can manipulate and reshape the electorate so as to tighten its grip. In Japan, the use of tax policy to favor corporate supporters and gerrymandering to overweight the votes of pliant rural constituencies put the opposition at a severe disadvantage. LDP dominance was accompanied and to some extent made possible by the extraction of financial support from business associations which reached scandalous proportions. Opposition parties were coopted or forced to accommodate themselves to the wishes of the ruling party. But the Japanese opposition shares the responsibility for its failure to capitalize on the LDP's failings. After World War II, the Japanese labor movement had a relatively weak tradition to draw upon, and only a small fraction of the work force was unionized. The LDP quickly gained the support of the cooperative movement that enrolled 99 percent of Japan's farming population.[37] Until 1986, when the Japan Socialist Party adopted a new platform replacing a Marxist-Leninist outlook with a more moderate Social Democratic platform, the opposition parties put so much emphasis on socialist principles that they alienated Japanese voters, especially as the LDP's policies turned Japan into an engine of economic growth. By denouncing Japan's ruling party as reactionary and fascist, they seemed to threaten the prosperity of an increasingly affluent, increasingly middle-class society. Their advocacy of unarmed neutrality also struck most Japanese voters as too risky a policy, given the realities of the Cold War, even though many were apprehensive about a resurgence of Japanese militarism.[38] Change may well be taking place in Japan. Over time, the socialist opposition party has considerably modified its positions both on domestic economic policy and foreign relations and the LDP's parliamentary behavior has shown a pattern of significant cooperation and agreement with other parties.[39] In 1993, popular anger over corruption led to a revolt within the LDP that led to a new multi-party coalition government committed to political reform. In November 1993, the lower house of the Diet passed legislation changing the way members of the house are elected. The lower house consists of 274 members from newly designed single-member districts and 226 elected by PR. These changes, coupled with a reapportionment designed to cut back the number of rural seats, are expected to help create a two-party system. Whether a more competitive party system will make Japan's economic policy bureaucracy more controllable by its elected representatives remains to be seen.

Latin America's Tentative Moves Toward Democracy

In Latin America, the revival of democracy is as impressive as it is in Eastern and Central Europe, but again the barriers to implementation are formidable. Although many factors now at play in the region tend to promote democratization, many others promote resistance. Political elites anxious to achieve a more efficient market economy recognize that democratization may help encourage foreign investment by providing some assurance of political stability and channels for discontent other than revolution. The interest of some members of the Latin American business elites in doing business in the United States is a potential force for democratization, but others are more interested in protecting domestic markets against foreign competition. The declining prestige of the Soviet model has dampened enthusiasm for the Cuban variant throughout Latin America and deprived right-wing forces of a rationale for suppression. Hard experience with violent military dictatorships and regimes dominated by oligarchies has led many Latin Americans to demand that their governments respect the belief in human rights, representation, and accountability which are central to democracy. Vested interests remain strongly entrenched and often in a position to foment resistance, however, and popular disillusionment with the failure to provide immediate economic improvement could well lead to reversals. A dramatic indication of change, as Huntington has pointed out, is that whereas in 1974, eight of ten South American countries were under nondemocratic rule, by 1990 nine had democratically elected governments.[40] The Caribbean countries seem firmly in the democratic orbit, apart from Cuba and from Haiti, whose democratic experiments have often been undermined by military coups. In the Dominican Republic, democratic strivings are once again challenging a tradition of authoritarianism.

The historic North American Free Trade Agreement (NAFTA) put into effect in 1993 has begun to affect the political character of its southernmost member. Mexico has been described as one of the few Latin American countries with a tradition of civilian rule but "no significant twentieth-century experience (and precious little prior experience) with democratic rule."[41] Under NAFTA, it is moving rapidly toward greater economic integration with the United States and Canada. The momentum of this economic integration, coupled with internal pressures for reform, may also promote the adoption of a democratic political system—much as happened when the southern European nations joined the Common Market. At least some leaders of the ruling *Partido Revolucionario Institucional* recognize that Mexico cannot have sustained economic growth without an end to corporatist control and the nepotism and general corruption that goes hand in hand with one-party rule and the wholesale use of patronage. Privatization of government enterprises has deprived the PRI of some sources of patronage.

Limits on campaign spending and contributions have been imposed for the first time. To curtail opportunities for electoral fraud in the 1994 national elections, the government distributed computerized voter cards with photographs, fingerprints, signature, and security data to 91 percent of the 42.6 million-member electorate. From voter lists, polling place officials were randomly chosen and trained for each of the country's 96,421 polling places. Other steps have since been taken to insulate the electoral process from political interference and assure access to the media for all parties. Unless the PRI allows more intraparty democracy and until other parties have a real opportunity to move from opposition to national office, however, Mexico's transition to democracy will not be secure. As the 1994 Zapatista rebellion in the state of Chiapas showed, a continued lack of political legitimacy could erode the popular support any Mexican government will need to continue economic modernization.

In Central America, democratic and peaceful Costa Rica, with its police force but no army, is increasingly considered a paradigm for emulation rather than an anomaly. Guatemala's democracy has survived military intervention, albeit precariously. In Nicaragua, a civil war was ended following a democratic election, and a difficult effort is underway to create a more prosperous and self-governing society. In Panama, a dictatorship was overthrown by United States military intervention and a democratic regime is struggling to overcome an ingrained pattern of corruption and economic dependency. In El Salvador, too, a vicious civil war has been ended and there are signs of real progress toward democracy.

Similar progress is evident in the rest of Latin America. Venezuela, thanks in part to the prosperity and rising educational levels resulting from the exploitation of oil discoveries, has become, since 1958, "the oldest and most stable mass democracy in South America."[42] With two major national political parties composed of diverse elements of the population competing effectively against each other, Venezuela has achieved a high degree of popular participation. Its democratic government has achieved growing legitimacy thanks both to its responsiveness to the demands of the electorate and efforts to make the political system "more efficient, more accountable, and ultimately more participatory."[43] In Venezuela, as in many other democracies, the greatest threat to the survival of democracy is the persistence of poverty and the urban underclass it tends to breed. Colombia, while it has not yet consolidated its democratic institutions, has endured a fierce attack on them from drug lords without succumbing either to military rule or social and economic instability.[44] Peru, having adopted a democratic constitution in 1980, is in very difficult straits, badly divided culturally as well in terms of income distribution between a dominant minority Hispanic population and a subordinate Indian majority, and besieged by a Maoist guerilla movement.[45] Efforts to deal with the problems by strengthening presidential power at the expense of the constitution may well be justifiable as temporary measures, but as has been the case so often in Latin America, they could also prove the undoing of the democratic experiment if allowed to continue indefinitely.

Developments in the more economically advanced countries of the Southern Cone have been no less dramatic. Although Uruguay was under military rule from 1973 to 1984, it has come to be considered one of the most democratic nations in Latin America, and its high and rising standards of living and education seem to assure the persistence of democracy.[46] In Brazil, which has lived under democracy for only about twenty-five years over the last century, the *distensao* or relaxation that began in 1974 has led to a restoration of elections and a civilian government, but the widening gap between the rich minority and the poor majority bodes ill for stability. Popular discontent with the government's failure to curb inflation, corruption, and lawlessness, and to improve living standards could provide support for a return to military rule. A populace hitherto excluded from politics must now learn how to engage in political activity rather than in acts of protest and revolution, transforming movements into political parties.[47] In Argentina, democracy has survived a change of government, and the apparently chastened attitude of the Peronista leadership now returned to power is an indication that a broad change of consciousness may be taking hold there as well. But corporatism and the personalistic populism reflected in Peronism will both need to be transformed if Argentine democracy is to be maintained and consolidated.[48] Chile, which had enjoyed stable democratic government for most of the preceding 100 years, until a military coup in 1973 toppled the duly-elected leftist government of Salvador Allende,[49] has now returned to the democratic fold, after almost two decades of harsh dictatorship ended when the junta made the mistake of risking a referendum in 1988. The impressive economic growth that the country has been experiencing improves the chances that Chile will remain true to its democratic tradition. In Paraguay, the death of a dictator has been followed by democratic elections.

Efforts of democratization in Latin America have failed in the past and still face formidable obstacles—not least from the violence and corruption that remain such potent forces throughout the region. Nevertheless, the balance in the southern hemisphere of the Americas appears to have shifted dramatically in favor of democracy, even if there can be no certainty yet that the trends will continue long enough to assure an irrevocable transition in all or even most of the countries of the region. The United States will have a critical role to play in reinforcing these tendencies. In the past, inconsistent policies with respect to the promotion of hemispheric democracy have been all too characteristic. As Abraham F. Lowenthal has noted, "From the turn of the century until the 1980s, the overall impact of U.S.

policy on Latin America's ability to achieve democratic politics was usually negligible, often counterproductive, and only occasionally positive."[50] But as Lowenthal also points out, "the citizens of the United States have good reason to want their government to foster open, participatory, and constitutional polities through the Western Hemisphere" because such polities are more humane and peaceful than authoritarian systems, more likely to promote the kind of economic and social reforms that will provide stability, and because they share the values toward which the United States itself aspires.[51]

Africa: Learning from Experience?

In sub-Saharan Africa, the hopes for democracy that followed decolonization were at first dashed virtually everywhere, but there have lately been some signs of renewal. In recent years, more than half the forty-eight states south of the Sahara have held or promised multi-party elections. Most have acquired vigorous, independent newspapers and human rights monitoring groups.[52] But the prospect that political reforms can take hold is gravely threatened by the collapse of development projects, which has paralyzed most of the continent since the spike in oil prices in the 1970s and the subsequent fall in the prices of Africa's export commodities. The countries in this region include eighteen of the world's poorest, thirty of the forty poorest, and, with a population of 600 million, had a combined 1991 Gross National Product about the same as that of Belgium, with a population of ten million.[53]

The initial difficulty was that the grafting of Western-style democracies onto African roots did not take, for reasons that in retrospect seem clear and compelling. Colonialism served to unify territorial regions in the form of nation-states, but although it deprived traditional local systems of authority, it did not generally provide the prosperity and education that would have transformed the village and tribal structures and turned the mass of the people into self-conscious citizens of the nation-state. At independence the greatest concern of the political leaders of the newly independent states was to preserve unity and centralization. Claiming that a strong central government was essential for modernization, the post-colonial governments set out to deprive local institutions of their residual authority and to head off any challenges. They placed formidable difficulties in the path of actual and potential opposition parties.

In virtually all African countries, one-party regimes emerged. Even in Uganda, where a liberal transition had been prepared by the British colonial authorities, the constitution was "suspended" in 1986 by Milton Obote, and then turned into a police state by Idi Amin. In Kenya, the euphoria over *uhuru* or freedom felt in December 1963, when the Union Jack was replaced by the Kenyan national flag, was soon dissipated, as the ruling faction tightened its control and cancelled elections promised for 1968, silencing opposition by making it seem that all criticism of them was tantamount to treason against the state. As E. S. Atieno Odhiambo summed up the situation in Kenya succinctly, "the country moved from the era of competitive politics to the era of preventive detentions."[54] In the 1980s, of the forty-nine independent states, fewer than five could be described as multi-party states. Only one, Botswana, has had a pattern of free competitive elections, but although political democracy has served effectively to contain the country's ethnic tensions, it is still subject to abridgement by an authoritarian social elite, and persisting economic inequality and a weak civil society have prevented its consolidation.[55] Under Robert Mugabe's leadership, Zimbabwe has managed to maintain the parliamentary institutions adapted from its previous existence as Rhodesia, though continuing racial and economic tensions remain dangerous.

Some African leaders argued that under African conditions, democracy might best flourish in one-party regimes. Thus Julius Nyerere of Tanzania contended that since democracy is an attitude of mind, its practice need not be confined to the multi-party system. He argued in favor of a single party identified with the nation as a whole, which would reflect the need for unity in overcoming the legacy of colonialism and would be best able to make socialism—*ujaama* or African socialism—the basis for development. In practice, this attitude has meant that African states have developed either de jure or de facto one-party systems, though these parties have been riddled with factionalism and internal rivalries, which have become the seedbeds of opposition parties. In Tanzania and Kenya, acts of parliament made opposition parties illegal. In other countries, smaller parties were induced to dissolve voluntarily and leaders and supporters were absorbed into the ruling party. At the same time, the one-party regimes sometimes extended their control to include all voluntary associations, which were made extensions of integral parts of the ruling party. In Tanzania, the ruling party, the trade unions, co-op organizations, and women's organizations were all brought under party control. In Guinea, Ahmed Sékou Touré's version of "African socialism" brought repressive government and impoverished a once prosperous nation. The formerly French colonies did not copy the parliamentary constitutions of France, but instead turned the presidentialism of De Gaulle's fifth republic into a system of presidential autocracy.[56]

The upshot of these efforts of centralization and consolidation was that the one-party regimes in effect became systems of personal rule which inhibited rather than promoted successful development. Rulers surrounded themselves with loyal sycophants and security forces to whom they gave special privileges, sometimes rationalizing their rule as a necessity for the sake of unity and development. Leaders were also apt to argue that Western democracy would be bad for Africa because it would create individualism and class-riven societies. But while they promised development and equal benefits for all, they actually created authoritarian systems in which the economy stagnated.

Dissatisfaction with the status quo in Africa has frequently led to military coups. By 1986, two-thirds of the forty-nine independent states were under a military government of one type or another, some having experienced several coups d'état. Peter Wanyande, an African political scientist, described the resulting polarization between government and people:

> The drift and growing gap between the rulers and the ruled, common to many African one-party states, has made those who control state power . . . increasingly insecure, sensitive, repressive, and less responsive to the wishes of society. The mass of the people in turn begin to regard the state and its organs with fear, suspicion and cynicism because as far as they are concerned, they are no longer legitimate. As a result of the feeling of insecurity on the part of the state, those who control state power no longer regard the various state institutions as instruments for the promotion of the common or national interest but more as instruments of controlling and promoting their own parochial interests as rulers and of those who identify with their policies and programmes. The masses on the other hand, sensing their inability to meaningfully influence the policies of state and the behaviour of those in positions of leadership, tend to develop apathy and to withdraw from participation in the political process. This they do also because as far as they are concerned, and out of experience, it is safer to do so. It is this limitation and restriction of individual rights and freedoms in African one-party states that poses one of the greatest threats to democratic politics in these states. Voluntary popular participation once restricted makes prospects for democratic politics very remote indeed. This unfortunately is the situation in most African one-party states.[57]

In recent years, dissatisfaction with these authoritarian regimes has led to popular manifestations in favor of democracy, which have sometimes been met by concessions. Early in 1990, the governments of Ivory Coast and Gabon both sought to quell riots and demonstrations by promising to open their political systems to opposition parties. Zaire's president for a quarter of a century, Mobutu Sese Seko, one of the continent's symbols of greed and corruption, also promised to allow opposition parties to function and convened a conference of government and opposition leaders that has preceded the transition from autocracy in other African countries. But the impoverished and fragmented people of Zaire were fearful that his removal might bring anarchy and even worse poverty. Kenneth Kaunda, president of Zambia since it gained independence, promised a referendum to decide whether the country should have a one-party or multi-party system. The new rulers of Ethiopia have pledged to build a democratic, market-oriented system, despite prior professions. The people of Eritrea have won their independence and committed themselves to building democracy. In the Francophone central African states of Togo, Cameroon, and the Central African Republic, popular protests have compelled military and single-party leaders to make concessions, but repressive elites still either cling to power or wait in the wings to resume control. The tentative moves in the direction of democracy leave most of the fifty-two members of the Organization of African Unity in the non-democratic column. The general outcome may well hinge on progress in Nigeria and South Africa.

Nigeria, with over 100 million people, or more than one-fifth of all Africans south of the Sahara, is the most populous country on the continent, and a society with a cultural tradition of outspokenness. The country has gone through three distinct efforts to establish democracy without achieving more than temporary success. The first, under British auspices in the 1950s and the second under the military in the 1970s, both ended in failure and military coups. Both efforts foundered on wholesale corruption, widespread failure to follow democratic norms of behavior, and regional and group conflicts. In the latest effort, civilian intellectuals and opinion leaders cooperated with the military in devising a scheme for a gradual evolution toward democracy. In 1993 the military regime reneged on its commitment to respect the outcome of elections and opted for repression rather than conciliation. But the will of the Nigerian people remains a force to be reckoned with. "Through their country's turbulent quarter-century of independence—which has encompassed eight governments, five successful military coups, a civil war, and a dizzying economic boom followed by a crushing depression," Larry Diamond notes, "Nigerians have maintained a profound commitment to personal freedom and political participation."[58]

The changes achieved in the Republic of South Africa are momentous and may well help reinforce democratization elsewhere in Africa. The interim constitutional compromise now adopted provides for universal suffrage but not for simple majority rule in a unitary state. Instead, a federal and divided system of government has been established to allow for group representation and to require power-sharing rather than simple majority rule for a period of five years, after which a new constitution is to take effect. The interim arrangement is in principle the version of democracy identified by Arend Lijphart as consociational or consensual, in contrast to the majority-rule "Westminster model."[59] The leaders of the African National Congress, which can plausibly claim to represent most of the black population, accepted the arrangement in the hope of avoiding civil war and preserving the South African economy. The election of the ANC's leader, Nelson Mandela, as the first democratically elected president, set the stage for a profound social and political transition. It remains to be seen whether the country will maintain its present power-sharing constitution or move toward a more majoritarian formula, and whether, in either case, what has so far been achieved can be consolidated by the great improvements in social welfare, education, and inter-group tolerance that will be necessary to cement adhesion to democratic norms.

Any movement toward democracy in Africa will represent a major change of direction for that continent. In the decades since decolonization, efforts to install and maintain democratic systems have proven vain in one country after another. The momentum for change in the direction of democracy is hardly yet well established. Liberia and Somalia have experienced intense civil war. Kenya and Malawi are notorious for the repression of dissent. Apart from South Africa and Botswana, only Ghana is making encouraging economic progress. In assessing prospects for South Africa, Donald L. Horowitz has properly called attention to the discouraging record throughout the continent:

> Since 1967, power has never passed from one elected government to another in Africa. Before 1967, although several states held free elections won by incumbents, almost no civilian government ever handed over power to a duly elected government from among the former opposition. There were, to be sure, two short-lived cases of peaceful alternation. In Benin, from 1957 to 1965, several civilian coalitions alternated in office, although usually with one of the coalition partners constant from one government to another, until a military coup ended the process. In the Sudan, power passed peacefully in 1956 from one party to a coalition of two others. In the elections that followed in 1958, a new coalition—including one party that had served in the former government—formed a majority. A coup later in the year put an end to that government and to alternation in office. There was also an aborted attempt at alternation in Sierra Leone in 1967. A new government had barely been sworn in when it was overthrown by the military. After that, alternation ended. No African political party has ever again moved from the opposition to the government benches after an election. Rather than turn power over, elected governments transformed themselves into single-party regimes. In several countries, continuing opposition electoral strength precipitated the declaration of a one-party state . . . In those few countries where an opposition functions and free elections are held—Senegal, Botswana, and the Gambia—the structure of cleavages is such as to give the ruling party a dominant position, free of any real prospect of losing power at the polls.[60]

Beneath this pattern of political failure is a pattern of economic hardship exacerbated by the persistence of ethnic and regional tensions. Successful democratization, in Africa as elsewhere, will require a combination of improvements aimed at promoting economic well being, dampening social conflicts, and providing experience in democratic procedures and a commitment to democratic norms.

The Arab and Muslim Middle East: An Exception?

Conditions seem even less favorable to democracy in the Arab countries and more broadly in those in which Islam is the predominant faith. Regimes in these countries have run from the theocratic to secular-authoritarian, with the important exceptions of Turkey and Malaysia, to some extent of Pakistan, and of Lebanon before the outbreak of civil war in 1975. There have recently been some tentative moves toward democratization in certain Arab countries, notably Jordan and Yemen. In May 1993 in Yemen, over 80 percent of the three million registered voters took part in what was by all accounts a free election—the country's first ever—under international supervision. Forty parties fielded candidates. Not only did women vote, but two were elected to the legislature. The party of the president who called the election, Colonel Ali Abdullah Saleh, gained the largest number of votes and announced afterward that it would form a governing coalition with the Socialist Party and the country's Islamic movement. The president also proposed that his office be limited to two terms. Alas, a year after this peaceful election a violent civil war broke out between the still not integrated armies of the two regions.

Students of Islamic societies sometimes argue that democracy cannot be achieved in societies in which traditional Islamic beliefs hold sway. From the traditional Islamic perspective, they point out, democracy is not among the ideals stipulated in the Koran; on the contrary, it is associated with secular modernism, which is considered a threat to Islamic values. Thus, in Pakistan, Iran, and the Sudan, recent efforts of "Islamization" have put in jeopardy human rights formerly protected by standards of due process in Western-style secular courts and Western-trained lawyers. These rights have been overridden as public law has been reformed to accord more with the *shari`a*, the body of Islamic law, and as judicial posts have been taken over by clerics or others trained in religious law.[61] Unlike the West, which had much experience with parliaments and church councils before the era of modern democracy, Islam, the historian Bernard Lewis points out, has no such pre-history: "There are no parliaments or representative assemblies of any kind, no councils or communes, no chambers of nobility or estates, no municipalities . . . nothing but the sovereign power to which the subject owed complete and unwavering obedience as a religious duty imposed by the Holy Law." For a thousand years, he adds, "the political thinking of Islam has been dominated by such maxims as 'tyranny is better than anarchy'. . ."[62] Similarly, the writer David Pryce-Jones observes that regardless of outward form the common political feature of all contemporary Muslim states is "the rule of a single power holder around whose ambitions the state has been arranged." The essential elements of democracy, he adds, are all but completely absent: "No parliament or assembly except by appointment of the power holder, no freedom of expression throughout rigidly state-controlled media, no opinion polls, nothing except a riot to determine what public opinion might be."[63]

The separation of church and state, which was a vital element in the Western transition to democracy, has no counterpart in Islamic experience. With the exception of Turkey, which has been more receptive to Western influence, countries with Muslim majorities have tended to make Islam the state religion and its law the basis of their constitutions or a major source of legislation.[64] Islamic fundamentalism arose early in this century in reaction to efforts to introduce a degree of separation between religion and politics and to adopt other attitudes and customs prevalent in the modern West. Its adherents denounce the very idea that any sphere of life, whether economic, social, or political, should lie outside the reach of religious law and authority. They believe it a religious duty to struggle, by force and violence wherever necessary, against leaders who would betray Islamic principles and forces both inside and outside the Islamic community which are said by religious authorities to pose a threat. The assassination of the Egyptian President, Anwar el-Sadat, by members of a cell connected to the Muslim Brotherhood, was one expression of this fundamentalist attitude, as it has appeared among Sunnis, who constitute 80 percent of the world's Muslims. The willingness of the Iranian Shiite regime to endorse a religious *fatwa* or pronouncement decreeing death as punishment for blasphemy against the writer Salman Rushdie, even though he is a citizen of another country and the alleged blasphemy occurred in a work of fiction, illustrates the glaring contrast between the modern democratic commitment to individual rights and the fundamentalist commitment to use the power of government to stamp out heresy wherever it appears.

The impact of Islamic belief is reinforced in Arab societies by ethnic attachments which take the political form of both pan-Arabism and narrower nationalism, both of which are themselves reinforced by poverty and a suspicion of outsiders inspired by long experience of colonial rule. The Arab states have been described as "tribes with flags" whose dominant psychology recognizes only shame and envy and all but requires authoritarian rule, since winning power provides honor, and losing power, whether in a coup or in an election, is too shameful to be willingly accepted.

In spite of these powerful anti-democratic influences, pro-democratic sentiments seem to be making headway in the Arab countries. The paradoxical state of current thinking is indicated by an unscientific poll carried out by the Egyptian newspaper *Al Ahram* of almost 5,000 people, chosen to be "a cross-section of the Arab world." The poll found that 56 percent of the respondents favored the introduction of Western-style democracy while 52.3 percent demanded the application of the *shari`a*, which would entail the banning of alcoholic beverages and the application of penalties laid down in the Koran. Support for democratization was said to be highest in the Gulf states (69 percent of Saudis, 71 per cent of Bahrainis, 87.5 percent of Kuwaitis, 89 percent of Qataris, and 90 percent of those from the United Arab Emirates).[65] But if democratization should require implementation of Islamic law, not only would there be no recognition of the individual rights protected in the modern form of democracy elsewhere, but in all likelihood the very commitment to democratic elections and procedures would be doubtful. In commenting on this poll, Elie Kedourie remarked that it is by no means clear what the respondents understood about the meaning of democracy if they also favored the introduction of Islamic law, for, as he put it, "the idea of democracy is quite alien to the mind-set of Islam,"[66] as indeed is the concept of the state. Islam posits the existence of a community, the *umma*, originally presided over by the Prophet Mohammed at Medina:

> Wherever the Muslim *umma* is, there is the polity of Islam. Elsewhere is the abode of war. This, in a nutshell, is the Islamic theory of international relations. The abode of Islam, *dar-al-Islam*, is not defined by permanent territorial frontiers. It is wherever Muslims exercise (or have exercised) dominion. *Dar-al-Islam* is not like the Roman Empire, a city-state developing into an extensive Empire; it is unlike the Greek *polis*, or the state as it has developed in Europe. Its basis is neither kinship, nor the occupation of a defined territory, and the bond between its members is not legal, as in the Roman empire, but religious: the members of the *umma* are such because they acknowledge the divine revelation as vouchsafed in the Koran, and obey its instructions.[67]

Because the ruler of the *umma* was the Prophet's successor, charged with maintaining the faith, defending the territory on which it had been established and extending that territory, it is considered the religious duty of Muslims to obey the ruler, at first the caliph, later the sultan. Anarchy is considered the worst evil because it makes the pursuit of holiness impossible and thus endangers eternal salvation. In the words of the great Islamic divine Ghazali (d. 1111), "The tyranny of a sultan for a hundred years causes less damage than one year's tyranny exerted by the subjects against each other."[68] As this attitude was inculcated over centuries of practice, a gulf developed between rulers and ruled in Islamic societies which allowed no room for representative institutions of any kind or for institutions of self-government, either in towns or villages. Craft and professional associations (which might have served as the nucleus of civil society) were also ruled out because they might have been suspected of seeking to limit the authority of the ruler over his subjects.

In the first half of the nineteenth century, however, Muslim rulers like Mohammed Ali in Egypt sought to emulate the enlightened absolutisms of Europe by enlarging their bureaucracies and centralizing power even more effectively by developing larger armies. Mohammed Ali took over practically all agricultural land and created monopolies for the sale and purchase of agricultural commodities and imports and exports. The interjection of Western methods of organization in the state apparatus, and with these methods western ways of thinking, widened the already existing gap between rulers and ruled, who, until then, had at least shared a common universe of discourse.[69] At the opening of the Suez Canal in 1869 the despot Ismail proclaimed that the country must become a part of Europe; because parliamentary institutions were part of European civilization, Egypt too would have a parliament. The members of this parliament were chosen by village headmen and divided by royal decree into two parties, one supporting the government, the other opposing. Since members were "understandably chary of being labelled as opponents of the government... the ruler himself had to designate who should sit on the opposition benches." This parliament had no real function, except as an instrument of the government. Ismail's more important contribution to the future of Egypt was to incite a mutiny by some Egyptian military officers against a ministry he had created to being some order into Egypt's public finances. This mutiny led to others against his successors, ending when King Farouk was overthrown and with him the monarchy.[70]

Meanwhile, the Ottoman empire was experiencing crises which led to an attempt to establish parliamentary government in Turkey. In 1876 the reigning sultan was deposed and replaced by another sultan who declared that he would rule "by the favor of the Almighty and the will of my subjects." He was succeeded shortly afterward by a new sultan who promulgated a constitution providing for a senate and a chamber of deputies. The powers of the parliament were very limited and its composition was either controlled or strongly influenced by the ruler. The second parliament elected under this constitution was dissolved in 1878. In 1908, a military coup by the Young Turks under Kemal Ataturk deposed the sultan, Abd al-Hamid, but the result was a replacement of the old autocracy by a military oligarchy riven by personal rivalries. A committee of military officers ruled the country until 1918, when the defeat of the Central Powers whom they had joined and which cost Turkey its empire forced them to flee. Those who engineered the coup did so because they recognized that autocracy was harmful, but they ended up substituting one form of autocracy for another.[71]

World War opened the Middle East to influences other than those of the Ottoman Empire. The two major colonial powers, Britain and France, set up states and governments to suit their interests, carving up the Ottoman-controlled territory to create Iraq, Syria, Lebanon, Palestine, and later Transjordan. In Iraq, where the populace was divided into Kurds, Sunni and Shiite Muslims, the majority Shiite, and a substantial Jewish population in the capital, Baghdad, the British mandatory gave power to a monarchy in the hands of a Sunni tribal leader, Faisal. The rulers took steps to keep down the Shiites, arousing their resentment against the new state. As a result, no common bond of citizenship developed between the small group of Sunni officials, who in effect were the state, and the Shiites, who were subjects rather than citizens. The Kurds refused to accept Arab rule. To make matters worse, the ex-Ottoman military officers who accompanied Faisal into power had imbibed from the Young Turks a taste for using conspiracy and violence in pursuit of political aims. The government did not rest on a base of popular support, and was therefore regularly overthrown once the mandate ended and British troops were withdrawn. Although parliamentary government was established, and parliaments were returned in elections, all of them conformed to the wishes of the government in power, until in May 1958 monarchy was abolished in a military coup. From then on, Iraq has been ruled by military dictatorships.[72]

In Syria, which had a Sunni majority but an even more mixed population, the French mandatory established separate states in Damascus, Aleppo, and the Druze country, and a separately governed Alawite territory. A constituent assembly was convened in 1928 and drafted a nationalist constitution, asserting Syria's claim to Lebanon and Palestine. The French High Commissioner reacted by dissolving the parliament and promulgating the constitution minus the claims to the other territories. The French had difficulty ending the mandate, until they finally agreed to the nationalists' demand for a unitary state ruled from Damascus. The nationalist bloc swept into power and, in imitation of what was happening in Europe, established a paramilitary organization, the Steel Shirts, to intimidate rivals and opponents. In 1941, Syria as well as Lebanon were invaded by the British, who feared that otherwise they might fall under Axis control, and a Syrian Republic came into existence. In 1949, in the aftermath of the Arab defeat in the war against Israel, a disgruntled army officer organized a coup d'état and was shortly thereafter declared president in a national referendum. A few months later he was toppled by another army officer and ordered executed. This officer was himself toppled in another military coup. Since then, Syria has been ruled autocratically.[73]

In Lebanon, the Arab world has had its first significant experience with democratization, but under unusual conditions which make its designation as the Switzerland of the Middle East especially apt. Lebanon too was created out of territorial units which had never been governed as a single entity and which were inhabited by differing ethnic and religious groups. In the nineteenth century, the Maronite Christians of Mount Lebanon had been hard pressed by their Muslim neighbors. A massacre in 1861 provoked the government of France to send an expeditionary force to Beirut with the object of protecting them. The other European Great Powers, concerned that France not act alone, entered into an agreement with the Ottoman rulers providing for a constitution for Mount Lebanon insulating the Maronites from direct interference and setting up an autonomous province in which both Christian and Muslim communities would have security. Government was to be placed in the hands of a non-Lebanese Christian who would be an Ottoman subject to be chosen in consultation with the European powers. He would be advised by an administrative council consisting of twelve members, two Maronites, two Druze, two Greek Catholic, two Greek Orthodox, two Sunnis, and two Shiites.

This system lasted until 1915, when, during the first World War, the Ottomans abolished the separate autonomous status for Mount Lebanon. After World War I, a much larger Lebanese Republic was created under a French mandate with a territory that included many more Sunnis than Shiites. The Sunnis, who had been a ruling group in their territory under the Ottomans, chafed at being subordinated and at being separated from their co-religionists in Syria. They also resented French partiality to the Maronites. Despite these differences, the Lebanese constitution of 1926 sought to maintain the spirit of the old autonomous entity by requiring that the various communities be equitably represented in public employments and in the composition of the cabinet, which would replace the administrative council. The scheme was implemented on the basis of a 1932 census which gave the Maronites a slight edge in population over the Sunnis and a larger one over the other groups. An informal agreement between the Maronites and the Sunnis, known as the "National Pact," pledged the Maronites to forego any attempt to seek foreign protection in exchange for which the Sunnis would give up their efforts to seek union with Syria.

This power-sharing arrangement worked tolerably well for a short time, but broke down twice, first in 1958, when the Sunnis were encouraged by Syria, which had not been a party to the National Pact and did not feel bound by it, to make Lebanon a more integral part of an Arab alliance committed to Nasserite pan-Arab goals. A civil war resulted which was ended only after American intervention. In the 1970s, another, far bloodier civil war broke out which left Lebanon effectively fragmented. One factor in provoking the wars was Sunni resentment over the failure of the government to take a new census which would have shifted the balance of political representation in their favor. Another was the increasing size and militancy of the exiled Palestinian Arab community in Lebanon, whose guerrilla factions operated against Israel beyond the control of the central government, creating a kind of state within the state. The Lebanese government was prevented from controlling or suppressing the Palestinians by pressure from other Arab governments and the Sunnis, who had the political power to veto any commitment of Lebanese forces. To compound the problem of achieving consensus, the Shiites, driven in great numbers to Beirut to escape Israeli attacks on the south, encouraged by the creation of an Islamic republic in Iran, and given tangible military support by Iran with the connivance of Syria, created their own militant movement and their own armed force. Gravely weakened by these internal strains, Lebanese self-government became all but a nominal exercise after Israel twice made incursions into its territory to suppress the Palestinian guerrillas and Syria stationed troops there in 1976-1977 and 1984. Syrian hegemony over most of the country was tacitly recognized by the Western powers, in exchange for Syrian support of the war to oust Iraq from Kuwait in 1990-1991.[74]

The Lebanese case shows that democratic arrangements can be made to work if there is a willingness on the part of the various factions to accommodate each other, but that such arrangements are precarious unless they are shored up by a sense of national identity strong enough to override communal loyalties in times of difficulty. In addition, an isolated democratic experiment is less likely to succeed in establishing itself than one that can draw support from its neighbors.

The difficulty facing democracy in the Arab and Islamic Middle East may not be quite as unique as it might seem to specialists, however. For many centuries, Christianity was no more hospitable to freedom of thought, free market economics, or political democracy than Islam is now. Heresy was severely punished, often through the agency of temporal authorities, and crusades were authorized against infidels. Strict rules governing usury prevented the development of capitalism in Europe for centuries. Jews played such a critical role in promoting trade and eventually a free market economy in medieval times because they were allowed to engage in these unclean activities that were forbidden to Christians. Christian fundamentalists promoted ideas of theocracy and called for holy wars; and intolerance on the scale of the Spanish inquisition is hardly inferior to anything practiced by the Ayatollahs in Iran. Democracy arose in Europe only after the Protestant revolt brought about an attack upon hierarchy in the church that served as a precedent (especially among English Puritans) for the democratization of politics and after bloody wars of religion led to toleration and the weakening if not the complete dissolution of ties between church and state. Political pluralism was modeled upon (and legitimated by) Protestant sectarianism. Recent developments in eastern Europe and Latin America have been considerably helped by the Second Vatican Council of 1963-1965, as a result of which the Roman Catholic church became less supportive of oligarchic regimes and readier to encourage opposition not only to communism but to other forms of authoritarianism.

This comparison suggests that democracy can come into being in the Arab and other Muslim countries—but only to the extent that Islam itself is made more compatible with secular rule. The key consideration with regard to Islam is the same as in regard to Christianity: democracy is possible only if the public sector is allowed to function without religious control. Otherwise corporate demands will override individual rights and traditional values incompatible with modernization will preclude the openness to change democracy necessarily entails. Such a change may happen because of the social transformation taking place in the Arab and more broadly Islamic world. As economic modernization takes place, especially in the wealthier Arab states of the Gulf, a middle class is being created with expectations and standards little different from those of middle classes elsewhere. The members of this class may very well force a transformation of Islam to accommodate the needs of modernization, just as the rising middle class transformed Christianity in Europe. That transformation will very likely be expressed in Islamic terms, much as it first found expression in the West in the Protestant version of Christianity, but it will also require a high degree of secularization similar to what was entailed in the separation of church and state in most of the Christian world.

Efforts to develop respect for human rights are bound to be resisted by traditionalists and are also likely to be criticized as efforts to impose Western values. The representative to the United Nations of the Islamic Republic of Iran, defending the regime of the Ayatollah Khomeini from charges of violating human rights, claimed, in a paraphrased version of his remarks, that "the Universal Declaration of Human Rights, which represented secular understanding of the Judaeo-Christian tradition, could not be implemented by Muslims and did not accord with the system of values represented by the Islamic Republic of Iran." A better way to understand the effort to promote respect for human rights in Muslim countries, as Anne Elizabeth Mayer has suggested in quoting this comment, is to see it as resting "on the premise that peoples in the West and East share a common humanity, which means that they are equally deserving of rights and freedoms." The evidence suggests, she points out, that concepts of international human rights are already "percolating through the tradition and becoming part of the apparatus Muslims use to determine what practices are or are not acceptable and to judge the adequacy of positive laws."[75] At least one Iranian cleric, Ayatollah Taleghani, has warned against the danger that Islam, which he described as "a religion of freedom," might be used by the clergy as a means "to enslave the masses" for the sake of clerical power.[76] Even his language is strongly reminiscent of Martin Luther's sermons on Christian liberty and his fulminations against the Roman Catholic hierarchy.

The Mixed Overall Picture: Avoiding Illusions

Overall, then, the global picture is mixed. Despite the upsurge in belief in democracy, only 37 percent of the world's people live in the fifty-one countries generally classified as stable democracies by the broadest criteria—as few as thirty if narrower criteria are used.[77] Still, there is plenty of evidence to support the view that real efforts are being made in many places to implement those ideals. These efforts may well prove abortive and deeply disappointing unless it is clear to those who make them that democracy is not a panacea and that democratization is hard to achieve and sustain. They may take inspiration, however, from the experienced of well-established democracies, which tends to show that once the foundations are in place, democracies are vigorous and resilient.

11

Autonomy Against Itself: Pitfalls and Pathologies

Democracies face two sets of problems, which may be distinguished as pitfalls and pathologies. The pitfalls are especially threatening while democratic norms and institutions are not yet well entrenched and forces hostile to democracy remain strong enough to capitalize on the difficulties of transition. The pathologies appear once democracy is firmly established, and may well be endemic because they arise from the very experience of autonomy. In ancient Athens, philosophers and dramatists played a constructive role as critics of democracy by calling attention to such dangers and difficulties. Modern democracies need the same critical scrutiny, even if the result is a catalogue of problems which enemies of democracy can exploit to shake confidence in it as an ideal and a working system.

Pitfalls: Crises of Confidence

Because the pitfalls have been outlined and illustrated in the preceding chapter, they require less elaboration than the pathologies. They can be summed up in a simple warning: the transition to democracy often inspires expectations of rapid improvement, in standards of living and in adherence to constitutional norms, which are not easily satisfied.

A new democratic government can be blamed for inherited hardships, as happened to the Weimar Republic during the difficulties experienced in Germany as a result of its defeat in war. In other cases, the inability of elected governments to fulfill hopes for immediate improvement can led to bitter disillusionment, as has happened recently in Russia and other eastern European countries. New democracies are likely to face a special threat from previously privileged groups deprived of power in the transition to democracy but still in a position to sabotage or corrupt efforts of social and political reform. This problem has often resulted in setbacks to democracy in Latin America.

When democratic regimes fail to satisfy expectations aroused in the transition, frustration and disenchantment invite a return to autocratic alternatives. Where democratic values and institutions are not yet well established, confidence in the new system of authority can easily be eroded, especially if those in authority are perceived to be inept and/or corrupt. "Widespread political cynicism," José María Maravall has noted, "can undermine support for economic reforms: if politicians are seen as corrupt, they cannot effectively demand austerity from the people." Unfortunately, he points out, "political mistrust and cynicism are prevalent in new democracies." In Spain, Hungary, Poland, for instance, surveys indicate that the great majority of people think their leaders are corrupt and care little about the interests of the people.[1]

In crises produced by the difficulties of transition, anti-democratic forces will inevitably seek to exploit popular discontent. The resulting scenario is all too familiar. Economic difficulties lead to a withdrawal of confidence in the government and to demands for leadership forceful enough to get things under control. Society becomes divided into hostile camps. The sense of solidarity is too weak to preserve unity. Protests and conspiratorial movements arouse alarm and threaten public order. The police and army are unable to exercise control; their overreaction provokes angry responses. Radical movements of the right and left led by populist demagogues propose simple solutions with popular appeal. Fearing that disorder will lead to anarchy or populist revolution, those with most to lose from disorder throw their support to the military leadership. Military coups result in "temporary" suspensions of democratic constitutions which threaten to become permanent.

The transition from communism poses similar but in some respects unfamiliar difficulties. There, crises of confidence are likely to arise from the effort to transform a command economy into a regulated market economy. The success of the transition depends upon whether enough citizens have enough patience to put up with hardships and dislocations, and whether governments provide necessary safety nets for those worst hurt by privatization and deregulation. Above all, the new governments must reassure citizens that their concerns will be heard because the government represents them, however imperfectly, and is sensitive to their grievances and petitions for help. Only when the democratic civic culture takes strong enough hold, and citizens refrain from rushing into the street to pull down the government over every grievance before electoral alternatives are exhausted, can the transition succeed.

In other cases, a crisis of confidence can arise because of tensions between cultural, ethnic, religious, and racial groups. These tensions are especially intense in multi-ethnic societies or in those assimilating immigrants whose ethnic and cultural backgrounds differ from that of the majority.

Even relatively heterogeneous societies are prey to xenophobia, but relatively homogeneous societies are apt to make minorities and immigrants scapegoats in times of difficulty. While the civic culture of democracy instils respect for the rights of all citizens, regardless of race or ethnicity, native birth or immigrant status, irrational fears and ingrained sentiments can be rooted out of popular consciousness only by prolonged and continuing reeducation and actual integration. Where democracy is not an ingrained tradition, it may have too shallow a hold on popular thinking to assure that such sentiments will be resisted. Well-intended efforts to offer opportunities for immigration and asylum may easily backfire if they result in large influxes that arouse fears of dispossession readily exploited by bigots hostile to democratic values.

Pathologies: The Paradoxes of Success

Whereas the pitfalls result from the failure of new democratic regimes to satisfy expectations, the pathologies appear paradoxically when democracy succeeds in providing opportunity for a high degree of autonomy. Anatole France put a finger on part of the problem when he observed of democracy: "I forgive it for governing badly because it governs so little."[2] Once a transition to democracy has been successfully achieved, democracy itself poses problems for its own maintenance because its very success in empowering people can make the social system more difficult to manage. It was just this achievement of freedom which aroused fears in the 1970s that because of "demand overload" democratic societies were becoming "ungovernable." But the problem is not just a matter of the demands people put upon government. It is also a matter of the ability of citizens to regulate their own behavior intelligently and responsibly and make informed judgments about public issues and candidates for office. In democracies, everything depends upon how well citizens regulate their own lives, how wisely they choose representatives to exercise the powers of government, and whether they have the good sense to endorse policies that promote the general welfare, rather than only their own narrow and immediate self-interest. The problem is compounded because in democracies virtually all politicians and many pundits court popularity by pandering to widely-held prejudices, no matter how ill-informed, rather than taking the risk of excoriating those who cling to them against all good sense. They do not often see their role to be that of latter-day Biblical prophets. In democracy, however, it can truly be said that the fault lies "not in our stars but in ourselves." When people do not take the trouble to inform themselves adequately about the public business or even to vote, they risk making the democratic process an unworkable sham, and they need to be reminded of their failings.

Under modern conditions, when so many public policies require so-phisticated scientific and technical understanding, democracy puts espe-cially heavy burdens on ordinary citizens. They are constantly asked to make judgments about economic policies, for example, about which pro-fessional economists disagree sharply and which are often not amenable to common-sense reasoning, because they involve unfamiliar concepts and estimates and forecasts that are subject to conjecture. Faced with the alarms raised by scientists, even well-educated and responsible citizens may not feel competent enough to decide whether a particular toxic pesticide is so harmful that it must be banned, or whether the risk posed by a new indus-trial technology or medical therapy outweighs the prospective benefits.[3] Nor can they always rely on the judgment of scientific experts, who may disagree among themselves or be biased because of various scientific and non-scientific commitments. At best, democratic polities must rely on the openness of the democratic process and on the adversary process it in-spires, to provide for informed debates and make possible intelligent deci-sions. But in the end citizens and their accountable representatives must make the decisions, and that responsibility requires that they be well-edu-cated and civic-minded enough to pay close attention to the arguments.

Even when democracy works well, it involves a series of delicate bal-ances—between the rights of individuals and sub-groups and the will of the majority; between particular and common interests; between citizens jealous of their independence and a government that must be intrusive and coercive in order to enforce the law; between the civility necessary for reasoned discourse and the angry and sometimes intolerant passions that freedom encourages. Personal liberty is not always compatible with the dictates of majority will. Group interests sometimes conflict with each other and with the general interest. When the urge for communal autonomy is allowed to become an intolerant ethnic nationalism, minorities are often relegated to second-class citizenship and even made victims of "ethnic cleansing."

These balances are constantly in danger of being upset. When the exer-cise of liberty leads to self-absorption and civic indifference, the civic cul-ture weakens and citizens behave irresponsibly. The political process be-comes a zero-sum game, a struggle for advantage marked by the exercise of vetoes rather than the pursuit of compromise and consensus. Conversely, democratic states which restrict individual liberty, even in the name of the common good, raise the specter of the tyranny of the majority.

The more successful is democratization, the more it tends to produce strong desires for personal and sub-group autonomy and resistance to ev-erything that smacks of external control. The spirit of democratic self-reli-ance readily becomes a kind of principled rebelliousness, especially among the young. For some, even the resort to violence becomes a perverse expression of the freedom of the individual from social control. A breakdown of the traditional family structure follows from the unwillingness of the individual to make commitments which are thought to compromise freedom and from the unwillingness of children, as though it were a matter of democratic principle, to respect the authority of parents and of school authorities acting *in loco parentis*. The weakness of family structures leads to an increase in single-parent families in which children do not receive the guidance they need to become responsible adults. The need for a sense of identity and security leads those in the social underclass to yield to peer pressures to act out frustrations in anti-social behavior by joining street gangs and engaging in criminal activity.

Difficulties in managing civil society and public government may interpenetrate and weaken the channelling mechanisms provided by organized interest groups, political parties, and the media of communications. Apathy toward public issues and resistance to taxation are not necessarily a result of the failure of the political process to engage the citizen or of a justifiable perception that the process is hopelessly corrupt and wasteful. They may also signify an indifference to public concerns in favor of self-absorption. When life in civil society is satisfying and well protected, it may give rise to the illusion that the regulatory and protective functions of government are not really needed. When citizens perceive that their government is mired in bureaucracy while private services are more efficient and "consumer-friendly," they may conclude erroneously that wholesale deregulation and privatization are always beneficial. By demanding cutbacks in public budgets and pay scales, they may create a self-fulfilling prophecy, by making the public sector less efficient in providing the services and infrastructure upon which civil society depends. By failing to support welfare programs for those who cannot fend for themselves or job programs for those willing to work but unable to find a job, they worsen problems of crime and violence. Ironically, they then find themselves compelled to hire their own private security police and live in gated residential facilities. By demanding wholesale deregulation, they may deprive the government of its ability to protect them against environmental pollution and similar hazards to health and safety.

Liberty and License: Pathologies of Individual Autonomy

The breakdown of the balance of autonomies appears most dramatically whenever the liberty that is indispensable to democracy degenerates into license, at its worst becoming a reckless disregard for civilized values.

The culture of democracy promotes individual self-assertiveness, expressiveness, and a consciousness of rights. Individualism is essential to democracy because it promotes the self-reliance and independence of judgment that enables citizens to discharge their responsibilities as democratic citizens. Although critics and detractors have feared that democracy would promote conformity and mass society, it is more likely, as it takes hold, to promote an intense individualism. Democratic systems promote an emphasis on the self-development and rights of the individual rather than on the more traditional subordination of individuals to collectivities of various kinds, from the family to the religious community to the nation. Many effects of individualism strongly reinforce democracy. Self-reliant citizens contribute to social stability, efficiency, and cooperation. Citizens lacking in self-confidence tend to become fearful and dependent and unable to shoulder responsibilities and make decisions independently, just as the crowd theorists suggested. The best antidote to the danger of mob rule is an ingrained capacity for self-reliance. Successful democracy fosters a sometimes bewildering menu of choices. Freedom means not only the right to elect representatives, but also the need to make choices of all sorts—from schooling to jobs and careers, from what consumer goods to buy to where to make one's home, from whether to follow the religion of one's parents or to adopt another, to whether and whom to marry. Although such choices are always constrained, democracy best exemplifies Pierre Mendès-France's remark that "to govern is to choose." If traditional society emphasizes order, Burkean prescription, and ascriptive status, democratic society emphasizes the freedom to choose.

But the very emphasis on the right to choose puts burdens on individuals which some may not be able to support. The incapable may find psychological security by conforming to group norms sometimes malevolently hostile to outsiders. They are readily manipulated by demagogues, especially those using modern techniques of advertising and propaganda. Even those capable of managing their own lives understandably defer to experts on matters in which they feel incompetent. But the more dependent they become, the more powerless they come to feel. A privatization takes place in the civic psyche, resulting in alienation at worst, indifference at best. The political arena becomes the preserve of political elites, and the citizenry at large is reduced to the role of spectators, giving occasional shouts of approval and disapproval. Government comes to seem remote and to some a conspiracy of the powerful against them and their freedom. Among the most immature and insecure, frustration may lead to anti-social behavior, including the use of violence.

Perhaps the most insidious paradox of all is that by promoting a sense of autonomy and empowerment, democracy tends to promote selfishness, opinionated arrogance, and an unwillingness to make sacrifices for the common good. This was a major fear of Tocqueville, when he examined American democracy, the fear that led him to use a newly coined word—"individualism"—to describe the ethos of democracy. He hoped that Americans would develop a sense of "individualism rightly understood,"[4] enabling them to recognize that their own welfare depends on that of others. Tocqueville's fear was not misplaced. In the process of promoting individualism, democracy inevitably stimulates egocentricity. "Question authority" becomes the slogan, especially among the young. Everyone comes to feel "empowered" to pursue his or her own interests, to make up his or her mind, to express an opinion. Conversely, there is a withdrawal of the deference to one's "betters" that is characteristic of non-democratic societies. Although individuals sometimes feel powerless when they must confront the power of collective authority in isolation, they are constantly made aware that they have rights, and the legal system often deliberately enables them to challenge authority. In the United States, where democracy is especially associated with the protection of individual rights, the result is that litigation is encouraged and that the administration of justice is made more complex and costly. Convicted murderers use the appeals process to avoid the death penalty for years; others accused or found guilty of lesser crimes can also put off paying the penalty by prolonging the process. Public prosecutors often offer reduced penalties to obtain plea bargains, and lawyers in civil cases often advise clients to settle early rather than enter into prolonged and costly court proceedings.

In the most extreme forms, individualism can promote an anarchistic frame of mind which leads to a withdrawal from social concern which is by no means always benign, as it was, for example, for Thoreau. The demand for absolute freedom from all social coercion is a self-assertiveness which may damage the consensual framework upon which democracy depends. In Robert Hughes' phrase, the result is a "culture of complaint."[5] When individualism results in a self-centeredness or egoism which leads people to become wholly absorbed in advancing their own cause and putting their claims ahead of all others, recognizing no responsibility to their fellow citizens, especially those less fortunate, individualism becomes inimical to citizenship.

Irresponsible egoism can take many different forms, some having in common a disdain or contempt for laws and practices embodying democratic norms. Greed tempts those inspired by the competitive norm of a free society to violate laws if they think they can get away with doing so and to solicit or offer bribes. A wealthy American recently convicted of evading taxation may or may not have said, as she has been reported to have, "Only the little people pay taxes," but the sentiment sums up an attitude which accounts for a good deal of willful tax evasion. The influence of money in elections makes democratically elected officials beholden to large contributors. Political corruption leads to the appointment of unqualified people to office and to the improper application of laws to benefit some rather than all. It also engenders a pervasive cynicism about the realities of democratic government that leads to an unwillingness to participate and a tendency to turn to authoritarian figures expressing populist protest. Self-absorption among the affluent also results in anti-social behavior. Business owners and managers cut corners and engage in fraudulent practices. Property owners rise up in tax revolts that hobble government and impoverish public services.

An effect of individualism more benign and important to protect because it is a form of free expression takes the form of artistic license or anarchic expressionism. Democracy puts a premium on individual self-expression and therefore protects the right to free expression, in contrast to totalitarian societies, which may prohibit "degenerate" art (*entartete Kunst*, as the Nazis called it), defined as art not in keeping with sanctioned standards. When popular artists and profit-minded purveyors transcend the limits of conventional taste and offend against commonly held standards of decency, they may not be entitled to public subsidy but they are entitled to the protection of their right to free expression. Only when the exercise of this freedom can be shown to endanger public safety or corrupt the immature is censorship warranted. Since tastes vary, even with respect to what may be thought decent and civil behavior, and since censorship can easily be abused, the grounds for limiting freedom of expression must be kept narrow. The anarchic impulse behind avant gardism is sometimes threatening to the fabric of consensus, and may promote extremist politics, as Italian futurism did fascism, but if the fabric of democracy is strong enough, expression alone will not seriously threaten it.

A similar problem arises on college and university campuses when concerns to protect minority groups against hate speech lead to the adoption of speech codes that restrict freedom of speech. Concern for civil liberties requires that no such codes be adopted. It is at least arguable that certain forms of speech are intimidating, inflammatory to the point of incitement, and harmful, especially when they are directed against members of minority groups who are made to feel inferior. Since universities are designed to promote freedom of inquiry, however, they need to take care not to inhibit freedom in the name of preserving it.

The tension between the freedom of the individual and the good of society also arises in many other respects. Even more than artists, scientists face an acute dilemma. Often they cannot pursue the work that concerns them without public or corporate subsidy of their research facilities. Corporate subsidies are usually provided in exchange for an explicit commitment to allow commercial exploitation of the research at the laboratory. Public subsidies are usually less targeted, but they are nevertheless couched in utilitarian terms. Scientists receive these subsidies by way of a sometimes tacit, sometimes explicit, bargain that the research they do will serve public priorities, whether these be national security or pressing health concerns. The autonomy that researchers crave can be protected to some extent by screening the process by which research priorities are set from political interference but to one degree or another it is bound to be influenced by public priorities, and scientists themselves are apt to tailor their work or at least to advertise its benefits in terms likely to appeal to the taxpaying public.

At its worst, psychological privatization promotes a pathological condition in which a pseudo-democratic mask covers the reality of a society dominated by the few—a plutocracy perhaps, or in some respects a technocracy, allied with people able to use the media for manipulative purposes. Civic consciousness increasingly takes the form of a blind patriotism rather than a critical awareness. The rulers are likely to whip up or take advantage of hostility to outsiders or to some internal minority, which is used as a scapegoat.

In such a social order, political campaigns become exercises in the selling of candidates and propaganda replaces debate and discussion of public policy. Everything depends on the mobilization of consent, and in pseudo-democratic societies this is accomplished by deception and appeals to emotional symbols rather than by appeals to reasoned self-interest and public spiritedness. Meanwhile, the real work of government is left to those with specialized functions and knowledge—the managers who staff the government agencies. Representative government, with its built-in systems of accountability, may act as a shield against some of the effects of mass indifference and incompetence, but it too is sometimes weak against the role of bureaucracy and special interests. When there is concerted cooperation among "iron triangles" of legislators, administrators, and interest groups, the popular will may be too diffuse to be mobilized effectively in opposition.

When citizens perceive that their government is in the hands of corruptible politicians and wealthy interests eager to corrupt them, the danger is they will develop resentment against politicians as a class, failing to discriminate between those who are self-serving and those who are dedicated public servants. This resentment can make them prey to demagogues who encourage them to believe in conspiracies, presumably undertaken in the name of powerful outside enemies. A typical expression of this misalliance is the opposition to salary increases for elected officials. Keeping these salaries low not only encourages inefficiency and corruption but discourages any but the wealthy from pursuing political careers. The declared intent may be to encourage amateurism in politics and to prevent the emergence of a ruling political class, but the effect is to reduce the competence of the government and make it even more vulnerable to the influence of well-organized and well-heeled interests. "Alienated voters" can be mobilized by idealistic campaigns to fight corruption or save the environment, but they are just as likely to succumb under the right circumstances to more ignoble appeals.

The economic inequality that free markets promote creates not just individualism but worse still, class consciousness and conflict. Class conflict leads the affluent to use their resources to shield themselves from the pathologies of poverty and blinds them to the recognition that their privileges are jeopardized by the gap between rich and poor. It leads the poor to resent the rich and to feel that they cannot improve their own condition except by emigrating or supporting populist crusades aimed at challenging the powerful and promising to transform the system. Democracy works best when there is a social commitment to the welfare of all, and when, in particular, the highest priority of public policy is the alleviation of poverty and the promotion of opportunities for social mobility among those handicapped by poverty and the disheartening attitudes it so often entails.

Individual autonomy is thus both a bulwark of democracy and a danger to it. By its very success in freeing human talents and aspirations, democracy creates a society in which individualism is apt to take the form of narcissistic self-absorption and hedonism. Unlike the Athenians celebrated by Pericles, those thus emancipated are apt to feel that their private business is their only or principal business. They are not indoctrinated with the aristocratic ideal of *noblesse oblige*, or the idea that those who enjoy privileges owe attention to the public business in exchange. In a democracy, the need to sacrifice for the common good arises only intermittently, in time of war, or during drives for blood donations and flood relief. Aristocrats are presumably led by notions of honor and duty to perform public service. The democrat has only a concern for personal fulfillment as a guide—coupled, however, with an ideal that somehow represents the strivings of humanity for a fairer and more cooperative way of life.

Majorities and Minorities: Pathologies of Communal Autonomy

Another class of paradoxes arises because democracy also embodies communal autonomy. The stage is set for a conflict between majorities and minorities. While the specter of a tyranny of the majority can be guarded against, there are some respects in which it must be a serious concern. In the French Revolution, the Terror reflected a popular demand for conformity and for the punishment of those considered enemies of the people, regardless of their rights to a fair trial. But this behavior was not, strictly speaking, adopted by anything resembling majority vote and should therefore not be considered evidence of the danger of a tyranny of the majority. In modern times, communal autonomy can sometimes express itself in ways that trample on the rights of individuals. The demand for the denial of citizenship to ethnic Russians in the re-created Baltic states is a case in point.

The justification offered in this case is that the former Soviet government deliberately attempted to Russify these provinces by encouraging immigration. But unless they are to be transferred back to their places of origin, the denial of citizenship violates democratic norms. An ordinance in Quebec that bans English-language signage in the name of preserving French-Canadian culture is considered by English-speaking Quebecers a denial of their right to self-determination under the Canadian constitution.

When factionalism takes the form of sub-nationalism, especially a sub-nationalism allied to ethnic loyalty, it poses perhaps the most serious problem for the maintenance of democracy, even though, in yet another irony, it may emanate from the spirit of democracy or take refuge under the shade of democracy. Sub-nationalism, like nationalism itself, is to some extent a product of democracy, in the sense that the autonomy democracy encourages can be easily find expression in the belief in self-determination by sub-groups of different descriptions. Since the belief in self-determination opens disputes over borders, it is likely to fan the flames of ethnic and regional sub-nationalism. It is no accident that the first American president to make a strong plea for democracy in international relations, Woodrow Wilson, should also have called for the self-determination of nations and the breakup of empires. The belief in autonomy has always implied group self-determination as much as that of the individual.

Intense nationalism involves so much that is exclusive and threatening to minorities that it can only inspire sub-nationalism among groups which feel their identity threatened by assimilation. Just as there is bound to be a tension between individualism and social belonging, so, in pluralistic societies, there is bound to be a tension between an all-embracing nationalism and various forms of sub-nationalism. Both forms, it must be emphasized, are reinforced if not necessarily inspired by the democratic ideal of autonomy. The more differences of ethnicity, language, religion, or culture are salient in a society, the more they will inspire conflict and separatism. Under certain circumstances, separatism may be the only viable option—the only alternative that prevents conflict and allows peaceful interaction between sub-cultural groups. Groups desperate for full autonomy cannot be satisfied by the partial fulfillment that arrangements like federalism and power-sharing make possible. To the extent that homogenization (of language and culture) overcomes pluralism, such pressures may abate, and it is therefore difficult to decide when a point has been reached where separation is the only practical solution.

Diversity and Intolerance: Pathologies of Plural Autonomy

Diversity should be one of the glories of democracy, but in reality it can pose serious difficulties. Democracy inevitably produces diversity because as an ideal it emphasizes freedom, toleration, and the equality of citizens without regard to race, color, gender, etc. At the same time, however, democracy also promotes a tendency to uniformity by emphasizing common standards. Some citizens may find lack of uniformity somehow unsettling, preferring a simpler world in which there are no cults (except one's own), no "foreigners," no physically or mentally handicapped people, no eccentrics, no homosexuals, no political mavericks. Democracy requires tolerance of diversity. So long as citizens pay taxes and otherwise discharge their democratic duties, they are fully entitled to be protected in pursuing whatever goals and lifestyles they may find appealing, so long as in so doing they deprive no one else of the same right. It is a disservice to the democratic ideal, however, to require that educational opportunities, public offices, and employment opportunities be distributed in proportion to group membership. The principle of equal liberty rules out such discrimination against qualified individuals, however well intended.

A kind of hyperactive citizenship takes the form of intense lobbying by groups with special interests and agendas. A group determined to pursue its own particular interest may not be powerful enough to withstand a majority or it may be checked by groups with countervailing interests; but in a complex representative system in which money is the "mother's milk of politics," the ability of a committed group to concentrate its resources on a single issue can enable it to exercise an influence disproportionate to its numerical strength. Preoccupation with a cause may promote a strong sense of civic activism, leading people to take part in broader movements, but it may also distort the expression of the public will by making it more the resultant of organized pressure group campaigns than of the will of the majority. While lobbying by organized groups is both a democratic right and a means by which citizens convey their views to others and to their elected representatives, it can have a distorting and corrupting effect unless measures are adopted to equalize opportunities and protect against what amounts to the buying and selling of legislative support.

As Tocqueville appreciated, democratic politics engenders a play of self-interested groups—the factions Madison warned against but expected to check each other in a large and complex republic. Tax revolts and the NIMBY ("not in my backyard") problem, the apathy of voters unwilling to take the trouble to vote, the refusal of people who complain about crime to support bond issues to build jails or programs to educate the children of the ghetto and help them find jobs and build constructive lives, make Tocqueville's fears seem more appropriate than his hopes. His deepest fear was that people would indulging their selfish concern for autonomy at the expense of wider concerns. That too is a very serious paradox of democracy, perhaps the most serious, because it suggests that autonomy can be its own worst enemy.

Remedies

There are no simple all-purpose remedies for these pathological symptoms. Perhaps the closest to a generalization that may be realistic is that because democracies depend so much on the exercise of responsibility by the citizenry, that sense of responsibility needs to be nurtured in many different ways.

Enable more citizens to experience democracy. Civic education should enable citizens to learn how democracy works, not just as an abstract learning exercise, but by active participation. They should be encouraged to understand public issues and to discuss and debate them with each other and their political leaders. The system of education must enable citizens to continue to educate themselves. Nothing can guarantee that they will take advantage of the opportunity to participate or to study the issues, but a deliberate effort to engage citizens in the process is more likely than not to encourage the habit of involvement.

Alleviate poverty. Education and freedom of information are of no avail in conditions of extreme poverty, or in a society in which there is such a wide disparity between the rich and the poor that class hatred dictates political outcomes. Poverty understandably makes people too concerned with their private benefits to worry about the public business. People in dire poverty are apt to become cynical about the democratic process and to be willing to sell their votes to politicians who can offer them any sort of benefits, even those that involve corruption and patronage. They are not apt to be censorious of politicians who enrich themselves so long as they behave liken Robin Hood and give at least some of the benefits to the poor. Extreme affluence engenders fear of the poor that leads the affluent to want to repress the poor protect their own advantages from redistributive programs. Not being dependent on public welfare programs, they become unwilling to contribute to them. Instead, those who can afford to do so withdraw to their own privileged enclaves, hiring their own security guards rather than relying on the guardians of public safety, and others shun the private associations that bring people together and encourage them to exchange views and concert their political behavior.[6] An extreme degree of privatization and withdrawal is as dangerous to democracy as is the alienation of the poor. It is just for this reason that theorists since Aristotle have emphasized the importance of a large middle class to social stability and democracy.

The alleviation of poverty and the culture of poverty is therefore the most critical item on the democratic agenda, whatever the risk that affluence may lead some to withdraw from public concern. To the extent that poverty breeds crime, it affects the rich as well as the poor. *Favelas* and ghettos are breeding grounds for anti-democratic forces, not for democratic caucuses and committees. The extreme inequalities that may result from an excessive individualism have long been recognized as a danger to democratic stability. Inequalities of wealth and income can result in the effective denial of equal rights (when, for example, the rich acquire better legal counsel than the poor) and in tensions between those in the socioeconomic middle class and in the urban underclass.[7] Inner city ghettoes breed discontent and lawlessness, as well as illiteracy and a turning to romantic and irrational cults. They may not produce movements of political rebellion, particularly if police forces are strong enough to repress such movements, but they may well produce antisocial behavior and a withdrawal of support from democracy. Society comes to be divided into very separate and antagonistic groupings and the affluent middle class finds itself threatened by an underclass without the means of escaping poverty and deprived even of hope for a better life.

Indeed, the single most important barrier to the viability of democracy is extreme economic inequality in conditions of significant and widespread poverty. The states in which democracy has been well established—India is arguably the one major exception—have one characteristic in common: they are all among those with relatively high per capita incomes and relatively widespread affluence and literacy. States like the Scandinavian, in which a moderate well being is common and in which basic security and health services are provided to all, are those in which democracy is most secure, provided the general economy is in good condition. The states in which democracy has failed to take root or in which it is in the most serious difficulty are those with relatively high rates of poverty, overpopulation, and illiteracy. Brazil can hardly be successfully democratized if thirty-five million of its 150 million people are desperately poor and malnourished. In Nigeria, where per capita income was only $250 in 1991, and where a military dictatorship has squandered the nation's wealth to create a system of rule based on patronage, major efforts to establish democratic processes have failed to take hold. The reasons democracy is incompatible with widespread poverty are all too obvious. People whose overriding concern must be with finding the food and shelter they need just to survive cannot easily concern themselves with public business. Often they lack the education necessary to understand the issues and appraise candidates they do not themselves know. Like the immigrants in the boss-ridden cities of the United States only a generation or two back, they are likely to be willing to sell their votes to those able to reward them with patronage. With well being and affluence come better education, better skills in communication, greater independence, and more interest in taking part in the affairs of the community. Even in relatively mature and stable democracies, poverty also tends to alienate those without hope of bettering their condition, to such an extent that they fail to take advantage of the franchise to direct attention to their needs. Instead they tend to act out their resentment by withdrawing from society, committing acts of crime, and in the process make things even worse for themselves and their neighborhoods. It would be a gross oversimplification to say that democracy is an automatic function of wealth, especially because affluence creates other forms of alienation from political commitment. But democracy is certainly made more difficult to establish and sustain by the persistence of poverty, either as a general condition or among elements of the population. Just as serious a defect of gross inequality is that it leads the wealthy to feel superior to their fellow citizens and to expect accommodations from those in power.

Limit the influence of wealth on elections. To counteract the danger that the democratic political process can be corrupted as a result of economic inequalities, the influence of wealthy contributors in election campaigns and the opportunities for well-financed lobbies to manipulate public opinion both need to be curbed. By putting a premium on public opinion, especially in large societies where the media of mass communications are well developed, democracy opens the possibility of demagogic manipulation on a scale and to a degree that are probably much greater than in small communities where people know each other and therefore can measure rhetoric and promises against character and performance. The selling of candidates, especially by negative advertising, and the ability of political leaders to display one character in public and quite another in the privacy of the Oval Office or a congressional suite is one of the more pernicious results of this paradox. In the age of television and satellite broadcasting, it invites manipulation of opinion. The definition of a California political rally as two people watching a television set is unfortunately apt. The media themselves can counteract this danger to some extent by exposing deceptive campaigning. Guaranteed television access for all candidates, coupled with limits on campaign advertising, may also be helpful, but in the end much depends both on the adoption of rules regulating campaigning and on the ability and determination of citizens not to allow themselves to be bamboozled.

Create political districts of manageable size. The very size of modern democracies poses difficulties for the expression of moral autonomy, because individuals feel a loss of identity in communities too large to give them a sense of citizenship.[8] To break these units into smaller ones is often self-defeating or at least costly, because it increases the cost of addressing common problems. Democracy requires that the size of units be taken seriously into account, because democracy works well as a political system only if citizens are engaged in the process of government. That engagement requires some degree of active participation. Those who never come together with others to compose their differences or to mount a challenge to some policy or ruling are not likely to acquire an understanding of their roles and responsibilities as citizens. Nor are they apt to have a realistic view of what the society's problems are or how they may be dealt with. It is therefore important that arrangements be in place to engage people in the actual process of government—not merely as voters—at levels of government which are accessible, such as school boards and zoning commissions. Experience on the governing committees of other private institutions is also valuable in acculturating people to democratic norms and processes. In democracies, every citizen should be expected to take part in some form of public management.

Strengthen the role of the media in public information and education. The public business is often too complex for anyone to understand fully enough on the basis of a limited experience in government. For just this reason, the media of communication are critically important. It is through them that citizens learn of the issues and personalities of democratic politics. The media must serve this purpose by accepting a role of civic responsibility. Insofar as they are profit-making enterprises, they are likely to become vehicles of entertainment rather than purveyors of political information, or, just as bad, to present political information as entertainment. Nothing prevents the media, moreover, from becoming partisan organs of opinion rather than sources of unbiased information. A diversity of viewpoints in the media serves a useful purpose, but there is a need for the media to restrain their partisanship, especially when they are monopolies or near-monopolies, so that real diversity of opinion can be assured and the presentation of information is balanced and factual. Libel laws alone cannot assure that reporting and commentary are kept within reasonable bounds of accuracy and fairness or that investigative journalism addresses itself to vital public issues. The "inner check" of professional responsibility and a more formal system of voluntary review, by press councils and in-house monitors must be relied upon even more than fear of legal action.

Inevitably, there is a curious paradox in the opportunity democracy offers for freedom of expression. The media are encouraged to provide the information citizens want to know, rather than necessarily what they need to know for the sake of conducting public business. They can therefore claim a democratic sanction if they give as much or more attention to gossip and reports of violence and other titillating news as they do public affairs. Whether the balance is redressed by some system of public information sponsored by the government or a system operating with public subsidy as well as private contributions, as in the United States, it is probably necessary to have some form of public media (preferably independent of the government of the day) to assure that those who wish to understand the public business have access to the information they need.

Encourage disciplined but pragmatic political parties. When political parties maintain reasonably tight internal discipline, voters are presented with clear choices. When they are also pragmatic rather than rigidly ideological, they can achieve compromises with each other which avoid stalemate. Parliamentary systems, in which the fate of incumbent legislators hangs on the success of their parties in forming or maintaining the governments are more likely to achieve such discipline. But even in systems with a separation of power between executive and legislature, coherent parties are vital in linking citizens to government and in making the representative system workable.

Regulate and diversify interest groups. Interest groups perform a legitimate and important function in a democracy by representing the views of groups of electors on issues that especially concern them. The role of such groups becomes abusive when their use of resources makes them so influential that they can distort the public agenda. Measures must be enacted to require disclosure of lobbying activity and to limit the role of lobbyists in providing campaign finance. Lobbying serves the purpose of alerting government officials to the point of view and concerns of major constituencies. It gives the members of the constituencies an opportunity to make their case. So long as the interest groups are not so dominant as to dictate outcomes, and so long as they are pluralized enough to exercise countervailing power against each other, the public interest is well served by lobbying. Where the public interest is inarticulate and undefined, or where particular lobbies are effective in gaining control over the direction of public policy, abuses occur. To correct for these abuses, it is important to keep legislators as insulated as possible from improper influence. The electoral process must be made open to candidates who do not depend on the support of wealthy individuals and interest groups. Reforms (such as taxpayer check-offs to support public interest lobbies) are also advisable to encourage better balance among lobbies.

Promote a balance of autonomies. Balance among the various forms of autonomy is essential to the stability of democracy. Since people are indeed social animals, they cannot achieve self-sufficiency in isolation; nor are they, like bees, so prone to accept the division of labor that some can be given the tasks of citizenship and others left to other business. The personality can be fulfilled only in the performance of multiple roles performed in contact with others and through the multiplicity of associations that enrich the fabric of society. Democracy requires life in communities, even though a life requiring total and constant subordination of the individual to the community would deprive him of liberty and therefore of the possibility of autonomy. But all the forms of autonomy require empathy—the ability to sympathize with the misfortune of others, to rejoice in another's accomplishments, above all to feel a responsibility for the success of the democratic ideal. When citizens become candidates for public office, serve on a jury, or vote in an election they are not simply advancing their own interests but engaging in the common work of democracy. In the design of residential areas and shopping centers, it is essential to provide public places where citizens can assemble for political purposes—substitutes for the town halls that were available in earlier urban communities. Television networks may have to be required to devote some of their broadcast schedules to public information and the debate of political questions, perhaps in the form of free time rather than paid advertising for elections.

Autonomy is not the be-all and end-all of life, but the opportunity to live a fulfilling life. The dangers that its several forms will be misused or used to excess, that freedom will unleash the "mad dogs," in Nietzsche's phrase, previously checked by the repressive external authorities, are real. But democracy is not anarchy; the rule of law protects autonomy even against itself.

12

Democracy and World Peace: Euphoria Limited

Reason makes [the achievement of] the state of peace a direct duty, and such a state of peace cannot be established or maintained without a treaty of the nations among themselves. Therefore there must exist a union of a particular kind which we may call the pacific union (foedus pacificum) which would be distinguished from a peace treaty (pactum pacis) by the fact that the latter tries to end merely one war, while the former tries to end all wars forever. This union is not directed toward the securing of some additional power of the state, but merely toward maintaining and making secure the freedom of each state by and for itself and at the same time of the other states thus allied with each other . . . It can be demonstrated that this idea of federalization possesses objective reality, that it can be realized by a gradual extension to all states, leading to eternal peace. For if good fortune brings it to pass that a powerful and enlightened people develops a republican form of government which by nature is inclined to peace, then such a republic will provide the central core for the federal union of other states. For they can join this republic and can thus make secure among themselves the state of peace according to the idea of a law of nations, and can gradually extend themselves by additional connections of this sort.

—Immanuel Kant[1]

Kant's vision of a federation of republics relies on political terminology similar to Rousseau's.[2] His usage hinges on a distinction between the state, which is democratic if the constitution provides for popular sovereignty, and government, which must be either republican or despotic. Because the form of the state depends on the number of people who hold ultimate authority, it will be autocratic, aristocratic, or democratic. The form of government is republican if legislative and executive powers are held separately and the laws are executed impartially; otherwise it is despotic. Kant favored the republican form of government as the only one in accord with law and right (*Recht*). He thought it would be easiest to achieve under monarchy, more difficult for an aristocracy, and impossible if the people as a whole were expected to compose the governing body, not only because of the practical difficulty in a large society of regularly assembling all the citizens, but also because people so empowered would insist on being their own executives as well as their own legislature and might not administer the laws impartially.

Strictly speaking, therefore, Kant's prophecy envisions a federation of republican governments so defined but not a federation of democracies in the governmental sense of the term. Nevertheless, it would be in keeping with the spirit of his prophecy to construe it to suggest, first, that democratic regimes as they are now understood are likely to be more pacific than autocratic regimes, and second, that widespread democratization will make possible federated systems of government, regional as well as global, which—just as Kant hoped—can greatly improve prospects for peace by deterring the resort to war and responding in concert to acts of aggression.

Some analysts have approached this question empirically, seeking to show that democratic nations have in fact not made war upon each other.[3] At least for the time being, this approach cannot yield robust and convincing results. Because the number of democratic regimes has been small and the duration of most of them comparatively short, any conclusion derived from the evidence of their behavior toward each other must be tentative. The same is true for the experience of international federations. Both the League of Nations and the United Nations have been weak federations, and in neither of them have democratic nations composed a majority of the member states. A significant test of Kant's prophecy in restated form will become possible only when a large number of democracies achieve the strong and close form of federation he foresaw.

Even now, however, the prophecy is plausible enough to warrant serious consideration, both with respect to its premises and actual experience. Restated to apply to modern democracies, it suggests three hypotheses: first, that states which adopt democratic principles and institutionalize democratic practices will be less inclined to settle international disputes by resorting to war; second, that they will be willing to enter into federations with other democratic nations for the purpose of achieving collective security against breaches of the peace and violations of human rights; and third, that as more and more states become democratic, such federations will gain strength because they will imply a widely shared moral consensus and draw upon the cooperation of enough states to provide serious sanctions against breaches of international order as well as peace keeping forces.

Each of these propositions is open to criticism, but even after the criticisms are taken into account, they remain sound. They are grounded in a profound historical transformation in the character of society and of the state. "Modernization" sums up a complex series of changes involving the spread of education, the advance of the sciences and technology, and the opening of opportunities for material consumption and an improved quality of life on an altogether unprecedented scale. As the opportunity for prosperity, health, and welfare becomes more and more widespread, insecurity, resentment, and the desire for conquest may well be diminished. Widespread democratization is now taken place against a background of millennia in which social life all too often resembled Thomas Hobbes' famous characterization in *Leviathan* (1651) of the state of nature:

> Whatsoever therefore is consequent to a time of Warre, where every man is Enemy to every man; the same is consequent to the time, wherein men live without other security, than what their own strength, and their own invention shall furnish them withall. In such condition, there is no place for Industry; because the fruit thereof is uncertain: and consequently no Culture of the Earth; no Navigation, nor use of the commodities that may be imported by Sea; no commodious Building; no Instruments of moving, and removing such things as require much force; no Knowledge of the face of the Earth; no account of Time; no Arts; no Letters; no Society; and which is worst of all, continuall feare, and danger of violent death; And the life of man, solitary, poore, nasty, brutish, and short.[4]

These insecure conditions bred attitudes which, as Hobbes also pointed out, made the threat and use of force inevitable. Even when life became more settled and secure, these attitudes persisted and were transmitted in social conditioning. The modern state arose in anarchic conditions. Every sovereign, like every individual in the state of nature, had no choice but, as Hobbes wrote, to "master the persons of all men he can, so long, till he see no other power great enough to endanger him: And this is no more than his own conservation requireth . . ."[5] Because of international insecurity, he contended, every sovereign state must be prepared to protect its survival: "In all times, Kings and Persons of Soveraigne authority, because of their Independency, are in continuall jealousies, and in the state and posture of Gladiators; having their weapons pointing, and their eyes fixed on one another; that is, their Forts, garrisons, and Guns upon the Frontiers of their Kingdomes, and continuall Spyes upon their neighbours; which is a posture of War . . ."[6]

The conditions Hobbes described were particularly characteristic of Europe during the period of history in which he wrote. "It is not surprising," Richard Rosecrance has observed, "that when territorial states began to take shape in the aftermath of the Reformation, they were organized for the purpose both of waging and resisting war, and the seventeenth century became the most warlike of epochs. Kings and statesmen could most rapidly enhance their positions through territorial combat." The unsettled boundaries of Europe, coupled with princely ambition, encouraged alliances, the acquisition of colonies, and the adoption of balance of power strategies. War and the threat of war became "omnipresent features of interstate relationships," arousing fears of loss and even extinction — not an idle concern considering that "95 percent of the state-units which existed in Europe in the year 1500 have now been obliterated, subdivided, or combined into other countries."[7]

Because international relations were so much a function of the play of force and the balance of power, international agreements to control armaments and to create mechanisms of collective security proved much too weak to exercise any influence. World War I and World II occurred in conditions that allowed and even encouraged ambitious autocrats to build armed forces without restraint and to seek to enlarge their territories and settle disputes by the use of force, and not necessarily only as a last resort. Peaceful commerce among nations depended on the role of force and alliances in maintaining spheres of influence and balances of power.

Increasingly, however, modern states—even those with great military resources—have found that negotiating arrangements for collective security is both a surer and more affordable way of protecting existence and promoting prosperity, and a practical way to minimize the prospects of an outbreak of war. The horrific costs of World War I showed that a Clausewitzian approach to war as an extension of foreign policy was irrational, but this lesson did not lead statesmen to take the concerted actions that could have prevented World War II. The advance of military technology has helped drive home the lesson of both these terrible conflicts. The advent of nuclear weapons and intercontinental delivery systems forced the two superpowers of the second half of the twentieth century and their dependents to recognize that war with these "doomsday weapons" could lead to their obliteration. The balance of power, Rosecrance observes,

> lasted so long as the waging of war was limited in its effects. In the eighteenth century war had a ritual character and, in contrast to the early seventeenth century, did not disrupt civilian life. Wars of maneuver and position were seldom decisive, and peace terms often restored the status quo that existed before the war. On the continent of Europe various coalitions were organized to restrain aggressive powers, and fighting was a tolerable, if not enjoyable, pursuit. In the nineteenth century the conquest of territory became easier with the development of new offensive capabilities, but with some exceptions, even losers in war did not emerge much worse off. Thus there was still a considerable incentive to engage in both offensive and defensive combat. One great power could seek to overturn and others to maintain a balance of power.[8]

The Cold War appeared at first to indicate that the even more horrific lesson of World War II had not sunk in, but as the new realities of nuclear war could not be avoided, political leaders on both sides of the iron curtain sought alternatives that did not require a sacrifice of sovereignty or hegemonic ambition. They found a half-way house in a series of arms control agreements that provided a framework for detente, on the basis of mutual deterrence. Politicians on both sides chafed at accepting the very concept of military parity that analysts tried to persuade them was inevitable, and constantly sought to gain advantages by developing weapons that did not come under arms control agreements and that threatened to undermine the very structure of arms control. In crisis situations, the framework threatened to disintegrate, but it was maintained, precariously, because the risks of allowing it to fail were so dangerously uncertain for both sides. The armed conflicts that did occur in the period between the end of World War II and the end of the Cold War took place in peripheral developing countries, where the risks of escalation to nuclear war were low enough to permit engagement. In those instances where the local conflict threatened to escalate into a nuclear confrontation between the superpowers, restraint and diplomatic initiatives came into play. A notable example is the Korean War, when the commander of United Nations forces, General Douglas MacArthur, sought permission to deprive the Chinese "volunteers" who were aiding North Korea of their sanctuary to the north by bombing their supply lines in China. When President Harry S Truman denied the request and fired MacArthur, out of fear that China might use atomic weapons and call in the aid of its Soviet ally, he in effect signalled that a great historical change had occurred. Henceforth regional wars had to be kept limited if they were to be waged at all. Whereas the Korean conflict ended in a stalemate, however, the subsequent conflicts in Vietnam and Afghanistan showed that the unwillingness of the superpowers to risk the consequences of the full use of their military power meant that they would have to accept a limitation on their ability to intervene in localized conflicts. The superpower confrontations in proxy wars in the Middle East also demonstrated both the risks of confrontation and the rise of prudential diplomacy, even if it sometimes involved the practice of "brinkmanship." As these conflicts threatened to involve direct confrontations between both superpowers, they forced their clients to agree to ceasefires and settlements. But the near-disaster in the 1962 Cuban missile crisis showed that brinkmanship and failures in communication could easily provoke a nuclear war.

The end of the Cold War has brought a dramatic change in international relations that would have seemed impossible while it was in process. Nuclear armaments have begun to be scaled back and defense budgets are being slashed, not only in the successor states of the Soviet Union but among the Western allies as well. The threat of nuclear proliferation remains a serious concern, but the major nuclear powers now have an interest in cooperating to prevent it. Economic cooperation between East and West is replacing military confrontation. As a result of the ending of this basic hostility, the former adversaries have been able to find common ground in dealing with conflicts in the developing countries instead of exploiting these conflicts for their own Cold War gain. By the end of 1980s, the conflict in Angola was settled, at least as far as the involvement of outside powers is concerned, and the United Nations Security Council achieved an unprecedented degree of unity in adopting effective sanctions to deal with Iraq's attempted annexation of Kuwait by force in 1990. Military conflicts have erupted in the wake of the ending of the Cold War, but they have mainly come in areas where either Soviet military power or the threat of Soviet intervention had previously held national aspirations and antagonisms at bay. These conflicts will subside only to the extent that the national aspirations can be appeased by territorial compromises and economic growth becomes a more pressing concern. Economic growth will require the same focus on the domestic economy and exports as it does in Western Europe and elsewhere. This focus will require a context of peaceful relations among neighboring states.

It seems, then, that major historical forces, having do with the character of modern society and the modern state, are leading away from a setting in which military force was an ever-present option and a threat, to one in which it may become more of a sentry protecting order. Because the United Nations is not a world government but rather an international forum and agency through which nations can concert their efforts, it cannot automatically respond to outbreaks of conflict or guarantee security. Only if consensus can be achieved among the permanent members of the Security Council and enough of the other members can the Council take action against aggression. In other instances, alliances provide an important form of deterrence. A formally anarchic system of states is therefore potentially a more managed system than it might appear in formal terms. To minimize the risk that this managed system will fail, states still need to work out agreements or "regimes" (like the General Agreement on Tariffs and Trade and more limited currency exchange mechanisms) to regulate conflicts over trade and other aspects of international commerce, including migration and environmental pollution. States need not be democratic to recognize the need for cooperation and enter into agreements to establish economic regimes (such as the oil production agreement among the Organization of Petroleum Exporting Countries and the tacit understandings between OPEC and the international oil companies and consumer states). For a variety of reasons, however, including the likelihood that a change of a democratic government will not casually nullify an agreement reached by a predecessor, it is plausible to suppose that democratization will enhance the prospects for peaceful relations.

Are Democracies Inherently Pacific?

The reasons for supposing that democracies are less likely to behave aggressively toward each other than other systems of society and government fall under four main headings:

1. *In democratic regimes wars can be declared and sustained only with the consent of a majority of citizens, acting through their representatives.* Because democratic procedures stipulate that decisions on such major issues as war and peace be taken after open discussion and with widespread consent by those who must bear the costs, a decision to go to war is not likely to be made capriciously. In democracies war will not be undertaken, as it may be in autocracies, to satisfy a ruler's vanity or delusions of grandeur. If the war-making power is conferred constitutionally on a representative assembly, the decision will be made after debate in which the nature and gravity of the *casus belli* are explored and weighed. It is therefore less likely than it is in autocracies that war will be initiated on the basis of incomplete or misleading information and without as full as possible a discussion of the alternatives. The media of information will be in a position to provide the public with independent assessments of the grounds for conflict and to publicize the debate over the issues. Since the representatives are accountable to the people, and the people must bear the risks and costs of the decision to go to war, they will be less inclined than autocratic regimes to initiate wars because they and their families must bear the burden. In addition, because modern democracy rests on the belief in the rights of the individual, conscientious objection to warfare or to a particular war is likely to be respected, thus potentially limiting the ability of a democratic regime to make or sustain an unpopular war. Even once wars are begun, democratic societies will be more inclined to terminate the war once opportunities for a peaceful settlement appear or as the war drags on inconclusively and no successful resolution seems possible. The American involvement in Vietnam during the 1960s and 1970s is often compared to the Soviet Union's involvement in Afghanistan as examples of wars that became quagmires for great powers, neither of which was fighting to achieve a vital national interest. But one difference between them is that the growing unpopularity of the war in the United States forced a change of government and an effort to extricate American forces. In the Soviet Union, popular disgruntlement could find no political outlet, so the war dragged on until the ruling oligarchy decided to terminate it because it could no longer sustain the drain on resources and began to fear, correctly but too late as it turned out, that the entire system in which its authority was embedded was becoming dysfunctional.

2. The principles that animate democracies are inherently less support-ive of the resort to war and to policies of expansion than those that moti-vate autocracies. Monarchic and autocratic regimes are often closely in-tertwined with the notion that honor and glory are more important vir-tues than mere survival and the opportunity to carry on trade with other nations. The prince, Machiavelli declared, should not be blamed for want-ing to acquire territory, for such a desire is natural to princes. Autocrats are often reared with the belief that their destiny is to rule over as ex-tended a realm as is within their power to grasp, whatever the cost to their subjects. They see the issues of trade in mercantilist terms. Territorial expansion is good because it provides guaranteed access to raw materials and markets and a source of cheap labor. Democratic societies are hardly immune to imperialistic fantasies or to mercantilism, but they are more likely to reflect the aims of people concerned rather with their own wel-fare than with either glory or hegemony over others. People reared in democratic societies are raised to be self-reliant, unlike those raised in more status-oriented societies where the privileged become dependent on do-mestic servants and carry the same attitude into their colonialism. The ambition to improve or expand standards of living need not require con-quest of territory or domination of other peoples. Whereas autocratic re-gimes often seek to foster a desire for national grandeur, in order to gain support for expansionism, democratic regimes are in principle opposed to militarism and to imperialism. Militarism is likely to arise with a pro-fessional army; democratic societies tend to rely on citizen armies. Impe-rialism is uncongenial to democratic nations because it contradicts the principle of national self-determination that these nations claim for them-selves. Democratic nations are also likely to respond to appeals from sis-ter democracies under attack. Thus, American intervention in World War I was justified as an effort to make the world safe for democracy. In the early years of World War II, the United States came perilously close to violating its Neutrality Act in order to help Great Britain survive German attack. While this assistance undoubtedly reflected a cultural bond, the adoption of the Four Freedoms expressed an ideological identification that was also at play.

3. Democratic societies tend to emphasize contractual and legal modes of dispute resolution and rely on the use of force only as a sanction, not as an alternative to peaceful means of conflict resolution. Autocratic regimes arise most often in circumstances in which force is a primary means of achieving social goals, especially security, and in which status hierarchies are considered indispensable to order. As contract replaces status, in Sir Henry Maine's phrase, social relations become more subject to law than to custom, and law is refashioned to respect equality of status. Older status hierarchies are challenged by a new emphasis on equality of opportunity, which leads not to a destruction of hierarchy, however, but its reconstitution in the form of socioeconomic classes less rigid and caste-defined than before. Tensions between classes sometimes lead to social convulsion until the extension of the suffrage enables the passage of legislation protecting the right of collective bargaining and providing welfare guarantees or "safety nets." As a result, the social contract becomes the basis of greater social harmony as it is interpreted to require state action to assure fairness in the operation of laws governing contracts, public welfare assistance when needed, and other measures to assure public health and the availability of health care. The managed economy aims to encourage initiative and market efficiency while preventing monopolistic practices and the exhaustion of natural resources. Environmental concerns loom larger as citizen groups react to the harmful effects of industrialization and governments respond by imposing environmental regulation.

   4. *Democratic states are apt to be "trading states" interested in doing business with other states rather than in dominating other states or becoming or remaining dependencies.* Under modern conditions, security requires alliances and conditions in which the temptation to use force is muted. When democratic states exist in sufficient number, circumstances change qualitatively. International relations may remain formally anarchic but regimes come into being which are based on common principles as well as interests and greatly minimize the likelihood of a resort to force. Nations which engage in trade must have secure and productive partners. To engage in military hostilities is to cut off some trading relationships and render others insecure. Even conducting a "beggar thy neighbor" trade policy or winning a "trade war" can produce a Pyrrhic victory by impoverishing customers and suppliers. Killing customers and suppliers and destroying their economic infrastructures makes even less sense. The democratic development of Germany after World War II contrasts dramatically with the consequences of the Carthaginian peace imposed upon Germany at Versailles. Japan's experience after its defeat in World War II has proven that it is far easier to establishing networks of suppliers and dealers than to attempting to impose by force a "greater east-Asia co-prosperity sphere." Nations that will fight to resist conquest will rush to enter into economic arrangements that serve their needs and interests as well as those of richer, more powerful countries. The rise of the multinational or transnational corporation both resulted from and furthered the tendency toward economic interdependence. By providing for technology transfer and stimulating industrial development in host countries, these firms in effect forge socioeconomic rather than exclusively political or military alliances among trading states.

These propositions are open to criticism on all four heads:

1. Empirical research suggests that democracies "are no less likely to become involved in foreign wars, crises, or potentially violent disputes than states organized under alternative governing arrangements."[9] Reasons why this should be so come readily to mind. The burden of war will not be born equally by all; the young invariably are called upon to sacrifice more than the old, men more than women. A society that does not rely on universal conscription will not distribute the sacrifice equally, and the increasing emphasis on specialized roles and economic incentives may well make military service less than fully universal. Mass electorates, in democracies as under autocracies, may clamor for war out of patriotic fervor and under the illusion that the war can be won without great sacrifices.

The historical evidence amply supports the view that although democracies have not made war on each other, they are not invariably pacifistic. Although the first World War was initiated by the German Kaiser's autocratic regime, it was joined by societies with strong parliamentary governments which voted for war on the wave of popular enthusiasm. The more recent example of the United States in the Vietnam conflict suggests that a democratic electorate can be misled into supposing that it has been the victim of aggression, as the American Congress was over the Tonkin Gulf episode. Under such circumstances, a legislature may be stampeded into commitments which will later be regretted. The assumption by executives of the power to commit armed forces is another development which weakens the argument that democracies require public consent. In the case of the Gulf War of 1990-91, President George Bush was prepared to order troops into battle without congressional authorization on the ground that United Nations resolutions accepted by the United States would authorize such action to be initiated by the president. Even though the American president is an elected official who can be held accountable for his conduct of office, the ability of the executive to act without direct popular authorization also weakens the argument. If the United States did not make war on other democracies, moreover, the reason may have been that it was preoccupied with domestic expansion and separated from most other nations by two great oceans. American policy toward the native North American population was sometimes as callous and harsh as that of European imperialists toward the native populations of Latin America and Africa. In the nineteenth century, some Americans coveted Canada and only gave up their designs after being rebuffed by military force. The United States has frequently intervened in Latin America to protect its economic interests and to prevent foreign penetration. These are hardly indications that democracy necessarily inspires pacifistic attitudes. Even when a populace is absorbed in materialistic pursuits, it may entertain notions of patriotism compatible with expansionism. What is to be made, for example, of the fact that the newly democratic French nation should have responded to Napoleon's call to national glory, using the very *levée en masse* that is supposed to make democratic warfare less likely? Under modern conditions, moreover, the expectation that a war can be conducted surgically and remotely with minimal loss of life may encourage even democratic electorates to suppose that war can be engaged in without high costs.

2. In order to resolve internal class tensions and enhance national power, even democratic societies able to do so are tempted to resort to imperialism or at least to quasi-imperialist efforts to achieve hegemony. Colonies provide an outlet for unemployed elements of the population and markets for goods which provide employment at home. Rather than give in to demands for redistribution at home, economic interest groups may in effect avoid redistribution by enlarging the domestic pie at the expense of exploited colonials. Once the era of colonialism ended as a result of colonial revolutions, the economic relationships did not completely disappear. However exaggerated is the case made by *dependentista* economists, there is a grain of truth in the contention that the countries at the periphery of the international system have been for the most part unequal partners in economic exchanges with the more developed countries. The rise of OPEC changed that relationship with respect to one important commodity, and the ability of developing countries to attract multinational companies on terms beneficial to their diversification has also helped alleviate this imbalance, but economic inequality creates political as well as economic dependence. Even to the extent that growing economic interdependence alleviates inequality and interdependence, other domestic pressures may lead democratic states to put national self-interest ahead of international obligations. Democracy alone does not free societies from a parochial sense of identity and national interest, as is evident from persisting support for economic protectionism even in relatively affluent societies. If the fulfillment of international obligations requires acceptance of sacrifices without a compelling national interest, democratic electorates may well prove unwilling to live up to democratic professions.

3. The persistence of war is a function less of the form of society or government and far more of the structural anarchy of international relations. So long as there are no tribunals to which grievances can be routinely addressed with the expectation that decisions will be enforced, nations will consider themselves justified in resorting to force as a last resort when conflicts cannot be peacefully resolved. Economic conflicts are often among the primary causes of conflict, so the mere fact that nations become dependent on each other for trade does not guarantee that they will not go to war to resolve a major trade dispute or, for that matter, because of some other dispute over territorial claims. World government will require a new global consciousness resting on more than agreement over universal codes of

rights and commitment to the same democratic systems of government. Even more important will be the development of a sense of identity that transcends tribal loyalties and territorial boundaries.

4. Trading states may still go to war over economic disputes if such disputes cannot be peacefully resolved and the matter at issue is vital enough to risk armed conflict. Rivalry over such issues as competitiveness and market access may begin peacefully enough, but there is no way to guarantee that such rivalries may not at some point lead to war. At the very least, the tensions they produce could produce arms races as the competitors revert to older methods of expressing the will to enforce national interest. While arms races in themselves do not necessarily lead to war, but may in fact lead to the sort of mutual deterrence that prevailed during the Cold War, accident or miscalculation in times of crisis could lead to the outbreak of war.

The Counter-Arguments Considered

Although such counter-arguments cannot easily be dismissed, they do not invalidate the hypotheses. Much of the warlike behavior that can be attributed to democratic nations has come early in their history. It is arguable that these states were still tainted with traditional fears and ambitions, now transferred from autocratic to democratic settings. Once domestic forces establish democratic procedures, a greater consciousness of individual rights and the validity of self-determination as a principle may be expected to take hold. It is certainly harder now in the United States to justify intervention in Latin America than it was for much of its earlier history. The reason may well be that having become better aware of what democratic norms require, democratic societies may be more sensitive to the rights of others. The cession of the Panama Canal to Panama is an example of historic significance. Even some recent American interventions— such as those in Panama, Grenada, and Nicaragua—were justified on the ground that they were undertaken to protect the right of other people to self-determination against domestic forces that would deny them that right. The British intervention in the case of the Falkland Islands was justified not only on grounds that this was British territory (however it was originally acquired), but on the ground that the Argentine invasion threatened the inhabitants of the Falklands with a deprivation of their right to self-determination.

As to federalism, the creation of the United Nations and recent efforts to achieve greater integration in Europe, Africa, and the Americas suggest that while Kant's vision of world federalism is still far from a reality, a federation of like-minded democracies is indeed the best hope for a peaceful world. Such federal systems, even when they involve only weak linkages, could help resolve conflicts by diplomacy wherever possible. Just as important, they provide mechanisms whereby gravely dangerous departures from international norms by non-democratic regimes are effectively sanctioned. The 1990-1991 Gulf War is a case in point. The reaction to Iraq's invasion of Kuwait indicates that at least where the vital economic interest of many nations is threatened, they can act in concert to repel aggression. It is worth noting, however, that economic self-interest helped create the problem. The nations that went to war with Iraq had previously been willing to sell the most advanced military technology to that country, even though they were well aware that was under the control of a dictatorial regime extremely repressive toward elements of its own population and bent on hegemony over its region.

The Evolution Toward International Federalism

The evolution toward federalism appears to be taking place, though not as Kant thought it would, because one exemplary republican state has been joined by others. The United Nations organization was conceived by many nations as an effort to achieve collective security, at a time when many of the member states did not suit Kant's definition and when antagonism between two major power blocs weakened its capacity to enforce norms affording collective security. As far as European integration is concerned, the United States may have played the role of an exemplary republic for its European allies, but the initial shoring up of democracy in Western Europe came as a result of a military alliance bolstered by economic aid, in the form of the Marshall Plan. The creation of the European Union, difficult as it will be to satisfy fears of the loss of national independence, is certainly a sign that a common commitment to the same basic principles, coupled with a desire to benefit from partnership, could end centuries of hatred and conflict. The potential expansion of the community to include the nations of central and eastern Europe is important in itself and as an example to other continents. The Organization of American States and the Organization of African Unity are other examples. Trade conflicts can of course engender forms of mercantilism, resulting in protectionism. It is possible that modern economic competition may engender a new period of mercantilism, especially inasmuch as security concerns no longer create conditions for bipolar hegemony. But some form of managed free trade is surely in the interests of all nations. Provided that negotiations can assure a reasonable balance of trade, open markets are preferable to closed. Democratic societies, moreover, are used to bargaining and negotiation as ways of resolving conflicts. They do not automatically suppose that the test of force is the only arbiter. They are inclined to follow the same habits in international relations as in domestic relations. As William J. Dixon has suggested, democratic norms of dispute resolution seem to restrain the escalation of conflicts to the stage of armed conflict by impeding escalation at an early stage of an evolving conflict situation.[10]

As democratic nations grope toward ways of addressing problems, a spirit of fellowship is likely to develop which will unite the peoples of the world around certain concerns. Democratic cultures breed the belief that all peoples share common goals and characteristics. They do not breed the supposition that some peoples are superior, others inferior. To that extent, they undermine the claim that some nations have an inborn right to dominate others. This universalism is reinforced by democratic culture, which emphasizes the common denominator of human wants and ways of living. To the extent that this common culture becomes universalized, it helps create the precondition for communication and understanding. In practical terms, this means that democracies are more likely to protect the environment and agree to provide development assistance to poorer countries, especially if those countries agree to cooperate by controlling population growth and using environmentally friendly technologies.

No less than others, democratic societies are also animated by considerations of interest, but this consideration too should form a basis for international peace. Although different nations will have different interests, which often lead to conflict, it is often the case, especially under modern conditions, that cooperation is in the common interest. Thus economic agreements that encourage open markets with some degree of regulation lower costs for all and allow each country to pursue its comparative advantages. The interconnectedness of the environment makes it especially obvious that international cooperation is in the interest of all. On a more subtle level, the interest of the advanced countries in the peaceful development of the developing countries suggests that they should be willing to cooperate to provide these countries with aid, both economic and technological, so as to help them overcome difficulties of overpopulation and resource use which are bound to have an impact of varying degrees on the rest of the world.

The end result in Europe and other regions and in the world as a whole could be a modified Kantianism: a federation of democratic nations with representative governments. Coupled with the spread of democracy in the Americas and elsewhere, this development in Europe could have such profound effects elsewhere as to make possible a growing world federalism of democratic states. Even if no formal federation proves feasible, the relations among these states could become far more cooperative than in the past.

In view of the tensions and violent clashes that have characterized the present century and all those before it, this prospect is bound to promote euphoric expectations because democratic nations have historically not made war upon each other. Could it be that at long last, the sorry record of constant war, which has had its chapters written on every continent and among every people, will finally come to an end? Will it be replaced by a "new world order" in which the various nations will join together in a global partnership, to address common needs and concerns and develop regimes of law governing international relations with as much force as domestic laws in the most stable states? If so, will the same principles govern international relations as govern the domestic polities of democratic nations?

These are such important questions and experience is so limited that they are probably best left to be addressed in the future, but it may not be altogether premature to think about them even now. Otherwise, too much may be expected too soon, and an unwarranted disillusionment with democratization could set in. Such disillusionment could well arise in the first place because in recent years many newly independent states have failed to make the transition to democracy, for various reasons. One of those most relevant to the East European cases is that they are apt to experience an emotional nationalism leading to conflicts with neighboring states over border issues. The same nationalism may also produce intolerance for the rights of minorities. Whatever else Soviet communism may have done, it kept a lid on the union's nationalistic antagonisms and on those of the Balkan states either controlled by the Soviet Union or held together, as in the case of Yugoslavia, by fear of Soviet control. Now that this lid has been removed, pent-up forces are being expressed. Despite the obvious economic and security attractions of federation, some of the newly independent states may not be ready to surrender any of their precious new sovereignty.

But Kant was not merely expressing a pious wish in forecasting "eternal peace" through world federalism. He recognized that differences of religion and language would keep people from wanting to amalgamate themselves completely into larger unitary societies, but he counted on the "spirit of commerce which cannot coexist with war, and which sooner or later takes hold of every nation," to keep these independent republics from making war upon each other. "In this way," he thought, "nature guarantees lasting peace by the mechanism of human inclinations . . ." Even so, he was not prepared to predict the rise of such an order as a certainty; instead he thought the idea sufficient to become a basis for a duty to work toward such a condition.[11] There are obvious limits to the capacity of any world system to prevent all aggression or to resolve all conflicts. Nations will understandably balk at intervention which aims to resolve internal disputes, lest their own sovereignty become similarly vulnerable. Some line must be drawn between grave violations of human rights, such as those that threaten genocide, and violations which may be regrettable but cannot be corrected without opening Pandora's box.

Autonomy, Statehood, and World Citizenship

As Kant well appreciated, the autonomy of the individual is grounded on beliefs in universal human rights that pertain to people in virtue of their characteristics as human beings, not their belonging to states. But these rights can be realized only in associations, and associations are strongest when they have the form of statehood—associations characterized by the legitimate monopoly of the means of physical coercion. It is therefore plausible to suppose that since the strongest state would be a universal state, protection of human rights would benefit from the creation of a universal state. There are other good reasons to suppose, however, that such a centralized state would be a bad idea for the same reason that centralized states have drawbacks on an even smaller scale: they impose cumbersome and remote bureaucracy and remove the capacity to make decisions from those at lower levels who are apt to be most affected by particular decisions. They tend to ride roughshod over local differences. Even apart from such theoretical objections, there are practical reasons why for the time being, the single world state ideal is likely to be resisted.

Nevertheless, the same belief in universal autonomy that lies at the root of the democratic ideal can serve as a basis for a morality of universal bearing. International justice requires a basis in reciprocity and voluntary undertakings among states whose constitutions respect human rights. Although national self-interest may dictate that intercourse be maintained even with states which do not live up to professions of human rights, to encourage states that practice torture or harbor terrorists is to deny the universal standard of moral behavior.

Does international morality require all states to admit refugees, whether from political persecution or economic hardship? This must depend on such practical considerations as the state's perceived carrying capacity and the effect of the migration. Scope for some degree of immigration or at least for residence without citizenship is as critical to the functioning of an international morality as is emergency aid and development assistance.

A concept of human rights adequate for the creation of a global moral order should not be overburdened with moral imperatives, however. It should provide first of all a respect for the rights of all people to basic standards of liberty. Democracy as a system of civil society and government follows logically from the guarantee of the right of liberty, but in the absence of explicit undertakings, states have no moral obligation to share resources equally and no right to intervene in the affairs of another state. National interest gives all states a concern for the preservation of international peace and cooperation in economic and environmental matters. Until the great disparities in wealth, health, and education are overcome, it is also in the interest of the advanced countries to assist the developing countries so as to promote their progress and their ability to enter the world order as equal partners. Democracy may well inspire a special solicitude for the peoples of developing countries, if only because the democratic commitment to universal autonomy implies the need to encourage self-government in the political dimension.

The danger of the democratic ideal for foreign policy is that it will promote a version of national self-absorption. The same insularity that prevented Athenians from seeing the universal potential of democracy as a force beyond the confines of the *polis* could prevent members of democracies from recognizing the need to help create a world of democratic nations. The recent experience of the results of a division of the world into democratic and non-democratic states could have the sobering counter-effect of enhancing concern for encouraging democratization.

Such a universal democratic order need not involve disrespect for differences of religion, language, and culture. On the contrary, the very pluralism autonomy inspires could guarantee respect for diversity. All that is required is a minimal commitment to the basic human rights of individuals, with the toleration that this respect implies. The forces making for intolerance are to some extent at least incidents of development. Nationalism and religious fundamentalism are functions of a sense of inferiority that may well diminish with successful development and social maturation. An international democratic order, moreover, should not eliminate all competition, all rivalry, but should channel that competition and rivalry into constructive and peaceful avenues—olympics of the mind as well as of the body—so that the world as a whole would benefit. Such a world order presupposes that war is no longer an acceptable instrument of international order. Aggressiveness would have to be dealt with by agreed international sanctions. How to assure that such sanctions will be made effective and that they will be administered fairly, given the division of the world into blocs of states with conflicting interests, is certainly difficult, and will not be accomplished in the short run. It can be accomplished only once international peace-keeping becomes a regular function. Everything must be done, however, to avoid the twentieth century's worst legacy, the horror of totalitarianism. If the travail of this century is to have a lasting meaning, it must be that it stands as a warning against the abandonment of the standards of human rights, against cynical perversion of such concepts as the people's will, against manipulation by elites using propaganda to turn one section of the people against another, to inflame feelings of exclusivism, and to make high-sounding ideals the basis for enslavement. The rebirth of democracy at the end of the twentieth century offers a promise of a brighter future. That promise will be realized only if the danger of the breakdown of democracy is fully appreciated and if there is enough patience and good will to enable democratic mechanisms to develop and to be used to resolve conflicts. Democracy, in short, must be understood as an aspiration common to people everywhere, one that should unite them rather than divide them into warring camps composed of insecure tribes.

Conclusion

13

Democracy and Its Prospects

The purpose of democracy—supplanting old belief in the necessary absoluteness of established dynastic rulership, temporal, ecclesiastical, and scholastic, as furnishing the only security against chaos, crime, and ignorance—is, through many transmigrations and amid endless ridicules, arguments, and ostensible failures, to illustrate, at all hazards, this doctrine or theory that man, properly trained in the sanest, highest freedom, may and must become a law, and a series of laws, unto himself, surrounding and providing for, not only his own personal control, but all his relations to other individuals, and to the State; and that, while other theories, as in the past histories of nations, have proved wise enough, and indispensable perhaps for their conditions, this, as matters now stand in our civilized world, is the only scheme worth working from, as warranting results like those of Nature's Laws, reliable, when once established, to carry on themselves.

—Walt Whitman[1]

In an age dominated by the progress of science and its applications along so many fronts, we are bound to wonder whether a poet's declaration that democracy is the most appropriate system for the modern age accords with the findings of the social sciences. Such a claim would not be easy to sustain, if only because the social sciences can offer no definitive answer. For the time being, an estimate of the prospects for democracy must rest on more tentative forms of reflection and empirical observation.

It is tempting to suppose that some principles of behavior and social interaction must operate in human affairs as they do in nature, even if human free will precludes a deterministic science of society. In the past, however, many efforts have been made to build such a science, all without lasting success. Thomas Hobbes' "civil science" adduced a "geometric method" (*more geometrico*) purporting to assimilate human behavior to a mechanistic conception of the universe, but this method was little more than rhetorical scaffolding for his intuitive assumption that fear, especially fear of violent death, would lead to insecurity unless a Leviathan state were accepted as a pacifying instrument. Auguste Comte's misnamed "social physics" described an evolutionary mental progression from theological to metaphysical to scientific or positive, but left altogether unclear how scientific thinking would address, let alone resolve, the persistent problems of human conflict and social organization. Social Darwinism made use of the discovery that natural selection is the mechanism of evolution, but the analogy between conflict and adaptation in nature and society was hardly strong enough to make the theory plausible, except to those seeking justification for predatory capitalism. Karl Marx's scientific socialism was more rigorous than the "utopian" versions he dismissed, but the economic analysis upon which his supposed laws of history rested turns out to have been gravely flawed, and history has hardly vindicated his forecast of the inevitable decline of capitalism and its replacement by socialism.

Nor is the scientific status of social theory much different in the final decade of the twentieth century. The remarkable advances lately achieved in the understanding of genetics and of the biochemistry and neural functioning of the brain make it likely that a great deal more may come to be understood about exactly how human beings perceive and think, and about their motivations. For the time being, however, evolutionary biology and its associated disciplines can make use of an understanding of the mechanisms of change and adaptation that social scientists can only envy. "What gives biological research its special flavor," Francis Crick has written, "is the long continued operation of natural selection. Every organism and all the large biochemical molecules are the end result of a long intricate process, often stretching back several billion years."[2] The discoveries that have followed the unravelling of the genetic code have greatly improved the understanding of the transmission of characteristics and of the role of natural selection. Genetic engineering is becoming practical and laboratory experiments are being conducted which simulate natural selection. By contrast, hardly anything can be said about the nature or possible evolution of human government with so high a degree of confidence. No genes or set of genes code for human rights or constitutional government or for privilege and authoritarianism.

Although some anthropologists maintain that an analogue of natural selection produces an evolution of societies, both in the general and particular sense, because the characteristics of some societies prove more adaptive than others, the theories hold better for pre-industrial societies than for those in the industrial-scientific phase of social history. In pre-industrial times and even to some extent in later periods, a "Law of Cultural Dominance" may well be said to operate according to which "that cultural system which more effectively exploits the energy resources of a given environment will tend to spread in that environment at the expense of less effective systems."[3] In earlier times, however, the challenges to survival came more from nature than from human activities, and even relatively primitive forms of organization and belief were ordinarily adequate to the circumstances. "They survive," C. R. Hallpike notes, "because in the circumstances of primitive society, small in scale and rudimentary in technology, where the demands on efficiency are low, where there are few, if any, variant forms to choose from, and where the level of competition is weak, even crude and inefficient forms will work, or seem to after a fashion, and will to some degree satisfy the desires of those who introduce or maintain them."[4] Modern societies are threatened not just by scarcity, calamity, and disease, but sometimes by social competitors, by dangers that arise from the misuse or careless use of human inventions, such as nuclear weapons and chlorofluorocarbons, and by difficulties (like the danger of global warming) that result from the societies' very success in manipulating the natural environment. Exploitation of finite natural resources cannot assure sustainable growth. Increasingly, adaptive success may depend not so much on the ability to compete with other societies and other species, but to the contrary, on the ability to cooperate with them and live in harmony with nature. Thus, even the theory of specific evolution is problematic.[5]

Since the work of E. B. Tylor, the broader evolutionary perspective has had to rely largely on cultural analysis.[6] It may now acquire fresh support from biological research, as advances in the understanding of human mental functioning are applied to the development of new forms of social theory, adumbrated in "biopolitics,"[7] perhaps grounded in "neurophilosophy,"[8] and issuing in applied and clinical sciences. These new understandings may better explain how and under what circumstances human beings behave peacefully or aggressively and how and with what institutions they can live together harmoniously and with mutual regard. "At this stage in their history," Patricia Churchland has exulted, anticipating developments comparable to the Copernican and Darwinian revolutions, "the brain and behavioral sciences are monumentally exciting, for we appear to have embarked upon a period when an encompassing scientific understanding of the mind-brain will, in some nontrivial measure, be ours."[9] Even before such an advanced scientific understanding can be attained, research on genetic intervention could make possible technologies with an impact on the manipulation of human nature comparable to that of the industrial revolution on physical nature. Gene therapy may soon be used not just to eliminate genetically caused diseases but also to improve mental functions and perhaps to rectify genetically-induced dispositions considered sociopathic.

Even as biological science advances, however, there will still be a need to supplement what comes to be understood about human mental functioning with an understanding of the role of sociocultural conditioning and the structure and functioning of social, economic, and political institutions. For the time being, no scientific alternative to multi-dimensional reflection and empirical observation is available, and no social engineering can be attempted which can claim to rest on laws of social interaction. Even sociobiologists, who attempt to assimilate human behavior to that of other animals, admit that the most important forms of human social behavior, such as the tendencies toward aggression and altruism, are much more subject to cultural conditioning in human beings than in other animals.[10]

On the basis of the evidence so far available, no conclusive determination can be made either that democracy is the form of government which nature or natural selection ordains or that nature commands us to live under some more authoritarian system of rule. Human beings are obviously life forms like other organisms, subject to the same laws of reproduction and transmission of characteristics, and society is the process of their interaction; but the links between the study of the organism and the study of human society are simply not strong enough to support any but the most tentative and equivocal conclusions. It is plausible to suppose that there has been a long historical evolution to democracy from the early tribal bands and through kingship and oligarchy. It is also possible that a kind of natural selection is at work in this evolution, in the sense that modern democracies, once well established, are better adapted to the social environment than other types of regime, but this hypothesis cannot easily be tested, either by observation or experiment.

Moral Autonomy as the Founding Principle

We are in no more advanced state with respect to these issues, then, than were the philosophers of antiquity, who could be sure only that the capacity for rationality and communication is far greater in human beings than in other animals. From this defining characteristic they proceeded to develop their political theories; and so must we. The ability to reason and communicate enables human beings to become self-determining creatures, capable not only of exercising "free will" but just as importantly of understanding their natural environmental and learning to survive its hazards as individuals and as a species. The first philosophers concluded that those few with the highest capacity to reason and communicate were most fit to rule. They recognized, however, that rule should be exercised in the interests of subjects, and that the best way to assure this was to educate the rulers to appreciate both their self-interest in ruling well and their duty to do so. Otherwise, they sought to make all human power subject to the rule of law, which they thought expressed "reason free from passion." In more recent times, philosophers have come to appreciate the universality of the aspiration for freedom. Hegel was so impressed by the yearning for autonomy that he could confidently sum up world history by observing that at first one is free, then some are free, and finally all are free.[11]

The modern movement for democracy rests on the rejection of the assumption that the best approximation to the rule of philosopher-kings is rule by those privileged by birth, wealth, or martial skills. Democracy invariably arises out of popular discontent with all forms of rule in which the majority is denied the opportunity of self-government. Modern democracy is not simply majority rule, however, because it rests more explicitly than ancient democracy and ancient republicanism on the belief that all human beings have the right to equal liberty. The philosophic assumption from which that belief follows is that insofar as human beings are not immature or incapacitated, they are fit to exercise the capacity for moral judgment, and therefore that they alone should have the responsibility for regulating their own lives and entering into agreements with others for their mutual benefit. Modern democrats share with their precursors the belief that what concerns all should be decided by all, but they also believe that the most practical way to do so in large and complex societies is through a representative process in which issues are openly debated and representatives are chosen and replaced in free and competitive elections. Democrats hardly reject the need for intelligence in public government, but they do reject the view that intelligence is a function of privilege. They also reject the assumption that if the privileged rule, the principle of *noblesse oblige* will lead them invariably to apply their intelligence for the good of all. They believe rather that properly-educated and well-informed citizens are the best judges of their own interests, and that they will want to elect to office those most capable of dealing with the public business. There is always a risk that elected and appointed officials will seek to arrogate power to themselves, but the electoral process and judicial safeguards can protect against usurpation, provided that the citizenry is not so cowed or cynical as to be unwilling to use the means it has available.

Autonomy and Representative Government

Democracy alone offers all citizens the opportunity to express and protect their right to autonomy by engaging in the process of self-government. Democratically adopted laws, basic and statutory, define the bounds of autonomy in civil society and assign the powers of government. Regular elections, conducted in settings in which information is available and debate allowed, and in which voting procedures are fair and open and there is competition among candidates and parties, make representative self-government practical. Elections enable citizens to register their convictions and change their leaders without having to resort to extra-constitutional means. One of the most important characteristics of democracy, often taken for granted, but precious in contrast to autocracy, is that it makes possible regular and peaceful succession in government. The experience of democracy is also a constant training in the need to take account of the concerns of others. It is therefore a constant schooling in toleration and compromise. Bargaining and negotiation are the hallmarks of democracy. The very fact that no one group is privileged over another compels those of every affiliation to learn to respect the rights of others. The religious preferences of a majority of the population, while they are bound to find expression in civil practice (as in the observance of major religious holidays) do not prevent others of different faiths from observing their own rites. Questions of exactly how and where to draw a line between church and state must be decided juridically and politically, and the answers will vary from one society to another, but the principle of separation is essential. Inasmuch as democracy fully respects the freedom of citizens to hold whatever beliefs they wish, it is eminently compatible with any and all religions, provided only that they do not require non-believers to adhere to their precepts.

Common standards are needed for the sake of peace and harmony. These standards must be determined by all who are subject to them, using the criterion of respect for the right to liberty, and not necessarily in accordance with individual or majority views of what is good, which are bound to differ. The common standards must respect the fundamental liberty of the individual, which is the core value of modern democracy, and may not impose other values, about which individuals may differ. The judgment of what is good is one all individuals must be free to make for themselves. In practice this means that people not only may hold whatever religious beliefs they choose but may practice whatever ways of life they choose—from monastic withdrawal to missionary zeal, from voluntary communism in property to the amassing of wealth—subject only to restrictions that may be necessary for good order and equality of opportunity.

Autonomy and the Market Economy

Market economies are advantageous because they promote prosperity and provide opportunities for the pursuit of diverse careers and enterprises. In a large society, specialized employment is more likely to be available, and organizations that succeed in one setting are replicated in many others. The field for achievement is greater and more rewarding. The opportunity for mobility is also enhanced. The competitive character of a market society makes it possible for some to achieve the means of greater autonomy than others, if autonomy is defined as the opportunity to pursue a self-chosen way of life. But the autonomy of all individuals and groups must be precarious to the extent that many are denied the opportunity to pursue goals for which they have a natural capacity. Just because democracy makes such a virtue of autonomy, those who are denied this opportunity are apt to be more discontented than people in nondemocratic societies who do not have the same expectation. Only democracy, in its modern form, is premised on the belief that all individuals, as equal citizens, are entitled to self-determination. Thus, while markets are inevitable and highly useful in free societies, democracies require that they work to the benefit of all, and not just for the welfare of the most fortunate.

Suitably regulated and stimulated, market economies encourage enterprise, innovation, and a general prosperity. Because economic activity is inherently social and takes advantage of resources that belong to all, there can be no right to "infinite appropriation." Socialists have argued that all acquisitiveness is an unmitigated evil, but much experience, including that of socialist societies, has shown that the profit incentive can be socially beneficial. Income differentials have been accepted as tools for increasing productivity in almost every society. The limit is breached when free trade chokes off competition and leads to grossly disproportionate benefits. Democratic societies do not fare well when great numbers of citizens are on the margins of poverty and must be so preoccupied with the task of survival that they cannot pay due attention to issues of social concern or acquire the education needed for an intelligent understanding of these issues. Because democracy aims to "empower" everyone, not just a privileged few, either the market economy must provide general prosperity, or income redistribution will be needed to assure that the majority is not forced to go without basic necessities so that the economically successful and fortunate may be protected. The right to autonomy may well be defined to include access to the basic means of welfare and health, insofar as the general productivity of the society makes that access affordable. But a redistribution so radical as to diminish incentives and dry up sources of investment is not in the interest of the society as a whole. A balance must be struck between the good of universal welfare and the good of promoting productivity.

Majority Rule and Power Sharing

When the principle of autonomy is made the basis for collective self-government, democratic societies face two options, which are often combined. One option is majority rule, the other consensual rule or power-sharing. Majority rule—in practice often plurality rule—has the effect of minimizing the fracturing of the electorate and promoting an aggregation of interests in two major parties which are apt to resemble each other in many respects because they must appeal to the same body of marginal voters. The two-party system has the advantage of enabling voters to hold the party in power responsible for its stewardship and to replace it with another party with a similarly identifiable point of view and leadership. Proportional representation is often considered a fairer form of representation because it assures that minorities will be represented in legislatures and sometimes in cabinets. In societies deeply divided along ethnic, religious, or cultural lines, constitutional guarantees of a share in power (such as the Swiss "magic formula" whereby each entity is guaranteed cabinet representation in rough proportion to its size) and other informal arrangements assure minorities that their interests will not be trampled. The social cost of such arrangements is that they may promote weak coalition governments liable to deadlock and fracturing and vulnerable to demands for patronage which may amount to blackmail. These arrangements may also have the bad tendency of freezing social cleavages rather than promoting associations that transcend the divisions. As guarantees for cultural autonomy are provided through federal and other arrangements, and feelings of national solidarity strengthen, such arrangements may become unnecessary. In societies in which the cleavages remain matters of intense concern, however, the only practical form of democracy may be consensual. G. Bingham Powell, Jr. is certainly correct in observing that different democratic political systems have both advantages and disadvantages, and that "creative political leadership can help to mitigate the undesirable qualities, or undermine the benefits, in any type of setting."[12]

Independence and Conformity

In all forms of democracy, there is bound to be a tension between the commitment to individual liberty and the pressures toward social solidarity and conformity. As Tocqueville was among the first to point out, the egalitarian individualism of democracy has the paradoxical outcome of promoting a skeptical independence of mind on the one hand and a belief in the superior claims of public opinion and conventional wisdom on the other. While persecution for secular heresy is in principle incompatible with democratic principles, in practice democratic societies are sometimes intolerant of dissenters, especially when they challenge widely held beliefs or seem to threaten national security. A vigorous climate of debate, coupled with continuing education on the nature of democracy, is probably the best long-term antidote.

Critics of democracy can cite some evidence for the tendency of democratic systems to bring about mob rule and tyranny, but the evidence is by no means an indictment of democracy under all circumstances. The French people did not rise in rebellion when Louis Napoleon, having been elected president, declared himself an emperor; the Nazis achieved power initially in a free election, after which they forcibly eliminated all opposition and nullified the democratic constitution. In both cases, democracy was not well established and socioeconomic conditions were difficult. Once well established, democratic systems are apt to nurture a suspicion of tyranny and a determination to resist it. Even under stress, people in democracies do not necessarily behave irrationally in large groups. In urban blackouts or riot conditions, most do not loot; even in heavy traffic, drivers who otherwise obey traffic signs and safe driving rules continue to do so. Contrary to the theorists of mass society, soldiers in democratic armies do not abandon the field in "panic dread" when their generals or even their platoon commanders are killed. People who belong to churches are not necessarily sheepish, nor are they necessarily intolerant toward others. There is a qualitative difference between a lynch mob and a political convention or a parliament. In democratic assemblies, discussion, bargaining, and negotiation are the rule, and allegiances given to leaders may be withdrawn. A revolutionary period, moreover, does not provide the best setting for an analysis applicable also to the more normal setting in which post-revolutionary politics is conducted. The theorists of mass society properly called attention to the irrational drives people undoubtedly feel and the dangers of crowd behavior that do characterize large urbanized societies, but they went much too far in claiming that all democratic behavior is mob behavior, that all groups must become masses and all leaders autocratic dictators. These days bearers of authority do not have an easy time of it, because democratic attitudes engender suspicion of all authority and an insistence on the right to exercise autonomy.

The Importance of Civic Culture

The theory of mass society is nevertheless useful in suggesting how important it is for democracies to encourage individual freedom and responsibility, and to allow a rich variety of associations to exist and flourish—so as to prevent the development of an amorphous mass of people who feel powerless and are ripe for the plucking by some would-be dictator. But the psychological and sociological assumptions upon which the theory relies take no account of the influence of democratic conditioning. Democratic citizenship both nurtures and depends upon a civic culture which promotes a strong sense of self-esteem, defined by a pervasive belief in the value and dignity of human life, a confidence in the human ability to deal with external forces and events, and a reasonable sense of security concerning social status.[13] Political extremism arises, as Paul N. Sniderman suggests, among those whose low self-esteem encourages fear, intolerance, cynicism, and a paranoid fear of obscure conspiracies: "They set little store by freedom of speech and assembly (unless it is theirs), the importance of diversity in an open society, the principle of equality. In sum, those with low self-esteem give evidence of a pronounced suspicion of—even a certain hostility toward—the democratic idea."[14]

What is also clearly harmful to democracy is the sort of social organization that divides citizens into antagonistic groupings, whether of ethnicity or social class. Ghettos enforcing involuntary segregation are both undemocratic and harmful to social harmony. Gerrymandered voting districts designed to provide representation for linguistic, ethnic, or racial groups may seem necessary in deeply divided societies, but it is better to use PR or cumulative voting in such conditions. Similarly, policies providing preferential treatment in employment and university admissions, however well intended, discriminate unfairly against individuals, promote resentment which undermines the belief in social justice and reform, and violate the democratic norm of equal treatment.

Debate and Deliberation in Voting and Elections

The prospects of democracy are greatly improved by systems of voting and election which put a premium on informed debate and deliberation and minimize the danger that votes can be bought or unduly influenced by advertising and other forms of mass propaganda.[15] In principle, representation allows for democracy in large settings because it enables citizens to engage the services of surrogates. Regular and frequent elections are necessary so that the citizens can register their approval or disapproval of their representatives' performance in office. Political parties enable those who join them to play a role in selecting leaders and shaping policy positions, and they help voters identify the views of candidates for office. These measures, coupled with judicial remedies for misfeasance in office, are effective devices for maintaining the integrity of the representative system. The major potential difficulties are that the need to obtain campaign financing makes representatives beholden to those who make large contributions and that campaigning in mass electorates requires great resources and operates through the mass media. The remedies for these potential abuses lie in regulating and limiting private campaign contributions and requiring more equal access to the mass media for all major candidates.

Protecting Democracy from Itself

Democracy is a difficult enterprise. It relies on representatives who may betray their trust, and it opens opportunities for the manipulation of public opinion and the concentration of resources by powerful interest groups. It relies on informed popular judgment and political vigilance. Intelligence is not equally distributed; nor are all voters equally well-informed or equally devoted to the common good. Moral judgments are not always made with the sublimely unconditioned rationality and universality that Kant called for. Many citizens who enjoy the right to vote may choose not to exercise it. Decisions made by majorities may be based on poor information and poor reasoning.

To counteract these weaknesses, protective measures are advisable. These must include a legal code guaranteeing basic rights and judicial systems independent enough to protect those rights even against abridgement by majorities. Checks and balances prevent those in control of one branch or part of the government from gaining so much control that they can do as they please without fear of being held accountable. A separation of church and state insures that freedom of conscience will not be abridged for minorities, and that no citizen will be penalized for non-conformity to an established religion. Subordination of the military to civilian control helps prevent unconstitutional interference with political democracy. An effective representative system requires effective leadership as well as respect for public opinion. Democratic politicians must also be able to communicate effectively. They must have a political temperament—the ability to conciliate, to listen, to persuade. Through the mass media and directly, leaders must be in constant touch with electorates, hearing their concerns, answering their questions, educating them as to what various policy options entail.

Democracy also requires active citizenship—in the sense that has been referred to as participatory democracy. Participation can be achieved in many ways and on many levels, but however it is accomplished, the actual experience of politics in some direct way is critical for the success of the democratic process. Jury duty, poll canvassing, attendance at a political rally, communicating with an elected official, contributing to a campaign, holding office, and myriad similar activities give citizens the experience of self-government and enable them to influence outcomes. Such active engagements work against an attitude of indifference which is harmful to democracy. They enable citizens to understand how the political system works and how to make use of it to further their own concerns. Without widespread participation, democracy risks becoming a facade behind which well-organized minorities and well-placed individuals have disproportionate influence.

The test of whether a system is democratic is not only the degree to which people participate actively in the process of government. Because democracy encompasses civil society as well as the public sector, it is in the broadest sense of the term a system of social life in which individuals exercise autonomy in private as well as public affairs. Anyone who makes use of civil freedom to manage his or her own life is experiencing a very real form of autonomy, and therefore of democracy. Whatever promotes prolonged dependence works against autonomy and therefore by definition against democracy. "Social democracy" does not mean that exactly the same rules must apply in industry or the church or professions as apply in politics. But it does mean that these settings too should respect and enhance individual autonomy. Individuals must be free to join and leave them voluntarily, and they should also have a voice in decisions that affect their welfare. Although organizations need hierarchy and chains of command in order to function effectively, they also benefit from committed employees and members. An organization which treats its members as humanoid robots to be tasked and exploited, and then discarded when they are no longer needed, will not have the flexibility to flourish in competitive and changing environments.

The cultural goal of a democratic society is to nurture the capacity for self-expression and self-fulfillment in as many people as possible and in all benign ways. A good democratic society is not one in which only the most popular forms of art and entertainment flourish. It is one that offers opportunities for people of all talents and tastes to pursue their interests, but which also recognizes that not all standards are equal. A democratic society should support cultural activities, even though they may not be appreciated equally by all, which are judged to be genuinely artistic by those qualified to do so—uncertain as judgments are bound to be in the case of avant garde art. Similarly, natural scientists should be given as much support as the society can reasonably afford to advance the understanding of nature and by so doing improve opportunities to make use of knowledge for human benefit. A democratic society should support scientific research as a basis of social progress, but also because research is an expression of a quest for human understanding, valuable in its own terms. Democracy benefits when standards of excellence are maintained, in culture and in science, and suffers when they are allowed to deteriorate.

Autonomy and Community

The evidence that democracies do not make war on each other is encouraging, but as has been noted previously, this evidence is as yet too limited to give the finding great predictive reliability. As an ethical ideal, however, democracy represents a respect for the unity of the human species. This unity is experienced best in love and friendship, sentiments which become attenuated in large societies and even more in an international order composed of separate and geographically distant peoples. As Aristotle first observed, large societies in which people cannot all know each other's characters are not conducive to an intense sense of community. But the mutual regard and respect that democracy promotes inspires a profound sense of community. As advances in communications and travel shrink the world and homogenize cultures, there may be good reason to lament the loss of differentiation, but there is compensation to be gained from the growing sense of mutual recognition. A world populated by peoples of different physical characteristics and cultural traditions, but with a common set of democratic social and political values, is likely to be more harmonious than any international order so far experienced.

Nationalism in its most strident and intolerant form represents a serious threat to this prospect. The new appeal of democracy will be sustainable only if it can be well established in more and more societies and if those societies can learn to live together in peace. Walt Whitman's dream that human beings trained in the exercise of freedom can become a law unto themselves echoes the sentiments of champions of autonomy from Pericles to Kant and beyond, and of ordinary people everywhere, in expressing the essence of the democratic aspiration.

Notes

Chapter 1

1. Quoted in David Goodman, *Beijing Street Voices: The Poetry and Politics of China's Democracy Movement* (London: K. Boyars, 1981), p. 95.

2. Plato, *Epistles*, trans. Glenn R. Morrow (Indianapolis: Bobbs-Merrill, 1962), seventh epistle, d 324, p. 216.

3. Francesco Guicciardini, *Maxims and Reflections of a Renaissance Statesman*, trans. Mario Domani (New York: Harper & Row, 1965), Series B, 5, p. 100.

4. See Larry Diamond and Marc F. Plattner, eds., *The Global Resurgence of Democracy* (Baltimore: The Johns Hopkins University Press, 1993).

5. John Stuart Mill, *Considerations on Representative Government* (1861; Chicago: Regnery, 1962), p. 57.

6. "East of Suez, however, 'democratic reins are impossible. India must be governed on old principles.' And he added: 'There! That is the creed of Tory Democracy. Peace & Power abroad—prosperity and progress at home.'" Quoted from a letter to his mother in 1897 in Martin Gilbert, *Churchill: A Life* (London: Heinemann, 1991), p. 69.

7. Churchill made his comment in a debate on Nov. 11, 1947. *Parliamentary Debates (Hansard): House of Commons Official Report*, 444, fifth series, vol. 2 (London: His Majesty's Stationery Office, 1947), p. 207. He does not appear to have outgrown his earlier view that non-white peoples were incapable of self-government: "By the standards of today—and probably even of his own time—Winston Churchill was a convinced racist. For all his public pronouncements on the 'Brotherhood of Man' he was an unrepentant white—not to say Anglo-Saxon—supremacist. For such a zealous child of the Empire anything else would have been astonishing." Andrew Roberts, "Winston Replied That He Didn't Like Blackamoors," *The Spectator* 272, 8648 (April 9, 1994), p. 11.

8. E. M. Forster, *What I Believe* (London: Edward Arnold, 1951), p. 79.

9. Leslie Bethell, "From the Second World War to the Cold War: 1944-1954," Abraham F. Lowenthal, ed., *Exporting Democracy: the United States and Latin America* (Baltimore: The Johns Hopkins University Press, 1991), p. 46.

10. Jonathan D. Spence, *The Search for Modern China* (New York: W. W. Norton, 1990), p. 487.

11. *Democracy in a World of Tensions* (Paris: UNESCO, 1951), Appendix 3, p. 527, quoted by S. I. Benn and R. S. Peters, *Social Principles and the Democratic State* (London: George Allen and Unwin, 1959), p. 332.

12. Raymond D. Gastil, *Freedom in the World: Political Rights and Civil Liberties 1980* (New York: Freedom House, 1980), pp. 5, 15-24; Arend Lijphart, *Democracies: Patterns of Majoritarian and Consensus Government in Twenty-One Countries* (New

Haven: Yale University Press, 1984), pp. 37-38.

13. Samuel P. Huntington, "Will More Countries Become Democratic?" *Political Science Quarterly* 99, 2 (Summer, 1984), p. 218.

14. George Steiner, *Granta* 30 (Winter 1990), p. 130. Anthony Lewis, who brought Steiner's remarks to American attention in the *New York Times* (June 1, 1990) criticized him for being "far too cynical in his dismissal of the longing for political freedom." The fact that dissident intellectuals have often been put in power by the same people who demonstrated in these "crowds" is evidence that this cynicism is unwarranted, but Steiner also misses the point that consumer sovereignty is an aspect of freedom that even Utilitarians like John Stuart Mill appreciated.

15. Frank E. Manuel, "A Requiem for Karl Marx," *Daedalus* 121, 2 (Spring 1992), p. 18, expanded as *A Requiem for Karl Marx* (Cambridge, Mass.: Harvard University Press, 1995).

16. Jagdish Bhagwati, "Democracy and Development," *Journal of Democracy* 3, 3 (July 1991), p. 41.

17. See especially Francis Fukuyama, *The End of History and the Last Man* (New York: The Free Press, 1992).

18. Adam Przeworski and Fernando Limongi, "Political Regimes and Economic Growth," *Journal of Economic Perspectives* 7, 3 (Summer 1993), p. 51.

19. Nicholas D. Kristof, "China Sees 'Market-Leninism' as Way to Future," *New York Times*, Sept. 6, 1993, pp. 1, 5.

20. Francis Fukuyama, "Capitalism & Democracy: the Missing Link," *Journal of Democracy* 3, 3 (July 1992), p. 105.

21. Przeworski and Limongi, "Political Regimes and Economic Growth," p. 65.

22. Lloyd I. Rudolph and Susanne Hoeber Rudolph, *In Pursuit of Lakshmi: The Political Economy of the Indian State* (Chicago: The University of Chicago Press, 1987), p. 223.

23. Przeworski and Limongi, "Political Regimes and Economic Growth," pp. 60-66, Table 1, p. 61.

24. Pranab Bardhan, "Symposium on Democracy and Development," *Journal of Economic Perspectives* 7, 3 (Summer 1993), p. 46. For a comprehensive analysis of the issue see Stephan Haggard and Robert R. Kaufman, *The Political Economy of Democratic Transitions* (Princeton: Princeton University Press, 1995).

25. Twenty of the most stable democracies show comparably high levels of both Gross National Product per capita and literacy. See G. Bingham Powell, Jr., *Contemporary Democracies: Participation, Stability, and Violence* (Cambridge, Mass.: Harvard University Press, 1982), Table 3.2, p. 36.

26. Zeev Maoz and Nasrin Abdolali, "Regime Types and International Conflict, 1816-1976," *The Journal of Conflict Resolution* 33, 1 (March 1989), p. 21. See also Zeev Maoz and Bruce Russett, "Normative and Structural Causes of Democratic Peace, 1946-1986," *American Political Science Review* 87, 3 (September 1993), pp. 624-39. Rudolph J. Rummel, "Libertarianism and International Violence," *The Journal of Conflict Resolution* 27, 1 (March 1983), pp. 27-71; Michael W. Doyle, "Liberalism and World Politics," *American Political Science Review* 80, 4 (December 1986), pp. 1151-69; Joshua Muravchik, *Exporting Democracy* (Washington: AEI Press, 1991), pp. 8-9; David A. Lake, "Powerful Pacifists: Democratic States and War," *American Political Science Review* 86, 1 (March 1992), pp. 24-37; Erich Weede, "Democracy and War Involvement," *The Journal of Conflict Resolution* 28, 4 (December 1984), pp. 649-64;

Bruce M. Russett, *Grasping the Democratic Peace: Principles for a Post-Cold War World* (Princeton: Princeton University Press, 1993); and William J. Dixon, "Democracy and the Peaceful Settlement of International Conflict," *American Political Science Review*, 88, 1 (March 1994), pp. 14-32.

27. Freedom House, *Freedom in the World* (Freedom House: New York, 1994).

Chapter 2

1. See Robert A. Dahl, *Polyarchy: Participation and Opposition* (New Haven: Yale University Press, 1971), p. 9, n. 4.

2. Charles F. Cnudde and Deane E. Neubauer, eds., *Empirical Democratic Theory* (Chicago: Markham, 1969), Introduction, p. 18.

3. Giovanni Sartori, *The Theory of Democracy Revisited* (Chatham, N.J.: Chatham House, 1987), vol. 1, p. 7.

4. Thus, in *Democracy and Its Critics* (New Haven: Yale University Press, 1989), p. 221, Dahl offers a definition of polyarchy which includes the rights to free political expression, alternative information, and association.

5. Dahl's theory is criticized for not directly including socioeconomic conditions by Bolivar Lamounier, "Brazil: Inequality Against Democracy," Larry Diamond, Juan J. Linz, and Seymour Martin Lipset, eds., *Democracy in Developing Countries*, vol. 4, *Latin America* (Boulder: Lynne Rienner, 1989), p. 145.

6. Robert D. Putnam, with Robert Leonardi and Raffaella Y. Nanetti, *Making Democracy Work; Civic Traditions in Modern Italy* (Princeton: Princeton University Press, 1993), p. 11.

7. T. D. Weldon, *The Vocabulary of Politics* (Baltimore: Penguin Books, 1953), p. 97.

8. See Bernard Gallie, "Essentially Contested Concepts," *Proceedings of the Aristotelian Society* 56 (1955), pp. 167-198.

9. See Thomas L. Thorson, *The Logic of Democracy* (New York: Holt, Rinehart & Winston, 1962).

10. Joseph A. Schumpeter, *Capitalism, Socialism and Democracy*, second edition (New York: Harper, 1947), chap. 21 and p. 269. For the view that the procedural approach has replaced the normative in political analysis, and for good reason, see Samuel P. Huntington, *The Third Wave: Democratization in the Late Twentieth Century* (Norman: University of Oklahoma Press, 1991), pp. 6-7.

11. See Jürgen Habermas, *The Philosophical Discourse of Modernity*, trans. Frederick Lawrence (Cambridge, Mass.: MIT Press, 1987).

12. Richard Rorty, *Contingency, Irony, and Solidarity* (Cambridge, England: Cambridge University Press, 1989), p. 67.

13. Brian Barry, "Is Democracy Special?," Peter Laslett and James Fishkin, eds., *Philosophy, Politics and Society*, fifth series (Oxford: Basil Blackwell, 1979), pp. 156-157.

14. Barry Holden, *The Nature of Democracy* (New York: Barnes and Noble, 1974), especially pp. 205-214. As examples of such analyses Holden cites Carl Cohen's chapter, "The Justification of Democracy," in his *Democracy* (Athens, Georgia: The University of Georgia Press, 1971), and J. H. Hallowell, *The Moral Foundations of Democracy* (Chicago: University of Chicago Press, 1954).

15. William E. Connolly, *The Terms of Political Discourse* (Lexington, Mass.: D. C. Heath, 1974), p. 32.

16. Athanasios Moulakis, "The Greeks and Democratic Theory: Moses I. Finley's *Democracy Ancient and Modern* Revisited," *Rivista internazionale di filosofia del diritto*, fourth series, 68, 1 (January–March 1991), p. 48.

17. List of rules given in the text of Aeschines' *Speech Against Timarchus* [I.35] quoted in David Stockton, *The Classical Athenian Democracy* (Oxford: Oxford University Press, 1990), p. 76.

18. See Walter Bagehot, *The English Constitution* (1867; Ithaca: Cornell University Press, 1966)

19. E. S. Staveley, *Greek and Roman Voting and Elections* (Ithaca: Cornell University Press, 1972), p. 202.

20. Ibid., pp. 62-69.

21. Quoted from Aeschines by Josiah Ober, *Mass and Elite in Democratic Athens: Rhetoric, Ideology, and the Power of the People* (Princeton: Princeton University Press, 1989), p. 296.

22. J. Peter Euben, *The Tragedy of Political Theory: the Road Not Taken* (Princeton: Princeton University Press, 1990), p. 55.

23. M. I. Finley, *The Ancient Greeks: An Introduction to Their Life and Thought* (New York: Viking Press, 1963), p. 82.

24. Chaim Wirszubski notes that "freedom of speech in the sense that any citizens had the right to speak, did not exist in the Roman Assemblies," but that in the Senate it was the right of those called upon by the presiding consul in order of rank. See his *Libertas as a Political Idea at Rome During the Late Republic and Early Principate* (Cambridge: Cambridge University Press, 1960), pp. 18, 20.

25. Ober, *Mass and Elite in Democratic Athens*, p. 35.

26. Ibid., p. 338.

27. Staveley, *Greek and Roman Voting and Elections*, p. 58.

28. Gregory Vlastos notes that Herodotus identifies the term *isonomia* with democracy "in the most positive and unmistakable way" and argues that other commentators are mistaken in supposing that *isonomia* connoted a constitutional regime, whether oligarchic or democratic. Instead, he suggests that *isonomia* was first used when the term democracy had not come into use and survived to mean "the standard by which constitutions can be evaluated." Gregory Vlastos, "Isonomia Politike," *Platonic Studies* (Princeton: Princeton University Press, 1973), pp. 164-174. Martin Ostwald also suggests, on the basis of persuasive if limited evidence, that *isonomia* was the term used before the term democracy was introduced, to refer to the principle of political equality rather than to some particular constitution, though it is more closely identified with the democratic constitution than with any other. See Martin Ostwald, *Nomos and the Beginnings of the Athenian Democracy* (Oxford: Oxford University Press, 1969), pp. 96-97.

29. Mattei Dogan, Introduction, Mattei Dogan, ed., *Comparing Pluralist Democracies; Strains on Legitimacy* (Boulder: Westview Press, 1988), p. 8.

30. Martin Ostwald, *From Popular Sovereignty to the Sovereignty of Law: Law, Society, and Politics in Fifth-Century Athens* (Berkeley: University of California Press, 1986), pp. 184-186. The translation from Thucydides' account of Pericles' Funeral Oration is Ostwald's.

31. Antoine-Nicolas de Condorcet, *Sketch for a Historical Picture of the Progress of the Human Mind* (1795), trans. J. Barraclough (London: Weidenfeld and Nicolson, 1955), p. 182.

32. Orlando Patterson, *Freedom: Volume 1: Freedom in the Making of Western Culture* (New York: Basic Books, 1991), pp. 404-405.

33. Ibid., pp. 134-135.

34. Ober, *Mass and Elite in Democratic Athens*, pp. 6-7.

35. Quoted from *Collections* of the Massachusetts Historical Society, 5th series, 3 (Boston, 1877), David Brion Davis, *The Problem of Slavery in the Age of Revolution* (Ithaca: Cornell University Press, 1975), p. 276.

36. See especially Alexis de Tocqueville, *Democracy in America*, ed. J. P. Mayer, trans. George Lawrence (Garden City, N.Y.: Anchor Books, 1969), vol. 2, 1, p. 432.

37. Ibid., p. 10.

38. W. G. Forrest, *The Emergence of Greek Democracy 800-400 BC* (New York: McGraw Hill, 1966), p. 44.

39. Mogens Herman Hansen, *The Athenian Democracy in the Age of Demosthenes: Structure, Principles, and Ideology*, trans. J. A. Crook (Oxford: Basil Blackwell, 1991), pp. 79-80.

40. Benjamin Constant, "The Liberty of the Ancients Compared With That of the Moderns," Benjamin Constant, *Political Writings*, ed. Biancamaria Fontana (Cambridge: Cambridge University Press, 1988), p. 327.

41. Tocqueville, *Democracy in America*, vol. 1, Author's Introduction, p. 9.

42. Donald Kagan, *Pericles and the Birth of Democracy* (New York: The Free Press, 1991), p. 2.

43. For the differences between the republics of Venice and Florence as perceived by contemporaries see J. G. A. Pocock, *The Machiavellian Moment* (Princeton: Princeton University Press, 1975), pp. 100-104.

44. Stephen R. Graubard, "Democracy," Philip P. Wiener, ed., *Dictionary of the History of Ideas* (New York: Charles Scribner's Sons, 1968), vol. 1, p. 653.

45. For a critical appraisal of the anti-democratic implications of the "Madisonian model" see Robert A. Dahl, *A Preface to Democratic Theory* (Chicago: University of Chicago Press, 1956).

46. See David Hume, "Idea of a Perfect Commonwealth" (1742), *Hume's Moral and Political Philosophy*, ed. Henry D. Aiken (New York: Hafner, 1948), pp. 384-385, and Douglass G. Adair, "That Politics May Be Reduced to a Science: David Hume, James Madison, and the Tenth *Federalist*," Jack P. Greene, ed., *The Reinterpretation of the American Revolution* (New York: Harper & Row, 1968), pp. 494-495.

47. William R. Everdell, *The End of Kings: A History of Republics and Republicans* (New York: Free Press, 1983), p. 6.

48. Robert A. Dahl, "Procedural Democracy," P. Laslett and J. Fishkin, eds., *Philosophy, Politics and Society* (Oxford: Basil Blakwell, 1979), fifth series, p. 115, n. 8. The figures are drawn from James C. Davis, *The Decline of the Venetian Nobility as a Ruling Class* (Baltimore: The Johns Hopkins Press, 1962), Table 1, p. 58.

49. Maurice Cranston, *Jean-Jacques; The Early Life and Work of Jean-Jacques Rousseau 1712-1754* (New York: W. W. Norton, 1983), pp. 15-16.

50. Jean-Jacques Rousseau, *The Social Contract*, trans. Maurice Cranston (Harmondsworth: Penguin Books, 1968), Book 3, chapter 4, p. 114.

51. See Keith M. Baker, *Condorcet: From Natural Philosophy to Social Mathematics* (Chicago: University of Chicago Press, 1975), especially pp. 236-244.

52. Quoted in R. R. Palmer, *The Age of the Democratic Revolution* (Princeton: Princeton University Press, 1959), vol. 1, pp. 16-17.

53. See Gordon S. Wood, *The Creation of the American Republic, 1776-1787* (Chapel Hill: University of North Carolina Press, 1969), p. 595.

54. A good example is the wording used in Article One of the constitution adopted in 1993 by the Russian Federation: "The Russian Federation/Russia is a democratic and federal state based on the rule of law, with a republican form of government." Article 3 specifies that the repository of sovereignty is the federation's "multinational people" and that the people exercise their authority directly and indirectly. The implication is that when popular authority is exercised directly, in elections and referenda, it is democratic, and when indirectly exercised through representatives, republican. "The Text of the Draft Constitution," *The Current Digest of the Soviet Press* 45, 45 (1993), p. 4.

55. George Orwell, "Politics and the English Language," in *A Collection of Essays* (Orlando: Harcourt Brace Jovanovich, 1946), p. 162.

56. C. B. Macpherson, *The Real World of Democracy* (Toronto: Canadian Broadcasting Corporation, 1965).

57. Quoted in James Seymour, ed., *The Fifth Modernization: China's Human Rights Movement, 1978-1979* (Stanfordville, N.Y.: Human Rights Publishing Group, 1980), p. 52. See also Spence, *The Search for Modern China*, pp. 662-664.

58. Philippe Lauvaux, *Les grands democraties contemporaine* (Paris: Presses universitaires de France, 1990), p. 17.

59. Philippe Bénéton, *Introduction à la politique moderne* (Paris: Hachette, 1987) p. 156; quoted in *Les grands democraties contemporaine*, p. 40.

60. See T. J. Pempel, ed., *Uncommon Democracies: The One-Party Dominant Regimes* (Ithaca: Cornell University Press, 1990).

61. For a different view, which argues that democracy is a term that should be understood to connote "a political system, separate and apart from the economic and social system to which it is joined," see Larry Diamond, Juan J. Linz, and Seymour Martin Lipset, eds., *Democracy in Developing Countries: Latin America*, preface, p. xvi. They propose that "issues of so-called economic and social democracy be separated from the question of governmental structure" lest empirical study be made too difficult. The contention that if reality is too complicated, only part of it should be singled out for study is a defensible research strategy, but it risks supposing that the political system can exist in a social void. The contention is especially puzzling in that the authors' own other writings and the country studies in the volume in which this preface appears sensibly ignore this injunction to treat political democracy without regard to the necessary reinforcements it requires in social and economic structure. Aristotle set the study of democracy on a better track when he observed that liberty is the underlying idea of the democratic constitution, and that liberty "has more than one form"—the political ("ruling and being ruled") and the civil ("living as you like"). *The Politics of Aristotle*, ed. and trans. Ernest Barker (Oxford: Oxford University Press, 1946), book 6, chap. 2, 1-4, p. 302. See for a Marxian critique of the Diamond, Lipset, and Linz view, arguing that democracy can only be understood in terms of the development of capitalist economies at their center and peripheries, Paul Cammack, "Democratization and Citizenship in Latin America," Geraint Parry and Michael Moran, eds., *Democracy and Democratization* (London: Routledge, 1994), chap. 8, pp. 174-195.

62. Kagan, *Pericles and the Birth of Democracy*, p. 9.

63. John Dunn, Preface, John Dunn, ed., *Democracy: the Unfinished Journey 500 BC to AD 1993* (Oxford: Oxford University Press, 1992), p. vi.

Chapter 3

1. Herodotus, [*Histories*] trans. A. D. Godley (Cambridge: Harvard University Press, Loeb Classical Library, 1957), vol. 5, p. 339.

2. Thucydides, *The Peloponnesian War*, book 2, chap. 64, 3, quoted by Donald Kagan, *Pericles of Athens and the Birth of Democracy* (New York: The Free Press, 1991), p. 9.

3. Quoted by Simon Hornblower, "Greece: The History of the Classical Period," John Boardman, Jasper Griffin, and Oswyn Murray, eds., *The Oxford History of the Classical World* (Oxford: Oxford University Press, 1986), p. 145.

4. See Henry Sidgwick, *The Development of European Polity* (London: Macmillan, 1903; New York: Kraus Reprint Co., 1969), p. 34.

5. Martin Ostwald, *From Popular Sovereignty to the Sovereignty of Law* (Berkeley: University of California Press, 1986), pp. 3-5.

6. Plato, *The Republic*, book 8.

7. Polybius, *The Histories of Polybius*, trans. Evelyn S. Schuckburgh from the text of F. Hultsch (Bloomington: Indiana University Press, 1982), book 6, 2-9, p. 459.

8. W. G. Forrest, *The Emergence of Greek Democracy 800-400 BC* (New York: McGraw Hill, 1966), p. 45.

9. Mogens Herman Hansen, *The Athenian Democracy in the Age of Demosthenes: Structure, Principles and Ideology*, trans J. A. Crook (Oxford: Basil Blackwell, 1991), p. 37.

10. Philip Brook Manville, *The Origin of Citizenship in Ancient Athens* (Princeton: Princeton University Press, 1990), p. 6.

11. Aristotle, *The Politics of Aristotle*, trans E. Barker (Oxford: Oxford University Press, 1948), book 1, chap. 2, 8, p. 5.

12. Edward Ch. L. Van Der Vliet, "Tyranny and Democracy: The Evolution of Politics in Ancient Greece," Henri J. M. Claessen and Peter van de Velde, eds., *Early State Dynamics* (Leiden: E. J. Brill, 1987), p. 87.

13. Hansen, *The Athenian Democracy*, p. 55.

14. George Forrest, "Greece: the History of the Archaic Period," *The Oxford History of the Classical World*, p. 20.

15. Hansen, *The Athenian Democracy*, p. 55.

16. Ibid.

17. As noted in 1864 by Numa Denis Fustel de Coulanges, *The Ancient City*, trans. Willard Small (Garden City, N.Y.: Doubleday, 1956), p. 203. For analyses of the term and its usage see Martin Ostwald, *Autonomia: Its Genesis and Early History* (New York: the American Philological Association, American Classical Studies, 11, 1982) and Cynthia Farrar, *The Origins of Democratic Thinking* (Cambridge: Cambridge University Press, 1988), pp. 103-106.

18. Hansen, *The Athenian Democracy*, p. 57.

19. H.D.F. Kitto, *The Greeks* (Harmondsworth: Penguin Books, 1951), p. 77.

20. Hansen, *The Athenian Democracy*, p. 19.

21. Ostwald, *From Popular Sovereignty*, p. 497.

22. Sidgwick, *The Development of European Polity*, p. 72

23. Ibid., p. 73.

24. Forrest, *The Emergence of Greek Democracy*, pp. 107-111.

25. Aristotle, *Politics*, book 6, chap. 5, 5, p. 314.

26. David Stockton, *The Classical Athenian Democracy* (Oxford: Oxford University Press, 1990), pp. 2-3.

27. Ibid., p. 20.

28. Hansen, *The Athenian Democracy*, p. 30.

29. Stockton, *The Classical Athenian Democracy*, pp. 6-7.

30. Hansen, *The Athenian Democracy*, p. 43.

31. Plutarch, *The Rise and Fall of Athens*, trans. Ian Scott-Kilvert (Harmondsworth: Penguin Books, 1960), p. 60. Solon's poem is among the fragmentary remains collected in Theodor Bergk, ed., *Poetae Lyrici Graeci* (Leipzig, 1843). Ibid., p. 45.

32. Ibid., p. 62.

33. Stockton, *The Classical Athenian Democracy*, p. 22.

34. Hansen, *The Athenian Democracy*, p. 34.

35. Ibid.

36. Ostwald, *From Popular Sovereignty*, p. 27.

37. Hansen, *The Athenian Democracy*, p. 50.

38. See in particular Ostwald, *From Popular Sovereignty*, pp. 3-84.

39. Manville, *The Origins of Citizenship in Ancient Athens*, p. 23.

40. Staveley, *Greek and Roman Voting and Elections*, p. 55.

41. Ostwald, *From Popular Sovereignty*, p. 79.

42. Quoted from Demosthenes, *First Philippic*, 4, 47, Hansen, *The Athenian Democracy*, p. 216.

43. Hansen, *The Athenian Democracy*, pp. 40-43.

44. Stockton, *The Classical Athenian Democracy*, pp. 15-16.

45. A. H. M. Jones, *Athenian Democracy* (Oxford: Basil Blackwell, 1957), p. 81.

46. Ibid., pp. 91-92.

47. Manville, *The Origins of Citizenship*, p. 8.

48. Ibid., pp. 8-9.

49. Ibid., pp. 8-10.

50. Ibid., p. 11.

51. Jones, *Athenian Democracy*, p. 11.

52. See Gregory Vlastos, "Slavery in Plato's Thought," in Vlastos, *Platonic Studies* (Princeton: Princeton University Press, 1973), p. 152, note 22.

53. Jones, *Athenian Democracy*, pp. 11-16.

54. M. I. Finley, *Democracy Ancient and Modern* (New Brunswick: Rutgers University Press, 1985), pp. 18-19.

55. Ibid., p. 3.

56. Ibid., p. 27.

57. Josiah Ober, *Mass and Elite in Democratic Athens: Rhetoric, Ideology, and the Power of the People* (Princeton: Princeton University Press), p. 328.

58. Thucydides, *History of the Peloponnesian War*, trans. Charles Forster Smith (Cambridge: Harvard University Press, Loeb Classical Library, 1920), vol. 2, book 3, chap. 43, 4-5, p. 77, quoted by Athanasios Moulakis, "The Greeks and Democratic Theory: Moses I. Finley's *Democracy Ancient and Modern* Revisited," *Rivista internazionale di filosofia del diritto*, fourth series, 68, 1, (January-March 1991), p. 69.

59. Moulakis, "The Greeks and Democratic Theory," pp. 69-70.

60. Manville, *The Origins of Citizenship in Ancient Athens*, p. 19.

61. Jones, *Athenian Democracy*, p. 107.

62. Ibid., p. 6.

63. Ibid., p. 3.

64. Hansen, *The Athenian Democracy*, p. 89

65. Ibid., p. 6.

66. Van der Vliet, "Tyranny and Democracy," p. 81.

67. Jones, *Athenian Democracy*, p. 5.

68. Finley, *Democracy Ancient and Modern*, p. 86.

69. Ibid., p. 7.

70. Jones, *Athenian Democracy*, pp. 41-42.

71. Stockton, *The Classical Athenian Democracy*, p. 169.

72. Thus "the diner — not the cook — will be the best judge of a feast." Aristotle, *Politics*, book 3, xi, 14, p. 126.

73. Jones, *Athenian Democracy*, p. 48.

74. See Ostwald, *From Popular Sovereignty*.

75. Jones, *Athenian Democracy*, pp. 56-57.

76. Ibid., p. 61.

77. Ibid., p. 62.

78. Ibid., p. 64.

79. Kagan, *Pericles*, pp. 269-270.

80. See Karl R. Popper, *The Open Society and Its Enemies* (Princeton: Princeton University Press, 1966, fifth edition, revised).

81. Quoted in Jones, *Athenian Democracy*, p. 47.

82. Ibid.

83. Farrar, *The Origins of Democratic Thinking*, p. 20.

84. Ibid., pp 21-22.

85. Ibid., pp. 25-26.

86. Ibid., pp. 37-38

87. Ibid., p. 43.

88. Ibid., p. 77.

89. Ibid., p. 83.

90. Forrest, *The Emergence of Greek Democracy*, pp. 65-66.

Chapter 4

1. A. N. Sherwin-White, *The Roman Citizenship* (Oxford: Oxford University Press, 1973), p. 3.

2. George Willis Botsford, *The Roman Assemblies* (New York: Macmillan, 1909), p. 177.

3. Frank Frost Abbott, *A History and Description of Roman Political Institutions* (New York: Biblo and Tannen, 1963), p. 10.

4. See Chaim Wirszubski, *Libertas as a Political Ideal at Rome During the Late Republic and Early Principate* (Cambridge: Cambridge University Press, 1950), p. 5.

5. Marcus Tullius Cicero, *On the Commonwealth*, trans. George Holland Sabine and Stanley Barney Smith (Columbus, Ohio: The Ohio State University Press, 1929), book 1, 28, pp. 132-133.

6. See the discussion of Sallust's account in P. A. Brunt, *Social Conflicts in the Roman Republic* (London: The Hogarth Press, 1986), pp. 75-76.

7. Michael Crawford, *The Roman Republic* (Glasgow: Fontana/Collins, 1978), p. 35.

8. Ibid., p. 14.

9. See Léon Homo, *Roman Political Institutions from City to State* (London: Routledge, Kegan Paul, 1929), pp. 3-8.

10. Abbott, *A History and Description of Roman Political Institutions*, p. 14.

11. Ibid., pp. 16-17.

12. Livy's account is quoted in Homo, *Roman Political Institutions*, p. 15.

13. Ibid., p. 17.

14. E. S. Staveley, *Greek and Roman Voting and Elections* (Ithaca: Cornell University Press, 1972), p. 121.

15. For a discussion of this institution and its modern applications see Clinton Rossiter, *Constitutional Dictatorship: Crisis Government in the Modern Democracies* (Princeton: Princeton University Press, 1948; reprinted Westport, Conn.: Greenwood Press, 1979).

16. Botsford, *The Roman Assemblies*, pp. 202-203.

17. Brunt, *Social Conflicts*, p. 61.

18. See Botsford, *The Roman Assemblies*, pp. 124-126.

19. Ibid., pp. 212-225.

20. See ibid., pp. 122-123.

21. Lily Ross Taylor, *The Voting Districts of the Roman Republic; The Thirty-five Urban and Rural Tribes* (Rome: The American Academy in Rome, 1960), pp. 8-9.

22. See Staveley, *Greek and Roman Voting and Elections*, pp. 129-131.

23. For an elaborate discussion of this status, stressing the Roman military interest in granting it to allies and changes over time see Sherwin-White, *The Roman Citizenship*, pp. 39-58, who points out (p. 35) that at a relatively late time in the history of the Republic, one tribe was set aside at Rome in the *Concilium plebis* in which Latin citizens could cast a vote.

24. Michel Serres, *Rome: The Book of Foundations*, trans. Felicia McCarren (Stanford: Stanford University Press, 1991), p. 153.

25. Ibid.

26. Wirszubski, *Libertas*, pp. 38-40.

27. William R. Everdell, *The End of Kings: A History of Republics and Republicans* (New York: The Free Press, 1983), p. 50.

28. Abbott, *A History*, p. 31.

29. Ibid., p. 65.

30. Everdell, *The End of Kings*, pp. 51-52. The *praetors* were executive officials who assigned legal cases and appointed district judges, among other duties. The *quaestors* were mainly in charge of caring for decrees of the Senate and otherwise serving the consuls. The *aediles* were in charge of public buildings and of maintaining public order. See Abbott, *A History*, pp. 376-379.

31. Cicero, *On the Commonwealth*, book 1, 25, p. 129.

32. See for an exposition of Cicero's views Wirszubski, *Libertas*, pp. 12-15.

33. Cicero, *On the Commonwealth*, book 1, 27, p. 132.

34. Ibid., book 1, 32, p. 136

35. Ibid., book 1, 5, p. 110.

36. See especially Staveley, *Greek and Roman Voting and Elections*, chap. 7, pp. 133-142.

37. Ibid., pp. 136-137.

38. Henry Sidgwick, *The Development of European Polity* (London: Macmillan, 1903; New York: Kraus Reprint Co., 1969), p. 144.

39. F. E. Adcock, *Roman Political Ideas and Practice* (Ann Arbor: University of Michigan Press, 1959), p. 23.

40. Sidgwick, *The Development of European Polity*, p. 148.

41. Adcock, *Roman Political Ideas and Practice*, p. 23.

42. *Bellum Jugurthinum* 41, 5, quoted by Michael Crawford, *The Roman Republic*, p. 160.

43. See especially Wirszubski, *Libertas*, pp. 115-118.

44. Wirszubski, *Libertas*, p. 169.

45. William J. Bouwsma, *Venice and the Defense of Republican Liberty* (Berkeley: University of California Press, 1968), p. 6.

46. Gianfranco Poggi, *The Development of the Modern State: A Sociological Introduction* (Stanford: Stanford University Press, 1978), pp. 25-26.

47. Ibid., pp. 42-44.

48. Hannah Arendt, *The Human Condition: A Study of the Central Dilemmas Facing Modern Man* (Garden City, N.Y.: Anchor Books, 1959), p. 65.

49. Ibid., p. 287.

50. Saint Augustine, *The City of God*, trans. Marcus Dods (New York: The Modern Library), book 15, 1, p. 479.

51. Ibid., book 19, 15, p. 596.

52. Ibid., 19, 21, p. 699

53. See Arthur P. Monahan, *Consent, Coercion, and Limit: The Medieval Origins of Parliamentary Democracy* (Kingston and Montreal: McGill-Queen's University Press, 1987), p. 30.

54. "What can be learned of the Christian attitude towards politics from the writings of early Christianity shows no express concern at all with the issue of consent as a feature of either the theory or the practise of political authority." Ibid., p. 42.

55. A. P. D'Entrèves, ed., *Aquinas: Selected Political Writings* (Oxford: Basil Blackwell, 1948), especially *Summa Theologica*, First Part, 1., qu. 92, 96, "Political life natural to man," pp. 103-106.

56. G. W. F. Hegel, "The Spirit of Christianity and its Fate," trans. T. M. Knox, *Early Theological Writings* (Chicago: University of Chicago Press, 1948), pp. 182-301.

57. Norman Cohn, *The Pursuit of the Millennium* (London: Secker & Warburg, 1957), especially chaps. 7 and 8, pp. 149-194.

58. See Jacob L. Talmon, *Political Messianism: The Romantic Phase* (New York: Praeger, 1960).

59. This discussion draws on Sanford A. Lakoff, *Equality in Political Philosophy* (Cambridge, Mass.: Harvard University Press, 1964) and "Christianity and Equality," in J. Roland Pennock and John W. Chapman, eds., *Equality/Nomos* 9 (New York: Atherton Press, 1967).

60. Alexis de Tocqueville, *Democracy in America*, trans. George Lawrence (New York: Harper & Row, 1969), vol. 1, Author's Introduction, p. 16.

61. G. P. Gooch, *English Democratic Ideas in the Seventeenth Century* (New York: Harper, 1959), p. 7.

62. Ibid., p. 48.

63. See for Suarez's views, Martin Sicker, *The Genesis of the State* (New York: Praeger, 1991), pp. 36-39.

64. Monahan, *Consent, Coercion, and Limit*, p. 135.

65. Ibid., pp. 137-143.

66. Ibid., p. 98.

67. Ibid., p. 99.

68. Ibid., p. 109.

69. Ibid., pp. 110-119.

70. Quoted by Bouwsma, *Venice*, p. 8. The interpretation that follows is indebted to Bouswma.

71. A. P. D'Entrèves, *The Notion of the State: An Introduction to Political Theory* (Oxford: Oxford University Press, 1967), p. 90.

72. Bouwsma, *Venice*, p. 16

73. Ibid., pp. 62-63.

74. J. G. A. Pocock, *The Machiavellian Moment: Florentine Political Thought and the Atlantic Republican Tradition* (Princeton: Princeton University Press, 1975), chaps. 5-8, pp. 114-271.

75. Gooch, *English Democratic Ideas*, p. 46.

76. A. S. P. Woodhouse, ed., *Puritanism and Liberty* (Chicago: University of Chicago Press, 1951), Putney Debates, October 28, 1647, p 56.

77. Quoted Gooch, *English Democratic Ideas*, p. 130.

78. See Caroline A. Robbins, *The Eighteenth-century Commonwealthman: Studies in the Transmission, Development and Circumstances of English Liberal Thought from the Restoration of Charles II until the War with the Thirteen Colonies* (Cambridge, Mass.: Harvard University Press, 1959) and Pocock, *The Machiavellian Moment*, chap. 12, pp. 401-422.

Chapter 5

1. Letter to Roger C. Weightman, June 24, 1826. Merrill D. Peterson, ed., *The Portable Jefferson* (New York: The Viking Press, 1975), p. 585.

2. Dorothy Pickles, *Democracy* (Baltimore: Penguin Books, 1970), p. 46.

3. Their relationship and the influence of the "exclusion crisis" on Locke's work are examined in Richard Ashcraft, *Revolutionary Politics & Locke's Two Treatises of Government* (Princeton: Princeton University Press, 1986).

4. John Locke, *Two Treatises of Government*, ed. Peter Laslett (Cambridge: Cambridge University Press, 1964), *Second Treatise*, 6, 61, p. 326.

5. Ibid., *Second Treatise*, 5, 51, p. 320.

6. Ibid., *Second Treatise*, 11, 135, pp. 375-6.

7. Ibid., *Second Treatise*, 5, 51, p. 320.

8. David Hume, *An Enquiry Concerning the Principles of Morals, Hume's Moral and Political Philosophy*, ed. Henry D. Aiken (New York: Hafner, 1948), Appendix 1, 5, p. 269.

9. See Adam Smith, *The Theory of Moral Sentiments*, ed. D.D. Raphael and A.L. Macfie (Oxford: Oxford University Press, 1976; reprinted, Indianapolis: Liberty Classics, 1982).

10. A. P. D'Entrèves, *The Notion of the State: An Introduction to Political Theory* (Oxford: Oxford University Press, 1967), p. 214.

11. Maurice Cranston, "Introduction," Jean-Jacques Rousseau, *The Social Contract* (Harmondsworth: Penguin Books, 1968), p. 31.

12. Rousseau, *The Social Contract*, chap. 3, 4, pp. 112-114.

13. Cranston, "Introduction," pp. 42-43.

14. See for a discussion of Rousseau's castigation of the substitution of "finance" for active engagement Robert Wokler, "Democracy's Mythical Ordeals: the Procrustean and Promethean Path to Popular Self-Rule," Geraint Parry and Michael Moran, eds., *Democracy and Democratization* (London: Routledge, 1994), chap. 1, pp. 35-36.

15. See Alan Craig Houston, *Algernon Sidney and the Republican Heritage in England and America* (Princeton: Princeton University Press, 1991).

16. Reviewing modern studies of the American Revolution, Jack P. Greene observes: "The prevailing view thus came to be that the Revolution was predominantly a conservative Whiggish movement undertaken in defense of American liberty and property, preoccupied throughout with constitutional and political problems, carried on with a minimum of violence—at least when seen in the perspective of other revolutions—and with little change either in the distribution of political power or in the structure and operation of basic social institutions, and reaching its logical culmination with the Federal Constitution." Although, as he also points out, recent historians acknowledge that more radical ideas played a role in the revolution, they generally agree that it was a supporting role, if only because ideas such as natural rights had already become part of American experience and expectations. Jack P. Greene, "The Reappraisal of the American Revolution in Recent Historical Literature," Jack P. Greene, ed., *The Reinterpretation of the American Revolution 1763-1789* (New York: Harper & Row, 1968), p. 54.

17. Gordon S. Wood, *The Radicalism of the American Revolution* (New York: Knopf, 1992), p. 233.

18. François Furet, *Interpreting the French Revolution*, trans. E. Forster (Cambridge: Cambridge University Press, 1981), p. 24

19. Ibid., p. 25.

20. Patrice Higonnet, *Sister Republics* (Cambridge, Mass.: Harvard University Press, 1988), pp. 1-2.

21. Quoted ibid., p. 2.

22. See for example A. R. M. Lower, *Colony to Nation: A History of Canada* (Toronto: Longmans, Green, 1946), pp. 114, 120.

23. Higonnet, *Sister Republics*, p. 189.

24. Ibid., p. 3.

25. David Ramsay, *A Dissertation on the Manner of Acquiring the Character and Privileges of a Citizen of the United States* (Charleston, 1789), p. 3, quoted by Wood, *The Radicalism of the American Revolution*, p. 169.

26. For the influence of Whig republicanism see Bernard Bailyn, *The Ideological Origins of the American Revolution* (Cambridge, Mass.: Harvard University Press, 1967), Gordon S. Wood, *The Creation of the American Republic 1776-1787* (Chapel Hill: The University of North Carolina Press, 1969), J. G. A. Pocock, *The Machiavellian Moment: Florentine Political Thought and the Atlantic Republican Tradition* (Princeton: Princeton University Press, 1975); and Robert Bellah, Richard Madsen, William M. Sullivan, Ann Swidler, and Stephen M. Tipton, *Habits of the Heart: Individualism and Commitment in American Life* (Berkeley: University of California Press, 1985) and *The Good Society* (New York: Knopf, 1991).

27. Ibid., p. 111.

28. Higonnet, *Sister Republics*, pp. 37-43.

29. Ibid., pp. 82-90.

30. See Louis Hartz, *The Liberal Tradition in America: An Interpretation of American Political Thought Since the Revolution* (New York: Harcourt Brace, 1955), especially chap. 1, pp. 3-32.

31. Quoted Higonnet, *Sister Republics*, p. 196.

32. Joyce O. Appleby, *Capitalism and a New Social Order: The Republican Vision of the 1790s* (New York: New York University Press, 1984), p. 15.

33. R. R. Palmer, *The Age of the Democratic Revolution* (Princeton: Princeton University Press, 1959), pp. 5-6.

34. Joshua Muravchik, *Exporting Democracy* (Washington: The AEI Press, 1991), pp. 72-88.

35. This analysis is presented in Maurice Duverger, *Modern Democracies: Economic Power versus Political Power*, trans. Charles L. Markmann (New York: Holt, Rinehart & Winston, 1974). The following paragraphs summarize the argument.

36. Ibid., p. 60.

37. Ibid., p. 91

Chapter 6

1. Benito Mussolini, in collaboration with Giovanni Gentile, "The Doctrine of Fascism" (1932), Adrian Lyttelton, ed., Douglas Parmée, trans. *Italian Fascisms: From Pareto to Gentile* (New York: Harper, 1973), p. 49.

2. See the discussion of Ruskin in Benjamin Evans Lippincott, *Victorian Critics of Democracy* (New York: Octagon, 1964), pp. 54-92.

3. For the views of Stephen and Maine see ibid., pp. 134-166, 167-206.

4. James Mill, "An Essay on Government," Terence Ball, ed., *James Mill, Political Writings* (Cambridge: Cambridge University Press, 1992), p. 21.

5. John Stuart Mill, "M. de Tocqueville on Democracy in America," Marshall Cohen, ed., *The Philosophy of John Stuart Mill, Ethical, Political and Religious* (New York: The Modern Library, 1961), pp. 123-126.

6. Ibid., p. 136.

7. Ibid., p. 137-138.

8. Ibid., p. 147.

9. Ibid., pp. 150-151.

10. "On Liberty," p. 259.

11. John Stuart Mill, *Considerations on Representative Government* (1861; Chicago: Henry Regnery, 1962), p. 35.

12. Dennis F. Thompson, *John Stuart Mill and Representative Government* (Princeton: Princeton University Press, 1976), p. 9 passim.

13. Quoted from Thomas Carlyle, *The French Revolution: A History*, Part One (London, 1891), p. 165 by Michael Levin, *The Spectre of Democracy* (New York: New York University Press, 1992), p. 141.

14. Quoted ibid., p. 142, from Carlyle, *The French Revolution*.

15. Ibid., p. 149.

16. Steven E. Aschheim, "The Myth of 'Judaization' in Germany," Jehuda Reinharz and Walter Schatzberg, eds., *The Jewish Response to German Culture: From the Enlightenment to the Second World War* (Hanover: University Press of New England, 1985), pp. 234-235.

17. Walter Kaufmann, *Nietzsche: Philosopher, Psychologist, Antichrist* (New York: Meridian Books, 1956), p. 272.

18. Friedrich Nietzsche, "Thus Spake Zarathustra," in Walter Kaufmann, ed., *The Portable Nietzsche* (New York: The Viking Press, 1954), p. 163. See also Tracy Strong, *Friedrich Nietzsche and the Politics of Transfiguration* (Berkeley: University of California Press, 1975).

19. Quoted from George Santayana, *The Life of Reason; or, the Phases of Human Progress*, vol. 2, *Reason in Society* (Scribner's, 1905-1906), p. 83 by David Spitz, *Patterns of Anti-Democratic Thought* (New York: Macmillan, 1049), p. 198.

20. H. L. Mencken, *Notes on Democracy* (London: Jonathan Cape, 1927), pp. 14-15.

21. Maurice Cranston, "The Ambiguity of Nationalism," *The Great Ideas Today* (Chicago: Encyclopedia Britannica, 1993), pp. 216-217.

22. Mill, *Considerations on Representative Government*, pp. 307-309.

23. Fritz Stern, *The Politics of Cultural Despair* (Berkeley: University of California Press, 1961), pp. 195-202.

24. Ibid.

25. See Mill's defense of British imperialism in India as the best way to facilitate a transition to self-government in *Considerations*, 350-365.

26. See Hannah Arendt, *The Origins of Totalitarianism* (New York: Harcourt Brace, 1951), p. 162.

27. Quoted Michael D. Biddiss, *Father of Racist Ideology: The Social and Political Thought of Count Gobineau* (New York: Weybright and Talley, 1970), p. 260.

28. Arthur, Comte de Gobineau, *Essai sur l'inégalité des races humaines* (1854; Paris: Firmin-Didot, 1940), vol. 1, chap. 16, pp. 215-216.

29. Ibid., vol. 1, chap. 9, p. 101.

30. Ibid., vol. 1, chap. 16, p. 220.

31. Ibid., vol. 2, chap. 8, p. 536.

32. Letter to Gobineau, January 14, 1857, John Lukacs ed. and trans., Alexis de Tocqueville, *The European Revolution and Correspondence with Gobineau* (Garden City, N.Y.: Anchor Books, 1959), p. 305.

33. Letter to Gobineau, January 24, 1857, ibid., pp. 309-310.

34. See Jacques Barzun, *Race, A Study in Modern Superstition* (New York: Harper, 1937; revised ed., 1965).

35. See Jules Isaac, *The Teaching of Contempt: Christian Roots of Anti-Semitism*, trans. Helen Weaver (New York: Holt, Rinehart & Winston, 1964) and Rosemary R. Ruether, *Faith and Fratricide: The Theological Roots of Anti-Semitism* (New York: Seabury Press, 1974).

36. See Bernard Lewis, *The Jews of Islam* (Princeton: Princeton University Press, 1984), p. 25.

37. Paul Johnson, *A History of the Jews* (New York: Harper and Row, 1987), p. 393.

38. "With trichinae and bacilli one does not negotiate, nor are trichinae and bacilli subjected to education; they are exterminated as quickly and as thoroughly as possible." Paul de Lagarde, *Ausgewählte Schriften*, ed. Paul Fischer (Munich, 1934; second edition) p. 239, translated and quoted, Stern, *The Politics of Cultural Despair*, pp. 61-63.

39. See Jean-Denis Brédin, *The Affair* (New York: Braziller, 1986), p. 26.

40. Carl E. Schorske, *Fin-de-Siecle Vienna: Politics and Culture* (New York: Knopf, 1980), pp. 120-146.

41. Houston Stewart Chamberlain, *Foundations of the Nineteenth Century* (1899), trans. John Lees (New York: Fertig, 1968), 1, pp. 253-257.

42. Ibid., p. 269.

43. Ibid., p. 261.

44. George L. Mosse, Introduction, Chamberlain, *Foundations of the Nineteenth Century*, p. xviii.

45. Lucy S. Dawidowicz, *The War Against the Jews 1933-1945* (New York: Holt, Rinehart & Winston, 1975), p. 20.

46. See Frank E. Manuel, introduction, Johann Gottfried Herder, *Reflections on the Philosophy of the History of Mankind*, trans. T. O. Churchill, abridged (Chicago: University of Chicago Press, 1968), pp. ix-xxv.

47. Richard Grunberger, *The 12-Year Reich: A Social History of Nazi Germany 1933-1945* (New York: Ballantine, 1971), pp. 269-271.

48. Quoted, James H. Meisel, *The Myth of the Ruling Class: Gaetano Mosca and the "Elite"* (Ann Arbor: The University of Michigan Press, 1962), p. 171.

49. Gaetano Mosca, *The Ruling Class*, trans. Arthur Livingston (New York: McGraw-Hill, 1939) p. 50.

50. Quoted, ibid., p. 106. For a similar modern approach, see Gary C. Jacobson and Samuel H. Kernell, *Strategy and Choice in Congressional Elections* (New Haven: Yale University Press, 1981).

51. Mosca, *The Ruling Class*, p. 126.

52. Ibid., p. 491.

53. Roberto Michels, *Political Parties: A Sociological Study of the Oligarchical Tendencies of Modern Democracies* (Glencoe, Ill.: Free Press, 1966).

54. See Walter Lippmann, *The Phantom Public* (New York: Harcourt Brace and Company, 1925) and Joseph A. Schumpeter, *Capitalism, Socialism and Democracy* (New York: Harper, 1950).

55. Peter Bachrach, *The Theory of Democratic Elitism: A Critique* (Boston: Little, Brown, 1967).

56. See Richard Hofstadter, *Social Darwinism in American Thought* (Boston: The Beacon Press, 1955), p. 33.

57. Gustave Le Bon, *The Crowd: A Study of the Popular Mind* (1896) (London: T. Fisher Unwin, 1920), p. 15.

58. Wilfred Trotter, *Instincts of the Herd in War and Peace* (1908; London: The Scientific Book Club, 1942) and Sigmund Freud, *Group Psychology [Massenpsychologie] and the Analysis of the Ego*, trans. James Strachey (New York: Liveright, 1949).

59. See especially Samuel P. Huntington, " Social and Institutional Dynamics of One-Party Systems" and Clement H. Moore, "The Single Party as Source of Legitimacy," Samuel P. Huntington and Clement H. Moore, eds., *Authoritarian Politics in Modern Society: The Dynamics of Established One-Party Systems* (New York: Basic Books, 1970), pp. 3-47; 48-72.

60. Theodor W. Adorno, Else Frenkel-Brunswik, Daniel J. Levinson, and R. Nevitt Sanford, *The Authoritarian Personality* (New York: Harper, 1950).

61. For Peronism in Argentina see Gino Germani, *Authoritarianism, Fascism, and National Populism* (New Brunswick: Transaction Books, 1978).

62. Quoted in Donald Cameron Watt, *How War Came: The Immediate Origins of the Second World War 1938-1939* (New York: Pantheon Books, 1989), p. 600.

63. Benito Mussolini, "Which Way is the World Going? (*Gerarchia*, February 25, 1922), *Italian Fascisms*, p. 66. See for the understanding of fascism by Mussolini and Gentile, A. James Gregor, *The Ideology of Fascism: The Rationale of Totalitarianism* (New York: The Free Press, 1969).

64. Mussolini, "The Doctrine of Fascism," *Italian Fascisms*, p. 49.

65. Quoted from Giovanni Gentile, *The Origins and Doctrine of Fascism* (1934), ibid., p. 311.

66. Leonard Schapiro, *Totalitarianism* (London: Macmillan, 1972), p. 13.

67. Ibid., pp. 14-15. See also Hannah Arendt, *The Origins of Totalitarianism* (New York: Harcourt Brace, 1851), Carl J. Friedrich and Zbigniew K. Brzezinski, *Totalitarian Dictatorship and Autocracy* (New York: Praeger, 1956; revised, 1961), Raymond Aron, *Democracy and Totalitarianism*, trans. V. Ionescu (London: Weidenfeld and Nicolson, 1968), Jeane Kirkpatrick, *Dictatorships and Double Standards: Rationalism and Reason in Politics* (New York: Simon and Schuster, 1982), Jean François Revel, *The Totalitarian Temptation*, trans. David Hapgood (Garden City, N.Y.: Doubleday, 1987).

68. Mussolini, *Italian Fascisms*, p. 39.

69. Ibid., p. 40.

70. Ibid., p. 44.

71. See Grunberger, *The 12-Year Reich*, pp. 443-444.

72. Ibid., p. 29.

73. Quoted by Schapiro, *Totalitarianism*, p. 34.

74. Gabriele d'Annunzio, "Letter to the Dalmatians" (January 15, 1915), *Italian Fascisms*, p. 185.

75. Filippo Tommaso Marinetti, "The Futurist Manifesto," *Italian Fascisms*, pp. 212-215.

76. Mussolini, *Italian Fascisms*, p. 43.

77. Ibid., p. 47.

78. Grunberger, *The 12 Year Reich*, p. 15.

Chapter 7

1. Ernst Cassirer, *Kant's Life and Thought*, trans. James Haden (New Haven and London: Yale University Press, 1981), pp. 243-244. Quotation from Kant is from the *Foundations of the Metaphysics of Morals* (1785), second section. See Immanuel Kant, *Foundations of the Metaphysics of Morals*, trans. Lewis White Beck, with Critical Essays Edited by Robert Paul Wolff (Indianapolis: Bobbs-Merrill, 1969), p. 59.

2. Kant, *Foundations of the Metaphysics of Morals*, p. 21.

3. Carl J. Friedrich, Introduction, Carl J. Friedrich, ed., *The Philosophy of Kant: Immanuel Kant's Moral and Political Writings* (New York: The Modern Library, 1949), p. xviii.

4. Kant, *Foundations of the Metaphysics of Morals*, p. 24.

5. William A. Galston, *Kant and the Problem of History* (Chicago: University of Chicago Press, 1975), p. 177.

6. Ibid., p. 51.

7. Ibid., pp. 54-55.

8. Hannah Arendt, *The Origins of Totalitarianism* (New York: Harcourt Brace, 1951), pp. 435-436.

9. Kant, "Theory and Practice; Concerning the Saying: this May Be True in Theory But Does Not Apply to Practice (1793)," Friedrich, *The Philosophy of Kant*, p. 416

10. Immanuel Kant, "Idea for a Universal History with Cosmopolitan Intent," Friedrich, *The Philosophy of Kant*, p. 121.

11. Ibid., p. 124-125.

12. Isaiah Berlin, *Four Essays on Liberty* (Oxford: Oxford University Press, 1969), pp. 152-153.

13. R. M. Hare, "Could Kant Have Been a Utilitarian?" *Utilitas* 5, 1 (May 1993), pp. 2-4.

14. Frederick Rosen, "Bentham and Mill on Liberty and Justice," George Feaver and Frederick Rosen, eds., *Lives, Liberties and the Public Good: New Essays in Political Theory for Maurice Cranston* (London: Macmillan, 1987), p. 125.

15. John Rawls, *A Theory of Justice* (Cambridge, Mass.: Harvard University Press, 1971).

16. See for such an argument Brian Barry, "Is Democracy Special?," Peter Laslett and James Fishkin, eds., *Philosophy, Politics and Society*, fifth series (Oxford: Basil Blackwell, 1979), pp. 155-96.

17. Giovanni Sartori, *The Theory of Democracy Revisited* (Chatham, N.J.: Chatham House, 1987), vol. 2, pp. 315-20.

18. Robert A. Dahl, *Democracy and Its Critics* (New Haven and London: Yale University Press, 1989), p. 91.

19. J. Roland Pennock, "The Justification of Democracy," Geoffrey Brennan and Loren E. Lomasky, eds., *Politics and Process: New Essays in Democratic Thought* (Cambridge: Cambridge University Press, 1989), p. 21. See also J. Roland Pennock, *Democratic Political Theory* (Princeton: Princeton University Press, 1979), p. 219.

20. Geraint Parry and Michael Moran, "Democracy and Denocratization," Geraint Parry and Michael Moran, eds., *Democracy and Democratization* (London: Routledge, 1994), chap. 12, p. 274.

21. Joseph Raz, *The Morality of Freedom* (Oxford: Clarendon Press, 1986), p. 425.

22. A considerable literature has appeared in recent times on the nature of liberalism and its relationship to democracy. See Bruce Ackerman, *Social Justice in the Liberal State* (New Haven: Yale University Press, 1980); Benjamin Barber, *The Conquest of Politics: Liberal Philosophy in Democratic Times* (Oxford: Oxford University Press, 1978); Richard Flathman, *Towards a Liberalism* (Ithaca: Cornell University Press, 1989); William A. Galston, *Liberal Purposes: Goods, Virtues, and Diversity in the Liberal State* (New York: Columbia University Press, 1989); Will Kymlicka, *Liberalism, Community, and Culture* (Oxford: Oxford University Press, 1989); Stephen Macedo, *Liberal Virtues: Citizenship, Virtue, and Community in Liberal Constitutionalism* (Oxford: Oxford University Press, 1990); Harvey Mansfield, *The Spirit of Liberalism* (Cambridge, Mass.: Harvard University Press, 1978); Margaret Moore, *Foundations of Liberalism* (New York: Oxford University Press, 1993); Nancy Rosenblum, *Another Liberalism: Romanticism and the Reconstruction of Liberal Thought* (Cambridge, Mass.: Harvard University Press, 1987); Michael Sandel, *Liberalism and the Limits of Justice* (Cambridge: Cambridge University Press, 1982), and Rogers Smith, *Liberalism and American Constitutional Law* (Cambridge, Mass.: Harvard University Press, 1985).

23. John Dewey, "The Democratic Form," from "Democracy and Educational Administration," *School and Society* (April 3, 1937), excerpted in *Intelligence in the Modern World: John Dewey's Philosophy*, ed. Joseph Ratner (New York: Modern Library, 1939), p. 400. For an examination of Dewey's views see Robert Westbrook, *John Dewey and American Democracy* (Ithaca: Cornell University Press, 1992).

24. See Ronald N. Dworkin, *Life's Dominion: An Argument About Abortion, Euthanasia, and Individual Freedom* (New York: Knopf, 1993).

25. See Gabriel Almond and Sidney Verba, *The Civic Culture* (Princeton: Princeton University Press, 1963).

26. Benjamin Barber, *Strong Democracy: Participatory Politics for a New Age* (Berkeley: University of California Press, 1984).

27. Robert D. Putnam, with Robert Leonardi and Raffaella Y. Nanetti, *Making Democracy Work; Civic Traditions in Modern Italy* (Princeton: Princeton University Press, 1993), p. 15.

28. Tocqueville, *Democracy in America*, ed. J. P. Mayer, trans. George Lawrence (Garden City, N.Y.: Anchor Books, 1969), vol. 1, Author's Introduction, p. 9.

29. Benjamin Constant, "The Liberty of the Ancients Compared with That of the Moderns," Biancamaria Fontana, ed. and trans., *Political Writings* (Cambridge: Cambridge University Press, 1988), p. 311.

30. Ibid., p. 311-312.

31. Ibid., p. 313.

32. The term "private government" was introduced by Charles E. Merriam in *Public and Private Government* (New Haven: Yale University Press, 1944). See also Grant McConnell, *Private Power and American Democracy* (New York: Knopf, 1966) and Sanford A. Lakoff with Daniel Rich, eds., *Private Government: Introductory Readings* (Reading, Mass.: Addison-Wesley, 1971).

33. See Charles Lindblom, *Politics and Markets* (New York: Basic Books, 1977), p. 356.

34. Daniel Bell, "The Old War," *The New Republic* 209, 8 & 9 (August 23 and 30, 1993), p. 18.

35. Robert A. Dahl, "Why Free Markets Are Not Enough," *Journal of Democracy* 3, 3 (July 1992), p. 82.

36. See Adam Przeworski, *Capitalism and Social Democracy* (New York: Cambridge University Press, 1985).

37. See especially Friedrich Hayek, *The Constitution of Liberty* (Chicago: University of Chicago Press, 1960) and Robert Nozick, *Anarchy, State, and Utopia* (New York: Basic Books, 1974).

38. Dennis C. Mueller, "Democracy: the Public Choice Approach," Geoffrey Brennan and Lauren E. Lomasky, eds., *Politics and Process: New Essays in Democratic Thought* (Cambridge, England: Cambridge University Press, 1989), p. 79.

39. James Q. Wilson, *Bureaucracy: What Government Agencies Do and Why They Do It* (New York: Basic Books, 1989), p. 346.

40. See Nozick, *Anarchy, State and Utopia*.

41. Mueller, "Democracy: the Public Choice Approach," p. 79.

42. Wilson, *Bureaucracy*, p. 347.

43. Peter H. Aronson, "The Democratic Order and Public Choice," Geoffrey Brennan and Loren E. Lomasky, eds., *Politics and Process: New Essays in Democratic Thought* (Cambridge, England: Cambridge University Press, 1989), p. 113.

44. See for an historical and analytical account of the differences between the two views, Hannah Fenichel Pitkin, *The Concept of Representation* (Berkeley: University of California Press, 1967).

45. Douglas J. Amy, *Real Choices/New Voices* (New York: Columbia University Press, 1993), p. 43.

46. Thucydides, *The Peloponnesian War*, trans. Rex Warner (Harmondsworth: Penguin Books, 1954), book 2, chap. 4, p. 119.

47. Mill, *Considerations on Representative Government* (Chicago: Henry Regnery, 1962), pp. 72-73.

48. For an innovative proposal to create sample assemblies for evaluating candidates and issues as well as effective criticisms of plebiscitary and representative democracy, see James Fishkin, *Democracy and Deliberation* (New Haven: Yale University Press, 1991).

49. See Frank Bryan and John McClaughry, *The Vermont Papers: Recreating Democracy on a Human Scale* (Post Mills, Vt.: Chelsea Green, 1989) for a proposal to renovate the principle of the town meeting by creating larger units to be called shires.

50. "This natural auditorium in the heart of Athens, about 300 yards from the foot of the Acropolis and the edge of the Agora, could accommodate about six thousand down to the end of the fifth century; at that point further work increased that number by about five hundred, and considerable enlargement round about 340 may have almost doubled its capacity." David Stockton, *The Classical Athenian Democracy* (Oxford: Oxford University Press, 1990), p. 71.

51. See Arthur Lupia, "Shortcuts Versus Encyclopedias: Information and Voting Behavior in California Insurance Reform Elections," *American Political Science Review* 88, 1 (March 1994), pp. 63-76.

52. Anne Rawley Saldich, *Electronic Democracy: Television's Impact on the American Political Process* (New York: Praeger, 1979).

53. California Commission on Campaign Financing, *Democracy By Initiative: Shaping California's Fourth Branch of Government* (Los Angeles: Center for Responsive Government, 1992), p. 3. Chapter ten of the report is devoted to suggestions for reform. For a generally favorable view of referenda, which, however, recognizes their susceptibility to manipulation, see Thomas E. Cronin, *Direct Democracy: the Politics of Initiative, Referendum, and Recall* (Cambridge, Mass.: Harvard University Press, 1989).

54. See Carol Pateman, *Participation and Democratic Theory* (Cambridge: Cambridge University Press, 1970) and Benjamin Barber, *Strong Democracy: Participatory Politics for a New Age* (Berkeley: University of California Press, 1984), and for criticisms of "pure" participatory democracy Sartori, *The Theory of Democracy Revisited* (Chatham, N.J.: Chatham House, 1987), vol. 1, pp. 115-123.

55. See Juan Linz, "The Perils of Presidentialism," *Journal of Democracy* 2, 1 (Winter 1990), pp. 51-69, and "The Virtues of Parliamentarism," *Journal of Democracy* 1, 4 (Fall 1990), pp. 84-91.

56. Arturo Valenzuela, "Latin America: Presidentialism in Crisis," *Journal of Democracy* 4, 4 (October 1993), pp. 3-16. See also Juan Linz and Arturo Valenzuela, eds., *The Failure of Presidential Democracy: Comparative Perspectives* (Baltimore: Johns Hopkins University Press, 1994), vol. 1.

57. Donald L. Horowitz, "Comparing Democratic Systems," *Journal of Democracy* 1, 4 (Fall 1990), pp. 73-79.

58. Seymour Martin Lipset, "The Centrality of Political Culture," *Journal of Democracy* 1, 4 (Fall 1990), pp. 80-83.

59. Ibid.

Chapter 8

1. Anthony Downs, *An Economic Theory of Democracy* (New York: Harper, 1957), p. 260.

2. Ibid., p. 39

3. Ibid., p. 246.

4. Ibid., p. 267.

5. William H. Riker and Peter C. Ordeshook, "A Theory of the Calculus of Voting," *American Political Science Review* 42, 1 (March, 1968), pp. 25, 28, cited in Raymond Wolfinger, "The Rational Citizen Faces Election Day," *Public Affairs Report* 33, 6 (November 1992), p. 10.

6. Raymond Wolfinger and Steven J. Rosenstone, *Who Votes?* (New Haven: Yale University Press, 1980).

7. See Robert A. Dahl, *Democracy and Its Critics* (New Haven: Yale University Press, 1991), pp. 42-51, and Robert Paul Wolff, *In Defense of Anarchism, with a Reply to Jeffrey H. Reiman's "In Defense of Political Philosophy"* (New York: Harper & Row, 1976).

8. Downs, *An Economic Theory of Democracy*, p. 45

9. David O. Sears and Carolyn L. Funk, "Self-Interest in Americans' Political Opinions," Jane Mansbridge, ed., *Beyond Self-Interest* (Chicago: University of Chicago Press, 1990), pp. 154-156.

10. Ibid., p. 158.

11. See Kenneth Arrow, *Social Choice and Individual Values* (New York: Wiley, 1963).

12. Peter H. Aranson, "The Democratic Order and Public Choice," Geoffrey Brennan and Loren Lomasky, eds., *Politics and Process: New Essays in Democratic Thought*, p. 107.

13. See William H. Riker, *Liberalism Against Populism: A Confrontation Between the Theory of Democracy and the Theory of Social Choice* (San Francisco: W. H. Freeman, 1982), pp. 132-137, and Dahl, *Democracy and its Critics*, pp. 144-146.

14. Riker, *Liberalism Against Populism*, especially pp. 241-246.

15. Aranson, "The Democratic Order and Public Choice," pp. 108-109.

16. See the argument of Samuel Popkin, *The Reasoning Voter* (Chicago: University of Chicago Press, 1993).

17. See Kaare Strom, *Minority Government and Minority Rule* (Cambridge: Cambridge University Press, 1990)

18. This discussion is much indebted to several sources. These are the drafts of two entries ("Electoral Systems" and "Proportional Representation") prepared by my colleague Arend Lijphart for the *Encyclopedia of Democracy* (Washington, D.C.: Congressional Quarterly Press, 1996) and two 1993 publications of the Working Party on Electoral Systems of the Labor Party of Great Britain, the second, interim report, "Democracy, Representation and Elections," and the third report containing recommendations for reforms affecting the House of Commons and the House of Lords. Both were kindly made available by the group's chair, Prof. Raymond Plant. For critiques of the working committee's recommendations, see the comments by David Butler and others with partisan perspectives in *Representation* 31, 16 (Autumn 1993), pp. 77-83. For a comparative examination of the role of electoral systems, emphasizing the criterion of proportionality of votes to seats in the

legislature, see Arend Lijphart, *Electoral Systems and Party Systems, A Study of Twenty-Seven Democracies, 1945-1990* (New York: Oxford University Press, 1994).

19. See especially Douglas J. Amy, *Real Choices/New Voices: the Case for Proportional Representation in the United States*, (New York: Columbia University Press, 1993), appendix B, pp. 234-236, for a description of the different allocation formulas.

20. Lijphart, *Electoral Systems*, pp. 45-46.

21. For the view that voters should be represented in accordance with their interests rather than by presumably arbitrary geographical districts and that majority rule necessarily denies fair representation to minority groups by wasting votes cast for small parties see Lani Guinier, *The Tyranny of the Majority: Fundamental Fairness in Representative Democracy* (New York: Martin Kessler Books/The Free Press, 1994).

22. J. Curtice and M. Steed, "Proportionality and Exaggeration in the British Electoral System," *Electoral Studies* (1986), cited, "Democracy, Representation and Elections," p. 18.

23. Downs, *An Economic Theory of Democracy*, pp. 114-115.

24. For a forceful presentation of the arguments for PR and a rebuttal of criticisms see *Real Choices/New Voices*.

25. Quoted, Curtice and Steed, "Democracy, Representation and Elections," p. 27.

26. As shown by Douglas W. Rae, *The Political Consequences of Electoral Laws* (New Haven: Yale University Press, 1967).

27. J. S. Mill, *Considerations on Representative Government* (Chicago: Henry Regnery, 1962), p. 35.

28. See especially Ferdinand A. Hermens, *Democracy and Anarchy: A Study of Proportional Representation* (1941; reprinted New York: Johnson Reprint Corp., 1972).

29. As pointed out by Rein Taagepara and Matthew Shugart, *Seats and Votes: The Effects and Determinants of Electoral Systems* (New Haven: Yale University Press, 1989), pp. 126-141.

30. "Democracy, Representation and Elections," p. 34.

31. Ibid., p. 12.

32. British Labor Party, "Report of the Working Party on Electoral Systems, 1993," pp. 20-24.

33. David Butler, "The Plant Report 1993: The Third Report of Labour's Working Party on Electoral Systems," *Representation* 31, 116 (Autumn 1993), pp. 77-9.

34. Thomas T. Mackie and Richard Rose, *The International Almanac of Electoral History* (New York: Free Press, 1974), Table A.5, cited, "Democracy, Representation and Elections," p. 25.

35. See for a discussion of the pros and cons of PR in Israel, Asher Arian, *Politics in Israel: The Second Generation* (Chatham, N.J.: Chatham House, 1985).

36. See especially Arend Lijphart, *Democracies: Patterns of Majoritarian and Consensus Government in Twenty-One Countries* (New Haven: Yale University Press, 1984).

37. See Donald L. Horowitz, *A Democratic South Africa? Constitutional Engineering in a Divided Society* (Berkeley: University of California Press, 1991), pp. 204-214.

38. Maurice Duverger, *Modern Political Parties: Their Organization and Activity in the Modern State*, trans. Barbara and Robert North (New York: John Wiley and Sons, 1954).

39. See Seymour Martin Lipset and Stein Rokkan, "Cleavage Structures, Party Systems, and Voter Alignments: An Introduction, in Lipset and Rokkan, eds., *Party*

Systems and Voter Alignments: Cross-National Perspectives (New York: Free Press, 1967).

40. See Taagepara and Shugart, *Seats and Votes*, Rae, *The Political Consequences of Electoral Laws,* and Bernard Grofman and Arend Lijphart, eds., *Electoral Laws and their Political Consequences* (New York: Agathon Press, 1986)

41. Giovanni Sartori, "The Influence of Electoral Systems: Faulty Laws or Faulty Method?" Grofman and Lijphart, *Electoral Laws,* p. 64.

42. Lijphart, *Electoral Systems,* p. 98.

43. See Steven J. Brams and Peter C. Fishburn, *Approval Voting* (Boston: Birkhauser, 1983).

44. Dennis C. Mueller, "Democracy: the Public Choice Approach," Geoffrey Brennan and Lauren E. Lomasky, eds., *Politics and Process: New Essays in Democratic Thought* (Cambridge, England: Cambridge University Press, 1989), p. 88.

45. Ibid.

Chapter 9

1. Alastair Hennessy, "The Renaissance of Federal Ideas in Contemporary Spain," Murray Forsyth, ed., *Federalism and Nationalism* (Leicester: Leicester University Press, 1989), p. 21.

2. Ibid., pp. 11-12.

3. See the text of the draft constitution as published in *Izvestia* Nov. 10, 1993, translated in *The Current Digest of the Soviet Press* 45, 45 (1993), pp. 4-16.

4. Murray Forsyth, "Introduction," Forsyth, *Federalism and Nationalism,* p. 3.

5. Donald V. Smiley, *Canada in Question: Federalism in the Seventies* (Toronto: McGraw Hill-Ryerson, 1972), p. 143.

6. Alain Gagnon, "Canadian Federalism: A Working Balance," in Forsyth, *Federalism and Nationalism,* p. 147.

7. Peter H. Russell, *Constitutional Odyssey: Can Canadians Be a Sovereign People?* (Toronto: University of Toronto Press, 1992), p. vii.

8. Ibid., p. 193.

9. This discussion draws heavily on Robert Senelle, "Constitutional Reform in Belgium: from Unitarism towards Federalism," Forsyth, *Federalism and Nationalism,* pp. 51-112.

10. Ibid., pp. 68-71.

11. Hennessy, "The Renaissance of Federal Ideas," Forsyth, *Federalism and Nationalism* , p. 12.

12. Audrey Brasslof, "Spain — the State of the Autonomies," Forsyth, *Federalism and Nationalism,* p. 31.

13. Ibid., p. 33.

14. Ibid., p. 21.

15. Reinhard Bendix, introduction to Reinhard Bendix et al., eds., *State and Society: A Reader in Comparative Political Sociology* (Boston: Little Brown, 1968), p. 7.

16. See especially the writings of Daniel J. Elazar, including *Exploring Federalism* (Tuscaloosa: The University of Alabama Press, 1987) and his edited colloquium volume, *Self Rule/Shared Rule: Federal Solutions to the Middle East Conflict* (Ramat Gan, Israel: Turtledove, 1979).

17. Ivo D. Duchacek, *The Territorial Dimension of Politics Within, Among, and Across Nations* (Boulder: Westview Press, 1986), p. 96.

18. As defined in the classic study by K. C. Wheare, *Federal Government* (London: Oxford University Press, 1946), p. 3.

19. See Quentin Skinner, *The Foundations of Modern Political Thought* (Cambridge: Cambridge University Press, 1978), vol. 2, pp. 254-301.

20. Julian H. Franklin, "Introduction," Jean Bodin, *On Sovereignty: Four Chapters from the Six Books of the Commonwealth* (Cambridge: Cambridge University Press, 1992), p. xv.

21. Ibid., p. 2.

22. Ibid., p. 3.

23. Ibid., Book 1, chap. 10, p. 46.

24. Ibid., Book 1, chap. 10, pp. 50, 54.

25. Ibid., Book 1, chap. 10, p. 53.

26. Thomas Hobbes, *De Cive or the Citizen*, (New York: Appleton Century Crofts, 1949), Author's Introduction, p. 11.

27. Thomas Hobbes, *Leviathan* (Harmondsworth: Pelican Books, 1968), part 2, chap. 21, p. 264.

28. Carl J. Friedrich, Introduction to *Politica Methodice Digesta of Johannes Althusius (Althaus)* (Cambridge, Mass.: Harvard University Press, 1932), p. xci.

29. Maurice Cranston, introduction to Jean-Jacques Rousseau, *The Social Contract* (Harmondsworth: Penguin Books, 1968), p. 27.

30. S. I. Benn and Richard Peters, *Social Principles and the Democratic State* (London: George Allen and Unwin, 1959), p. 334.

31. Alexis de Tocqueville, *Democracy in America*, ed. J. P. Mayer, trans. George Lawrence (Garden City, N.Y.: Anchor Books, 1969), vol. 1, chap. 4, p. 59.

32. James Madison, *Federalist* 46, Clinton Rossiter, ed., Alexander Hamilton, John Jay, and James Madison, *The Federalist Papers* (New York: Mentor, 1961), p. 294. See the illuminating discussion of Madison's argument for a "compound republic" in Samuel F. Beer, *To Make a Nation: The Rediscovery of American Federalism* (Cambridge, Mass.: Harvard University Press, 1993), chap. 8, pp. 244-278.

33. Tocqueville, *Democracy in America*, vol. 1, chap. 4, p. 60.

34. Leo Gross, "The Peace of Westphalia: 1648-1948," in R. A. Falk and W. F. Hanrieder, eds., *International Law and Organization: An Introductory Reader* (Philadelphia: Lippincott, 1969), pp. 53-54, quoted in Gianfranco Poggi, *The Development of the Modern State* (Stanford: Stanford University Press, 1987), p. 89.

35. See ibid., p. 88.

36. Benn and Peters, *Social Principles*, p. 257.

37. Stanley I. Benn, "The Uses of 'Sovereignty,'" *Political Studies* 3, 2 (June 1955), pp. 109-122; reprinted in W. J. Stankiewicz, ed., *In Defense of Sovereignty* (New York: Oxford University Press, 1969), p. 85.

38. Benn and Peters, *Social Principles*, pp. 257-263.

39. F. H. Hinsley, *Sovereignty* (New York: Basic Books, 1966), p. 25.

40. Ibid., pp. 227-228.

41. A. P. D'Entrèves, *The Notion of the State: An Introduction to Political Theory* (Oxford: Oxford University Press, 1967), pp. 6, 92-93.

42. Ibid., p. 117.

43. Ibid., p. 131.

44. W. J. Stankiewicz, "In Defense of Sovereignty: A Critique and Interpretation," in Stankiewicz, *In Defense of Sovereignty*, pp. 3-38.

45. Robert O. Keohane, *After Hegemony: Cooperation and Discord in the World's Political Economy* (Princeton: Princeton University Press, 1984), p. 130.

46. Ernst Haas, *Beyond the Nation-State: Functionalism and International Organization* (Stanford: Stanford University Press, 1964).

47. Raymond Vernon, *Sovereignty at Bay: the Multinational Spread of U.S. Enterprises* (New York: Basic Books, 1971).

48. But see Joseph A. Camilleri and Jim Falk, *The End of Sovereignty?* (Aldershot: Edward Elgar Publishing Limited, 1992), p. 9, for the view that "the theory of sovereignty serves us poorly" already.

49. See the earlier discussion of *autonomia* in chapter three and in Martin Ostwald, *Autonomia: Its Genesis and Early History* (Chico, Ca.: Scholars Press, 1982) and Cynthia Farrar, *The Origins of Democratic Thinking: The Invention of Politics in Classical Athens* (Cambridge: Cambridge University Press, 1988), pp. 103-104.

50. Daniel J. Elazar, "Options, Problems and Possibilities in Light of the Current Situation," introduction to Daniel J. Elazar, ed., *Self Rule/Shared Rule*, p. 10.

Chapter 10

1. Samuel P. Huntington, *The Third Wave: Democratization in the Late Twentieth Century* (Norman: University of Oklahoma Press, 1991), pp. 16-26.

2. *Freedom in the World* (New York: Freedom House, 1994).

3. See the seminal essay by Seymour Martin Lipset, "Some Social Requisites of Democracy: Economic Development and Political Legitimacy," *American Political Science Review* 53, 1 (March 1959), pp. 69-105, incorporated into chap. 2 of his *Political Man: The Social Bases of Politics* (Garden City, N.Y.: Doubleday & Co., 1960)

4. See especially Larry Diamond, "Economic Development and Democracy Reconsidered," Gary Marks and Larry Diamond, eds., *Reexamining Democracy: Essays in Honor of Seymour Martin Lipset* (Newbury Park, Ca.: SAGE Publications, 1992), p. 127.

5. Philippe Schmitter, "An Introduction to Southern European Transitions from Authoritarian Rule: Italy, Greece, Portugal, Spain, and Turkey," Guillermo O'Donnell, Philippe Schmitter, and Laurence Whitehead, eds., *Transitions from Authoritarian Rule* (Baltimore: Johns Hopkins University Press, 1986), p. 6.

6. Yuri N. Afanasyev, "Russian Reform is Dead," *Foreign Affairs* 73, 2 (March/April 1994), p. 22.

7. Victor Perez-Diaz, *The Return of Civil Society* (Cambridge, Mass.: Harvard University Press, 1993), p. 55.

8. Ibid.

9. Ibid., p. 59.

10. See Frederick C. Engelmann, "How Austria Has Coped With Two Dictatorial Legacies," in John H. Herz, ed., *From Dictatorship to Democracy: Coping with the Legacies of Authoritarianism and Totalitarianism* (Westport, Conn.: Greenwood Press, 1982), pp. 135-160.

11. For the return to democracy in Italy see Giuseppe Di Palma, "Italy: Is There A Legacy and Is It Fascist?" *From Dictatorship to Democracy* pp. 107-134.

12. Harry J. Psomiades, "Greece from the Colonels' Rule to Democracy," *From Dictatorship to Democracy*, pp. 251-252.

13. Stephan Haggard and Richard Kaufman, "The Challenges of Consolidation," *Journal of Democracy* 5, 4 (October 1994), p. 7. See also their *The Political Economy of Democratic Transitions* (Princeton: Princeton University Press, 1995).

14. *New York Times*, Oct. 7, 1974.

15. See Martin Jacques, "The Godmother," *The New Republic* 4, 205-206 (September 20 and 27, 1993), pp. 23-28.

16. See Michael Hechter, *Internal Colonialism: the Celtic Fringe in British National Development, 1536-1966* (Berkeley: University of California Press, 1975).

17. See Philippe C. Schmitter, "An Introduction to Southern European Transitions from Authoritarian Rule: Italy, Greece, Portugal, Spain, and Turkey," Guillermo O'Donnell, Philippe C. Schmitter, and Laurence Whitehead, eds., *Transitions from Authoritarian Rule; Southern Europe* (Baltimore, Johns Hopkins University Press, 1986), p. 4.

18. See Timothy Garton Ash, *We The People: the Revolution of '89 Witnessed in Warsaw, Budapest, Berlin and Prague* (Cambridge: Granta Books, 1990), especially pp. 131-138.

19. See for this contention Vladimir Tismaneanu, *Reinventing Politics: Eastern Europe from Stalin to Havel* (New York: The Free Press, 1992) and the critical review of the thesis by Gale Stokes in *The New Leader* (June 29, 1992), pp. 18-19.

20. Gyorgy Szobsolai, "Parliamentarism in the Making: Crisis and Political Transformation in Hungary," prepared for the Conference on Institutional Design and Democratization, May 13-15, 1993, Center for Iberian and Latin American Studies, University of California, San Diego.

21. János Kis, "Postcommunist Politics in Hungary," *Journal of Democracy* 2, 3 (Summer 1991), p. 4.

22. Ibid., p. 171.

23. See Jeffrey C. Goldfarb, *Beyond Glasnost* (Chicago: University of Chicago Press, 1989).

24. "Post-Communist Politics in Hungary," p. 4.

25. See Kenneth Jowitt, *The New World Disorder: The Extinction of Leninism* (Berkeley: University of California Press, 1992).

26. Drawn from Stanislaw Gebethner, "Proportional Representation Versus Majoritarian Systems: Free Elections and Political Parties in Transitions to Democracy in Central and Eastern Europe," prepared for the Conference on Institutional Design and Democratization, May 13-15, Center for Iberian and Latin American Studies, University of California, San Diego.

27. For an analysis of the 1993 Russian constitution and other developments in the Confederation of Independent States see Philip G. Roeder, "Varieties of Post-Soviet Authoritarian Regimes," *Post-Soviet Affairs* (forthcoming).

28. Flemming Christiansen, "Democratization in China: Structural Constraints," Geraint Parry and Michael Moran, eds., *Democracy and Democratization* (London: Routledge, 1994), chap. 7, p. 153.

29. Nicholas D. Kristof, "China Sees 'Market-Leninism' as Way to Future," *New York Times*, Sept. 6, 1993, pp. A1, A5.

30. Guillermo O'Donnell, "Corporatism and the Question of the State," James Malloy, ed., *Authoritarianism and Corporatism in Latin America* (Pittsburgh: University of Pittsburgh Press, 1977), pp. 47-87.

31. Robert A. Dahl, *Polyarchy: Participation and Opposition* (New Haven: Yale University Press, 1971), pp. 78-79.

32. Lloyd I. Rudolph and Susanne Hoeber Rudolph, *In Pursuit of Lakshmi: The Political Economy of the Indian State* (Chicago: The University of Chicago Press, 1987), p. 46.

33. Edward A. Gargan, "The Once and Future Powder Keg: South Asia," *New York Times*, May 23, 1993, p. E3.

34. Ellis S. Krauss and Takeshi Ishida, "Japanese Democracy in Perspective," in Takeshi Ishida and Ellis S. Krauss, eds., *Democracy in Japan* (Pittsburgh: University of Pittsburgh Press, 1989), pp. 328-329.

35. See especially Chalmers Johnson, *MITI and the Japanese Miracle* (Stanford: Stanford University Press, 1982) and Karel van Wolferen, *The Enigma of Japanese Power: People and Politics in a Stateless Nation* (New York: Knopf, 1989).

36. T. J. Pempel, "Introduction," in Pempel, ed., *Uncommon Democracies* (Ithaca: Cornell University Press, 1990), pp. 2-3.

37. Ibid., p. 27.

38. Hideo Otake, "Defense Controversies and One-Party Dominance: The Opposition in Japan and West Germany, *Uncommon Democracies*, p. 129.

39. See Ellis S. Krauss and Jon Pierre, "The Decline of Dominant Parties: Parliamentary Politics in Sweden and Japan in the 1970s, *Uncommon Democracies*, pp. 226-259.

40. Huntington, *The Third Wave*, p. 25.

41. Daniel C. Levy, "Mexico: Sustained Civilian Rule Without Democracy," Larry Diamond, Juan J. Linz, and Seymour Martin Lipset, eds., *Democracy in Developing Countries*, vol. 4, *Latin America* (Boulder:Lynn Rienner, chap. 11, p. 459.

42. Daniel H. Levine, "Venezuela: The Nature, Sources, and Prospects of Democracy," *Democracy in Developing Countries*, vol. 4, *Latin America*, chap. 6, p. 247.

43. Ibid., p. 276.

44. See Jonathan Hartlyn, "Colombia: The Politics of Violence and Accommodation," *Democracy in Developing Countries*, vol. 4, *Latin America*, chap. 7, pp. 291-334.

45. See Cynthia McClintock, "Peru: Precarious Regimes, Authoritarian and Democratic," *Democracy in Developing Countries*, vol. 4, *Latin America*, chap. 8, pp. 335-385.

46. See Charles Guy Gillespie and Luis Eduardo Gonzalez, "Uruguay: the Survival of Old and Autonomous Institutions," *Democracy in Developing Countries*, vol. 4, *Latin America*, chap. 5, pp. 207-245.

47. See the exhortation to Brazilians, particularly those on the left, to devote themselves to political rather than revolutionary activity by a leader of the democratic opposition, in Francisco Weffort, "Why Democracy?," Alfred Stepan, ed., *Democratizing Brazil* (New York: Oxford University Press, 1989), pp. 327-349.

48. See Carlos H. Waisman, "Argentina: Autarkic Industrialization and Illegitimacy," *Democracy in Developing Countries*, vol. 4, *Latin America*, chap. 2, pp. 59-109.

49. See the especially valuable historical and analytical account in Arturo Valenzuela, "Chile: Origins, Consolidation, and Breakdown of a Democratic Regime," *Democracy in Developing Countries*, vol. 4, *Latin America*, chap. 4, pp. 159-206, which draws on his *The Breakdown of Democratic Regimes* (Baltimore: Johns Hopkins University Press, 1978).

50. Abraham F. Lowenthal, "The United States and Latin American Democracy: Learning from History," Abraham F. Lowenthal, ed., *Exporting Democracy: the United States and Latin America* (Baltimore: the Johns Hopkins University Press, 1991), p. 383.

51. Ibid., pp. 401-402.

52. John Darnton, "Africa Tries Democracy, Finding Hope and Peril," *New York Times*, June 21, 1994, pp. A1, A6-7.

53. John Darnton, "In Decolonized, Destitute Africa Bankers Are the New Overlords," *New York Times*, June 20, 1994, pp. A1, A6-7.

54. E. S. Atieno Odhiambo, "Democracy and the Ideology of Power in Kenya: 1968-1986," in Walter O. Oyugi, E.S. Atieno Odhiambo, Michael Chege, and Afrika K. Gityonga, eds., *Democratic Theory & Practice in Africa* (Portsmouth, N.H.: Heinemann Educational Books, 1988), p. 130.

55. See John D. Holm, "Botswana: A Paternalistic Democracy," Larry Diamond, Juan J. Linz, and Seymour Martin Lipset, eds., *Democracy in Developing Countries*, vol. 2, *Africa* (Boulder: Lynne Rienner, 1988), chap. 5, pp. 179-215.

56. Franz Ansprenger, "External Relations of the African Democratic Experience," *Democratic Theory*, p. 161.

57. Peter Wanyande, "Democracy and the One-Party State: the African Experience," *Democratic Theory*, p. 77.

58. Larry Diamond, "Nigeria: Pluralism, Statism, and the Struggle for Democracy," *Democracy in Developing Countries*, vol. 4, *Africa*, chap. 2, p. 33.

59. See Arend Lijphart, *Power-Sharing in South Africa* (Berkeley: Institute of International Studies, University of California, Berkeley, Policy Papers in International Affairs, no. 24, 1985).

60. Donald L. Horowitz, *A Democratic South Africa?* (Berkeley: University of California Press, 1991), pp. 240-241.

61. Anne Elizabeth Mayer, *Islam and Human Rights: Tradition and Politics* (Boulder: Westview Press, 1991), pp. 34-35.

62. Bernard Lewis, "Communism in Islam," Walter Laqueur, ed., *The Middle East in Transition* (London: Routledge, Kegan Paul, 1958), pp. 318-319.

63. David Pryce-Jones, *The Closed Circle: An Interpretation of the Arabs* (New York: Harper & Row, 1989), p. 17.

64. Bernard Lewis, *The Political Language of Islam* (Chicago: The University of Chicago Press, 1988), p. 4.

65. According to a report by Christopher Walker in *The Times* (London), May 24, 1991, p. 9.

66. Elie Kedourie, *Democracy and Arab Political Culture* (Washington: The Washington Institute for Near East Policy, 1992), p. 1.

67. Ibid., p. 6.

68. Quoted ibid., p. 8

69. Ibid., pp. 8-10.

70. Ibid., pp. 15-16.

71. Ibid., pp. 18-19.

72. Ibid., p. 31.

73. Ibid., p. 45.

74. Ibid., pp. 47-61.

75. Mayer, *Islam and Human Rights*, pp. 9-10.

76. Ibid., pp. 32-33.

77. The figure of fifty-one countries with 37 per cent of the population is given in Raymond D. Gastil, *Freedom in the World: Political Rights and Civil Liberties 1980* (New

York: Freedom House, 1980), pp. 5, 15-24. The stricter estimate of thirty is given in Arend Lijphart, *Democracies: Patterns of Majoritarian and Consensus Government in Twenty-One Countries* (New Haven: Yale University Press, 1985), pp. 38-39.

Chapter 11

1. José María Maravall, "The Myth of the Authoritarian Advantage," *Journal of Democracy* 5, 4 (October 1994), pp. 28-29.

2. Quoted by Maurice Duverger, in *Modern Democracies: Economic Power versus Political Power* (New York: Holt, Rinehart & Winston, 1974), p. 101.

3. See the cases reviewed in Aaron Wildavsky, *But Is It True? A Citizen's Guide to Environmental Health and Safety Issues* (Cambridge, Mass.: Harvard University Press, 1995).

4. See Alexis de Tocqueville, *Democracy in America*, ed. J. P. Mayer, trans. George Lawrence (Garden City: Anchor Books, 1969), vol. 2, chap. 8, pp. 525-528.

5. See Robert Hughes, *The Culture of Complaint: the Fraying of America* (New York: Oxford University Press, 1993).

6. Robert Putnam has pointed out that insofar as association is critical to the vitality of democracy (as Tocqueville suggested), there is reason to be concerned about the decline in associational activity in the U.S. in recent years. He cites evidence not only from bowling leagues but virtually across the board, in trade unions, fraternal and veterans' organizations, church attendance, school-service groups, and political organizations. See his "Bowling Alone," *Journal of Democracy* (January 1995), pp. 65-78.

7. See Robert A. Dahl, *A Preface to Democratic Theory* (Chicago: Phoenix Books, 1985), p. 60. See also David Held, *Models of Democracy* (Oxford: Basil Blackwell, 1987), pp. 202-203.

8. See Robert A. Dahl and Edward R. Tufte, *Size and Democracy* (Stanford: Stanford University Press, 1973).

Chapter 12

1. "Eternal Peace" [1795], Carl J. Friedrich, ed. and trans. *The Philosophy of Kant* (New York: Modern Library, 1949), p. 444.

2. In *The Social Contract* and the *Émile*, Rousseau defines democracy as direct popular self-government and dismisses it as an impractical form of government. He makes the state the expression of the sovereign people and considers small-scale republican (but not representative) government most likely to preserve liberty.

3. See the references in chap. 1, note 25.

4. Thomas Hobbes, *Leviathan*, ed. C.B. Macpherson (Harmondsworth: Penguin Books, 1968), part 1, chap. 13, 62, p. 186.

5. Ibid., part 1, chap. 13, 60, p. 184.

6. Ibid., part 1, chap. 13, 63, pp. 187-188.

7. Richard Rosecrance, *The Rise of the Trading State: Commerce and Conquest in the Modern World* (New York: Basic Books, 1984), p. 8.

8. Ibid., p. 19

9. William J. Dixon, "Democracy and the Peaceful Settlement of International Conflict," *American Political Science Review* 88, 1 (March 1994) p. 14.

10. Ibid., p. 30.
11. Immanuel Kant, "Eternal Peace," pp. 454-455.

Chapter 13

1. *Democratic Vistas* [1871] (New York: Liberal Arts Press, 1949), p. 15.

2. Francis Crick, *What Mad Pursuit? A Personal View of Scientific Discovery* (New York: Basic Books, 1988), p. 137.

3. Marshall D. Sahlins and Elman R. Service, eds., *Evolution and Culture* (Ann Arbor: University of Michigan Press, 1960), P. 75.

4. C. R. Hallpike, *The Principles of Social Evolution* (Oxford: Oxford University Press, 1986), p. 372.

5. It can lead too easily to the rationalization of collectivistic forms of repression no less objectionable than the Spencerian rationalization of ruthless capitalism as an evolutionary necessity. Thus the explanation given for "forced-draft" strategy of industrialization adopted by Soviet and Chinese Communist leaders is that "because of lack of capital they are forced to terrorize their own people." Sahlins, *Evolution and Culture*, p. 119. Other developing countries have adopted different strategies, sometimes more successfully.

6. Ibid., p. 4. For a very suggestive analysis of how social evolution may have taken place in the distant past, extrapolating backwards from modern anthropological study, see Eli Sagan, *At the Dawn of History* (New York: Knopf, 1985).

7. One of the first uses of the term is Thomas Landon Thorson, *Biopolitics* (New York: Holt, Rinehart & Winston, 1970).

8. See Patricia Smith Churchland, *Neurophilosophy: Toward a Unified Science of the Mind/Brain* (Cambridge, Mass.: MIT Press, 1986)

9. Ibid., p. 481.

10. E. O. Wilson, *On Human Nature* (Cambridge, Mass.: Harvard University Press, 1978) and *Sociobiology: the New Synthesis* (Cambridge, Mass.: Harvard University Press, 1975).

11. "The Eastern nations knew only that *one* is free; the Greek and Roman world only that *some* are free; whilst *we* know that all men absolutely (man *as man*) are free . . ." G.W.F. Hegel, "Introduction to the Philosophy of History," J. Lowenberg, ed., trans. J. Sibree, *Hegel Selections* (New York: Scribner's, 1929), p. 362.

12. G. Bingham Powell, Jr., *Contemporary Democracy: Participation, Stability, and Violence* (Cambridge, Mass.: Harvard University Press, 1982), p. 226.

13. Paul N. Sniderman, *Personality and Democratic Politics* (Berkeley: University of California Press, 1975), p. 48.

14. Ibid., p. 305.

15. See James S. Fishkin, *Democracy and Deliberation: New Directions for Democratic Reform* (New Haven: Yale University Press, 1991).

Select Bibliography

Abbott, Frank Frost. *A History and Description of Roman Political Institutions.* New York: Biblo and Tannen, 1963.

Adcock, F. E. *Roman Political Ideas and Practice.* Ann Arbor: University of Michigan Press, 1959.

Almond, Gabriel, and Sidney Verba. *The Civic Culture.* Princeton: Princeton University Press, 1963.

Amy, Douglas J. *Real Choices/New Voices.* New York: Columbia University Press, 1993.

Appleby, Joyce. *Capitalism and a New Social Order: the Republican Vision of the 1760s.* New York: New York University Press, 1984.

Arendt, Hannah. *The Origins of Totalitarianism.* New York: Harcourt Brace, 1951.

Aron, Raymond. *Democracy and Totalitarianism.* Trans. Valence Ionescu. London: Weidenfeld and Nicolson, 1968.

Arrow, Kenneth. *Social Choice and Individual Values.* New York: Wiley, 1963.

Ashcraft, Richard. *Revolutionary Politics & Locke's Two Treatises of Government.* Princeton: Princeton University Press, 1986.

Bachrach, Peter. *The Theory of Democratic Elitism: A Critique.* Boston: Little, Brown, 1967.

Bailyn, Bernard. *The Ideological Origins of the American Revolution.* Cambridge, Mass.: Harvard University Press, 1967.

Barber, Benjamin. *Strong Democracy: Participatory Politics for a New Age.* Berkeley: University of California Press, 1984.

_____ . *The Conquest of Politics: Liberal Philosophy in Democratic Times.* Oxford: Oxford University Press, 1978.

Barry, Brian. "Is Democracy Special?" Peter Laslett and James Fishkin, eds., *Philosophy, Politics and Society.* Fifth series. Oxford: Basil Blackwell, 1979, pp. 155-196.

_____ . *Sociologists, Economists, and Democracy.* London: Collier/Macmillan, 1970.

Barzun, Jacques. *Race, A Study in Modern Superstition.* New York: Harper, 1937.

Beer, Samuel F. *To Make a Nation: The Rediscovery of American Federalism.* Cambridge, Mass.: Harvard University Press, 1993.

Benn, S. I. *A Theory of Freedom.* Cambridge: Cambridge University Press, 1988.

_____ and R. S. Peters. *Social Principles and the Democratic State.* London: George Allen and Unwin, 1959.

Benoit, Francis Paul. *La democratie liberale.* Presses universitaires de France, 1978.

Berlin, Isaiah. *Four Essays on Liberty.* Oxford: Oxford University Press, 1969.

Bhagwati, Jagdish. "Democracy and Development." *Journal of Democracy* 3,3 (July 1992), pp. 37-44.

Biddiss, Michael D. *Father of Racist Ideology: The Social and Political Thought of Count Gobineau.* New York: Weybright and Talley, 1970.

Birnbaum, Pierre, Jack Lively and Geraint Parry, eds. *Democracy, Consensus and Social Contract*. Beverly Hills: Sage, 1978.

Boardman, John, Jasper Griffin, and Oswyn Murray, eds. *The Oxford History of the Classical World*. Oxford: Oxford University Press, 1986.

Bobbio, Norberto. *Democracy and Dictatorship*. Trans. Peter Kennealy. Minneapolis: University of Minnesota Press, 1989.

Boeker, Paul H. ed. *Lost Illusions: Latin America's Struggle for Democracy, as Recounted by its Leaders*. New York: M. Wieners, 1990.

Bogner, Hans. *Die verwirklichte Demokratie Idee; Lehren der Antike*. Hamburg: Hanseatische Verlagsanstalt, 1930.

Botsford, George Willis. *The Roman Assemblies*. New York: Macmillan, 1909.

Bouwsma, William J. *Venice and the Defense of Republican Liberty*. Berkeley: University of California Press, 1968.

Bowles, Samuel and Gintis, Herbert. *Democracy and Capitalism: Property, Community, and the Contradictions of Modern Social Thought*. New York: Basic Books, 1986.

Brennan, Geoffrey and Loren E. Lomasky, eds. *Politics and Process: New Essays in Democratic Thought*. Cambridge: Cambridge University Press, 1989.

Brunt, P.A. *Social Conflicts in the Roman Republic*. London: The Hogarth Press, 1986.

Bryan, Frank, and John McClaughry. *The Vermont Papers; Recreating Democracy on a Human Scale*. Post Mills, Vt.: Chelsea Green Publishing Co., 1989.

Buchanan, James M. and Gordon Tullock. *The Calculus of Consent*. Ann Arbor: University of Michigan, 1962.

Butler, David. "The Plant Report 1993: The Third Report of Labour's Working Party on Electoral Systems." *Representation* 31, 116 (Autumn 1993), pp. 77-9.

California Commission on Campaign Financing. *Democracy By Initiative: Shaping California's Fourth Branch of Government*. Los Angeles: Center for Responsive Government, 1992.

Camilleri, Joseph A. and Jim Falk. *The End of Sovereignty?* Aldershot: Edward Elgar Publishing Limited, 1992.

Cassirer, Ernst. *Kant's Life and Thought*. Trans. James Haden. New Haven: Yale University Press, 1981.

Chamberlain, Houston Stewart. *The Foundations of the Nineteenth Century*. Trans. John Lees. New York: Howard Fertig, 1968.

Christophersen, Jens A. *The Meaning of Democracy as Used in European Ideologies*. Oslo: Universitets forlaget, 1966.

Cnudde, Charles F. and Deane E. Neubauer, eds. *Empirical Democratic Theory*. Chicago: Markham, 1969.

Cohen, Carl. *Democracy*. Athens, Georgia: The University of Georgia Press, 1971.

Connolly, William E. *The Terms of Political Discourse*. Lexington, Mass.: D.C. Heath, 1974.

Constant, Benjamin. *Political Writings*. Ed. Biancamaria Fontana. Cambridge: Cambridge University Press, 1988.

Cranston, Maurice. *What Are Human Rights?* New York: Basic Books, 1962.

_____ . "The Ambiguity of Nationalism." *The Great Ideas Today*. Chicago: Encyclopedia Britannica, 1993.

Crawford, Michael. *The Roman Republic*. Glasgow: Fontana/Collins, 1978.

Cronin, Thomas E. *Direct Democracy: the Politics of Initiative, Referendum, and Recall*. Cambridge, Mass.: Harvard University Press, 1989.

Crozier, Michel, Samuel P. Huntington, and Joji Watanuki. *The Crisis of Democracy: Report on the Governability of Democracies to the Trilateral Commission*. New York: New York University Press, 1975.

D'Entrèves, A.P. *The Notion of the State: An Introduction to Political Theory*. Oxford: Oxford University Press, 1967.

Dahl, Robert A. *A Preface to Democratic Theory*. Chicago: University of Chicago Press, 1956.

_____ . *Democracy and its Critics*. New Haven: Yale University Press, 1989.

_____ . *Polyarchy: Participation and Opposition*. New Haven: Yale University Press, 1971.

_____ . "Why Free Markets Are Not Enough." *Journal of Democracy* 3, 3 July 1992), pp. 82-89.

_____ and E.R. Tufte. *Size and Democracy*. Stanford: Stanford University Press, 1973.

Davis, David Brion. *The Problem of Slavery in the Age of Revolution*. Ithaca, N.Y.: Cornell University Press, 1975.

Diamond, Larry, and Marc F. Plattner, eds. *The Global Resurgence of Democracy*. Baltimore: Johns Hopkins University Press, 1993.

Diamond, Larry, Juan Linz, and Seymour Martin Lipset, eds. *Democracy in Developing Countries*. Boulder: Lynne Rienner, 1989, vols. 2 (Africa), 3 (Asia), 4 (Latin America).

Di Nunzio, Mario R. *American Democracy and the Authoritarian Tradition of the West*. Lanham, Md.: University Press of America, 1987.

Di Palma, Giuseppe. *To Craft Democracies: An Essay on Democratic Transitions*. Berkeley: University of California Press, 1990.

Dixon, William J. "Democracy and the Peaceful Settlement of International Conflict." *American Political Science Review* 88, 1 (March 1994), pp. 14-32.

Dogan, Mattei, ed. *Comparing Pluralist Democracies; Strains on Legitimacy*. Boulder: Westview, 1988.

Downs, Anthony. *An Economic Theory of Democracy*. New York: Harper, 1957.

Doyle, Michael W. "Liberalism and World Politics." *American Political Science Review* 80, 4 (December 1986), pp. 1151-1169.

Drake, Paul, and Silva, Eduardo, eds. *Elections and Democratization in Latin America, 1980-85*. San Diego: Center for Iberian and Latin American Studies, University of California, San Diego, 1986.

Duchacek, Ivo D. *The Territorial Dimension of Politics Within, Among, and Across Nations*. Boulder: Westview Press, 1986.

Dunn, John, ed. *Democracy: The Unfinished Journey 500 BC to AD 1993*. Oxford: Oxford University Press, 1992.

Duverger, Maurice. *Modern Democracies: Economic Power vs. Political Power*, trans. Charles L. Markmann. New York: Holt, Rinehart & Winston, 1974.

Elazar, Daniel. *Exploring Federalism*. Tuscaloosa: The University of Alabama Press, 1987

Elshtain, Jean Bethke. *Democracy on Trial*. New York: Basic Books, 1995.

Euben, J. Peter. *The Tragedy of Political Theory: the Road Not Taken*. Princeton: Princeton University Press, 1990.

Everdell, William R. *The End of Kings: A History of Republics and Republicans*. New York: Free Press, 1983.

Farrar, Cynthia. *The Origins of Democratic Thinking: the Invention of Politics in Classical Athens*. Cambridge: Cambridge University Press, 1988.

Field, Geoffrey G. *Evangelist of Race: The Germanic Vision of Houston Stewart Chamberlain*. New York: Columbia University Press, 1988.

Finley, M. I. *Democracy Ancient and Modern*. New Brunswick: Rutgers University Press, 1973.

————. *The Ancient Greeks: An Introduction to Their Life and Thought*. New York: Viking Press, 1963.

Fishkin, James. *Democracy and Deliberation: New Directions for Democratic Reform*. New Haven: Yale University Press, 1991.

Flathman, Richard. *Towards a Liberalism*. Ithaca: Cornell University Press, 1989.

Forrest, W. G. *The Emergence of Greek Democracy 800-400 BC*. New York, McGraw Hill, 1966.

Forster, E. M. *What I Believe*. London: Edward Arnold, 1951.

Forsyth, Murray, ed. *Federalism and Nationalism*. Leicester: Leicester University Press, 1989.

Friedrich, Carl J. and Zbigniew Brzezinski. *Totalitarian Dictatorship and Autocracy*. Revised edition. New York: Praeger, 1961.

Fukuyama, Francis. "Capitalism and Democracy: the Missing Link." *Journal of Democracy* 3,3 (July 1992), pp. 100-110.

————. *The End of History and the Last Man*. New York: Free Press, 1992.

Furet, François, *Interpreting the French Revolution*. Trans. Elborg Forster. Cambridge: Cambridge University Press, 1981.

Fustel de Coulanges, Numa Denis, *The Ancient City*, trans. Willard Small. Garden City, N.Y.: Anchor Books, n.d.

Galasso, Giuseppe, *Italia democratica: dai Giacobini al Partito d'azione*. Florence: F. Le Monnier, 1986.

Gallie, Bernard. "Essentially Contested Concepts." *Proceedings of the Aristotelian Society* 56 (1955), pp. 167-198.

Galston, William A. *Kant and the Problem of History*. Chicago: University of Chicago Press, 1965.

————. *Liberal Purposes: Goods, Virtues, and Diversity in the Liberal State*. New York: Columbia University Press, 1989.

Gastil, Raymond, *Freedom in the World*. New York: Freedom House, 1994.

Germani, Gino. *Authoritarianism, Fascism, and National Populism*. New Brunswick: Transaction Books, 1978.

Gobineau, Arthur Comte de. *Essai sur l'Inégalité des Races Humaines*. Paris: Firmin-Didot, 1940.

Goldfarb, Jeffrey C. *Beyond Glasnost*. Chicago: University of Chicago Press, 1989.

Gooch, G.P. *English Democratic Ideas in the Seventeenth Century*. New York: Harper, 1959.

Goodman, David. *Beijing Street Voices: The Poetry and Politics of China's Democracy Movement*. London: K. Boyars, 1981.

Graubard, Stephen R. "Democracy." Philip P. Wiener, ed., *Dictionary of the History of Ideas*. New York: Scribner's, 1968, vol. 1, pp. 652-667.

Greene, Jack P., ed. *The Reinterpretation of the American Revolution*. New York: Harper and Row, 1968.

Gregor, A. James. *The Ideology of Fascism: The Rationale of Totalitarianism*. New York: Free Press, 1969.

Grunberger, Richard. *The 12-Year Reich: A Social History of Nazi Germany 1933-1945*. New York: Holt, Rinehart & Winston, 1971.

Guicciardini, Francesco. *Maxims and Reflections of a Renaissance Statesman.*Trans. Mario Domani. New York: Harper & Row, 1965.

Guinier, Lani. *The Tyranny of the Majority: Fundamental Fairness in Representative Democracy*. New York: Martin Kessler Books/The Free Press, 1994.

Haas, Ernst. *Beyond the Nation-State: Functionalism and International Organization*. Stanford: Stanford University Press, 1964.

Habermas, Jürgen. *The Philosophical Discourse of Modernity*. Trans. Frederick Lawrence. Cambridge, Mass.: MIT Press, 1987.

Haggard, Stephan, and Robert R. Kaufman. *The Political Economy of Democratic Transitions*. Princeton: Princeton University Press, 1995.

Hallowell, J.H. *The Moral Foundations of Democracy*. Chicago: University of Chicago Press, 1954.

Hamilton, Alexander, John Jay, and James Madison. *The Federalist Papers*. Ed. Clinton Rossiter. New York: Mentor, 1961.

Hansen, Mogens Herman. *The Athenian Democracy in the Age of Demosthenes: Structure, Principles, and Ideology*. Trans. J.A. Crook. Oxford: Blackwell, 1991.

Hare, R.M. "Could Kant Have Been A Utilitarian?" *Utilitas* 5, 1 (May 1993), pp. 1-16.

Hartz, Louis. *The Liberal Tradition in America*. New York: Harcourt Brace, 1955.

Hayek, Friedrich. *The Constitution of Liberty*. Chicago: University of Chicago Press, 1960.

Held, David. *Models of Democracy*. Oxford: Basil Blackwell, 1987.

Hermens, Ferdinand A. *Democracy and Anarchy: A Study of Proportional Representation*. New York: Johnson Reprint Co., 1972).

Hermet, Guy. *Aux Frontiéres de la Democratie*. Paris: Presses Universitaires de France, 1983.

Herz, John, ed. *From Dictatorship to Democracy: Coping with the Legacies of Authoritarianism and Totalitarianism*. Westport, Conn.: Greenwood Press, 1982.

Higgonet, Patrice. *Sister Republics*. Cambridge, Mass.: Harvard University Press, 1988.

Hinsley, F.H. *Sovereignty*. New York: Basic Books, 1966.

Hofstader, Richard. *Social Darwinism in American Thought*. Boston: The Beacon Press, 1955.

Holden, Barry. *The Nature of Democracy*. New York: Barnes and Noble, 1974.

Homo, Léon. *Roman Political Institutions: From City to State* London: Routledge, Kegan Paul, 1929.

Horowitz, Donald L. *A Democratic South Africa? Constitutional Engineering in a Divided Society*. Berkeley: University of California Press, 1989.

Houston, Alan Craig. *Algernon Sidney and the Republican Heritage in England and America*. Princeton: Princeton University Press, 1991.

Huntington, Samuel P. *The Third Wave: Democratization in the Late Twentieth Century*. Norman: University of Oklahoma Press, 1991.

Isnardi Parente, Margherita. *Sofistica e democrazia antica*. Florence: Sansoni, 1977.

Jones, A. H. M. *Athenian Democracy*. Oxford: Blackwell, 1957.

Journal of Democracy. Vol I (1990) - .

Jowitt, Kenneth. *The New World Disorder: the Extinction of Leninism*. Berkeley: University of California Press, 1992.

Kagan, Donald. *Pericles and the Birth of Democracy.* New York: The Free Press, 1991.

Kant, Immanuel. *Foundations of the Metaphysics of Morals.* Trans. Lewis White Beck. Indianapolis: Bobbs Merrill, 1969

Kariel, Henry S., ed. *Frontiers of Democratic Theory.* New York: Random House, 1970.

Kaufmann, Walter. *Nietzsche: Philosopher, Psychologist, Antichrist.* New York: Meridian Books, 1956.

Kedourie, Elie. *Democracy and Arab Political Culture.* Washington: The Washington Institute for Near East Policy, 1992.

Keohane, Robert O. *After Hegemony: Cooperation and Discord in the World's Political Economy.* Princeton: Princeton University Press, 1984.

Kirkpatrick, Jeane. *Dictatorships and Double Standards: Rationalism and Reason in Politics.* New York: Simon and Schuster, 1982.

Kitto, H.D.F. *The Greeks.* Harmondsworth: Penguin Books, 1951.

Kloppenberg, James T. *Uncertain Victory: Social Democracy and Progressivism in European and American Thought, 1870-1920.* New York: Oxford University Press, 1986.

Krauss, Ellis S., and Takeshi Ishida, eds. *Democracy in Japan.* Pittsburgh: University of Pittsburgh Press, 1989.

Kristol, Irving. *On the Democratic Idea in America.* New York: Harper & Row, 1972.

Kymlicka, Will. *Liberalism, Community, and Culture.* Oxford: Oxford University Press, 1990.

Lake, David. "Powerful Pacifists: Democratic States and War." *American Political Science Review* 86, 1 (March 1992), pp. 24-37.

Lakoff, Sanford. "Autonomy and Liberal Democracy." *Review of Politics,* 52, 3 (Summer 1990), pp. 378-96.

_____. "Between Either/Or and More or Less: Sovereignty vs. Autonomy Under Federalism." *Publius, The Journal of Federalism,* 24, 1 (Winter 1994) pp. 63-78.

_____. "Christianity and Equality." *Equality/Nomos IX,* ed. Roland Pennock and John Chapman. New York: Atherton Press, 1967, pp. 115-133.

_____. *Equality in Political Philosophy.* Cambridge, Mass.: Harvard University Press, 1964.

_____. "Knowledge, Power and Democratic Theory." *The Annals of the American Academy of Political and Social Sciences,* 394 (March 1971), pp. 5-12.

_____. "Liberty, Equality, Democracy: Tocqueville's Answer to Rousseau." George Feaver and Frederick Rosen, eds., *Lives, Liberties and the Public Good: New Essays in Political Theory for Maurice Cranston.* London: Macmillan, 1987.

Laqueur, Walter, ed. *The Middle East in Transition.* London: Routledge, Kegan Paul, 1958.

Laslett, Peter, and James Fishkin, eds. *Philosophy, Politics, and Society.* Fifth Series. Oxford: Basil Blackwell, 1979.

Lauvaux, Philippe. *Les grands democraties contemporaine.* Paris: Presses Universitaires de France, 1990.

Le Bon, Gustave. *The Crowd: A Study of the Popular Mind.* London: T. Fisher Unwin, 1920.

Levin, Michael. *The Spectre of Democracy.* New York: New York University Press, 1992.

Lewis, Bernard. *The Political Language of Islam.* Chicago: University of Chicago Press, 1988.

Lijphart, Arend, *Democracies: Patterns of Majoritarian and Consensus Government in Twenty-One Countries*. New Haven: Yale University Press, 1984.

————. *Electoral Systems and Party Systems, A Study of Twenty-Seven Democracies, 1945-1990*. New York: Oxford University Press, 1994.

————. *Power Sharing in South Africa*. Berkeley: Institute of International Studies, University of California, 1985.

Lindblom, Charles. *Politics and Markets*. New York: Basic Books, 1977.

Lindsay, A. D. *The Modern Democratic State*. New York: Oxford University Press, 1962.

Linz, Juan and Arturo Valenzuela, eds. *The Failure of Presidential Democracy: Comparative Perspectives*. Baltimore: Johns Hopkins University Press, 1994.

Lippincott, Benjamin Evans. *Victorian Critics of Democracy*. New York: Octagon Books, 1964.

Lippmann, Walter. *The Phantom Public*. New York: Harcourt Brace, 1925.

Lipset, Seymour M. *The First New Nation: The United States in Historical and Comparative Perspective*. Garden City, N.Y.: Doubleday, 1967.

————. *Political Man: Where, How, and Why Democracy Works in the Modern World*. Garden City, N.Y.: Doubleday & Co., 1960.

————. and Stein Rokkan, eds. *Party Systems and Voter Alignments: Cross National Perspectives*. New York: The Free Press, 1967.

————. et al., eds. *The Encyclopedia of Democracy*. Four volumes. Washington: Congressional Quarterly Press, 1996.

Lively, Jack, *Democracy*. Oxford: Basil Blackwell, 1975.

Lowenthal, Abraham F., ed. *Exporting Democracy: The United States and Latin America* Baltimore: Johns Hopkins University Press, 1993.

Lyttelton, Adrian, ed. *Italian Fascisms: From Pareto to Gentile*. Trans. Douglas Parmée. New York: Harper Torchbook, 1973.

Macedo, Stephen. *Liberal Virtues: Citizenship, Virtue, and Community in Liberal Constitutionalism*. Oxford: Oxford University Press, 1990.

Mackie, Thomas T. and Richard Rose. *The International Almanac of Electoral History*. New York: The Free Press, 1974.

Macpherson, C. Brough. *Democratic Theory: Essays in Retrieval*

————. *The Political Theory of Possessive Individualism*. Oxford: Clarendon Press, 1962.

————. *The Real World of Democracy*. Toronto: Canadian Broadcasting Corporation, 1965.

Malloy, James M., ed. *Authoritarianism and Corporatism in Latin America*. Pittsburgh: University of Pittsburgh Press, 1977.

————. and Mitchell A. Seligson, eds., *Authoritarians and Democrats: Regime Transition in Latin America*. Pittsburgh: University of Pittsburgh Press, 1987.

Mansbridge, Jane J., ed. *Beyond Self-Interest*. Chicago: University of Chicago Press, 1990.

Mansfield, Harvey. *The Spirit of Liberalism*. Cambridge, Mass.: Harvard University Press, 1978.

Manuel, Frank E. *A Requiem for Karl Marx*. Cambridge, Mass.: Harvard University Press, 1995.

Manville, Philip Brook. *The Origins of Citizenship in Ancient Athens* Princeton: Princeton University Press, 1990.

Maoz, Zeev and Bruce Russett. "Normative and Structural Causes of Democratic Peace, 1946-1986." *American Political Science Review* 87, 3 (September 1993) pp. 624-639.

_____ and Nasrin Abdolali. "Regime Types and International Conflict, 1816-1976." *The Journal of Conflict Resolution* 33, 1 March 1989, pp. 3-36.

Maravall, José Maria. "The Myth of the Authoritarian Advantage." *Journal of Democracy* 3, 4 (October 1994), pp. xx.

Marks, Gary and Larry Diamond, eds. *Reexamining Democracy: Essays in Honor of Seymour Martin Lipset.* Newbury Park, Ca.: Sage Publications, 1992.

Mayer, Anne Elizabeth. *Islam and Human Rights: Tradition and Politics.* Boulder: Westview Press, 1991.

Mayo, H.B. *An Introduction to Democratic Theory.* New York: Oxford University Press, 1960.

McClosky, Herbert and John Zaller. *The American Ethos: Public Attitudes toward Capitalism and Democracy.* Cambridge, Mass.: Harvard University Press, 1984.

McConnell, Grant. *Private Power and American Democracy.* New York: Knopf, 1966.

McCormack, Gavan, and Yoshio Sugimoto. *Democracy in Contemporary Japan.* Armonk, N.Y.: M.E. Sharpe, 1986.

Meisel, James H. *The Myth of the Ruling Class: Gaetano Mosca and the "Elite."* Ann Arbor: The University of Michigan Press, 1962.

Mencken, H.L. *Notes on Democracy.* New York: Knopf, 1926.

Mill, John Stuart. *Considerations on Representative Government.* Chicago: Henry Regnery, 1962.

Millon-Delsol, Chantal. *Essai sur le pouvoir occidental: democratie et despotisme dans l'antiquité.* Paris: Presses Universitaires de France, 1985.

Milone, Jorge E. *La democracia en occidente.* Buenos Aires: AZ Editoria, 1984.

Monahan, Arthur P. *Consent, Coercion and Limit: The Medieval Origins of Parliamentary Democracy.* Kingston and Montreal: McGill-Queen's University Press, 1987.

Moore, Barrington, Jr. *Authority and Inequality Under Capitalism and Socialism.* Oxford: Clarendon Press, 1987.

_____. *Social Origins of Dictatorship and Democracy": Lord and Peasant in the Making of the Modern World.* Boston: Beacon Press, 1966.

Moore, Margaret. *Foundations of Liberalism.* New York: Oxford University Press, 1990.

Mosca, Gaetano. *The Ruling Class.* Trans. Arthur Livingston. New York: McGraw-Hill, 1939.

Muravchik, Joshua. *Exporting Democracy.* Washington: AEI Press, 1991.

Nordlinger, Eric. *On the Autonomy of the Democratic State.* Cambridge, Mass.: Harvard University Press, 1981.

Nozick, Robert. *Anarchy, the State, and Utopia.* New York: Basic Books, 1974.

O'Donnell, Guillermo, Philippe C. Schmitter, and Laurence Whitehead. *Transitions From Authoritarian Rule: Prospects for Democracy.* Baltimore: Johns Hopkins University Press, 1986.

Ober, Josiah. *Mass and Elite in Democratic Athens: Rhetoric, Ideology, and the Power of the People.* Princeton: Princeton University Press, 1989.

Ortega y Gasset, Jose. *The Revolt of the Masses.* Trans. Arthur Kerrigan, ed. Kenneth Moore. Notre Dame, Ind.: University of Notre Dame Press, 1985.

Orwell, George. *A Collection of Essays.* Orlando: Harcourt Brace Jovanovich, 1946.

Ostwald, Martin. *Nomos and the Beginnings of the Athenian Democracy*. Oxford: Oxford University Press, 1969.

————. *Autonomia: Its Genesis and Early History*. Chico, Ca.: Scholars Press, 1982.

————. *From Popular Sovereignty to the Sovereignty of Law: Law, Society, and Politics in Fifth-Century Athens*. Berkeley: University of California Press, 1986.

Oyugi, Walter O. et al., eds. *Democratic Theory & Practice in Africa*. Portsmouth, N.H.: Heinemann Educational Books, 1988.

Pae, Sung M. *Testing Democratic Theories in Korea*. Lanham, Md.: University Press of America, 1986.

Palmer, R.R. *The Age of the Democratic Revolution*. 2 vols. Princeton University Press, 1959-64.

Parenti, Michael. *Democracy For the Few*. New York: St. Martin's Press, 1974.

Parry, Geraint and Michael Moran, eds. *Democracy and Democratization*. London: Routledge, 1994.

Pateman, Carol. *Participation and Democratic Theory*. Cambridge: Cambridge University Press, 1970.

Patterson, Orlando. *Freedom: Volume I: Freedom in the Making of Western Culture*. New York: Basic Books, 1991.

Pempel, T.J., ed. *Uncommon Democracies*. Ithaca: Cornell University Press, 1990.

Pennock, Roland. *Democratic Political Theory*. Princeton: Princeton University Press, 1979.

Perez-Diaz, Victor. *The Return of Civil Society*. Cambridge, Mass.: Harvard University Press, 1993.

The Philosophy of Kant: Immanuel Kant's Moral and Political Writings. Ed. Carl J. Friedrich. New York: The Modern Library, 1949.

The Portable Jefferson. Ed. Merrill Peterson. New York: The Viking Press, 1975.

Pickles, Dorothy. *Democracy*. Harmondsworth: Penguin Books, 1970.

Pitkin, Hanna Fenichel. *The Concept of Representation*. Berkeley: University of California Press, 1993.

Plamenatz, John. *Democracy and Illusion: An Examination of Certain Aspects of Modern Democratic Theory*. London: Longmans, 1973.

Plutarch. *The Rise and Fall of Athens*, trans. Ian Scott-Kilvert. Harmondsworth: Penguin Books, 1960.

Pocock, J.G.A. *The Machiavellian Moment: Florentine Political Thought and the Atlantic Republican Tradition*. Princeton: Princeton University Press, 1975.

Poggi, Gianfranco. *The Development of the Modern State: A Sociological Introduction*. Stanford: Stanford University Press, 1978.

Polybius. *The Histories of Polybius*. Trans. Evelyn S. Schuckburgh. Bloomington: Indiana University Press, 1982.

Popkin, Samuel. *The Reasoning Voter*. Chicago: University of Chicago Press, 1993.

Popper, Karl R. *The Open Society and Its Enemies*. Princeton: Princeton University Press, 1996, fifth edition, revised.

Powell, G. Bingham, Jr. *Contemporary Democracies: Participation, Stability, and Violence*. Cambridge, Mass.: Harvard University Press, 1982.

Przeworski, Adam. *Capitalism and Social Democracy*. New York: Cambridge University Press, 1985.

———— and Fernando Limongi, "Political Regimes and Economic Growth," *Journal of Economic Perspectives* 7, 3 (Summer 1993), pp. 51-70.

Putnam, Robert. "Bowling Alone: America's Declining Social Capital." *Journal of Democracy* 6, 1 (January 1995), pp. 65-78.

_____ with Robert Leonardi and Raffaela Y. Nanetti. *Making Democracy Work; Civic Traditions in Modern Italy* Princeton: Princeton University Press, 1993.

Rae, Douglas W. *The Political Consequences of Electoral Laws*. New Haven: Yale University Press, 1967.

_____ . "Political Democracy as a Property of Political Institutions." *American Political Science Review* 65, 1 (March 1971), pp. 111-19.

_____ and Douglas Yates. *Equalities*. Cambridge, Mass.: Harvard University Press, 1967.

Raphael, D.D., ed. *Political Theory and the Rights of Man*. Bloomington: Indiana University Press, 1967.

Rawls, John. *A Theory of Justice*. Cambridge, Mass.: Harvard University Press, 1971.

_____ . "Kantian Constructivism in Moral Theory: The Dewey Lectures 1980." *The Journal of Philosophy* 77, 9 (September 1980), pp. 515-72.

Raz, Joseph. *The Morality of Freedom*. Oxford: Oxford University Press, 1986.

Revel, Jean François, with the assistance of Branko Lazitch. Trans. William Byron. *How Democracies Perish*. Garden City, N.Y.: Doubleday, 1983.

Revel, Jean François. *The Totalitarian Temptation*. Trans David Hapgood. Garden City, N.Y.: Doubleday, 1987.

Riker, William H. *Liberalism Against Populism: A Confrontation Between the Theory of Democracy and the Theory of Social Choice*. San Francisco: W.H. Freeman, 1982.

Robbins, Caroline. *The Eighteenth-Century Commonwealthsman: Studies in the Transmission, Development, and Circumstance of English Liberal Thought from the Restoration of Charles II until the War with the Thirteen Colonies*. Cambridge, Mass.: Harvard University Press, 1959.

Rorty, Richard. *Contingency, Irony, and Solidarity*. Cambridge: Cambridge University Press, 1989.

Rosecrance, Richard. *The Rise of the Trading State: Commerce and Conquest in the Modern World*. New York: Basic Books, 1984.

Rosen, Frederick. "Bentham and Mill on Liberty and Justice." George Feaver and Frederick Rosen, eds., *Lives, Liberties and the Public Good: New Essays in Political Theory for Maurice Cranston*. London: Macmillam, 1987, pp. 121-38.

Rosenblum, Nancy. *Another Liberalism: Romanticism and the Reconstruction of Liberal Thought*. Cambridge, Mass.: Harvard University Press, 1987.

_____ . ed. *Liberalism and the Moral Life*. Cambridge, Mass.: Harvard University Press, 1989.

Rossiter, Clinton. *Constitutional Dictatorship: Crisis Government in the Modern Democracies*. Princeton: Princeton University Press, 1948.

Rouland, Norbert. *Rome, democratie impossible? les acteurs du pouvoir dans la cité romaine*. Paris: Presses universitaires de France, 1981.

Rudolph, Lloyd I. and Suzanne Hoeber Rudolph. *In Pursuit of Lakshmi: The Political Economy of the Indian State*. Chicago: The University of Chicago Press, 1987.

Ruether, Rosemary R. *Faith and Fratricide: The Theological Roots of Anti-Semitism*. New York: Seabury Press, 1974.

Rummel, Rudolph J. "Libertarianism and International Violence," *Journal of Conflict Resolution* 27,1 (March 1983), pp. 27-71.

Russell, Peter H. *Constitutional Odyssey: Can Canadians Be a Sovereign People?* Toronto: University of Toronto Press, 1992.

Russett, Bruce M. *Grasping the Democratic Peace: Principles for a Post-Cold War World.* Princeton: Princeton University Press, 1993.

Sagan, Eli. *At the Dawn of History.* New York: Knopf, 1985.

Salditch, Anne Rawley. *Electronic Democracy: Television's Impact on the American Political Process.* New York: Praeger, 1979.

Sandel, Michael. *Democracy's Discontent.* Cambridge, Mass.: Harvard University Press, 1996.

————. *Liberalism and the Limits of Justice.* Cambridge: Cambridge University Press, 1982.

Sartori, Giovanni. *The Theory of Democracy Revisited.* Two vols. Chatham, N.J.: Chatham House, 1987.

Schapiro, Leonard. *Totalitarianism.* London: Macmillan, 1972.

Schumpeter, Joseph A. *Capitalism, Socialism and Democracy,* second edition. New York: Harper, 1947.

Scott, Jonathan. *Algernon Sidney and the English Republic, 1623-1677.* Cambridge: Cambridge University Press, 1988.

Serres, Michel. *Rome: The Book of Foundations,* trans. Felicia McCarren. Stanford: Stanford University Press, 1991.

Seymour, James, ed. *The Fifth Modernization: China's Human Rights Movement, 1978-1979.* Stanfordville, N.Y.: Human Rights Publishing Group, 1980.

Sherwin-White, A.N. *The Roman Citizenship.* Oxford: Oxford University Press, 1973.

Sicker, Martin. *The Genesis of the State.* New York: Praeger, 1991.

Sidgwick, Henry. *The Development of European Polity.* London: Macmillan, 1903; New York: Kraus Reprint Co., 1969.

Skinner, Quentin. "The Empirical Theorists of Democracy and their Critics: A Plague on Both their Houses." *Political Theory* 5 (1973), pp. 287-306.

————. *The Foundations of Modern Political Thought.* 2 vols. Cambridge: Cambridge University Press, 1978.

Smiley, Donald V. *Canada in Question: Federalism in the Seventies.* Toronto: McGraw-Hill-Ryerson, 1972.

Smith, Rogers. *Liberalism and American Constitutional Law.* Cambridge, Mass.: Harvard University Press, 1985.

Smith, Tony. *America's Mission: The United States and the Worldwide Struggle for Democracy in the Twentieth Century.* Princeton: Princeton University Press, 1994.

Snell, John L. *The Democratic Movement in Germany, 1789-1914.* Ed. and completed, Hans A. Schmitt. Chapel Hill: University of North Carolina, 1976.

Sniderman, Paul N. *Personality and Democratic Politics.* Berkeley: University of California Press, 1975.

Spence, Jonathan D. *The Search for Modern China.* New York: W. W. Norton, 1990.

Spitz, David. *Patterns of Anti-Democratic Thought.* New York: Macmillan, 1949.

Stankiewicz, W.J. *In Defense of Sovereignty.* New York: Oxford University Press, 1969.

Staveley, E.S. *Greek and Roman Voting and Elections.* Ithaca, N.Y.: Cornell University Press, 1972.

Stepan, Alfred, ed. *Democratizing Brazil: Problems of Transition and Consolidation.* New York: Oxford University Press, 1989.

————— and Juan Linz, eds. *The Breakdown of Democratic Regimes.* Baltimore: Johns Hopkins Press, 1978.

Stern, Fritz. *The Politics of Cultural Despair*. Berkeley: University of California Press, 1961.

Stockton, David. *The Classical Athenian Democracy*. Oxford: Oxford University Press, 1990.

Stojanovic, Svetozar, *In Search of Democracy in Socialism: History and Party Consciousness*. Trans. Gerson S. Sher. Buffalo, N.Y.: Prometheus Books, 1981.

Strom, Kaare. *Minority Government and Minority Rule*. Cambridge: Cambridge University Press, 1990.

Strong, Tracy. *Friedrich Nietzsche and the Politics of Transfiguration*. Berkeley: University of California Press, 1975.

Taagepara, Rein, and Matthew Shugart. *Seats and Votes: The Effects and Determinants of Electoral Systems*. New Haven: Yale University Press, 1989.

Taylor, Lily Ross. *The Voting Districts of the Roman Republic; The Thirty-Five Urban and Rural Tribes*. Rome: The American Academy in Rome, 1960.

Thompson, Dennis F. *John Stuart Mill and Representative Government*. Princeton: Princeton University Press, 1976.

Thomson, David. *Democracy in France Since 1870*. New York: Oxford Pres, 1964.

Thorson, Thomas L. *The Logic of Democracy*. New York: Holt, Rinehart and Winston, 1962.

Tismaneanu, Vladimir. *Reinventing Politics: Eastern Europe from Stalin to Havel*. New York: The Free Press, 1992.

Tocqueville, Alexis de. *Democracy in America*. Ed. J.P. Mayer, trans. George Lawrence. Garden City, N.Y.: Anchor Books, 1969.

_____ . *The European Revolution and Correspondence with Gobineau*. Ed. and trans. J. Lukacs. Garden City, N.Y.: Anchor Books, 1959.

Trotter, Wilfred. *Instincts of the Herd in War and Peace*. London: The Scientific Book Club, 1942.

Valenzuela, Arturo. *The Breakdown of Democratic Regimes: Chile*. Baltimore: Johns Hopkins University Press, 1978.

Van Wolferen, Karel. *The Enigma of Japanese Power: People and Politics in a Stateless Nation*. New York: Knopf, 1989.

Vanhanen, Tatu, ed. *Strategies of Democratization*. Washington, D.C.: Crane Russak, 1992.

_____ . *The Emergence of Democracy: a Comparative Study of 119 States, 1850-79*. Helsinki: Societas Scientarium Fennica. 1984.

_____ . *The Process of Democratization: A Comparative Analysis of 147 States, 1980-88*. New York: Crane Russak, 1990.

Vernon, Raymond. *Sovereignty at Bay: the Multinational Spread of U.S. Enterprises*. New York: Basic Books, 1971.

Waltz, Kenneth. *Man, the State, and War: A Theoretical Analysis*. New York: Columbia University Press, 1969.

Weede, Erich. "Democracy and War Involvement." *The Journal of Conflict Resolution* 28, 4 (December, 1984), pp. 649-664.

Westbrook, Robert. *John Dewey and American Democracy*. Ithaca: Cornell University Press, 1992.

Wheare, K.C. *Federal Government*. London: Oxford University Press, 1978.

Whitman, Walt. *Democratic Vistas*. New York: Liberal Arts Press, 1949.

Wildavsky, Aaron. *But Is It True? A Citizen's Guide to Environmental Health and Safety Issues.* Cambridge, Mass.: Harvard University Press. 1995.

Wilson, E.O. *On Human Nature.* Cambridge, Mass.: Harvard University Press, 1978.

_____ . *Sociobiology: The New Synthesis.* Cambridge, Mass.: Harvard University Press, 1975.

Wilson, James Q. *Bureaucracy: What Government Agencies Do and Why They Do It.* New York: Basic Books, 1989.

Wirszubski, Chaim. *Libertas as a Political Idea at Rome During the Late Republic and Early Principate.* Cambridge: Cambridge University Press, 1960.

Wolff, Robert Paul. *In Defense of Anarchism.* New York: Harper & Row, 1976.

Wolfinger, Raymond and Steven J. Rosenstone. *Who Votes?* New Haven: Yale University Press, 1980.

Wood, Gordon S. *The Creation of the American Republic 1776-1787.* Chapel Hill: University of North Carolina Press, 1969.

_____ . *The Radicalism of the American Revolution.* New York: Knopf, 1992.

Woodhouse, A.S.P., ed. *Puritanism and Liberty.* Chicago: University of Chicago Press, 1951.

Index

About the Author

Sanford Lakoff is Research Professor of Political Science at the University of California, San Diego. He has taught at UCSD since being appointed founding chair of the department in 1974. Previously, he held faculty positions at Harvard University, SUNY/Stony Brook, and the University of Toronto, and served as visiting professor at the European University Institute in Florence, the University of Rochester, and MIT. He has also been a fellow of the Woodrow Wilson Center for Scholars and the National Humanities Center. His other writings include *Equality in Political Philosophy* and (with Herbert F. York) *A Shield in Space?* He has written numerous journal articles and chapters for edited volumes as well as entries for the *Dictionary of the History of Ideas*, the *Encyclopedia of Democracy*, and the *Encyclopedia of U.S. Foreign Policy.*